ACCA

Applied Skills

Taxation (TX - UK) FA 2022

Practice & Revision Kit

For exams in June 2023, September 2023, December 2023 and March 2024

Seventeenth edition 2022

ISBN 9781 0355 0288 2

e-ISBN 9781 0355 0297 4

British Library Cataloguing-in-Publication Data

A catalogue record for this book is available from the British Library

Published by

BPP Learning Media Ltd

BPP House, Aldine Place

London W12 8AA

www.bpp.com/learningmedia

Printed in the United Kingdom

Your learning materials, published by BPP Learning Media Ltd, are printed on paper obtained from traceable, sustainable sources.

We are grateful to the Association of Chartered Certified Accountants for permission to reproduce past examination questions. The suggested solutions in the Practice & Revision Kit have been prepared by BPP Learning Media Ltd, except where otherwise stated.

A note about copyright

Dear Customer

What does the little © mean and why does it matter?

Your market-leading BPP books, course materials and e-learning materials do not write and update themselves. People write them on their own behalf or as employees of an organisation that invests in this activity. Copyright law protects their livelihoods. It does so by creating rights over the use of the content. Breach of copyright is a form of theft – as well as being a criminal offence in some jurisdictions, it is potentially a serious breach of professional ethics. With current technology, things might seem a bit hazy but, basically, without the express permission of BPP Learning Media:

- Photocopying our materials is a breach of copyright
- Scanning, ripcasting or conversion of our digital materials into different file formats, uploading them to social media or emailing them to a third party is a breach of copyright

You can, of course, sell your books, in the form in which you have bought them – once you have finished with them. (Is this fair to your fellow students? We update for a reason.) Please note the e-products are sold on a single user licence basis: we do not supply 'unlock' codes to people who have bought them second-hand.

And what about outside the UK? BPP Learning Media strives to make our materials available at prices students can afford by local printing arrangements, pricing policies and partnerships which are clearly listed on our website. A tiny minority ignore this and indulge in criminal activity by illegally photocopying our material or supporting organisations that do. If they act illegally and unethically in one area, can you really trust them?

Contents

Question index

The headings in this checklist/index indicate the main topics of questions, but questions may cover several different topics.

Questions set under the old F6 Taxation (UK) exam format are included in this Kit because their style and content are similar to those that may appear in the Taxation (TX – UK) exams from 1 September 2016.

Some of these questions have been amended to reflect the new exam format and this is shown by (amended) in the title of the question.

	Marks	Time allocation (mins)	Page number	
			Questions	Answers
Section B				
78-82 OT case – Ann, Basil and Chloe (December 2008) (amended)	10	18	27	178
83-87 OT case – Ae, Bee, Cae, and Eu (December 2018) (amended)	10	18	28	179
88-92 OT case – Rosie and Sam (December 2012) (amended)	10	18	29	180
93-97 OT case – Fang and Hong (December 2013) (amended)	10	18	31	182
98-102 OT case – Chi (June 2014) (amended)	10	18	33	183
Section C				
103 Kagan (September/December 2019)	10	18	35	185
104 Michael and Sean (June 2012) (amended)	10	18	37	188
105 Paul and Palu Ltd (March/June 2021) (amended)	10	18	38	189
106 Robinette (September/December 2019)	15	27	38	191
107 Lucy	10	18	39	194
108 Daniel, Francine and Gregor (September/December 2015)	10	18	40	196
109 George (March/June 2016)	10	18	41	198
110 Joe (December 2010) (amended)	15	27	41	200
111 Sammi (December 2010)	15	27	42	201
112 Simon (December 2009)	15	27	43	203
113 Alfred and Amaia (March/June 2021) (amended)	15	27	44	206
114 John (June 2013) (amended)	15	27	45	208
115 Ronald (June 2014) (amended)	15	27	46	212
116 Wai (June 2015) (amended)	15	27	47	214
117 Samson and Delilah (September/December 2015) (amended)	15	27	48	217
118 Patience (March/June 2016)	15	27	49	220
119 Petula (March/June 2017)	15	27	50	223
120 Dill (September/December 2017) (amended)	15	27	51	227
121 Danh (March/June 2018)	15	27	53	230
122 Martin (September/December 2018)	15	27	54	232

BPP

Topic index

Listed below are the key Taxation (TX – UK) syllabus topics and the numbers of the questions of this Kit (excluding the Mock exams) covering those topics.

If you need to concentrate your practice and revision on certain topics, or if you want to attempt all available questions that refer to a particular subject, you will find this index useful.

Syllabus topic	Question numbers
Syllabus section A:	
Overall function and purpose of tax	1, 8, 31, 41, ME1 Q7, ME2 Q2
Principal sources of revenue law and practice	2, 16, 25, 32, 322, ME3 Q5
Systems for self-assessment and returns	4, 18, 19, 22, 41, ME1 Q 8, ME2 Q22
Time limits	7, 9, 10, 11, 12, 14, 21, 26, 27, 29, 36, 38, 42, 122, 251, 253, 257, 325, ME1 Q15, ME2 Q5, ME2 Q13, ME3 Q6, ME3 Q12, ME3 Q19, ME4 Q4, ME4 Q8, ME4 Q9
Procedures for compliance checks, appeals and disputes	3, 24, 39, 40, 41, ME3 Q10, ME4 Q2, ME4 Q9
Penalties for non-compliance	5, 6, 13, 15, 17, 20, 23, 28, 30, 33, 34, 35, 37, 41, 253, ME1 Q12
Syllabus section B:	
The scope of income tax	43, 123, 124, ME1 Q9, ME2 Q 15, ME3 Q9, ME4 Q6
Employment income	47, 50, 51, 52, 54, 106, 107, 108, 109, 110, 1011, 114, 116, 117, 118, 119, 120, 121, 122, 123, 325, ME1 Q10, ME1 Q31, ME1 Q32, ME2 Q31, ME2 Q32, ME3 Q32
Self-employment	59, 60, 61, 62, 63, 64, 65, 66, 67,68, 69, 70, 83, 84, 85, 86, 87, 93, 94, 95, 96, 97, 98, 100, 101, 102, 104, 105, 106, 107, 108, 109, 112, 113, 115, 118, 122, 124, ME1 Q32, ME2 Q32, ME4 Q16, ME4 Q17, ME4 Q19, ME4 Q20
Property and investment income	44, 53, 56, 57, 58, 91, 92, 106, 115, 117, 118, 121, 122, 123, 247, 248, 249 ME2 Q12, ME2 Q32, ME3 Q8, ME3 Q11, ME3 Q31, ME4 Q5
Taxable income	45, 46, 48, 49, 80, 81, 103, 113, 115, 117, 118, 119, 122, 123, 124, 217, 247, 248, 249 ME1 Q31, ME2 Q3, ME2 Q31, ME3 Q13
National insurance	71, 72, 99, 107, 109, 111, 112, 124, 247, 248, ME1 Q16, ME1 Q31, ME2 Q1, ME2 Q31, ME3 Q7, ME3 Q32, ME4 Q1
Income tax exemptions and reliefs	55, 78, 79, 82, 88, 89, 90, 115, 118, 119, 217, ME1 Q3, ME3 Q31

Syllabus section C:	
The scope of the taxation of capital gains	112, 124, 162, ME2 Q11
The basic principles of computing gains and losses	118, 125, 126, 127, 136, 141, 143, 150, 151, 158, 160, 169, 170, 171, 213, 217, 249
Gains and losses on the disposal of movable and immovable property	128, 129, 130, 135, 142, 157, 162, 169, ME1 Q2, ME2 Q7, ME2 Q18, ME3 Q4, ME4 Q7
Gains and losses on the disposal of shares and securities	132, 139, 140, 141, 147, 149, 173, ME2 Q16, ME3 Q18
Computing capital gains tax	120, 132, 145, 146, 148, 152, 153, 159, 170, 171, 172, 213, ME1 Q25, ME3 Q20, ME4 Q3
Syllabus section D:	
Transfers of value	173, 174, 176, 180, 188, 189, 190, 194, 199, 201, 206, 210, 211, 214, 215, 216, ME3 Q23
Liabilities on chargeable lifetime transfers and on death	175, 177, 180, 181, 183, 186, 191, 192, 195, 197, 200, 202, 203, 204, 205, 208, 209, 213, 214, 215, 217, ME1 Q11,ME1 Q16, ME1 Q17, ME1 Q19, ME1 Q20, ME2 Q8, ME2 Q21, ME2 Q22, ME2 Q23,ME2 Q24, ME3 Q3, ME3 Q14, ME3 Q21, ME3 Q25, ME3 Q31 Q8,ME2 Q21,ME2 Q22, ME2 Q23, ME2 Q24, ME3 Q3, ME3 Q14, ME4 Q11, ME4 Q12, ME4 Q26, ME4 Q27
Exemptions	178, 184, 187, 193, 198, 207, 212, 214, 215, 216, 217, ME1 Q1, ME2 Q9, ME2 Q25, ME3 Q24, ME4 Q28, ME4 Q29, ME4 Q30
Payment of IHT	182, 185, 196, ME1 Q18, ME3 Q22
Syllabus section E:	
Scope of corporation tax	219, 254, 258, ME3 Q33
Taxable total profits	106, 218, 220, 221, 223, 224, 244, 245, 247, 248, 249, 250, 256, 249, 250, 252, 253, 254, 255, 256, 257, 258, 259, ME1 Q5, ME1 Q13, ME1 Q33, ME2 Q14, ME2 Q33, ME3 Q33, ME4 Q15
Chargeable gains for companies	222, 228, 229, 230, 231, 232, 233, 234, 235, 236, 237, 243, 245, 249, 257, 258, 259, ME1 Q21, ME1 Q22,ME1 Q23,ME1 Q24, ME4 Q10
Corporation tax liability	245, 247, 248, 250, 251, ME1 Q31, ME2 Q33, ME3 Q33
Groups	225, 226, 227, 238, 239, 240, 241, 242, 246, 247, 251, 254, 258, 259 ME1 Q13, ME2 Q4, ME2 Q14, ME3 Q2, ME3 Q33

Syllabus section F:	
VAT registration	269, 285, 298, 299, 304, 310, 315, 321, 322, ME1 Q26, ME3 Q26, ME4 Q13, ME4 Q25
Computing VAT liabilities	269, 285, 298, 299, 304, 310, 316, 317, 318, 319, 321, 322, ME1 Q26, ME3 Q26, ME4 Q14, ME4 Q21, ME4 Q22, ME4 Q23, ME4 Q24
Special schemes	272, 273, 274, 278, 279, 292, 293, 294, 308, 309, 319, 320, 321, 323, 324, ME2 Q10

About this Practice & Revision Kit

This Practice & Revision Kit is valid for exams from the June 2023 sitting through to the March 2024 sitting and, in this Practice & Revision Kit, you will find questions in both multiple choice question (MCQ) and objective testing question (OTQ) format. OTQs include a wider variety of question types including MCQ as well as number entry, multiple response and drag and drop. More information on these question types will be available on the ACCA website.

More information on the exam formats can be found on page **xvii**.

The TX exam is 3 hours in duration and the timings of the questions are based on this time allocation. Prior to the start of each exam there will be time allocated for students to be informed of the exam instructions.

These materials are reviewed by the ACCA examining team. The objective of the review is to ensure that the material properly covers the syllabus and study guide outcomes, used by the examining team in setting the exams, in the appropriate breadth and depth. The review does not ensure that every eventuality, combination or application of examinable topics is addressed by the ACCA Approved Content. Nor does the review comprise a detailed technical check of the content as the Approved Content Provider has its own quality assurance processes in place in this respect.

BPP Learning Media do everything possible to ensure the material is accurate and up to date when sending to print. In the event that any errors are found after the print date, they are uploaded to the following website: https://learningmedia.bpp.com/catalog?pagename=Errata

Revising Taxation (TX – UK)

Topics to revise

All questions are compulsory so you must revise the **whole** syllabus. Since the exam includes 15 objective test questions in Section A and 15 objective test questions in Section B, you should expect questions to cover a large part of the syllabus. Selective revision **will limit** the number of questions you can answer and hence reduce your chances of passing. It is better to go into the exam knowing a reasonable amount about most of the syllabus rather than concentrating on a few topics to the exclusion of the rest.

Question practice

This is the most important thing to do if you want to get through. Many of the most up-to-date exam questions are in this Kit. Practice doing them under timed conditions, then go through the answers and go back to the Workbook for any topic you are really having trouble with. Come back to a question a week later and try it again – you will be surprised at how much better you are getting. Be very ruthless with yourself at this stage – you have to do the question in the time, without looking at the answer. This will really sharpen your wits and make the exam experience less worrying. Just keep doing this and you will get better at doing questions and you will really find out what you know and what you don't know.

Passing the Taxation (TX – UK) exam

Displaying the right qualities

- You will be required to identify the requirements of objective test questions quickly, so that you can make your answers confidently within the available time.
- In constructed response questions you will be required to carry out calculations, with clear workings and a logical structure. If your numbers are not perfect, you will not necessarily lose too many marks so long as your method is correct and you have stated any assumptions you have made.
- You will also be expected to apply your tax knowledge to the facts of each particular question and also to identify the compliance issues for your client.
- You may also be required to describe rules and conditions, so take care to practise the descriptive elements of the answers.

Avoiding weaknesses

- There is no choice in this exam, all questions have to be answered. You must therefore study the entire syllabus, there are no short-cuts.
- Ability to answer objective test questions and cases improves with practice. Try to get as much practice with these questions as you can.
- The constructed response questions will be based on simple scenarios and answers must be focused and specific to the requirement of the question.
- Answer all parts of the constructed response questions. Even if you cannot do all the calculation elements, you will still be able to gain marks in the descriptive parts.

Gaining the easy marks

Easy marks in this exam tend to fall into three categories.

Objective test questions (OTQs)

Some OTQs are easier than others. Answer those that you feel fairly confident about as quickly as you can. Come back later to those you find more difficult. This could be a way of making use of the time in the examination most efficiently and effectively. Some OTQs will not involve calculations. Make sure that you understand the wording of 'written' OTQs before selecting your answer.

Calculations in Section C questions

There will always be basic marks available for straightforward tasks such as putting easy figures into proformas, for example putting the cost figure for an addition into a capital allowances proforma. Do not miss out on these easy marks by not learning your proformas properly.

Discussions in Section C questions

A constructed response question may separate descriptive requirements from calculations, so that you do not need to do the calculations first in order to answer the descriptive parts. This means that you should be able to gain marks from the descriptive parts without having to complete the calculations.

Descriptive requirements may focus on administrative, or compliance, details such as filing deadlines and tax payment dates. Make your points concisely, bearing in mind that one mark usually equates to one point to be made.

Read the question carefully and more than once, to ensure you are actually answering the specific requirements. Don't write about matters which are not specifically required – even if these are technically correct, you will not gain any marks and will waste valuable time.

Tackling objective test case questions

First, read the whole case scenario. Highlight any specific instructions or assumptions, such as 'Ignore the annual exempt amount' in a capital gains tax question. Then skim through the requirements of the five questions. If you are sitting your exam in-centre you can make notes either on the on-screen scratchpad or on the scrap paper available to you in the exam. If you are sitting your exam via remote invigilation only the on-screen scratchpad can be used. You can familiarise yourself with the on-screen scratchpad by testing it on the Practice Platform.

The questions are independent of each other and can be answered in any order. Some of the OTQs will be easier than others. For example, you may be asked to identify the filing date for a tax return and the penalty for late filing. Answer these OTQs quickly.

Other OTQs will be more difficult and/or complex. There are two types of OTQ that may take you longer to answer.

The first more time-consuming OTQ will involve doing a computation. For example, you may be asked to calculate the personal allowance available to a taxpayer whose adjusted net income exceeds £100,000. You will probably need to use a quick pro-forma to answer a computational question like this.

If the OTQ is a multiple-choice question, remember that the wrong answers will usually involve common errors, so don't assume that because you have the same answer as one of the options that your answer is necessarily correct! Double check to make sure you haven't made any silly mistakes, such as deducting the whole of the excess of adjusted net income over the £100,000 threshold (instead of half of it) when working out the restriction for the personal allowance. If you haven't got the same answer as any of the options, rework your computation, thinking carefully about what errors you could have made. If you still haven't got one of the options, choose the one which is nearest to your answer.

The second more time-consuming OTQ is one where you are asked to consider a number of statements and identify which one (or more) of them is correct. Make sure that you read each statement at least twice before making your selection. Be careful to follow the requirements of the OTQ exactly, for example if you are asked to identify **TWO** correct statements.

Exam information

Computer-based exams

Applied Skills exams are all computer-based exams.

Format of the exam

The exam format will comprise three exam sections.

Section	Style of question type	Description	Proportion of exam (%)
A	Objective test (OT)	15 questions × 2 marks	30
B	Objective test (OT) case	3 questions × 10 marks Each question will contain 5 subparts each worth 2 marks	30
C	Constructed Response (Long questions)	1 question × 10 marks 2 questions × 15 marks	40
Total			100

Section A and B questions will be selected from the entire syllabus. The responses to each question or subpart in the case of OT cases are marked automatically as either correct or incorrect by computer.

The 10-mark Section C question can come from any part of the syllabus. The 15-mark Section C questions will mainly focus on the following syllabus areas, but a minority of marks can be drawn from any other area of the syllabus:

- Income tax (syllabus area B)
- Corporation tax (syllabus area E)

The responses to these questions are human marked.

CBE practice platform

Practising as many exam-style questions as possible in the ACCA CBE practice platform will be the key to passing this exam. You must do questions under timed conditions and ensure you produce full answers to the discussion parts as well as doing the calculations.

Also ensure that you attempt all mock exams under exam conditions.

ACCA have launched a free on-demand resource designed to mirror the live exam experience helping you to become more familiar with the exam format. You can access the platform via the Study Support Resources section of the ACCA website navigating to the CBE question practice section and logging in with your myACCA credentials.

Additional information

The study guide provides more detailed guidance on the syllabus and can be found by visiting the exam resource finder on the ACCA website.

Useful websites

The websites below provide additional sources of information of relevance to your studies for Taxation (TX – UK).

- www.accaglobal.com

  ACCA's website. The students' section of the website is invaluable for detailed information about the qualification, past issues of Student Accountant (including technical articles) and a free downloadable Student Planner App.
- www.bpp.com

  Our website provides information about BPP products and services, with a link to the ACCA website.

Remote invigilated exams

In certain geographical areas it may be possible for you to take your exam remotely. This option, which is subject to strict conditions, can offer increased flexibility and convenience under certain circumstances. Further guidance, including the detailed requirements and conditions for taking the exam by this method, is contained on ACCA's website at: https://www.accaglobal.com/an/en/student/exam-entry-and-administration/about-our-exams/remote-exams/remote-session-exams.html.

Helping you with your revision

BPP Learning Media – Approved Content Provider

As an ACCA **Approved Content Provider**, BPP Learning Media gives you the **opportunity** to use revision materials reviewed by the ACCA examining team. By incorporating the ACCA examining team's comments and suggestions regarding the depth and breadth of syllabus coverage, the BPP Learning Media Practice & Revision Kit provides excellent **ACCA approved** support for your revision.

Tackling revision and the exam

Using feedback obtained from the ACCA examining team review:

- We look at the dos and don'ts of revising for, and taking, ACCA exams.
- We focus on Taxation (TX – UK); we discuss revising the syllabus, what to do (and what not to do) in the exam, how to approach different types of question and ways of obtaining easy marks.

Selecting questions

We provide signposts to help you plan your revision.

- A full question index
- A topic index listing all the questions that cover key topics, so that you can locate the questions that provide practice on these topics, and see the different ways in which they might be examined

Making the most of question practice

At BPP Learning Media we realise that you need more than just questions and model answers to get the most from your question practice.

- Our Top tips included for certain questions provide essential advice on tackling questions, presenting answers and the key points that answers need to include.
- We show you how you can pick up easy marks on some questions, as we know that picking up all readily available marks often can make the difference between passing and failing.
- We include marking guides to show you what the examining team rewards.
- We include comments from the examining team to show you where students struggled or performed well in the actual exam.
- We refer to the FA 2022 Workbook (for exams in June 2023, September 2023, December 2023 and March 2024) for detailed coverage of the topics covered in questions.

Attempting mock exams

There are four mock exams that provide practice at coping with the pressures of the exam day. We strongly recommend that you attempt them under exam conditions.

Mock exam 1 is the September 2016 exam, **Mock exam 2** is the Specimen exam, **Mock exam 3** is the December 2016 exam and **Mock exam 4** is the March/June 2022 exam.

Essential skills areas to be successful in Taxation (TX – UK)

We think there are three areas you should develop in order to achieve exam success in TX:

(a) Knowledge application

(b) Specific ATX skills

(c) Exam success skills

These are shown in the diagram below.

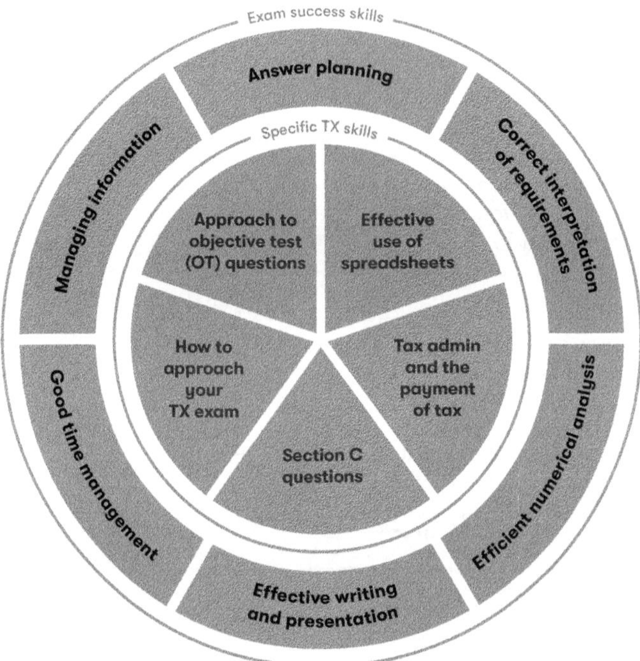

Specific TX skills

These are the skills specific to ATX that we think you need to develop in order to pass the exam.

In the BPP TX Workbook, there are five **Skills Checkpoints** which define each skill and show how it is applied in answering a question. A brief summary of each skill is given below.

Skill 1: Approach to objective test (OT) questions

Section A of the exam will include 15 OT questions worth two marks each. Section B of the exam will include three OT cases, worth 10 marks each. Each OT case contains a group of five OT questions based around a single scenario. 60% of your TX exam is therefore made up of OT questions. It is essential that you have a good approach to answering these questions. OT questions are auto-marked; your workings will therefore not be considered; you have to answer the whole question correctly to earn their two marks.

A step-by-step technique for tackling OT questions is outlined below:

General guidance for approaching OT questions

STEP 1: Answer the questions you know first.

If you're having difficulty answering a question, move on and come back to tackle it once you've answered all the questions you know.

It is often quicker to answer discursive style OT questions first, leaving more time for calculations.

General guidance for approaching OT questions

STEP 2: Answer all questions.

There is no penalty for an incorrect answer in ACCA exams; there is nothing to be gained by leaving an OT question unanswered. If you are stuck on a question, as a last resort, it is worth selecting the option you consider most likely to be correct and moving on. Make a note of the question, so if you have time after you have answered the rest of the questions, you can revisit it.

Guidance for answering specific OT questions

STEP 3: Read the requirement first!

The requirement will be stated in bold text in the exam. Identify what you are being asked to do, any technical knowledge required and **what type of OT question** you are dealing with. Look for key words in the requirement such as "which **TWO** of the following," "which of the following is **NOT**"

Guidance for answering specific OT questions

STEP 4: Apply your technical knowledge to the data presented in the question.

Take your time working through questions, and make sure to read through each answer option with care. OT questions are designed so that each answer option is plausible. Work through each response option and eliminate those you know are incorrect.

Skills checkpoint 1 in the BPP TX – UK Workbook covers this technique in detail through application of an OT case question.

Skill 2: Effective use of spreadsheets

It is very likely that you will be required to use the spreadsheet response option in the constructed workspace for Section C questions. It is imperative that you know how to use the spreadsheet functions to prepare accurate and easy to follow calculations.

The key steps are outlined below:

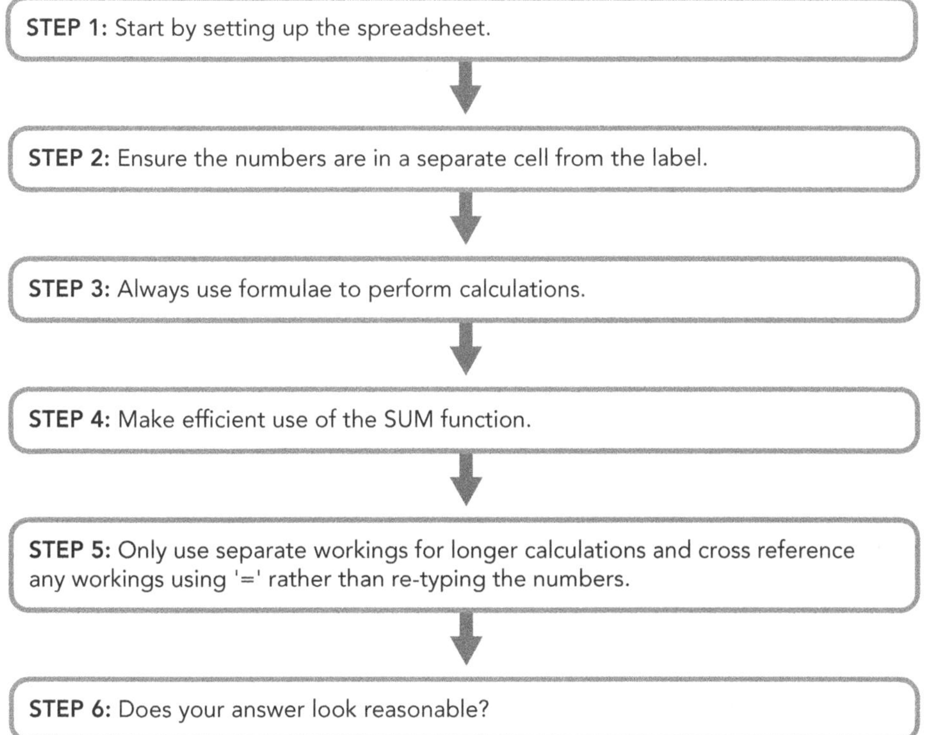

STEP 1: Start by setting up the spreadsheet.
STEP 2: Ensure the numbers are in a separate cell from the label.
STEP 3: Always use formulae to perform calculations.
STEP 4: Make efficient use of the SUM function.
STEP 5: Only use separate workings for longer calculations and cross reference any workings using '=' rather than re-typing the numbers.
STEP 6: Does your answer look reasonable?

Skills checkpoint 2 in the BPP TX – UK Workbook covers this technique in detail through application to a question.

Skill 3: The UK tax system and its administration

You must study the whole syllabus in order to pass the TX exam but having the administration knowledge at your fingertips will give you extra time in the exam to answer the more difficult questions.

This skills checkpoint gives you a list of quickfire questions to help you learn the basic information.

Skill 4: Section C questions

Section C questions contain one 10-mark question and two 15-mark questions. One 15-mark question will focus on income tax and the other one will focus on corporation tax. This means that you know roughly what to expect and you can use proformas where relevant to help with the long calculations. Discursive elements will be relatively short. 10-mark questions often cover more than one tax and are designed to act as a bridge question between TX and the higher-level exam, ATX.

A step-by-step technique for attempting these questions is outlined below:

STEP 1: Read the requirements first and read them carefully.

↓

STEP 2: Learn and use the proformas where relevant.

↓

STEP 3: Input easy numbers from the question directly into your proforma.

↓

STEP 4: Always use formulae to perform basic calculations.

↓

STEP 5: Show longer workings separately.

Skills checkpoint 4 in the BPP TX – UK Workbook covers this technique in detail through application to a question.

Skill 5: How to approach your TX exam

You can answer your TX exam in whatever order you prefer. It is important that you adopt a strategy that works best for you. We would suggest that you decide on your preferred approach and practice it by doing a timed mock exam before your real exam.

A suggested approach to tackling your TX exam is outlined below.

Complete Section A first – allocated time 54 minutes

Tackle any easier OT questions first. Often discursive style questions can be answered quickly, saving more time for calculations. Do not leave any questions unanswered. Even if you are unsure make a reasoned guess.

Complete Section B next – allocated time 54 minutes

You will have 18 mins of exam time to allocate to each of the three OT case questions in Section B. Use the same approach to OT questions as discussed for Section A.

There will normally be discursive and numerical questions within each case. Again, it is better to tackle the discursive type questions first and make a reasoned guess for any questions you are unsure on.

Finally, complete Section C – allocated time 72 minutes

Start with the question you feel most confident with.

Skills checkpoint 5 covers this technique in more detail.

Exam success skills

Passing the TX exam requires more than applying syllabus knowledge and demonstrating the specific TX skills; it also requires the development of excellent exam technique through question practice.

We consider the following six skills to be vital for exam success. The Skills Checkpoints show how each of these skills can be applied in the exam.

Exam success skill 1

Managing information

Questions in the exam will present you with a lot of information. The skill is how you handle this information to make the best use of your time. The key is determining how you will approach the exam and then actively reading the questions.

Advice on developing Managing information

Approach

The exam is 3 hours long. There is no designated 'reading' time at the start of the exam, however, one approach that can work well is to start the exam by spending 10–15 minutes carefully reading through all of the questions to familiarise yourself with the exam.

Once you feel familiar with the exam, consider the order in which you will attempt the questions; always attempt them in your order of preference. For example, you may want to leave to last the question you consider to be the most difficult.

If you do take this approach, remember to adjust the time available for each question appropriately – see Exam success skill 6: Good time management.

If you find that this approach doesn't work for you, don't worry – you can develop your own technique.

Active reading

You must take an active approach to reading each question. Focus on the requirement first, underlining/highlighting key verbs such as 'prepare', 'comment', 'explain', 'discuss', to ensure you answer the question properly. Then read the rest of the question, underlining/highlighting and annotating important and relevant information, and making notes of any relevant technical information you think you will need.

Exam success skill 2

Correct interpretation of the requirements

The active verb used often dictates the approach that written answers should take (eg 'explain', 'discuss', 'evaluate'). It is important you identify and use the verb to define your approach. The **correct interpretation of the requirements** skill means correctly producing only what is being asked for by a requirement. Anything not required will not earn marks.

Advice on developing correct interpretation of the requirements

This skill can be developed by analysing question requirements and applying this process:

Step 1 Read the requirement

Firstly, read the requirement a couple of times slowly and carefully and highlight the active verbs. Use the active verbs to define what you plan to do. Make sure you identify any sub-requirements and any topics which you are specifically told you do not need to cover in your answer. Also note the number of marks available for each requirement or sub-requirement, as this will indicate the time available and hence the level of depth required in your answer.

Step 2 Read the rest of the question

By reading the requirement first, you will have an idea of what you are looking out for as you read through the scenario. This is a great time saver and means you don't end up having to read the whole question in full twice. You should do this in an active way – see Exam success skill 1: Managing Information.

Step 3 Read the requirement again

Read the requirement again to remind yourself of the exact wording before starting your answer. This will capture any misinterpretation of the requirements or any missed requirements entirely. This should become a habit in your approach and, with repeated practice, you will find the focus, relevance and depth of your answer plan will improve.

Exam success skill 3

Answer planning: Priorities, structure and logic

This skill requires the planning of the key aspects of an answer which accurately and completely responds to the requirement.

Advice on developing Answer planning: Priorities, structure and logic

Everyone will have a preferred style for an answer plan. For example, it may be a mind map, bullet-pointed lists or simply making some notes. Choose the approach that you feel most comfortable with, or, if you are not sure, try out different approaches for different questions until you have found your preferred style.

For 10-mark Section C questions, it can be useful to draw up a separate answer plan in the format of your choosing (eg a mind map or bullet-pointed lists). You will want to remind yourself of key facts from the scenario to avoid having to re-read the question – you should at the very least make a few notes including vital information such as the following key factors:

- Nature of the taxpayer: is it an individual or a company?
- For individuals: their age, any family relationships, their residence and domicile status, whether they're a basic, higher or additional rate taxpayer, and whether they've used their CGT annual exempt amount/IHT exemptions
- For companies: their ownership structure and group relationships
- Relevant dates: the year end(s) of businesses, dates of actual or proposed transactions, the date that a business started, dates of gifts (or death!) for IHT

Exam success skill 4

Efficient numerical analysis

This skill aims to maximise the marks awarded by making clear to the marker the process of arriving at your answer. This is achieved by laying out an answer such that, even if you make a few errors, you can still score subsequent marks for follow-on calculations. It is vital that you do not lose marks purely because the marker cannot follow what you have done.

Advice on developing Efficient numerical analysis

This skill can be developed by applying the following process:

Step 1 Use a standard proforma working where relevant

If answers can be laid out in a standard proforma then always plan to do so. This will help the marker to understand your working and allocate the marks easily. It will also help you to work through the figures in a methodical and time-efficient way.

Step 2 Show your workings

Keep your workings as clear and simple as possible and ensure they are cross-referenced to the main part of your answer.

Step 3 **Keep moving!**

It is important to remember that, in an exam situation, it is difficult to get every number 100% correct. The key is therefore ensuring you do not spend too long on any single calculation. If you are struggling with a solution then make a sensible assumption, state it and move on.

Exam success skill 5

Effective writing and presentation

Written answers should be presented so that the marker can clearly see the points you are making, presented in the format specified in the question. The skill is to provide efficient written answers with sufficient breadth of points that answer the question, in the right depth, in the time available.

Advice on developing Effective writing and presentation

Step 1 **Use headings**

Using the headings and sub-headings from your answer plan will give your answer structure, order and logic. This will ensure your answer links back to the requirement and is clearly signposted, making it easier for the marker to understand the different points you are making. Underlining your headings will also help the marker.

Step 2 **Write your answer in short, but full, sentences**

Use short, punchy sentences with the aim that every sentence should say something different and generate marks. Write in full sentences, ensuring your style is professional.

Step 3 **Do your calculations first and explanation second**

Questions sometimes ask for an explanation with supporting calculations. The best approach is to prepare the calculation first then add the explanation. Performing the calculation first should enable you to explain what you have done.

Exam success skill 6

Good time management

This skill means planning your time across all the requirements so that all tasks have been attempted at the end of the 3 hours available and actively checking on time during your exam. This is so that you can flex your approach and prioritise requirements which, in your judgement, will generate the maximum marks in the available time remaining.

Advice on developing Good time management

The exam is 3 hours long, which translates to 1.8 minutes per mark. At the beginning of a question, work out the amount of time you should be spending on each requirement. If you take the approach of spending 10–15 minutes reading and planning at the start of the exam, adjust the time allocated to each question accordingly.

Keep an eye on the clock

Aim to attempt all requirements but be ready to be ruthless and move on if your answer is not going as planned. The challenge for many is sticking to planned timings. Be aware this is difficult to achieve in the early stages of your studies and be ready to let this skill develop over time.

Questions

Part A: The UK tax system and its administration

Part A covers the UK tax system and its administration, the subject of Chapters 1, 17 and 23 of the BPP Workbook for Taxation (TX – UK).

Section A

OTQ bank – The UK tax system and its administration 1

(36 mins)

1 Which TWO of the following statements are true about inheritance tax?

- ☐ It is an indirect tax.
- ☐ It is a progressive tax.
- ☐ It is an environmental tax.
- ☐ It is a redistributive tax.

(2 marks)

---

2 Which TWO of the following have legal force?

- ☐ Revenue and Customs Brief
- ☐ A Statutory Instrument
- ☐ An Act of Parliament
- ☐ An Extra Statutory Concession

(2 marks)

---

3 Fare plc wishes to appeal against the assessment of £10,000,000 of corporation tax by HM Revenue & Customs (HMRC).

By whom is Fare plc's appeal most likely to be heard?

- O By the First Tier Tribunal
- O By the Upper Tribunal
- O By the Supreme Court
- O By the Court of Appeal

(2 marks)

---

4 Daren made a chargeable gain of £50,000 on the sale of a painting on 30 June 2022. This was Daren's only disposal in the tax year 2022/23. He had previously paid his income tax through deduction at source so has not had to submit a self-assessment tax return.

By what date must Daren notify HM Revenue & Customs (HMRC) of his chargeability to capital gains tax in relation to the gain made on 30 June 2022 and by what date must he pay the capital gains tax liability?

	Notification	Payment
O	31 January 2024	31 January 2024
O	5 October 2023	31 January 2024
O	5 October 2023	31 July 2024
O	31 January 2024	31 July 2024

(2 marks)

---

5 Sarah received NS&I investment account interest of £5,300 in the tax year 2022/23 which she deliberately omitted from her self-assessment tax return for that tax year. She did not attempt to conceal the omission. HM Revenue & Customs (HMRC) discovered the error from records collected from NS&I and Sarah then made a prompted disclosure of the error. Sarah is a higher rate taxpayer and she had already used her savings income nil rate band on other income.

What is the minimum penalty that HMRC may impose on Sarah in respect of this error?

- O £742
- O £1,484
- O £424
- O £1,855

(2 marks)

---

6 For the year ended 30 June 2022, Forgetful Ltd had a corporation tax liability of £166,250, which it did not pay until 31 July 2023. Forgetful Ltd is not a large company.

How much interest will Forgetful Ltd be charged by HM Revenue & Customs (HMRC) in respect of the late payment of its corporation tax liability for the year ended 30 June 2022?

- O £450
- O £2,701
- O £5,403
- O £1,801

(2 marks)

---

7 Mammoth Ltd commenced trading on 1 January 2023. The company's profits have been as follows:

Period	£
Year ended 31 December 2023	524,000
Year ended 31 December 2024	867,000
Year ended 31 December 2025	912,000

Throughout all of these periods, Mammoth Ltd had one related 51% group company.

What is the first year for which Mammoth Ltd will be required to pay its corporation tax liability by quarterly instalments?

- O Year ended 31 December 2024
- O None of the years ended 31 December 2023, 2024 or 2025
- O Year ended 31 December 2025
- O Year ended 31 December 2023

(2 marks)

---

8 Taxes can be either capital taxes or revenue taxes, although some taxes are neither type of tax.

Identify, by clicking on the relevant boxes in the table below, the correct classification for the following three taxes.

Value added tax	NEITHER TYPE	CAPITAL TAX	REVENUE TAX
Inheritance tax	NEITHER TYPE	CAPITAL TAX	REVENUE TAX
National insurance contributions	NEITHER TYPE	CAPITAL TAX	REVENUE TAX

(2 marks)

---

9 In the year ended 31 March 2023, Luck Ltd had taxable total profits of £400,000 and received the following dividends:

	£
From unconnected companies	5,200
From a company in which Luck Ltd has an 80% shareholding	4,300
From a company in which Luck Ltd has a 45% shareholding	1,400

What is the value of Luck Ltd's profits for the year ended 31 March 2023 for the purposes of determining whether it should pay corporation tax in instalments?

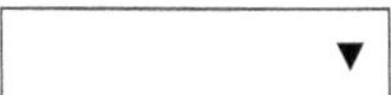

Pull down list

- £405,200
- £405,700
- £406,600
- £410,900

(2 marks)

---

10 On 10 August 2024, Zahra submitted her income tax return electronically for the tax year 2022/23. She paid the tax due of £8,400 on the same day.

What is the MAXIMUM penalty that can be imposed by HM Revenue and Customs (HMRC) in respect of the late filing of Zahra's income tax return?

You are not required to consider penalties for the late payment of tax. ***(March/June 2021)***

- O £100
- O £1,000
- O £1,420
- O £1,300

(2 marks)

(Total = 20 marks)

OTQ bank – The UK tax system and its administration 2

(36 mins)

11 HM Revenue & Customs (HMRC) issued Lenny with a notice to file his self-assessment tax return for the tax year 2022/23 on 30 April 2023. Lenny submitted the return online on 15 March 2024.

Match the due date for submission of the online return and the date by which HMRC will have to notify Lenny of a compliance check into this return.

31 October 2023		Submission
31 January 2024		Notification
15 March 2025		
30 April 2025		

(2 marks)

---

12 Gareth's tax payable for 2021/22 and 2022/23 is as follows:

	2021/22	*2022/23*
	£	£
Income tax	10,000	12,500
Class 2 NIC	159	164
Class 4 NIC	2,000	2,500
Capital gains tax	1,000	2,000

Gareth always pays the correct amount of tax on each due date.

What is the amount payable by Gareth to HM Revenue & Customs (HMRC) on 31 January 2024 in respect of the tax year 2022/23?

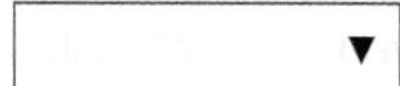

Pull down list

- £4,005
- £4,164
- £5,000
- £5,164

(2 marks)

---

13 For the year to 31 March 2023 Key Ltd, which is not a large company, had a corporation tax liability of £22,400. It paid £10,000 of this liability on 1 December 2023 and the remaining £12,400 on 1 February 2024.

What is the interest payable by Key Ltd on late paid tax?

£ [ ] **(2 marks)**

---

14 Jess plc is required to pay corporation tax by instalments. It had prepared accounts to 31 March each year but decided to prepare accounts for the ten-month period to 31 January 2023. Jess plc's corporation tax liability for the period to 31 January 2023 was £500,000.

What is the amount of the final instalment of corporation tax for the period ended 31 January 2023 and when is it due?

- O £125,000 due on 1 November 2023
- O £166,667 due on 14 January 2023
- O £50,000 due on 14 May 2023
- O £150,000 due on 14 May 2023

(2 marks)

---

15 More Ltd prepares accounts to 30 September each year. It was given notice by HM Revenue & Customs (HMRC) to submit its corporation tax return for the year to 30 September 2022 on 30 November 2022. The return was submitted on 1 December 2023. This was the first late return for the company.

What is the maximum penalty payable by More Ltd as a result of its late submission?

£ [ ] **(2 marks)**

---

16 Mick has already realised a capital gain on the disposal of Asset 1 but is proposing to pretend that the disposal date actually falls into next tax year.

Mick is also planning to dispose of Asset 2 but is proposing to delay the actual sale until after 5 April.

In relation to which disposal(s) is Mick committing tax evasion?

- O Both disposals
- O Neither disposal
- O Asset 1 only
- O Asset 2 only

(2 marks)

---

17 Quinn will not make the balancing payment in respect of her tax liability for the tax year 2021/22 until 17 October 2023.

What is the total percentage penalty which Quinn will be charged by HM Revenue & Customs (HMRC) in respect of the late balancing payment for the tax year 2021/22?

[▼]

Pull down list

- 10%
- 15%
- 30%
- 5%

(2 marks)

---

18 Dennis has made a deliberate error in his self-assessment tax return for the tax year 2022/23.

What is the time limit for HM Revenue & Customs (HMRC) to issue a discovery assessment? ***(June 2018)***

- O 5 April 2024
- O 5 April 2027
- O 5 April 2029
- O 5 April 2043

(2 marks)

---

19 Daljit received a notice from HM Revenue & Customs (HMRC) to submit his self-assessment tax return for the tax year 2022/23. He did not submit the return by the due date.

What can HMRC do to collect any tax owing in respect of Daljit's unfiled return? ***(March 2017)***

[▼]

Pull down list

- Make a determination
- Offer an internal review
- Raise a discovery assessment
- Start a compliance check enquiry into the return

(2 marks)

---

20 Based on her income tax liability of £15,600 for the tax year 2021/22, Sarah was liable to make two payments on account for the tax year 2022/23 of £7,800 each.

In May 2023, Sarah made a claim to reduce her second payment on account to £6,000. This reduced payment was made on 30 September 2023.

Sarah's actual income tax liability for the tax year 2022/23 was £16,000, and she paid the full balance outstanding on 31 January 2024.

How much interest is payable by Sarah to HM Revenue & Customs (HMRC) in respect of her second payment on account for the tax year 2022/23? ***(March 2017)***

- O £62
- O £65
- O £30
- O £20

(2 marks)

(Total = 20 marks)

OTQ bank – The UK tax system and its administration 3 (18 mins)

21 Little Fence Ltd has made up accounts for the 15-month period ended 31 March 2023.

By which date(s) must Little Fence Ltd file its corporation tax self-assessment tax return(s) for the 15-month period ended 31 March 2023? ***(September 2017)***

- O The return for the year ended 31 December 2022 must be filed by 31 October 2023. The return for the period ended 31 March 2023 must be filed by 31 December 2023.
- O One return for the 15-month period ended 31 March 2023 must be filed by 31 March 2024.
- O The return for the year ended 31 December 2022 must be filed by 31 December 2023. The return for the period ended 31 March 2023 must be filed by 31 March 2024.
- O The returns for the year ended 31 December 2022 and the period ended 31 March 2023 must both be filed by 31 March 2024. **(2 marks)**

---

22 Dayfis Ltd was incorporated on 1 October 2022. The company started to trade on 1 December 2022 and made up its first accounts for the period to 30 June 2023.

By which date must Dayfis Ltd notify HM Revenue & Customs (HMRC) of its first accounting period? ***(September 2017)***

- O 1 December 2022
- O 1 January 2023
- O 1 March 2023
- O 30 June 2024 **(2 marks)**

---

23 Dee Ltd has been late in filing its last two self-assessment corporation tax returns. The company's self-assessment corporation tax return for the year ended 31 December 2022 shows corporation tax due of £7,000.

If Dee Ltd files its self-assessment tax return for the year ended 31 December 2022 on 31 August 2024, what amount of penalty will be charged by HM Revenue & Customs (HMRC)? ***(December 2017)***

- O £1,200
- O £700
- O £1,000
- O £1,700

(2 marks)

---

24 Petula filed her self-assessment tax return for the tax year 2021/22 on 20 September 2022. She subsequently amended the return on 29 March 2023.

What is the latest date by which HM Revenue & Customs (HMRC) can give written notice of its intention to commence a compliance check into items changed by the amended tax return? ***(December 2017)***

- O 31 January 2024
- O 20 September 2023
- O 29 March 2024
- O 30 April 2024

(2 marks)

---

25 Certain individuals are required to complete a self-assessment tax return. The taxpayer must sign a declaration that the information given on the tax return and any supplementary pages is correct and complete to the best of the taxpayer's knowledge.

Which of the following statements is FALSE? ***(March 2018)***

- O The tax return comprises a main return form, together with supplementary pages for particular sources of income
- O Partnerships must file a separate return and account for each partner's tax through this return
- O If HM Revenue & Customs (HMRC) calculates the tax for the taxpayer, it merely does so based on the information provided and does not judge the accuracy of it
- O An employee who only has employment income, with the tax collected under PAYE, is not required to complete a tax return

(2 marks)

(Total = 10 marks)

Section B

OT case – Domingo and Fargo (June 2009) (amended) (18 mins)

The following scenario relates to the next five questions.

Domingo and Fargo are brothers. In the tax year 2022/23, Domingo is employed and Fargo is self-employed. Fargo is required to make a balancing payment of £1,800 in respect of his income tax liability for the tax year 2022/23 and payments on account for the tax year 2023/24.

For the tax year 2022/23 Domingo wants to file a paper self-assessment tax return. Fargo wants to file his tax return online. Both notices to file returns were issued by HM Revenue & Customs (HMRC) to Domingo and Fargo on 1 July 2023.

26 What are the latest dates for Domingo and Fargo to submit their respective self-assessment tax returns for the tax year 2022/23 given their stated filing preferences?

	Domingo	Fargo
O	31 October2023	31 October 2023
O	31 October2023	31 January 2024
O	31 January 2024	31 October 2023
O	31 January 2024	31 January 2024

(2 marks)

---

27 How long must Domingo and Fargo retain the records used in preparing their respective tax returns for the tax year 2022/23?

	Domingo	Fargo
O	31 January 2029	31 January 2024
O	31 January 2029	31 January 2026
O	31 January 2025	31 January 2025
O	31 January 2025	31 January 2029

(2 marks)

---

28 What is the maximum penalty that may be imposed on Domingo and Fargo for not retaining their records for the required period?

O £100

O £500

O £1,500

O £3,000

(2 marks)

---

29 What are the dates by which Fargo should make the balancing payment for the tax year 2022/23 and the first payment on account for the tax year 2023/24, and the second payment on account for the tax year 2023/24?

	Balancing payment 2022/23 and first POA 2023/24	Second POA 2023/24
O	31 July 2023	31 July 2024
O	31 July 2023	31 January 2025
O	31 January 2024	31 July 2024
O	31 January 2024	31 January 2025

(2 marks)

---

30 What is the interest payable and the maximum penalty payable if Fargo makes the balancing payment for the tax year 2022/23 exactly four months late?

- O Interest £20, penalty £90
- O Interest £59, penalty £90
- O Interest £20, penalty £180
- O Interest £59, penalty £180

(2 marks)

(Total = 10 marks)

OT case – Ernest (June 2010) (amended) (18 mins)

The following scenario relates to the next five questions.

You should assume that today's date is 30 June 2023.

You are a trainee Chartered Certified Accountant and your firm is dealing with the tax affairs of Ernest.

Ernest's self-assessment tax return for the tax year 2021/22 was submitted to HM Revenue & Customs (HMRC) on 15 May 2022 and Ernest paid the resulting income tax liability by the due date. However, you have just discovered that during the tax year 2021/22 Ernest disposed of a freehold non-residential property, the details of which were omitted from his self-assessment tax return. The capital gains tax liability in respect of this disposal is £18,000 and this amount has not been paid.

Ernest has suggested that since HMRC's right to make a compliance check enquiry into his self-assessment tax return for the tax year 2021/22 expired on 15 May 2023, no disclosure should be made to HMRC of the capital gain.

31 Identify, by clicking on the relevant boxes in the table below, whether each of the following statements concerning tax evasion and tax avoidance is true or false.

Tax evasion is illegal.	TRUE	FALSE
Both tax evasion and tax avoidance are illegal.	TRUE	FALSE
Tax avoidance is legal but may fail if challenged in the courts by HMRC.	TRUE	FALSE
Tax evasion always involves providing HM Revenue & Customs with false information.	TRUE	FALSE

(2 marks)

32 Which TWO of the following statements are correct about how your firm should deal with the suggestion from Ernest that no disclosure is made to HMRC of his capital gain?

- ☐ Ernest should be advised to disclose details of the capital gain to HMRC.
- ☐ If Ernest does not disclose the gain, your firm can still continue to act for him.
- ☐ If your firm ceases to act for Ernest, it must disclose this to HMRC and provide detailed reasons why it has ceased to act.
- ☐ If Ernest does not disclose the gain to HMRC, your firm would be obliged to report under the money laundering regulations.

(2 marks)

---

33 What is the maximum penalty that could be imposed on Ernest for the error by omission in his tax return, assuming that it is considered to be deliberate but not concealed?

- O £18,000
- O £12,600
- O £9,000
- O £5,400

(2 marks)

---

34 Assuming that HMRC discovers the capital gain and Ernest then makes a disclosure of it, what is the minimum penalty that could be imposed on Ernest for the error if it is considered to be deliberate but not concealed?

[▼]

Pull down list

- £0
- £2,700
- £6,300
- £9,000

(2 marks)

---

35 If Ernest pays the capital gains tax liability on 31 July 2023, what is the interest that will be charged on this late payment?

- O £585
- O £506
- O £293
- O £254

(2 marks)

(Total = 10 marks)

OT case – Thai Curry Ltd **(18 mins)**

The following scenario relates to the next five questions.

Thai Curry Ltd prepares accounts for the year ended 31 March 2023 and has taxable total profits of £171,705, resulting in a corporation tax liability of £32,624.

Thai Curry Ltd has previously always submitted its corporation tax returns on time and had a corporation tax liability for the year to 31 March 2022 of £22,000.

The company is in dispute with HM Revenue & Customs (HMRC) in relation to its corporation tax return for the year ended 31 March 2022 and has been offered an internal review of the case.

The case is likely to be allocated to either the complex track or the standard track if it instead chooses to go to a formal appeal.

36 What is the date by which Thai Curry Ltd's self-assessment corporation tax return for the year ended 31 March 2023 should be submitted?

31 December 2023 | 31 January 2024 | 31 March 2024 | 31 July 2024

(2 marks)

---

37 What is the total amount of late filing penalties that will be charged on Thai Curry Ltd if it submits its return for the year ended 31 March 2023 and pays the corporation tax due eight months late?

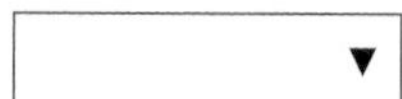

Pull down list

- £3,262
- £3,462
- £6,525
- £6,725

(2 marks)

---

38 How should Thai Curry Ltd's corporation tax liability for the year ended 31 March 2023 be paid?

○ £32,624 on 1 January 2024

○ £11,000 on 31 January 2023 and 31 July 2023, £10,624 on 31 January 2024

○ £8,156 on 14 October 2022, 14 January 2023, 14 April 2023 and 14 July 2023

○ £5,500 on 14 October 2022, 14 January 2023 and 14 April 2023, £16,124 on 14 July 2023 **(2 marks)**

---

39 Which TWO of the following statements are correct about the internal review procedure?

☐ An internal review is a less costly and more effective way to resolve disputes informally than a formal appeal.

☐ The review is carried out by the HMRC officer who has previously dealt with the case.

☐ HMRC must usually carry out the review within 45 days.

☐ After the review conclusion is notified, the company cannot make a further appeal.

(2 marks)

---

40 Match what body is initially likely to hear Thai Curry Ltd's appeal if it does not take up the offer of an internal review.

First tier		Complex track
Upper tier		Standard track

(2 marks)

(Total = 10 marks)

Section C

41 John **(18 mins)**

(a) **You should assume today's date is 30 November 2022.**

John is a new client whom you met today. On 6 April 2021, he commenced in self-employment and prepared his first set of accounts to 5 April 2022. John had not previously filed a self-assessment tax return and has not received any communication from HM Revenue & Customs (HMRC) about his tax affairs. As this will be his first self-assessment tax return, John is also concerned that HMRC might carry out a compliance check.

Required

(i) Advise John of the latest date by which he should have notified HMRC of his chargeability to income tax for the tax year 2021/22 and the maximum and minimum penalties for late notification if he immediately notifies HMRC of his chargeability and is deemed to have been careless. **(3 marks)**

(ii) State the period during which HMRC will have to notify John if it intends to carry out a compliance check in respect of his self-assessment tax return for the tax year 2021/22, and the possible reasons why such a check would be made.

Note. You should assume for part (ii) that John will file his tax return by the due date. **(3 marks)**

(b) The UK Government uses tax policies to encourage certain types of activity.

Required

Briefly explain how the UK Government's tax policies encourage:

(i) Individuals to save **(1 mark)**

(ii) Individuals to support charities **(1 mark)**

(iii) Entrepreneurs to build their own businesses and to invest in plant and machinery **(2 marks)**

(Total = 10 marks)

42 Sugar plc **(18 mins)**

Sugar plc has been in business for many years. It owns 45% of the ordinary shares of Honey plc and 75% of the ordinary shares of Molasses plc. Molasses plc owns 70% of the ordinary shares of Treacle plc. This structure has existed for many years.

In the year to 31 March 2023, Sugar plc had taxable total profits of £470,000. It also received dividends of £50,000 from Honey plc. In the year to 31 March 2024, Sugar plc will have taxable total profits of £600,000. It will not receive any dividends in that year.

Required

(a) Define what is meant by a related 51% group company and explain which companies are related 51% group companies of Sugar plc. **(3 marks)**

(b) Explain whether or not Sugar plc is a large company for the purposes of payment of corporation tax for the years ended 31 March 2023 and 31 March 2024. **(3 marks)**

(c) Assuming that Sugar plc is a large company in both years but was not a large company for any previous year, calculate Sugar plc's corporation tax liabilities for the years ended 31 March 2023 and 31 March 2024 and explain when these will be paid. **(4 marks)**

(Total = 10 marks)

Part B: Income tax and NIC liabilities

Part B covers income tax and NIC liabilities, the subject of Chapters 2 to 12 of the BPP Workbook for Taxation (TX – UK).

Section A

OTQ bank – Income tax and NIC liabilities 1 (36 mins)

43 Hana was UK resident in the tax year 2021/22. He worked full-time in Egypt throughout the tax year 2022/23.

What is the maximum number of days which Hana can spend in the UK and be treated as automatically not resident in the UK for the tax year 2022/23? ***(March 2019)***

- O 15
- O 45
- O 90
- O 182

(2 marks)

---

44 Which TWO of the following types of income are exempt from income tax?

- ☐ Interest on an NS&I Investment account
- ☐ Premium bond prizes
- ☐ Interest on UK government stocks ('gilts')
- ☐ Dividends on shares held in an Individual Savings Account **(2 marks)**

---

45 In the tax year 2022/23 Claudio has taxable income (after deduction of his personal allowance) consisting of £3,000 of non-savings income and £12,500 of savings income.

What is Claudio's income tax liability for the tax year 2022/23?

- O £2,500
- O £2,900
- O £2,700
- O £3,100 **(2 marks)**

---

46 Mike and Delia are a married couple. In the tax year 2022/23, Mike has taxable non-savings income (after deducting his personal allowance) of £13,500.

Delia has no income in the tax year 2022/23. Delia has made an election in relation to her personal allowance for the tax year 2022/23.

What is Mike's income tax liability for the tax year 2022/23?

- O £186
- O £2,448
- O £1,440
- O £2,700 **(2 marks)**

---

47 John is employed by Zebra plc. He was provided with a computer for private use on 6 November 2021.

The market value of the computer when first provided to an employee for private use was £3,600 and the computer had a market value of £2,000 when first provided to John for private use. Zebra plc gave the computer to John on 5 April 2023 when it had a market value of £1,000.

What are the total taxable benefits for John in respect of the computer for the tax year 2022/23?

- O £2,880
- O £3,300
- O £1,720
- O £1,833

(2 marks)

---

48 In the tax year 2022/23 Susie receives employment income of £170,000. She made a gross gift aid donation of £10,000 in January 2023.

What is Susie's income tax liability for the tax year 2022/23?

- O £59,460
- O £61,460
- O £58,960
- O £53,432

(2 marks)

---

49 Petunia is a single parent with a two-year old son. She receives child benefit of £1,134 in the tax year 2022/23. Petunia has net income of £57,000 in 2022/23 and she made gross personal pension contributions of £2,000 during 2022/23.

What is Petunia's child benefit income tax charge for the tax year 2022/23?

- O £1,134
- O £454
- O £567
- O £794

(2 marks)

---

50 Judith works for Sabre Ltd for an annual salary of £18,000. On 30 September 2022, she received a bonus of £4,000 in respect of Sabre Ltd's trading results for the year ended 31 March 2022. She expects to receive a bonus of £4,800 on 30 September 2023 in respect of Sabre Ltd's results for the year ended 31 March 2023. Judith also received £500 from a customer on 1 December 2022 as a gratuity for good service.

What is Judith's employment income for the tax year 2022/23?

- O £22,000
- O £22,800
- O £22,500
- O £23,300

(2 marks)

---

51 Which TWO of the following are qualifying travel expenses?

- ☐ Travel from employer's office to visit a client
- ☐ Travel from home to a workplace to which an employee has been seconded for 36 months

☐ Travel from home to a permanent place of work

☐ Travel from home to visit a trade fair relevant to the employer's business 100 miles away from permanent place of work **(2 marks)**

---

52 Since 2018, Sergey has lived in job-related accommodation provided by his employer for Sergey's personal security. He has an annual gross salary of £60,000 for the tax year 2022/23.

Throughout the tax year 2022/23, Sergey's employer paid for heating, cleaning and lighting the accommodation at a cost of £7,000. His employer also provided Sergey with furniture on 6 April 2022 at a cost of £10,000.

What is the amount assessable on Sergey in the tax year 2022/23 in relation to the furniture, heating, cleaning and lighting costs? ***(March 2018)***

O £6,000

O £9,000

O £7,000

O £8,000 **(2 marks)**

(Total = 20 marks)

OTQ bank – Income tax and NIC liabilities 2 (36 mins)

53 Marion bought £20,000 (nominal value) 5% UK Government Loan Stock on 1 July 2022. Interest is payable on 30 June and 31 December each year. Marion sold the loan stock to Gerald on 31 October 2022 including interest.

Match the amounts amount of savings income taxable on Marion and Gerald in respect of the loan stock for the tax year 2022/23.

£0		Marion
£333		Gerald
£500		
£167		

(2 marks)

---

54 Trevor is employed by Cress plc. He is provided with a car available for private use for the tax year 2022/23. The car has CO_2 emissions of 102 g/km and a list price of £20,000 although Cress plc actually paid £18,000 for the car as the result of a dealer discount.

The car has a diesel engine which does not meet the RDE2 standard. No private fuel is provided.

What is Trevor's taxable car benefit for the tax year 2022/23?

O £4,500

O £5,220

O £5,000

O £5,800 **(2 marks)**

---

55 Troy is a sole trader who had trading income of £60,000 in the tax year 2021/22 and £80,000 in the tax year 2022/23. He has no other income. He joined a personal pension scheme on 6 April 2021 and made gross contributions of £25,000 in 2021/22. This was the first pension provision that Troy had made.

What gross amount can Troy contribute to his personal pension scheme in March 2023 without incurring an annual allowance charge?

[▼]

Pull down list

- £135,000
- £25,000
- £40,000
- £55,000

(2 marks)

---

56 Luke rents out a room in his own residence throughout 2022/23. The rent is £150 a week. Luke's expenses of the letting are £20 per week, none of which is loan interest on the property.

What is the amount of property business income taxable on Luke for 2022/23 if he makes any relevant election?

O £6,760

O £0

O £7,800

O £300 **(2 marks)**

---

57 Susie rents out a furnished house. The house does not qualify as a furnished holiday letting. The furnishings include a new sofa which was bought in the tax year 2022/23 to replace an old one which was disposed of at the same time. The old sofa cost £3,000 in 2015 and was disposed of in January 2023 for proceeds of £200. The new sofa was bought in January 2023 for £5,500 and was larger than the old one. If Susie had bought a newer sofa of the same model as the old one, it would have cost £4,000.

What deduction against property business income can Susie claim for the cost of the sofa bought in 2022/23?

O £5,500

O £3,800

O £5,300

O £4,000 **(2 marks)**

---

58 Amrul bought a house on 1 September 2022 and immediately let it out on a quarterly tenancy with rent of £900 being payable in advance on 1 September, 1 December, 1 March and 1 June each year. The tenant also paid a security deposit of £500. The tenant was still in the property on 5 April 2023.

Amrul paid a buildings insurance premium of £150 on 1 September 2022 for a 12-month period from that date.

Amrul drove 178 miles in his own car in relation to the letting during the period 1 September 2022 to 5 April 2023. He wishes to use approved mileage allowances to calculate his motoring expenses.

What is Amrul's property business income for the tax year 2022/23?

▼

Pull down list

- £1,932
- £2,470
- £2,505
- £2,970

(2 marks)

---

59 Harry is a sole trader. He prepares accounts for the year ended 5 April 2023 and has deducted the following items of expenditure in the statement of profit or loss:

	£
Depreciation	3,000
Accountancy fees for preparing accounts	1,000
Entertainment of:	
Staff (party at £300 per person for 6 employees)	1,800
Customers	2,400

How much should be added back to Harry's net profit to arrive at his adjusted taxable profit?

£ ______ **(2 marks)**

---

60 Rose is a sole trader who prepares accounts to 5 April each year using the cash basis of accounting. Her results for the period of account to 5 April 2023 show the following:

	£
Cash sales	41,000
Invoice sales	4,000
Cash expenses	20,200

The figure for invoice sales includes an invoice for £1,500 which was paid on 10 April 2023. In addition to the cash expenses of £20,200, Rose incurred motoring expenses of £2,800 for driving 8,000 miles of which 6,500 miles were for business purposes. Rose wishes to use approved mileage allowances for motoring.

What is Rose's taxable trading income for the tax year 2022/23?

£ ______ **(2 marks)**

---

61 Olive is self-employed, preparing her accounts to 5 April each year. She claims capital allowances on a car used in her business. The car has a CO_2 emission rate of 145 grams per kilometre, with 40% of Olive's mileage for private purposes. The car had a tax written down value of £12,000 at 6 April 2022. Olive sold the car for £6,000 on 1 November 2022.

What amount of capital allowances can Olive claim in respect of the car for the tax year 2022/23? ***(June 2019)***

- O £3,600
- O £648
- O £2,400
- O £216

(2 marks)

---

62 Ella started in business as a sole trader on 6 November 2022 and prepared her first set of accounts to 5 April 2023. On 6 December 2022 she acquired plant at a cost of £430,000.

What are the maximum capital allowances that Ella can claim for the period of account to 5 April 2023?

[▼]

Pull down list

- £339,133
- £417,667
- £419,067
- £430,000

(2 marks)

(Total = 20 marks)

OTQ bank – Income tax and NIC liabilities 3 (36 mins)

63 Joe has been in business for many years preparing accounts to 5 April each year. The tax written down value of his main pool at 6 April 2022 was £12,000. Joe sold machinery on 10 June 2022 for £11,900 which had originally cost £11,600. He made no acquisitions during the year ended 5 April 2023.

What is the maximum capital allowance that Joe can claim for the period of account to 5 April 2023?

- O £1,000
- O £400
- O £100
- O £72

(2 marks)

---

64 Alexandra started in business as a sole trader on 1 August 2021 and prepared her first set of accounts to 30 April 2023.

Match the start date and the end date of Alexandra's basis period for the tax year 2022/23, her second tax year of trading.

1 August 2021		Start date
6 April 2022		End date
1 May 2022		
31 July 2022		
5 April 2023		
30 April 2023		

(2 marks)

---

65 Timothy started in business as a sole trader on 1 February 2021. He prepared his first set of accounts to 30 November 2021 and his second set of accounts to 30 November 2022. His taxable trading profits were as follows:

p/e 30 November 2021	£30,000
y/e 30 November 2022	£42,000

What are Timothy's overlap profits?

£ [ ] **(2 marks)**

---

66 Abida ceased trading on 31 January 2023. Her recent trading profits were as follows:

Year ended 30 June 2021	£18,400
Year ended 30 June 2022	£11,200
Seven-month period ended 31 January 2023	£7,300

Abida has unused overlap profits of £2,600.

What amount of trading profit will Abida be assessed on for the tax year 2022/23?

(March/June 2021)

£ [ ] **(2 marks)**

---

67 Joyce started in business as a sole trader on 1 January 2022 and prepared her first set of accounts to 30 September 2022 and her second set of accounts to 30 September 2023.

She made the following losses in her first two periods of trading:

	£
p/e 30 September 2	(9,000)
y/e 30 September 2023	(14,400)

Match the amounts of the trading losses with the tax years.

£3,000		2021/22
£9,000		2022/23
£9,600		
£11,400		
£12,600		
£14,400		

(2 marks)

---

68 Humphrey is a sole trader who has been trading for a number of years.

Humphrey incurred a trading loss in the tax year 2022/23. He wishes to make a claim to offset this loss against his total income of the tax year 2021/22.

What is the deadline for Humphrey to claim this relief? ***(December 2018)***

- O 31 January 2024
- O 31 January 2025
- O 5 April 2026
- O 5 April 2027

(2 marks)

---

69 Peter and Jane have been in partnership for many years preparing accounts to 31 July each year and sharing profits equally. On 1 September 2021, they changed their profit-sharing agreement so that Peter was entitled to a salary of £9,000 each year and the remaining profits were then split two parts to Peter and three parts to Jane. The partnership made a trading profit of £96,000 in the year to 31 July 2022.

What is Peter's taxable trading profit for the tax year 2022/23?

£ [ ] **(2 marks)**

---

70 Robin and Stuart had been in partnership for many years preparing accounts to 31 December each year and sharing profits equally. On 1 January 2023, Tania joined the partnership and profits were then split 2:2:1. The partnership made a profit of £96,000 in the year to 31 December 2022 and £112,000 in the year to 31 December 2023.

Match the taxable trading profits of the partners for 2022/23.

£5,600		Robin and Stuart each
£11,200		Tania
£22,400		
£47,200		
£48,000		

(2 marks)

---

71 Shona started in business on 1 January 2023 as a sole trader and prepared her first set of accounts for the 14 weeks to 5 April 2023. Her taxable trading profit for that period was £13,500.

What are Shona's total national insurance contributions for the tax year 2022/23?

£ [ ] **(2 marks)**

---

72 Mark has been in business as a sole trader for many years preparing accounts to 5 April. He made a trading loss of £(2,000) in the year to 5 April 2022 and has not made any claim in respect of this loss. In the year to 5 April 2023, he made a trading profit of £16,700.

What are Mark's Class 4 national insurance contributions for the tax year 2022/23?

£ [ ] **(2 marks)**

(Total = 20 marks)

OTQ bank - Income tax and NIC liabilities 4 (18 mins)

73 Katya is provided with a hybrid-electric company car from 1 July 2022 to 31 December 2022. The car has a list price of £26,000 with CO_2 emissions of 35g/km and an electric range of 39 miles.

What is Katya's car benefit for 2022/23?

£ [ ] **(2 marks)**

---

74 Elsa is employed by Bee Ltd. During the tax year 2022/23, Bee Ltd provided Elsa with the following benefits:

- A private gym membership
- A contribution of £1,800 into Elsa's private pension scheme

Elsa had use of the private gym membership throughout the tax year. The normal membership fee is £1,000, but Bee Ltd negotiated a discount and paid £900 for it.

What amount of class 1A national insurance contributions (NICs) are payable by Bee Ltd in respect of Elsa for the tax year 2022/23? ***(September 2019)***

- O £135
- O £151
- O £406
- O £421

(2 marks)

---

75 Johan is provided with an electric company car throughout the tax year 2022/23. The car has a list price of £30,000 with zero CO_2 emissions. Johan made a capital contribution of £5,550.

What is Johan's car benefit for 2022/23?

£ [ ] **(2 marks)**

---

76 Niamhe has adjusted income for the tax year 2022/23 of £270,000.

During the year, she made personal pension scheme contributions of £100,000 (gross).

Niamhe has no brought forward unused annual allowances.

What is the amount of annual allowance charge to be added to Niamhe's taxable income for the tax year 2022/23? ***(December 2019)***

- O £75,000
- O £60,000
- O £90,000
- O £25,000

(2 marks)

---

77 Dane and Zara are a married couple.

They jointly own a residential property which is let to tenants. In the tax year 2022/23 the property business income from the property is £20,000. Dane owns 25% of the property and Zara owns the other 75%. No election has been made in relation to the ownership of the property.

Zara earns employment income of £65,000 and Dane receives £1,885 of child benefit in the tax year 2022/23. Dane has no other income.

Which TWO of the following statements are true in relation to Zara's income tax liability for the tax year 2022/23? ***(March 2020)***

- ☐ Zara's taxable income is £62,430.
- ☐ Zara can reduce her income tax liability by claiming the transferable personal allowance (the 'marriage allowance').
- ☐ It would be beneficial to Zara if the couple were to make a joint election to HM Revenue and Customs (HMRC) specifying their actual ownership share in the residential property.
- ☐ A child benefit charge of £1,885 will be added to Zara's income tax liability. **(2 marks)**

(Total = 10 marks)

Section B

OT case – Ann, Basil and Chloe (December 2008) (amended) (18 mins)

The following scenario relates to the next five questions.

Ann

Ann is self-employed. Her taxable income for the tax year 2022/23 was £76,000 which was all trading income. Ann made contributions of £49,000 (gross) into a personal pension scheme between September 2022 and March 2023. This was the second year that she had been a member of a pension scheme and she had an unused annual allowance of £20,000 brought forward from 2021/22.

Basil

Basil is employed. During the tax year 2022/23 Basil had taxable income of £250,000 which was all employment income. Basil made contributions of £50,000 (gross) into a personal pension scheme during the tax year 2022/23. This was the first year that he had been a member of a pension scheme. In future, his employer may contribute to Basil's personal pension scheme.

Chloe

Chloe lets out an unfurnished property. For the tax year 2022/23, her taxable income was £16,630 which was all property business income. Chloe made contributions of £8,200 (gross) into a personal pension scheme during the tax year 2022/23. This was the first year that she had been a member of a pension scheme. Chloe does not have any interest payable on her buy-to-let property.

78 Which TWO of the following statements about relevant earnings are correct?

- ☐ Individuals can always make gross pension contributions of £3,600 in 2022/23 even if they do not have any relevant earnings in that tax year.
- ☐ Relevant earnings relate both to contributions to personal pension schemes and to occupational pension schemes.
- ☐ If an individual makes pension contributions less than relevant earnings in a tax year, the excess can be carried forward for three years and used to cover pension contributions.
- ☐ Relevant earnings do not include income from furnished holiday lettings. **(2 marks)**

---

79 Identify, by clicking on the relevant boxes in the table below, whether each of the following statements about the annual allowance is true or false.

Employer contributions do not count towards the annual allowance.	**TRUE**	**FALSE**
The annual allowance can be carried forward for three years to the extent that it is unused in the tax year.	**TRUE**	**FALSE**
The annual allowance is available even if the individual is not a member of a pension scheme in a tax year and so can be carried forward.	**TRUE**	**FALSE**
If tax-relievable pension contributions exceed the annual allowance, there is a charge to income tax.	**TRUE**	**FALSE**

(2 marks)

---

80 What is Ann's income tax liability for the tax year 2022/23?

£ [ ] **(2 marks)**

---

81 What is Basil's annual allowance charge for the tax year 2022/23?

£ [ ] **(2 marks)**

---

82 What is Chloe's tax relief on her pension contribution for the tax year 2022/23?

- O £0
- O £1,640
- O £900
- O £720

(2 marks)

(Total = 10 marks)

OT case – Ae, Bee, Cae, and Eu (December 2018) (amended) (18 mins)

The following scenario relates to the next five questions.

Ae, Bee and Cae

Ae and Bee commenced in partnership on 1 July 2020 preparing accounts to 30 April. Cae joined as a partner on 1 July 2022. Profits were always shared equally. The partnership's trading profits since the commencement of trading have been as follows:

	£
Period ended 30 April 2021	54,000
Year ended 30 April 2022	66,000
Year ended 30 April 2023	87,000

Eu

Eu ceased trading on 30 September 2024, having been self-employed since 1 July 2013.

(1) Eu's trading profits for the final three periods of trading were as follows:

These figures are before taking account of capital allowances.

	£
Year ended 30 June 2023	62,775
Year ended 30 June 2024	57,600
Three-month period ended 30 September 2024	14,400

(2) Eu's capital allowances in the year to 30 June 2023 were £1,575 and in the year to 30 June 2024 were £1,292.

(3) The tax written down value of the capital allowances main pool at 1 July 2024 was £5,883. On 15 September 2024, Eu purchased office furniture for £2,400. All of the items included in the main pool were sold for £5,175 (all for less than cost) on 30 September 2024.

(4) Until the final period of trading Eu had always prepared accounts to 30 June. Her overlap profits for the period 1 July 2013 to 5 April 2014 were £9,800.

83 What is Ae's trading income assessment for the tax year 2021/22?

- O £27,000
- O £24,300
- O £32,500
- O £33,000

(2 marks)

---

84 What is Cae's trading income assessment for the tax year 2022/23?

- O £26,583
- O £24,167
- O £29,000
- O £21,750

(2 marks)

---

85 What is Eu's trading income assessment for the tax year 2023/24?

- O £56,025
- O £62,775
- O £57,600
- O £61,200

(2 marks)

---

86 What are Eu's capital allowances for the three-month period ended 30 September 2024?

- O £3,108
- O £1,491
- O £2,775
- O £559

(2 marks)

---

87 Assuming that the capital allowances for the three-month period ended 30 September 2024 were £3,000, what is Eu's trading income assessment for the tax year 2024/25?

- O £1,600
- O £57,908
- O £62,200
- O £67,708

(2 marks)

(Total = 10 marks)

OT case – Rosie and Sam (December 2012) (amended) (18 mins)

The following scenario relates to the next five questions.

You should assume that today's date is 15 February 2023.

Rosie

Rosie has recently been promoted to managing director at Hornburg plc. During the tax year 2022/23, Rosie will be paid gross director's remuneration of £260,000 and she has received dividend income of £500,000. She had income of £130,000 in 2019/20, 2020/21 and 2021/22.

She has made the following gross personal pension contributions:

Tax year	*Pension contribution*
	£
2020/21	26,000
2021/22	Nil

Rosie has been a member of a pension scheme since the tax year 2020/21 and Hornburg plc makes an employer's contribution of £10,000 per year.

Sam

In September 2020, Sam invested £7,000 in a flexible cash ISA. In May 2022, he invested a further £6,000 in that cash ISA. He withdrew £5,000 from the cash ISA in October 2022. Sam is now considering investing more cash into the cash ISA before 5 April 2023. He also invested £4,000 in premium bonds and government securities ('gilts') in the tax year 2022/23.

88 What is the total pension scheme annual allowance that Rosie has available for the tax year 2022/23?

- O £74,000
- O £38,000
- O £114,000
- O £78,000

(2 marks)

---

89 Use ONE of the following to complete the sentence below:

If Rosie makes pension contributions in excess of her available annual allowances, there will be a charge to income tax at [▼] % on the excess contributions.

Pull down list

- 20
- 25
- 45
- 55

(2 marks)

---

90 What are the tax consequences for Rosie if she takes pension benefits under flexible access drawdown?

	Lump sum	*Rest of pension fund*
O	Up to 10% of fund can be taken tax free	Taxable as pension income when received
O	Up to 10% of fund can be taken as tax-free lump sum	5% of fund taxable as pension income each year whether or not received
O	Up to 25% of fund can be taken as tax-free lump sum	5% of fund taxable as pension income each year whether or not received
O	Up to 25% of fund can be taken as tax-free lump sum	Taxable as pension income when received

(2 marks)

91 What is the maximum amount that Sam can invest into the cash ISA for the tax year 2022/23 in addition to his investments already made?

Pull down list

- £12,000
- £14,000
- £15,000
- £19,000

(2 marks)

---

92 Match the income tax and capital gains tax treatments of Sam's investments in premium bonds and government securities.

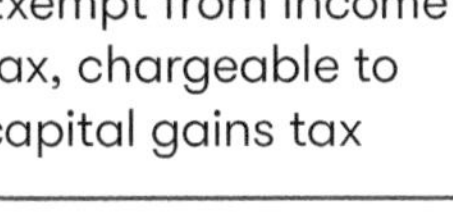

Exempt from income tax, chargeable to capital gains tax

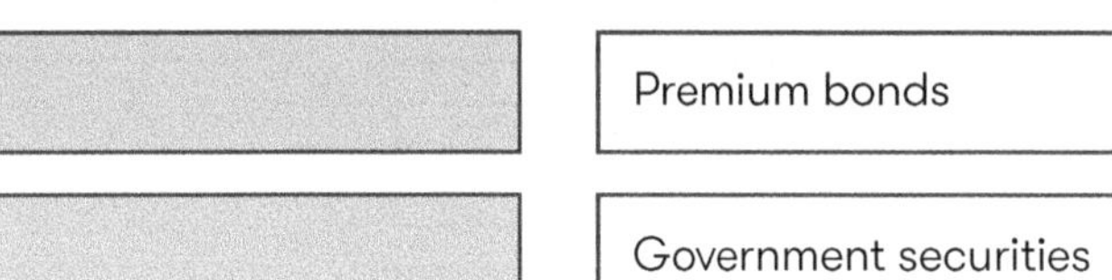

Chargeable to income tax and capital gains tax

Exempt from both income tax and capital gains tax

Chargeable to income tax, exempt from capital gains tax

(2 marks)

(Total = 10 marks)

OT case – Fang and Hong (December 2013) (amended) (18 mins)

The following scenario relates to the next five questions.

Fang

Fang commenced self-employment on 1 August 2020. She has a trading profit of £45,960 for the year ended 31 July 2021, and a trading profit of £39,360 for the year ended 31 July 2022. Fang has overlap profits on commencement.

Hong

Hong has been in self-employment since 2007, preparing accounts to 5 April. For the year ended 5 April 2023 she made a trading loss of £45,800, and has claimed this against her total income for the tax year 2021/22. For the year ended 5 April 2022, Hong made a trading profit of £29,700. She also has a property business profit of £3,900 for the tax year 2021/22. Hong has an unused trading loss of £2,600 brought forward from the tax year 2020/21.

During the tax year 2021/22, Hong disposed of an investment property and this resulted in a chargeable gain. As Hong has claimed relief against total income of this tax year, she may include a further claim to set the trading loss against her chargeable gain for the year.

93 Match the amount of trading profit which will have been assessed on Fang for each of the tax years 2020/21 and 2021/22.

Amounts		Tax years
£30,640		2020/21
£39,360		2021/22
£45,960		
£48,000		

(2 marks)

94 In which of the following ways can overlap profits be relieved?

- O Against first available current year basis profits
- O Against trading income on cessation
- O Against general income of tax year of commencement and/or preceding tax year
- O Against general income in the three tax years preceding the year of commencement

(2 marks)

95 How could Fang have obtained relief for trading expenditure incurred prior to 1 August 2020 and for computer equipment which Fang already owned which was brought into business use on 1 August 2020?

	Trading expenditure	*Computer equipment*
O	Added to overlap profit and relieved on cessation	Addition for capital allowances purposes based on its original cost
O	Treated as incurred on 1 August 2020	Addition for capital allowances purposes based on its original cost
O	Added to overlap profit and relieved on cessation	Addition for capital allowances purposes based on market value at 1 August 2020
O	Treated as incurred on 1 August 2020	Addition for capital allowances purposes based on market value at 1 August 2020

(2 marks)

96 What was the amount of loss for the year ended 5 April 2023 which was relieved against Hong's income for the tax year 2021/22?

[▼]

Pull down list

- £18,430
- £2,600
- £31,000
- £33,600

(2 marks)

---

97 Which TWO of the following statements about the further claim to set Hong's trading loss against her chargeable gain for the tax year 2021/22 are correct?

☐ The trading loss is first set against general income of the tax year 2021/22 and only any excess loss is set against chargeable gains of that year.

☐ The amount of chargeable gains for the tax year 2021/22 is computed ignoring the annual exempt amount for the purposes of this relief.

☐ Capital losses of the tax year 2021/22 are taken into account, but not brought forward losses, for the purposes of this relief.

☐ Hong can specify the amount to be set against chargeable gains, so her annual exempt amount for the tax year 2021/22 is not wasted. **(2 marks)**

(Total = 10 marks)

OT case – Chi (June 2014) (amended) (18 mins)

The following scenario relates to the next five questions.

Chi commenced self-employment on 6 April 2022, and for the year ended 5 April 2023 her trading profit using the normal accruals basis was £53,000, calculated as follows:

	Note	£	£
Revenue	1		72,500
Expenses			
Motor expenses	2	4,400	
Other expenses	3	8,200	
Capital allowances	4	6,900	
			(19,500)
Trading profit			53,000

Notes.

1 **Revenue**

The revenue figure of £72,500 includes receivables of £1,600 which were owed as at 5 April 2023.

2 **Motor expenses**

The total motor expenses for the year ended 5 April 2023 were £5,500, of which 20% was for private journeys. This proportion has been disallowed in calculating the trading profit. During the year ended 5 April 2023, Chi drove 13,200 business miles.

3 **Other expenses**

The other expenses figure of £8,200 includes payables of £900 owed as at 5 April 2023.

4 **Capital allowances**

Capital allowances consist of an annual investment allowance claim of £4,020 in respect of office equipment purchased on 6 April 2022, and a writing down allowance of £2,880 claimed in respect of Chi's car. The car had cost £20,000 on 6 April 2022.

98 Based on the trading profit of £53,000 for the year ended 5 April 2023, what is Chi's income tax liability for the tax year 2022/23?

£ [ ] **(2 marks)**

---

99 Based on the trading profit of £53,000 for the year ended 5 April 2023, what are the Class 4 national insurance contributions payable by Chi for the tax year 2022/23?

£ [ ] **(2 marks)**

---

100 Which TWO of the following statements about the cash basis of assessment are correct?

☐ The trader must prepare accounts to 5 April each year.

☐ The trader can deduct capital expenditure on plant and machinery (other than cars) as business expenses rather than using capital allowances.

☐ A trader can start to use the cash basis if his receipts for the tax year do not exceed £150,000.

☐ Under the cash basis, a trader can offset losses against other income or gains.

(2 marks)

---

101 If Chi uses the cash basis and claims approved mileage allowances, what is the amount of motor expenses (Note 2) which are allowable?

○ £4,400

○ £5,300

○ £5,940

○ £8,180 **(2 marks)**

---

102 If Chi uses the cash basis, what is the amount of revenue which is chargeable (Note 1) and the other expenses (Note 3) which are allowable for the year ended 5 April 2023?

○ Revenue £72,500, other expenses £8,200

○ Revenue £70,900, other expenses £8,200

○ Revenue £72,500, other expenses £7,300

○ Revenue £70,900, other expenses £7,300 **(2 marks)**

(Total = 10 marks)

Section C

103 Kagan (September/December 2019) (18 mins)

This scenario relates to four requirements.

You should assume that today's date is 4 April 2022.

On 2 April 2022, Kagan inherited some quoted ordinary shares valued at £510,000 following the death of his aunt. Kagan is unsure whether to retain the shares or sell some of them in order to make some alternative investments.

Kagan is aged 61 and is an additional rate taxpayer. Prior to the inheritance, his taxable income, consisting entirely of employment income, for the tax year 2022/23 would have been £400,000. The income tax liability on this income for the tax year 2022/23 would have been £165,000.

Prior to receiving the inheritance, Kagan's chargeable estate for inheritance tax (IHT) purposes was valued at £1,700,000. IHT of £550,000 would be payable were he to die in the near future.

Retain the inherited shares

If Kagan simply retains the inherited shares, then he will receive dividend income of £15,300 during the tax year 2022/23. This is in addition to his employment income of £400,000.

Sell some inherited shares and make four alternative investments

Kagan is considering selling some of his inherited shares (for which there has only been a minimal increase in value since he inherited them) to fund the following four investments, all of which will be made at the start of the tax year 2022/23:

(1) Kagan will make a gross personal pension contribution of £100,000. Kagan is a member of a pension scheme but has not made any contributions in recent years because his income has been substantially lower than it is for the tax year 2022/23. Kagan will immediately withdraw £25,000 of the pension fund tax free. This is the permitted 25% tax-free lump sum. However, no pension will be taken during the tax year 2022/23.

(2) Kagan will invest £50,000 in premium bonds. The expected amount of premium bond prizes which will be received during the tax year 2022/23 is £700.

(3) Kagan will invest the maximum permitted amount of £20,000 in a cash individual savings account (ISA). This ISA will pay interest of £400 during the tax year 2022/23.

(4) Kagan will purchase a freehold property for £295,000 (including all costs of purchase). The property will be let out unfurnished, with Kagan receiving property income of £9,600 during the tax year 2022/23.

After making these four investments, Kagan will be left with £65,000 of inherited shares, on which he will receive dividend income of £1,950 during the tax year 2022/23. He will also have his employment income of £400,000.

Kagan will not make any other disposals during the tax year 2022/23.

Required

(a) Calculate Kagan's revised income tax liability for the tax year 2022/23 if he retains the inherited shares. **(1 mark)**

(b) Answer the following questions:

(i) Explain why little or no capital gains tax (CGT) will be payable if Kagan sells some of his inherited shares. **(1 mark)**

(ii) Calculate Kagan's revised income tax liability for the tax year 2022/23 if he sells some of his inherited shares and makes the four alternative investments.

Notes.

1 For this part, you are expected to produce a full income tax computation.

2 You should indicate by use of zero (0) any items which are not taxable. **(6 marks)**

(c) For each of the four alternative investments (pension contribution, premium bonds, ISA and freehold property), state whether the investment will reduce Kagan's potential IHT liability compared to him retaining the inherited shares.

Note. For this part of the question, no computations are required. **(2 marks)**

(Total = 10 marks)

104 Michael and Sean (June 2012) (amended) **(18 mins)**

You are a trainee Chartered Certified Accountant and your manager has asked for your help regarding two taxpayers who have both made trading losses.

Michael

Michael commenced in self-employment on 1 July 2021, preparing accounts to 5 April. His results for the first two periods of trading were as follows:

	£
Nine-month period ended 5 April 2022 – Trading loss	(26,230)
Year ended 5 April 2023 – Trading profit	9,665

For the tax years 2017/18 to 2019/20, Michael had the following income from employment:

	£
2017/18	45,100
2018/19	20,365
2019/20	57,095

Michael did not have any income during the period 6 April 2020 to 30 June 2021.

Sean

Sean has been in self-employment since 2010 but ceased trading on 31 December 2022. He has always prepared accounts to 31 December. His results for the final five years of trading were:

	£
Year ended 31 December 2018 – Trading profit	21,300
Year ended 31 December 2019 – Trading profit	14,400
Year ended 31 December 2020 – Trading profit	18,900
Year ended 31 December 2021 – Trading profit	3,700
Year ended 31 December 2022 – Trading loss	(23,100)

For each of the tax years 2018/19 to 2022/23, Sean has property business profits of £12,600.

Sean has unused overlap profits brought forward of £3,600.

Required

For each of the two taxpayers, Michael and Sean, identify the loss relief claims that are available to them, and explain which of the available claims would be the most beneficial.

Notes.

1 You should clearly state the amount of any reliefs claimed and the rates of income tax saved. However, you are not expected to calculate any income tax liabilities.

2 Assume that the tax rates and allowances for the tax year 2022/23 apply throughout.

3 The following mark allocation is provided as guidance for this requirement:

Michael, 4½ marks Sean, 5½ marks

(Total = 10 marks)

105 Paul and Palu Ltd (March/June 2021) (amended) (18 mins)

This scenario relates to one requirement.

You should assume that today's date is 15 March 2022.

Paul is the managing director of, and 100% shareholder in, Palu Ltd.

For the year ended 5 April 2023, Palu Ltd's tax adjusted trading profit, before taking account of director's remuneration, is forecast to be £175,000. Paul intends to extract all of Palu Ltd's profits (after allowing for corporation tax). This will be achieved by paying himself gross director's remuneration of £8,000 and dividends of £135,270.

Paul wants to know if it would be beneficial to cease trading via Palu Ltd on 5 April 2022, and instead run his business from 6 April 2022 onwards as a sole trader. His tax adjusted trading profit for the year ended 5 April 2023 would remain unchanged at £175,000.

Paul will not have any other income for the tax year 2022/23.

Required

Determine whether or not there will be an overall saving of tax and national insurance contributions (NICs) for the year ended 5 April 2023 if Palu Ltd's business is instead run by Paul as a sole trader from 6 April 2022.

Notes.

1 You are expected to calculate the income tax payable by Paul, any NICs payable by Paul and Palu Ltd, and the corporation tax liability of Palu Ltd for the year ended 5 April 2023 assuming that he continues to run the business via the company.

2 You should then compare this total amount with the income tax and NICs payable by Paul assuming that he runs the business as a sole trader.

3 You should assume that the rate of corporation tax remains unchanged.

(Total = 10 marks)

106 Robinette (September/December 2019) (27 mins)

This scenario relates to three requirements.

Robinette ceased self-employment on 30 June 2022. She was then employed by Bird plc for the six-month period from 1 August 2022 to 31 January 2023. Robinette commenced self-employment again, in a new business, on 1 February 2023.

Self-employment ceasing on 30 June 2022

(1) Robinette's trading profit for the final 14-month period of trading from 1 May 2021 to 30 June 2022 was £106,900. This figure is **before** taking account of capital allowances.

(2) The tax written down value of the capital allowances main pool at 1 May 2021 was £15,300. On 11 June 2021 Robinette purchased a laptop computer for £2,600.

On the cessation of trading, Robinette personally retained the laptop computer. Its value on 30 June 2022 was £1,750. The remaining items included in the main pool were sold for £7,300 on 30 June 2022.

(3) Robinette had unused overlap profits brought forward of £22,700.

Employment from 1 August 2022 to 31 January 2023

(1) During the six-month period from 1 August 2022 to 31 January 2023, Robinette was paid a gross monthly salary of £10,600 in respect of her employment with Bird plc.

(2) Throughout the period from 1 August 2022 to 31 January 2023, Bird plc provided Robinette with living accommodation. The property was rented by Bird plc at a cost of £690 per month (this is higher than the annual value of the property). Bird plc also paid for the running costs relating to the property, and for the period 1 August 2022 to 31 January 2023 these amounted to £1,440.

(3) Throughout the period from 1 August 2022 to 31 January 2023, Robinette's two-year old son was provided with a place at Bird plc's workplace nursery. The total cost to the company of providing this nursery place was £4,800 (120 days at £40 per day).

(4) Robinette used her private car for business purposes. During the period from 1 August 2022 to 31 January 2023, she drove 5,200 miles in the performance of her duties for Bird plc, for which the company paid an allowance of 35 pence per mile.

Self-employment from 1 February 2023

(1) Robinette's trading profit for the first five-month period of trading from 1 February to 30 June 2023 was £55,700. This figure is **before** taking account of capital allowances.

(2) The only item of plant and machinery owned by Robinette, and used in this business, is office equipment which was purchased for £26,200 on 1 February 2023.

Property income

(1) During the period 1 August 2022 to 31 January 2023, Robinette let out her main residence at a monthly rent of £1,100. Robinette lived in this property up to 31 July 2022 and then again from 1 February 2023 onwards.

(2) The only expenditure incurred by Robinette in respect of the letting was property insurance, which cost £624 for the year ended 5 April 2023.

(3) Robinette has opted to calculate her property income using the accruals basis. Rent-a-room relief is not available in respect of the letting.

Self-assessment tax return

Robinette filed her self-assessment tax return for the tax year 2022/23 on 14 August 2023. She is quite confident that all of her income for the tax year 2022/23 was correctly declared and that no deductions were incorrectly claimed.

Required

(a) Calculate Robinette's taxable income for the tax year **2022/23.**

Note. You should indicate by the use of zero (0) any items which are not taxable or deductible. **(12 marks)**

(b) (i) State the period during which HM Revenue and Customs (HMRC) will have to notify Robinette if they intend to carry out a compliance check in respect of her self-assessment tax return for the tax year 2022/23, and the likely reason why such a check would be made. **(2 marks)**

(ii) Advise Robinette as to how long she must retain the records used in preparing her self-assessment tax return for the tax year **2022/23.** **(1 mark)**

(Total = 15 marks)

107 Lucy (18 mins)

Assume that it is 1 March 2022.

Lucy is considering two work arrangements. She will start her chosen arrangement on 6 April 2022 and will continue with that arrangement for the whole of the tax year 2022/23.

Employment with Red plc

Lucy has been offered employment with Red plc. She would be paid a salary of £36,000 and would be required to work at Red plc's offices.

Lucy would travel from home to Red plc's offices by train and would buy an annual season ticket costing £1,500.

Self-employment

Lucy would work for a number of clients at their offices. She would receive fees of £36,000 from her clients in the year to 5 April 2023.

Lucy would travel from home to client offices in her own car. Her business mileage would be 4,600 miles during the year and she estimates this would actually cost 40p per mile.

Lucy would prepare accounts to 5 April 2023 and elect to use the cash basis and approved mileage allowances.

Required

Determine which of the work arrangements would result in Lucy having a higher amount of disposable income after deducting income tax, national insurance contributions and travel costs.

Note. You are expected to calculate the income tax and NIC liability for Lucy for each arrangement and then calculate her disposable income in each case, taking into account her travel costs.

(Total = 10 marks)

108 Daniel, Francine and Gregor (September/December 2015) (18 mins)

(a) Amanda, Beatrice and Claude have been in partnership since 1 November 2013, preparing accounts to 31 October annually. Daniel joined as a partner on 1 May 2022. Profits have always been shared equally. The partnership's recent tax adjusted trading profits are as follows:

	£
Year ended 31 October 2021	147,000
Year ended 31 October 2022	96,000
Year ended 31 October 2023 (forecast)	180,000

Required

Calculate Daniel's trading income assessment for the tax year 2022/23. **(3 marks)**

(b) Francine is employed by Fringe plc. On 1 August 2022, Fringe plc provided Francine with a loan of £96,000 to help her purchase a holiday cottage. On 1 October 2022, the loan was increased by a further £14,000 so that Francine could renovate the cottage. Francine pays interest at an annual rate of 1.5% on this loan.

The taxable benefit in respect of this loan is calculated using the average method.

Required

Calculate Francine's taxable benefit for the tax year 2022/23 in respect of the loan from Fringe plc. **(3 marks)**

(c) Gregor has been self-employed since 6 April 2005. He has the following income and chargeable gains for the tax years 2021/22 and 2022/23:

	2021/22	*2022/23*
	£	£
Trading profit/(loss)	14,700	(68,800)
Business property profit/(loss)	4,600	(2,300)
Building society interest (gross)	1,300	900
Chargeable gain/(loss)	(2,900)	17,400

Required

On the assumption that Gregor relieves his trading loss of £68,800 as early as possible, calculate the amount of trading loss carried forward to the tax year 2023/24.

Note. You should assume that the tax allowances for the tax year 2022/23 apply throughout. **(4 marks)**

(Total = 10 marks)

109 George (March/June 2016) (18 mins)

You should assume that today's date is 1 March 2022.

George is a software developer. He has accepted a one-year contract to update software for Xpee plc.

(1) The contract will run from 6 April 2022 to 5 April 2023, with a fee of £40,000 payable for the entire year of the contract. A condition of the contract is that George will have to do the work personally and not be permitted to sub-contract the work to anyone else.

(2) George will work from home but will have to attend weekly meetings at Xpee plc's offices to receive instructions regarding the work to be performed during the following week.

(3) George will not incur any significant expenses in respect of the contract apart from the purchase of a new laptop computer for £3,600 on 6 April 2022. This laptop will be used 100% for business purposes.

(4) During the term of the contract, George will not be permitted to work for any other clients. He will therefore not have any other income during the tax year 2022/23.

(5) George's tax liability for the tax year 2021/22 was collected through PAYE, so he will not be required to make any payments on account in respect of the tax year 2022/23.

George has several friends who are also software developers. He understands that his employment status is not clear cut but that his income tax liability for the tax year 2022/23 will be the same regardless of whether he is treated as employed or as self-employed. However, George appreciates that there are advantages to being classed as self-employed.

Required

(a) List **FOUR** factors which are indicators of George being treated as an employee in relation to his contract with Xpee plc rather than as self-employed.

Note. You should confine your answer to the information given in the question. **(2 marks)**

(b) Calculate George's income tax liability and national insurance contributions for the tax year 2022/23 if he is treated as self-employed in respect of his contract with Xpee plc. **(4 marks)**

(c) If George is treated as being an employee of Xpee plc instead of self-employed:

(i) Explain why George's income tax liability will be payable earlier. **(2 marks)**

(ii) Calculate the additional amount of national insurance contributions which he personally will suffer for the tax year 2022/23. **(2 marks)**

(Total = 10 marks)

110 Joe (December 2010) (amended) (27 mins)

On 31 December 2022, Joe resigned as an employee of Firstly plc, and on 1 January 2023 commenced employment with Secondly plc. The following information is available for the tax year 2022/23:

Employment with Firstly plc

(1) From 6 April 2022 to 31 December 2022, Joe was paid a salary of £6,360 per month. In addition to his salary, Joe was paid a bonus of £12,000 on 12 May 2022. He had become entitled to this bonus on 22 March 2022.

(2) Joe contributed 6% of his monthly gross salary of £6,360 into Firstly plc's occupational pension scheme. Firstly, plc contributed 3%.

(3) On 1 May 2022, Firstly plc provided Joe with an interest-free loan of £120,000 so that he could purchase a holiday cottage. Joe repaid £50,000 of the loan on 31 July 2022 and repaid the balance of the loan of £70,000 when he ceased employment with Firstly plc on 31 December 2022.

(4) During the period from 6 April 2022 to 31 December 2022, Joe was provided with a company van that he used as his only vehicle. The van had emissions of 40g/km CO_2.

(5) Firstly plc provided Joe with a home entertainment system for his personal use costing £4,400 on 6 April 2022. The company gave the home entertainment system to Joe for free when he left the company on 31 December 2022, although its market value at that time was £3,860.

Employment with Secondly plc

(1) From 1 January 2023 to 5 April 2023, Joe was paid a salary of £6,565 per month. He worked one day a week at home and the remainder at Secondly plc's offices.

(2) During the period 1 January 2023 to 5 April 2023, Joe contributed a total of £3,000 (gross) into a personal pension scheme.

(3) From 1 January 2023 to 5 April 2023, Secondly plc provided Joe with living accommodation. The property has an annual value of £10,400 and is rented by Secondly plc at a cost of £2,250 per month. On 1 January 2023, Secondly plc purchased furniture for the property at a cost of £16,320.

(4) From 1 January 2023 to 5 April 2023, Secondly plc paid Joe £15 per month to cover additional household costs incurred when he worked at home.

Required

Calculate Joe's employment income for the tax year 2022/23.

(Total = 15 marks)

111 Sammi (December 2010) (27 mins)

You should assume that today's date is 20 March 2022.

Sammi is a director of Smark Ltd, a profitable company. The company has given her the choice of being provided with a leased company car or alternatively being paid additional director's remuneration and then privately leasing the same car herself.

Company car

The car will be provided throughout the tax year 2022/23 and will be leased by Smark Ltd at an annual cost of £27,630. The car will be petrol powered, will have a list price of £80,000, and will have an official CO_2 emission rate of 185 grams per kilometre.

The lease payments will cover all the costs of running the car except for fuel. Smark Ltd will not provide Sammi with any fuel for private journeys.

Additional director's remuneration

As an alternative to having a company car, Sammi will be paid additional gross director's remuneration of £27,000 during the tax year 2022/23. She will then privately lease the car at an annual cost of £27,630.

Other information

The amount of business journeys that will be driven by Sammi will be immaterial and can therefore be ignored.

Sammi's current level of director's remuneration is over £150,000 which means that she will pay income tax at the additional rate of 45% in 2022/23. Smark Ltd prepares its accounts to 5 April. The lease of the car will commence on 6 April 2022.

Required

(a) Advise Sammi of the income tax and national insurance contribution implications for the tax year 2022/23 if she (1) is provided with the company car, and (2) receives additional director's remuneration of £27,000. **(5 marks)**

(b) Advise Smark Ltd of the corporation tax and national insurance contribution implications for the year ended 5 April 2023 if the company (1) provides Sammi with the company car, and (2) pays Sammi additional director's remuneration of £27,000.

Note. You should ignore value added tax (VAT). **(5 marks)**

(c) Determine which of the two alternatives is the more beneficial from each of the respective points of view of Sammi and Smark Ltd. **(5 marks)**

(Total = 15 marks)

112 Simon (December 2009) (27 mins)

On 19 April 2022, Simon purchased a derelict freehold house for £127,000. Legal fees of £1,800 were paid in respect of the purchase.

Simon then renovated the house at a cost of £50,000, with the renovation being completed on 6 August 2022. He immediately put the house up for sale, and it was sold on 27 August 2022 for £260,000. Legal fees of £2,600 were paid in respect of the sale.

Simon financed the transaction by a bank loan of £150,000 that was taken out on 19 April 2022 at an annual interest rate of 6%. The bank loan was repaid on 28 August 2022.

Simon had no other income or capital gains for the tax year 2022/23 except as indicated above.

Simon has been advised that whether or not he is treated as carrying on a trade will be determined according to the six following 'badges of trade':

(1) Subject matter of the transaction

(2) Length of ownership

(3) Frequency of similar transactions

(4) Work done on the property

(5) Circumstances responsible for the realisation

(6) Motive

Required

(a) Briefly explain the meaning of each of the six 'badges of trade' listed in the question.

Note. You are not expected to quote from decided cases. **(3 marks)**

(b) Calculate Simon's income tax liability and his Class 2 and Class 4 national insurance contributions for the tax year 2022/23, if he is treated as carrying on a trade in respect of the disposal of the freehold house. **(8 marks)**

(c) Calculate Simon's capital gains tax liability for the tax year 2022/23, if he is not treated as carrying on a trade in respect of the disposal of the freehold house. **(4 marks)**

(Total = 15 marks)

113 Alfred and Amaia (March/June 2021) (amended) (27 mins)

Alfred and Amaia are a married couple.

Alfred

Alfred commenced trading as a sole trader on 1 September 2022. He prepared his first set of accounts for the seven-month period ended 31 March 2023, and his draft tax adjusted trading profit before capital allowances was £63,000.

The draft tax adjusted trading profit is **before** adjusting for any deductions arising from the following:

(1) £5,000 incurred during January and February 2022 on a marketing campaign for his business

(2) A premium of £30,000 paid on 1 September 2022 to acquire a ten-year lease on a workshop used for trade purposes

(3) Cost of a golf day on 31 March 2023 for a group of Alfred's largest clients totalling £1,000

(4) Expenditure of £116,000 on 1 September 2022 for plant and equipment

(5) The purchase of a car on 15 December 2022 for £24,000. The car has a CO_2 emissions rate of 24 grams per kilometre, and is used by Alfred's employee.

Amaia

Amaia is employed by Argole Ltd and her remuneration package comprises:

(1) A gross annual salary of £80,000

(2) From 1 January 2023, Argole Ltd provided Amaia with a petrol-powered company car. The car had a list price of £25,000, although Argole Ltd received a discount and only paid £23,500. The car has a CO_2 emissions rate of 52 grams per kilometre. Argole Ltd did not provide any fuel for Amaia's private use.

(3) Since 6 April 2020, Argole Ltd has provided Amaia with living accommodation which qualifies as job-related accommodation. The annual value of the property is £23,000 and Argole Ltd pays rent of £2,500 per month.

Argole Ltd deducted income tax under PAYE of £19,240 from Amaia's salary during the tax year 2022/23.

Since 6 April 2020, Amaia has let out her own house unfurnished at a rent of £1,200 per month. Amaia received 13 months' rent during the tax year 2022/23. Amaia has a mortgage which she took out to acquire the house and, in the tax year 2022/23, she made mortgage payments of £6,000, including interest of £2,600.

On 1 December 2021, Amaia paid an insurance premium of £800 for the house in respect of the year ended 31 December 2022. Then on 1 December 2022, she paid an insurance premium of £1,250 for the year ended 31 December 2023.

Required

(a) Calculate Alfred's revised tax adjusted trading profit or loss for the seven-month period ended 31 March 2023.

Notes.

1 Your computation should commence with the draft tax adjusted trading profit of £63,000 and list all of the items referred to in the notes, indicating with the use of zero (0) any items which do not require adjustment.

2 You should assume Alfred claims the maximum amount of capital allowances. **(6 marks)**

(b) Calculate the income tax payable by Amaia for the tax year 2022/23.

Note. Your computation should list all of the items referred to in the scenario, indicating with the use of zero (0) any items which are not taxable. **(9 marks)**

(Total = 15 marks)

114 John (June 2013) (amended) (27 mins)

John is employed by Surf plc. The following information is available for the tax year 2022/23:

(1) During the tax year 2022/23, John was promoted and paid gross remuneration of £328,318. In each of the tax years 2019/20, 2020/21 and 2021/22 his adjusted income was below £150,000.

(2) During the tax year 2022/23, John contributed £18,000 into Surf plc's occupational pension scheme. The company contributed a further £12,000 on his behalf. Both John and Surf plc have made exactly the same contributions for the previous five tax years.

(3) During 2019 Surf plc provided John with a loan which was used to purchase a yacht. The amount of loan outstanding at 6 April 2022 was £84,000. John repaid £12,000 of the loan on 31 July 2022, and then repaid a further £12,000 on 31 December 2022. He paid loan interest of £90 to Surf plc during the tax year 2022/23. The taxable benefit in respect of this loan is calculated using the average method.

(4) During the tax year 2022/23, John made personal pension contributions up to the maximum amount of available annual allowances, including any unused amounts brought forward from previous years. These contributions were in addition to the contributions he made to Surf plc's occupational pension scheme (see note (2)). John has not made any personal pension contributions in previous tax years.

(5) John owns a holiday cottage which is let out as a furnished holiday letting, although the letting does not qualify as a trade under the furnished holiday letting rules. The property business profit for the year ended 5 April 2023 was £14,855 before taking into account interest and £1,875 paid to a letting agent. John paid loan interest of £7,500 for the year in respect of a loan to buy this property.

Required

(a) Calculate John's income tax liability for the tax year 2022/23. **(12 marks)**

(b) State THREE tax advantages of a rental property qualifying as a trade under the furnished holiday letting rules. **(3 marks)**

(Total = 15 marks)

115 Ronald (June 2014) (amended) (27 mins)

Ronald is employed and also self-employed. Ronald has tried to prepare his own income tax computation for the tax year 2022/23, but he has found it more difficult than expected. Although the sections which Ronald has completed are correct, there are a significant number of omissions. The omissions are marked as outstanding (O/S). The partly completed income tax computation is as follows:

RONALD – INCOME TAX COMPUTATION 2022/23

	Note	£
Trading income	1	O/S
Employment income		70,065
Property business profit	2	O/S
Building society interest		1,260
Dividends		O/S
		O/S
Personal allowance		(12,570)
Taxable income		O/S
Income tax		
Non-savings income: £37,700 @ 20%		7,540
Non-savings income: O/S @ 40%		O/S
Savings income: £500 @ 0%		0
Savings income: O/S @ 40%		O/S
Dividend income: O/S @ 0%		0
Dividend income: £800 @ 33.75%		270
O/S		—
Income tax liability		O/S
Tax suffered at source		
PAYE		(11,513)
Income tax payable		O/S

Notes.

1 **Trading profit**

Ronald commenced self-employment on 1 January 2022. He had a tax adjusted trading profit of £3,840 for the four-month period ended 30 April 2022, and £12,060 for the year ended 30 April 2023. These figures are **before** taking account of capital allowances.

The only item of plant and machinery owned by Ronald is his car, which cost £24,000 on 1 September 2022.

The car has a CO_2 emission rate of 122 grams per kilometre, and 70% of the mileage driven by Ronald is for private journeys.

2 **Property business profit**

Ronald owns a freehold shop. The 10-year old shop was purchased on 1 October 2022, and during October 2022 Ronald spent £8,400 replacing the roof. The shop was not usable until this work was carried out, and this fact was represented by a reduced purchase price.

On 1 December 2022, the property was let to a tenant, with Ronald receiving a premium of £12,000 for the grant of a 30-year lease. The monthly rent is £768 payable in advance, and during the period 1 December 2022 to 5 April 2023 Ronald received five rental payments.

Due to a fire, £8,600 was spent on replacing the roof of the shop during February 2023. Only £8,200 of this was paid for by Ronald's property insurance.

Ronald paid insurance of £156 in respect of the property. This was paid on 1 October 2022 and is for the year ended 30 September 2023.

Other information

Ronald did not make any personal pension contributions during the tax year 2022/23. He has never been a member of a pension scheme.

Required

(a) Calculate the income tax payable by Ronald for the tax year 2022/23. **(11 marks)**

(b) Advise Ronald why the maximum gross amount of tax relievable personal pension scheme contribution which he could have made for the tax year 2022/23 is £40,000, and the method by which tax relief would have been given if he had made this amount of contribution. **(4 marks)**

(Total = 15 marks)

116 Wai (June 2015) (amended) (27 mins)

Wai is employed as a sales manager by Qaz plc, and the following information is available in respect of the tax year 2022/23:

(1) During the tax year 2022/23, Wai was paid a gross monthly salary of £10,200.

(2) In addition to her salary, Wai has been paid the following bonuses:

Amount	*Date of payment*	*Date of entitlement*	*In respect of the six-month period ended*
£			
4,600	25 April 2022	31 March 2022	31 December 2021
8,100	20 August 2022	3 July 2022	30 June 2022
2,900	3 May 2023	15 April 2023	31 December 2022

(3) During the period 6 April to 31 August 2022, Wai used her private car for both private and business journeys. She was reimbursed by Qaz plc at the rate of 55p per mile for the following mileage:

	Miles
Normal daily travel between home and Qaz plc's offices	2,420
Travel between home and the premises of Qaz plc's clients (none of the clients' premises were located near the offices of Qaz plc)	8,580
Travel between home and a temporary workplace (the assignment was for ten weeks)	2,860
Total mileage reimbursed by Qaz plc	13,860

(4) During the period 1 September 2022 to 5 April 2023, Qaz plc provided Wai with a new diesel-powered car which meets the RDE2 standard. The car has a list price of £10,013 and an official CO_2 emission rate of 86 grams per kilometre. Qaz plc does not provide Wai with any fuel for private journeys.

(5) During January 2023, Wai spent ten nights overseas on company business. Qaz plc paid Wai a daily allowance of £10 to cover the cost of personal incidental expenses, such as telephone calls to her family.

(6) Throughout the tax year 2022/23, Qaz plc allowed Wai the use of two mobile telephones. The telephones had each cost £400 when purchased by the company in March 2022.

(7) Throughout the tax year 2022/23, Qaz plc provided Wai with living accommodation. The company had purchased the property on 1 June 2019 for £142,000, and it has been provided to Wai since 1 February 2021. Improvements costing £24,200 were made to the property during October 2019, and further improvements costing £9,800 were made during August 2022. The annual value of the property is £4,828.

Qaz plc does not payroll employee benefits.

Required

(a) Calculate Wai's taxable income for the tax year 2022/23. **(12 marks)**

(b) Briefly outline the information to be included in PAYE forms P60 and P11D, and state the dates by which they should have been provided to Wai for the tax year 2022/23.

Note. Your answer should be confined to the details which are relevant to Wai, although no figures are required. **(3 marks)**

(Total = 15 marks)

117 Samson and Delilah (September/December 2015) (amended) (27 mins)

Samson and Delilah are a married couple. They are both employed by Rope plc, and Delilah is also a partner in a partnership. The following information is available in respect of the tax year 2022/23:

Samson

During the tax year 2022/23, Samson was paid a gross annual salary of £112,000 in respect of his employment with Rope plc.

Delilah

(1) During the tax year 2022/23, Delilah was paid a gross annual salary of £184,000 in respect of her employment with Rope plc.

(2) Throughout the tax year 2022/23, Rope plc provided Delilah with a petrol powered car which has a list price of £67,200, and an official CO_2 emission rate of 147 grams per kilometre. Rope plc does not provide Delilah with any fuel for private journeys. Delilah was unable to drive her car for a period during the tax year 2022/23 because of a skiing accident, and during this period Rope plc provided her with a chauffeur at a total cost of £9,400.

(3) Rope plc provided all its employees with a hamper of groceries costing £42 each in December 2022.

(4) Delilah spent £70 in July 2022 on travelling by train to visit a customer of Rope plc. This amount was reimbursed by Rope plc in August 2022.

(5) During the tax year 2022/23, Delilah donated £250 (gross) per month to charity under the payroll deduction scheme operated by Rope plc.

(6) Delilah has been in partnership with Esther and Felix for a number of years. The partnership's tax adjusted trading profit for the year ended 31 December 2022 was £93,600. Esther is paid an annual salary of £8,000, with the balance of profits being shared 40% to Delilah, 30% to Esther and 30% to Felix.

(7) During the tax year 2022/23, Delilah paid interest of £6,200 (gross) on a personal loan taken out to purchase her share in the partnership.

(8) During the tax year 2022/23, Delilah made charitable gift aid donations totalling £4,864 (net).

Joint income – building society deposit account

Samson and Delilah have savings in a building society deposit account which is in their joint names. During the tax year 2022/23, they received building society interest totalling £9,600 from this joint account.

Required

(a) Calculate Samson and Delilah's respective income tax liabilities for the tax year 2022/23.

Note. The following mark allocation is provided as guidance for this requirement:

Samson (4 marks)

Delilah (9 marks) **(13 marks)**

(b) Calculate Samson's income tax saving for the tax year 2022/23 if the building society deposit account had been in Delilah's sole name instead of in joint names for the entire year. **(2 marks)**

(Total = 15 marks)

118 Patience (March/June 2016) (27 mins)

Patience retired on 31 December 2022, and on that date ceased employment and self-employment. The following information is available in respect of the tax year 2022/23:

Employment

(1) Patience was employed by a private school as a teacher. From 6 April to 31 December 2022, she was paid a salary of £3,750 per month.

(2) During the period 6 April to 31 December 2022, Patience contributed 6% of her monthly gross salary of £3,750 into her employer's occupational pension scheme. Patience's employer contributed a further 10% on her behalf.

(3) During the period 6 April to 30 June 2022, Patience's granddaughter was given a free place at the private school run by Patience's employer. The normal fee payable would have been £4,600. The additional marginal expense of providing the place was £540.

(4) On 25 June 2022, Patience was given a clock valued at £600 as an award for her 25 years of teaching at her employer's school. She has not previously received any similar awards.

(5) Patience's employer provided her with an interest-free loan so that she could purchase a season ticket for the train to work. The balance of the loan outstanding at 6 April 2022 was £8,000, and Patience repaid the loan in full on 31 December 2022.

Self-employment

(1) Patience was self-employed as a private tutor. Her trading profit for the year ended 31 July 2022 was £14,800. This figure is **after** taking account of capital allowances.

(2) Patience's trading profit for the final five-month period of trading from 1 August to 31 December 2022 was £6,900. This figure is **before** taking account of capital allowances.

(3) The tax written down value of the capital allowances main pool at 1 August 2022 was £2,200. On 10 August 2022, Patience purchased a laptop computer for £1,700.

On the cessation of trading, Patience personally retained the laptop computer. Its value on 31 December 2022 was £1,200. The remainder of the items included in the main pool were sold for £800 on 31 December 2022.

(4) Patience has unused overlap profits brought forward of £3,700.

Personal pension contributions

During the period 6 April to 31 December 2022, Patience contributed a total of £3,600 (net) into a personal pension scheme.

Pension income

During the period 1 January to 5 April 2023, Patience received the state pension of £1,450, a pension of £7,000 from her employer's occupational pension scheme, and a private pension of £3,650. These were the total gross amounts received.

Property

Patience owned two properties which were let out unfurnished until both properties were sold on 31 December 2022. The following information is available in respect of the two properties:

	Property one	*Property two*
	£	£
Rent received during the tax year 2022/23	3,600	7,200
Sale proceeds on 31 December 2022	122,000	98,000
Allowable revenue expenditure paid during the tax year 2022/23 (no finance costs)	(4,700)	(2,600)
Purchase cost	(81,000)	(103,700)

Patience has never occupied either of the two properties as her main residence.

Required

Calculate Patience's income tax and capital gains tax liabilities for the tax year 2022/23.

Notes.

1 You should indicate by the use of zero (0) any items which are not taxable or deductible.

2 The following mark allocation is provided as guidance for this question:

Income tax (13 marks)

Capital gains tax (2 marks)

(Total = 15 marks)

119 Petula (March/June 2017) (27 mins)

Petula has been employed as a sales manager by Downtown plc since 6 April 2013. The following information is available in respect of the tax year 2022/23:

(1) During the tax year 2022/23, Petula was paid a gross annual salary of £260,000.

(2) In addition to her salary, Petula has been paid the following bonuses by Downtown plc:

Amount	*Date of payment*	*Date of entitlement*	*In respect of the six-month period ended*
£			
21,200	30 April 2022	1 April 2022	31 December 2021
18,600	31 October 2022	1 October 2022	30 June 2022
22,400	30 April 2023	1 April 2023	31 December 2022

(3) During the tax year 2022/23, Petula used her private car for both private and business journeys. The total mileage driven by Petula throughout the tax year was 26,000 miles, with all of this mileage reimbursed by Downtown plc at the rate of 60p per mile. However, only 21,000 miles were in the performance of Petula's duties for Downtown plc.

(4) Petula pays an annual professional subscription of £630 which is relevant to her employment with Downtown plc. Petula also pays an annual subscription membership fee of £1,840 to a golf club which she uses to entertain Downtown plc's clients. Downtown plc does not reimburse Petula for either of these costs.

(5) During the tax year 2022/23, Petula paid interest of £140 on a personal loan taken out on 6 April 2022 to purchase a computer for sole use in her employment with Downtown plc.

(6) Each tax year since 6 April 2015 (including the tax year 2022/23), Downtown plc has contributed £25,000 into the company's occupational pension scheme on Petula's behalf. Petula has never personally made any pension contributions. Petula's adjusted income for 2019/20, 2020/21 and 2021/22 was below £150,000.

(7) Petula owns a freehold house which was let out furnished throughout the tax year 2022/23. The total amount of rent received during the tax year was £12,000.

During August 2022, Petula purchased a new washer-dryer for the property at a cost of £730. This was a replacement for an old washing machine which was scrapped, with nil proceeds. The cost of a similar washing machine would have been £420.

During November 2022, Petula purchased a new dishwasher for the property at a cost of £580. The property did not previously have a dishwasher.

The other expenditure on the property paid in the tax year 2022/23 amounted to £1,640, none of which is loan interest, and all of this is allowable.

(8) During the tax year 2022/23, Petula rented out one furnished room of her main residence. During the year, she received rent of £8,900 and incurred allowable expenditure of £2,890 in respect of the room. Petula always uses the most favourable basis as regards the tax treatment of the furnished room.

(9) On 1 July 2022, Petula purchased £250,000 (nominal value) of gilts paying interest at the rate of 3% for £300,000. Interest is paid half-yearly on 30 June and 31 December based on the nominal value. Petula sold the gilts on 31 October 2022 for £302,500 (including accrued interest).

Required

(a) Calculate Petula's taxable income for the tax year 2022/23.

Note. Your computation should list all of the items referred to in notes (1) to (9), indicating with the use of zero (0) any items which are not taxable or deductible. **(12 marks)**

(b) Advise Petula of the total amount of her unused pension annual allowances which are available to carry forward to the tax year 2023/24. **(3 marks)**

(Total = 15 marks)

120 Dill (September/December 2017) (amended) (27 mins)

Up to and including the tax year 2020/21, Dill was always resident in the United Kingdom (UK), being in the UK for more than 300 days each tax year. She was also resident in the UK for the tax year 2022/23. However, during the tax year 2021/22, Dill was overseas for 305 days, spending just 60 days in the UK. Dill has a house in the UK and stayed there on the 60 days which she spent in the UK. She also has a house overseas. For the tax year 2021/22, Dill did not have any close family in the UK, did not do any work in the UK and was not treated as working full-time overseas.

On 6 April 2022, Dill returned to the UK and commenced employment with Herb plc as the IT manager. She also set up a small technology business which she ran on a self-employed basis, but this business failed and Dill ceased self-employment on 5 April 2023. The following information is available for the tax year 2022/23:

Employment

(1) During the tax year 2022/23, Dill was paid a gross annual salary of £430,000.

(2) In addition to her salary, Dill has been paid the following bonuses by Herb plc:

Amount	*Date of payment*	*Date of entitlement*	*In respect of the four-month period*
£			
16,200	31 December 2022	1 November 2022	31 July 2022
29,100	30 April 2023	1 March 2023	30 November 2022

(3) Throughout the tax year 2022/23, Dill had the use of Herb plc's company gym which is only open to employees of the company. The cost to Herb plc of providing this benefit was £780.

(4) Throughout the tax year 2022/23, Herb plc provided Dill with a home entertainment system for her personal use. The home entertainment system cost Herb plc £5,900 on 6 April 2022.

(5) During the tax year 2022/23, Dill's three-year-old son was provided with a place at Herb plc's workplace nursery. The total cost to the company of providing this nursery place was £7,200 (240 days at £30 per day).

(6) On 1 June 2022, Herb plc provided Dill with an interest-free loan of £96,000 which she used to renovate her main residence. No loan repayments were made before 5 April 2023.

(7) On 25 January 2023, Herb plc paid a health club membership fee of £990 for the benefit of Dill.

(8) During the tax year 2022/23, Dill used her private car for both private and business journeys. The total mileage driven by Dill throughout the tax year was 16,000 miles, with all of this mileage reimbursed by Herb plc at the rate of 25p per mile. However, only 14,500 miles were in the performance of Dill's duties for Herb plc.

(9) During the tax year 2022/23, Dill paid an annual professional subscription of £560 which is relevant to her employment with Herb plc. She also paid an annual membership fee of £1,620 to a golf club which she uses to entertain Herb plc's suppliers. Herb plc did not reimburse Dill for either of these costs.

(10) During the tax year 2022/23, Dill contributed the maximum possible tax relievable amount into Herb plc's occupational pension scheme. The company did not make any contributions on her behalf. Dill has never previously been a member of a pension scheme.

Self-employment

For the tax year 2022/23, Dill's self-employed business made a tax adjusted trading loss of £58,000. Dill will claim relief for this loss against her total income for the tax year 2022/23.

Other information

(1) On 1 November 2022, Dill received a premium bond prize of £1,000.

(2) On 28 February 2023, Dill received interest of £1,840 on the maturity of savings certificates from NS&I (National Savings and Investments).

Required

(a) Explain why Dill was treated as not resident in the United Kingdom for the tax year 2021/22. **(3 marks)**

(b) Calculate Dill's taxable income for the tax year 2022/23.

Note. You should indicate by the use of zero (0) any items which are not taxable or deductible. **(12 marks)**

(Total = 15 marks)

121 Danh (March/June 2018) (27 mins)

Up to and including the tax year 2019/20, Danh was always automatically treated as not resident in the UK, spending fewer than 46 days in the UK each year. Danh knows that for the tax year 2022/23, he will automatically be treated as resident in the UK, but is unsure of his residence status for the tax years 2020/21 and 2021/22. For these two tax years, Danh was neither automatically not resident in the UK nor automatically resident. For both of these tax years, Danh spent 100 days in the UK, with the remainder of each tax year spent in the same overseas country. Throughout both tax years, Danh had a property in the UK and stayed there on the 100 days which he spent in the UK. Danh also did substantive work in the UK during both tax years. He does not have any close family in the UK.

On 6 August 2022, Danh commenced self-employment as a sole trader. In addition, on 6 September 2022, Danh joined an existing partnership run by Ebele and Fai. The following information is available for the tax year 2022/23:

Self-employment

(1) Danh's statement of profit or loss for the eight-month period ended 5 April 2023 is:

	Note	£
Income		96,400
Expenses		
Depreciation		(2,300)
Motor expenses	2	(3,300)
Professional fees	3	(1,800)
Other expenses (all allowable)		(18,800)
Net profit		70,200

(2) During the eight-month period ended 5 April 2023, Danh drove a total of 12,000 miles, of which 4,000 were for private journeys.

(3) The figure for professional fees consists of £340 for accountancy and £1,460 for legal fees in connection with the grant of a new five-year lease for business premises.

(4) Danh runs his business using one of the six rooms in his private house as an office. The total running costs of the house for the eight-month period ended 5 April 2023 were £4,200. No deduction has been made for the cost of using the office in calculating the net profit of £70,200.

(5) The only item of plant and machinery owned by Danh is his car. This was purchased on 6 August 2022 for £14,800, and has a CO_2 emission rate of 40 grams per kilometre.

Partnership loss

(1) For the year ended 5 April 2023, the partnership made a tax-adjusted trading loss of £12,600. Until 5 September 2022, profits and losses were shared 60% to Ebele and 40% to Fai. Since 6 September 2022, profits and losses have been shared 20% to Danh, 50% to Ebele and 30% to Fai.

(2) Danh will claim to relieve his share of the partnership's loss against his total income for the tax year 2022/23.

(3) During the tax year 2022/23, Danh paid interest of £875 (gross) on a personal loan taken out to purchase his share in the partnership.

Property income

(1) On 6 April 2022, Danh purchased a freehold house which was then let out. The total amount of rent received during the tax year 2022/23 was £14,400.

(2) Danh partly financed the purchase of the property with a repayment mortgage, paying mortgage interest of £10,000 during the tax year 2022/23.

(3) The other expenditure on the property for the tax year 2022/23 amounted to £3,980, and this is all allowable.

Required

(a) Explain whether Danh was treated as resident or not resident in the UK for each of the tax years 2020/21 and 2021/22. **(3 marks)**

(b) Calculate Danh's income tax liability for the tax year 2022/23.

Note. When calculating Danh's trading profit from self-employment for the eight-month period ended 5 April 2023, your computation should commence with the net profit figure of £70,200, indicating by the use of zero (0) any items which do not require adjustment. **(12 marks)**

(Total = 15 marks)

122 Martin (September/December 2018) (27 mins)

Martin is employed by Global plc and he is also a member of a partnership. The following information is available in respect of the tax year 2022/23.

Employment

(1) During the tax year 2022/23, Martin was paid a gross annual salary of £144,000 in respect of his employment with Global plc.

(2) In addition to his salary, Martin was paid the following bonuses by Global plc:

Amount	*In respect of the six-month period ended*	*Date of payment*	*Date of entitlement*
£			
18,200	28 February 2022	31 March 2022	20 March 2022
21,400	31 August 2022	31 August 2022	20 September 2022
13,700	28 February 2023	30 April 2023	20 March 2023

(3) During the tax year 2022/23, Global plc provided Martin with the following petrol-powered cars:

Period provided	*List price*	*CO_2 emission date*
	£	
6 April to 31 December 2022	18,450	57 grams per kilometre
1 January to 5 April 2023	24,905	72 grams per kilometre

Martin was not provided with any fuel for private use.

(4) On 6 April 2022, Global plc provided Martin with an interest free loan of £8,000 which he used to purchase a motor bike. No loan repayments were made during the year.

(5) Throughout the tax year 2022/23, Global plc allowed Martin private use of a home entertainment system owned by the company. The home entertainment system cost Global plc £7,400 on 6 April 2022.

(6) During the tax year 2022/23, Martin donated a total of £1,000 (gross) to charity under the payroll deduction scheme operated by Global plc.

(7) Martin paid an annual professional subscription of £560 which is relevant to his employment with Global plc. Martin also paid an annual membership fee of £1,240 to a health club which he used to entertain Global plc's clients. Global plc did not reimburse Martin for either of these costs.

Partnership

(1) Martin has been in partnership with Norma and Oprah since 1 January 2008. The partnership's trading profit for the year ended 31 December 2022 was £54,600.

(2) Until 30 September 2022, profits were shared 40% to Martin, 30% to Norma and 30% to Oprah. Since 1 October 2022, profits have been shared equally.

Other income

(1) During the tax year 2022/23, Martin rented out one furnished room of his main residence, receiving rent of £9,200 for the year. No additional expenditure was incurred as a result of the letting.

(2) During the tax year 2022/23, Martin received dividends of £440.

(3) On 30 November 2022, Martin received interest of £1,330 on the maturity of savings certificates from NS&I (National Savings and Investments).

Self-assessment tax return

Martin always files his self-assessment tax return online on 26 December, so his tax return for the tax year 2022/23 will be filed on 26 December 2023.

Because more than 80% of Martin's tax liability is paid under PAYE, he is not required to make self-assessment payments on account.

Required

(a) Calculate Martin's taxable income for the tax year 2022/23.

Note. You should indicate by the use of zero (0) any items which are not taxable or deductible. **(11 marks)**

(b) (i) Advise Martin of the deadline for making an amendment to his self-assessment tax return for the tax year 2022/23, and state how HM Revenue and Customs (HMRC) will calculate interest if such an amendment results in additional tax becoming payable. **(2 marks)**

(ii) State the latest date by which HMRC will have to notify Martin if they intend to carry out a compliance check in respect of his self-assessment tax return for the tax year 2022/23, and (assuming the check is not made on a completely random basis) the possible reasons why such a check would be made. **(2 marks)**

(Total = 15 marks)

123 Tonie (March/June 2019) (27 mins)

Up to and including the tax year 2020/21, Tonie was resident in the UK for tax purposes, spending more than 300 days in the UK each year. Tonie understands that for the tax year 2022/23, she will again automatically be treated as resident in the UK, but is unsure of her residence status for the tax year 2021/22. For this tax year, Tonie was neither automatically resident in the UK nor automatically not resident. Throughout the tax year 2021/22, Tonie was travelling around the world and did not stay in any one country for longer than 30 days, although she did spend a total of 50 days in the UK. Tonie has a house in the UK, but it was let out throughout the tax year 2021/22. She is single, has no children, and stayed with a friend on the 50 days which she spent in the UK. Tonie did not do any substantive work in the UK during the 2021/22.

The following information is available for the tax year 2022/23:

Employment

On 6 April 2022, Tonie, who is a software developer, accepted a one-year contract to maintain websites for Droid plc. Droid plc treated the contract as one of employment, with the payments to Tonie being subject to PAYE. However, Tonie thought that, because she was working from home, her employment status should instead have been one of self-employment.

(1) For the term of the contract, from 6 April 2022 to 5 April 2023, Tonie was paid a fixed gross amount of £6,200 a month. During the term of the contract, Tonie was not permitted to work for any other clients. She was required to do the work personally, not being permitted to sub-contract the work to anyone else.

(2) During the term of the contract, Tonie worked from home, but had to attend weekly meetings at Droid plc's offices to receive instructions regarding the work to be performed during the following week. During the period 6 April 2022 to 5 April 2023, Tonie used her private car for business visits to Droid plc's clients. She drove 2,300 miles, for which Droid plc paid an allowance of 60 pence per mile.

(3) During the term of the contract, Tonie leased computer equipment at a cost of £180 a month. This was used 100% for business purposes.

Property income

(1) Tonie owns a freehold house which is let out (this is not a furnished holiday letting). The total amount of rent received during the tax year 2022/23 was £10,080.

(2) Tonie partly financed the purchase of the property with a repayment mortgage, paying mortgage interest of £8,400 during the tax year 2022/23.

(3) During May 2022, Tonie purchased a new washer-dryer for the property at a cost of £640. This was a replacement for an old washing machine which was scrapped, with nil proceeds. The cost of a similar washing machine would have been £380.

(4) During November 2022, Tonie purchased a new dishwasher for the property at a cost of £560. The property did not previously have a dishwasher.

(5) The other expenditure on the property for the tax year 2022/23 amounted to £3,210, and this is all allowable.

(6) During the tax year 2022/23, Tonie rented out one furnished room of her main residence. During the year, she received rent of £8,580 and incurred allowable expenditure of £870 in respect of the room. Tonie always uses the most favourable basis as regards the tax treatment of the furnished room.

Other income

(1) On 1 July 2022, Tonie inherited £100,000 (nominal value) of gilts paying interest at the rate of 3%. The inheritance was valued at £120,000. Interest is paid half-yearly on 30 June and 31 December based on the nominal value. Tonie sold the gilts on 30 November 2022 for £121,250 (including accrued interest).

(2) On 31 January 2023, Tonie received a premium bond prize of £100.

(3) On 31 March 2023, Tonie received interest of £520 on the maturity of savings certificates from NS&I (National Savings and Investments).

Required

(a) Explain why Tonie was treated as not resident in the UK for the tax year 2021/22. **(2 marks)**

(b) List FOUR factors which are indicators of Tonie being treated as employed in relation to her contract with Droid plc rather than as self-employed.

Note. You should confine your answer to the information given in the question. **(2 marks)**

(c) On the basis that Tonie is treated as employed in relation to her contract with Droid plc, calculate her taxable income for the tax year 2022/23.

Note. You should indicate by the use of zero (0) any items which are not taxable or deductible. **(11 marks)**

(Total = 15 marks)

QUESTIONS

PART C: CHARGEABLE GAINS FOR INDIVIDUALS

Part C covers chargeable gains for individuals, the subject of Chapters 13 to 16 of the BPP Workbook for Taxation (TX – UK).

Section A

OTQ bank – Chargeable gains for individuals 1 (18 mins)

124 Which of the following gifts made by an individual is exempt from capital gains tax? *(March 2019)*

- O Gift of a motor boat valued at £10,000 (cost £5,000) to his aunt
- O Gift of unquoted shares in a United Kingdom company valued at £2,500 (cost £1,800) to his brother
- O Gift of antique jewellery valued at £6,800 (cost £3,200) to his sister
- O Gift of a sculpture valued at £3,000 (cost £10,000) to his nephew **(2 marks)**

---

125 Trudy sold a house in November 2022. She had never lived in the house.

Her chargeable gain on the sale was £26,300. Trudy has taxable income of £25,620 in the tax year 2022/23.

The house does not qualify for business asset disposal relief.

What is Trudy's capital gains tax liability for the tax year 2022/23 assuming that she has no other disposals in that year?

- O £2,712
- O £3,920
- O £6,156
- O £1,592 **(2 marks)**

---

126 Clive purchased a ten-hectare plot of land in May 2011 for £80,000.

In January 2023, Clive sold three of the hectares for £36,000 with expenses of sale amounting to £1,000.

The market value of the remaining seven hectares of land in January 2023 was £90,000.

What is Clive's chargeable gain on the disposal of the three hectares of land in the tax year 2022/23?

Pull down list

- £11,000
- £12,143
- £12,600
- £13,143

(2 marks)

---

127 James has the following gains and losses arising from disposals of chargeable assets:

Tax year	*2020/21*	*2021/22*	*2022/23*
	£	£	£
Gains	2,000	4,000	14,900
Losses	(14,000)	(2,000)	(2,000)

The allowable loss carried forward to 2023/24 will be:

- O £0
- O £2,000
- O £11,400
- O £100

(2 marks)

---

128 Ellen purchased an antique vase for £1,500. In October 2022 she sold the vase for £7,000.

What is Ellen's chargeable gain on the sale of the vase?

- O £0
- O £1,000
- O £1,667
- O £5,500

(2 marks)

(Total = 10 marks)

OTQ bank – Chargeable gains for individuals 2 (36 mins)

129 Harold bought a painting for £8,500. In December 2022 he sold the painting for £5,000.

What is Harold's allowable loss on the sale of the painting?

£ [ ]

(2 marks)

---

130 Angela purchased a house and lived in it for three years. The house was then unoccupied for five years because Angela was seconded to an overseas office. She then lived in the house for two years. Angela then went to live with her sister and the house was unoccupied for four years. Angela then lived in the house for the last year of ownership.

How many years of Angela's 15-year period of ownership of the house will be exempt for the purposes of private residence relief?

[▼]

Pull down list

- 11 years
- 14 years
- 14½ years
- 15 years

(2 marks)

131 Sascha owned a factory which had always been used in her business. She sold the factory on 14 May 2022 and realised a gain of £60,000. On 12 August 2022, she purchased a 20-year lease on a warehouse using all the proceeds from the sale of the factory. A claim for relief for replacement of business assets was made. The warehouse will continue to be used in Sascha's trade until it is sold on 14 October 2032.

When will the deferred gain of £60,000 become chargeable to capital gains tax?

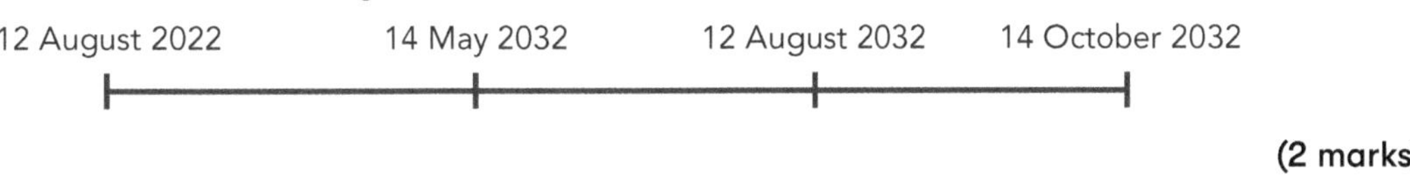

(2 marks)

---

132 Louise has two chargeable gains from the disposal of shares in the tax year 2022/23:

- £8,000 – claim made for business asset disposal relief
- £14,100 – claim not made for business asset disposal relief

Louise has taxable income of £38,000 in the tax year 2022/23.

What is Louise's capital gains tax liability for the tax year 2022/23?

£ [ ] **(2 marks)**

---

133 Neil bought 1,000 shares in Garden plc for £1,500 in October 2004. In November 2006, there was a 1 for 2 bonus issue when the shares had a market value of £2.40 each. In July 2011, there was a 3 for 1 rights issue when the shares had a market value of £3 but were offered to existing shareholders for £2.70 each. Neil took up his full entitlement to shares under the rights issue. Neil sold all of his shares in Garden plc in February 2023.

What is the cost of the shares sold in February 2023?

£ [ ] **(2 marks)**

---

134 On 10 January 2023, a freehold property owned by Winifred was damaged by a fire. The property had been purchased on 29 May 2004 for £73,000. Winifred received insurance proceeds of £37,200 on 23 February 2023, and she spent a total of £41,700 during March 2023 restoring the property. Winifred has elected to disregard the part disposal.

What is the base cost of the restored freehold property for capital gains tax purposes?

- O £68,500
- O £77,500
- O £114,700
- O £35,800

(2 marks)

---

135 On 31 March 2023, Jessica sold a copyright for £28,800. The copyright had been purchased on 1 April 2017 for £21,000 when it had an unexpired life of 15 years.

What is Jessica's chargeable gain in respect of the disposal of the copyright?

- O £0
- O £20,400
- O £16,200
- O £7,800

(2 marks)

---

136 For the tax year 2022/23, Nog has a chargeable gain of £24,400 and a capital loss of £10,000. She has unused capital losses of £6,100 brought forward from the tax year 2021/22.

What amount of capital losses can Nog carry forward to the tax year 2023/24?

£ [ ]

(2 marks)

---

137 Alice is in business as a sole trader. On 13 May 2022, she sold a freehold warehouse for £184,000, and this resulted in a chargeable gain of £38,600. Alice purchased a replacement freehold warehouse on 20 May 2022 for £143,000. Where possible, Alice always makes a claim to roll over gains against the cost of replacement assets. Both buildings have been, or will be, used for business purposes by Alice.

What is the base cost of the replacement warehouse for capital gains tax purposes?

£ [ ]

(2 marks)

---

138 Larry is a sole trader who made a disposal of a factory on 31 July 2022.

Match the earliest date and the latest date that Larry can make an acquisition of a new qualifying business asset and claim replacement of business asset (rollover) relief.

Options	Answer	Date
1 August 2019		Earliest date
31 July 2023		Latest date
1 August 2021		
31 July 2025		

(2 marks)

(Total = 20 marks)

Section B

OT case – Nim (June 2009) (amended) **(18 mins)**

The following scenario relates to the next five questions.

Nim disposed of the following assets during the tax year 2022/23:

(1) On 20 July 2022 Nim made a gift of 10,000 £1 ordinary shares in Kapook plc to his daughter. On that date the shares were quoted on the stock exchange at £3.70–£3.80. Nim has made the following purchases of shares in Kapook plc:

19 February 2004	8,000 shares for £16,200
6 June 2009	1 for 2 rights issue at £3.65 per share
24 July 2022	2,000 shares for £5,800

Nim's total shareholding was less than 5% of Kapook plc, and so gift holdover relief is not available.

(2) On 13 August 2022 Nim transferred his entire shareholding of 5,000 £1 ordinary shares in Jooba Ltd, an unquoted company, to his wife. On that date the shares were valued at £28,200. Nim's shareholding had been purchased on 11 January 2010 for £16,000.

(3) On 26 November 2022 Nim sold an antique table for net proceeds of £8,700 after deducting the sale costs of £300. The antique table had been purchased for £5,200.

Other information

Nim has unused capital losses of £15,800 brought forward from the tax year 2021/22.

139 What are the deemed proceeds of the shares in Kapook plc sold on 20 July 2022?

O £37,000

O £37,250

O £37,500

O £38,000 **(2 marks)**

---

140 What is the total cost of the shares in Kapook plc sold on 20 July 2022?

O £26,333

O £28,500

O £25,667

O £20,533 **(2 marks)**

---

141 Which TWO of the following statements about capital gains tax for Nim and his wife are correct?

☐ Nim's wife will take the Jooba Ltd shares at market value at the date of the transfer.

☐ Nim will have deemed proceeds on the transfer of the Jooba Ltd shares to his wife so that neither a gain nor a loss will arise.

☐ The transfer of the Jooba Ltd shares is exempt from capital gains tax because it is between spouses.

☐ Nim's wife will not be able to transfer her annual exempt amount to Nim. **(2 marks)**

142 What is the gain on the sale of the antique table on 26 November 2022?

[▼]

Pull down list

- £3,500
- £4,500
- £5,000
- £800

(2 marks)

---

143 Assuming that Nim had chargeable gains of £21,000 in the tax year 2022/23, what is the amount of the loss brought forward from 2021/22 which will be carried forward to 2023/24?

£ [ ]

(2 marks)

(Total = 10 marks)

OT case – Aloi, Bon and Dinah (June 2011) (amended) (18 mins)

The following scenario relates to the next five questions.

On 15 October 2022 Alphabet Ltd, an unquoted trading company, was taken over by XYZ plc. Prior to the takeover Alphabet Ltd's share capital consisted of 100,000 £1 ordinary shares, and under the terms of the takeover the shareholders received for each £1 ordinary share in Alphabet Ltd either cash of £6 per share or one £1 ordinary share in XYZ plc worth £6.50. The following information is available regarding three of the shareholders of Alphabet Ltd:

Aloi

Aloi has been the managing director of Alphabet Ltd since the company's incorporation on 1 January 2012, and she accepted XYZ plc's cash alternative of £6 per share in respect of her shareholding of 60,000 £1 ordinary shares in Alphabet Ltd. Aloi had originally subscribed for 50,000 shares in Alphabet Ltd on 1 January 2012 at their par value and purchased a further 10,000 shares on 20 May 2013 for £18,600.

On 6 February 2023 Aloi sold an investment non-residential property, and this disposal resulted in a chargeable gain against which her annual exempt amount will be set.

For the tax year 2022/23 Aloi has taxable income of £60,000. All her income tax has previously been collected under PAYE, so she has not received a notice to file a return for the tax year 2022/23 and so is required to give notice of her chargeability to capital gains tax to HMRC.

Bon

Bon has been the sales director of Alphabet Ltd since 1 February 2021, having not previously been an employee of the company, although she had been a shareholder since 1 March 2020. She accepted XYZ plc's share alternative of one £1 ordinary share for each of her 25,000 £1 ordinary shares in Alphabet Ltd. Bon had purchased her shareholding on 1 March 2020 for £92,200.

On 4 March 2023 Bon made a gift of 10,000 of her £1 ordinary shares in XYZ plc to her brother. On that date the shares were quoted on the stock exchange at £7.10 – £7.14. Gift holdover relief is not available in respect of this disposal.

Dinah

Dinah has been an employee of Alphabet Ltd since 1 May 2020. She accepted XYZ plc's share alternative of one £1 ordinary share for each of her 3,000 £1 ordinary shares in Alphabet Ltd. Dinah had purchased her shareholding on 20 June 2019 for £4,800.

On 13 November 2022 Dinah sold 1,000 of her £1 ordinary shares in XYZ plc for £6,600.

Dinah died on 5 April 2023, and her remaining 2,000 £1 ordinary shares in XYZ plc were inherited by her daughter. On that date these shares were valued at £16,000.

For the tax year 2022/23 Dinah had taxable income of £12,000.

144 Which TWO of the following statements are correct about Bon and Dinah's entitlement to business asset disposal relief in relation to their shares in Alphabet Ltd if they had accepted the cash alternative on the takeover by XYZ plc?

☐ Alphabet Ltd was not Bon's personal company for the requisite time before disposal.

☐ Bon was not an officer or employee of Alphabet Ltd for the requisite time before disposal.

☐ Dinah was not an officer or employee of Alphabet Ltd for the requisite time before disposal.

☐ Alphabet Ltd was not Dinah's personal company for the requisite time before disposal.

(2 marks)

---

145 What is Aloi's capital gains tax liability on the disposal of her shares in Alphabet Ltd assuming that the gain qualifies for business asset disposal relief?

O £31,000

O £52,452

O £29,140

O £81,592

(2 marks)

---

146 Match the the latest dates by which Aloi must:

(1) Give notice of her chargeability to capital gains tax for the tax year 2022/23 to HMRC.

(2) Pay her capital gains liability for the tax year 2022/23 in order to avoid interest and penalties.

5 October 2023		Notification
31 January 2024		Payment
31 December 2023		
31 July 2024		

(2 marks)

---

147 What is the chargeable gain arising on Bon's gift of her shares in XYZ plc to her brother?

O £34,320

O £6,200

O £34,220

O £61,200

(2 marks)

---

148 What is Dinah's capital gains tax liability for the tax year 2022/23?

- O £610
- O £0
- O £900
- O £1,090

(2 marks)

(Total = 10 marks)

OT case – Ginger, Innocent and Nigel (June 2013) (amended) (18 mins)

The following scenario relates to the next five questions.

You should assume that today's date is 1 March 2023.

Ginger

Ginger has a holding of 10,000 £1 ordinary shares in Nutmeg Ltd, an unquoted trading company, which she had purchased on 13 February 2005 for £2.40 per share. The current market value of the shares is £6.40 per share, but Ginger intends to sell some of the holding to her daughter at £4.00 per share during March 2023. Ginger and her daughter will elect to use gift holdover relief to hold over any gain. For the tax year 2022/23, Ginger will not make any other disposals, and has therefore not utilised her annual exempt amount. She has a loss brought forward from 2021/22 of £(800).

Innocent and Nigel

Innocent and Nigel, a married couple, both have shareholdings in Cinnamon Ltd, an unquoted trading company with a share capital of 100,000 £1 ordinary shares.

Innocent has been the managing director of Cinnamon Ltd since the company's incorporation on 1 July 2008, and she currently holds 20,000 shares (with matching voting rights) in the company. These shares were subscribed for on 1 July 2008 at their par value. Nigel has never been an employee or a director of Cinnamon Ltd, and he currently holds 3,000 shares (with matching voting rights) in the company. These shares were purchased on 23 April 2012 for £46,200.

Either Innocent or Nigel will sell 2,000 of their shares in Cinnamon Ltd during March 2023 for £65,000 but are not sure which of them should make the disposal. For the tax year 2022/23, both Innocent and Nigel have already made disposals which will fully utilise their annual exempt amounts, and they will each have taxable income of £80,000.

149 What is the chargeable gain per share that Ginger will make on her disposal of shares in Nutmeg Ltd to her daughter?

- O £4.00
- O £1.60
- O £2.40
- O £0

(2 marks)

---

150 If the chargeable gain per share on Ginger's disposal of shares in Nutmeg Ltd had been £1.54 per share, what would be the maximum number of shares that Ginger could have sold to her daughter without incurring a charge to capital gains tax?

- O 2,046
- O 7,207
- O 8,506
- O 3,275

(2 marks)

151 Which TWO of the following statements about business asset disposal relief are correct?

- ☐ Business asset disposal relief is only available on shareholdings owned by a director.
- ☐ There is a lifetime limit of £1,000,000 for business asset disposal relief.
- ☐ Business asset disposal relief is only available on shareholdings if they are held in a trading company.
- ☐ The conditions for business asset disposal relief in relation to a shareholding must be satisfied for five years before the disposal. **(2 marks)**

---

152 What would Innocent's capital gains tax liability be if she sold her shares in Cinnamon Ltd during March 2023?

£ ☐ **(2 marks)**

---

153 What would Nigel's capital gains tax liability be if he sold his shares in Cinnamon Ltd during March 2023?

£ ☐ **(2 marks)**

(Total = 10 marks)

OT case – Jerome (March/June 2016) (amended) (18 mins)

The following scenario relates to the next five questions.

Jerome made the following disposals of assets to family members during the tax year 2022/23:

(1) On 28 May 2022, Jerome sold a house to his wife for £140,000. The value of the house at that date was £187,000. Jerome's uncle had purchased it on 14 July 1995 for £45,900. The uncle died on 12 June 2005, and it was inherited by Jerome. On that date, the house was valued at £112,800. Jerome has never occupied the house as his main residence.

(2) On 24 June 2022, Jerome made a gift of his entire 12% holding of 12,000 £1 ordinary shares in Reward Ltd, an unquoted trading company, to his son. The market value of the shares on that date was £98,400. The shares had been purchased on 15 March 2006 for £39,000. On 24 June 2022, the market value of Reward Ltd's chargeable assets was £540,000, of which £460,000 was in respect of chargeable business assets. Jerome and his son will elect to use gift holdover relief to hold over the gain on this gift of a business asset.

(3) On 7 November 2022, Jerome made a gift of an antique bracelet valued at £12,200 to his granddaughter. The antique bracelet had been purchased on 1 September 2001 for £2,100.

(4) On 29 January 2023, Jerome made a gift of nine hectares of land valued at £78,400 to his brother. He had originally purchased ten hectares of land on 3 November 2005 for £37,800. The market value of the unsold hectare of land as at 29 January 2023 was £33,600. The land has never been used for business purposes.

154 What is the base cost of the house for capital gains tax purposes for Jerome's wife?

- O £45,900
- O £187,000
- O £112,800
- O £140,000 **(2 marks)**

---

155 What is the amount of gift holdover relief that can be claimed on the gift of the Reward Ltd shares?

£ [ ] **(2 marks)**

---

156 Match the latest date for submission of the election for gift holdover relief on the gift of the Reward Ltd shares and person(s) who must make the election.

Options		
31 January 2024		Latest date for election
5 April 2027		Person(s) making election
Jerome		
Jerome and his son		

(2 marks)

---

157 What is the amount of the chargeable gain on the disposal of the antique bracelet?

[▼]

Pull down list

- £10,000
- £10,100
- £10,333
- £3,900

(2 marks)

---

158 What is the amount of the chargeable gain on the disposal of the nine hectares of land?

- O £66,200
- O £40,600
- O £44,380
- O £51,940

(2 marks)

(Total = 10 marks)

OT case – Hali and Goma (March/June 2019) (18 mins)

The following scenario relates to the next five questions.

You should assume that the tax allowances for the tax year 2022/23 applied in previous tax years.

Hali and Goma are a married couple.

Capital losses brought forward

Hali had capital losses of £39,300 for the tax year 2020/21. He had chargeable gains of £16,300 for the tax year 2021/22.

Goma had capital losses of £9,100 and chargeable gains of £6,900 for the tax year 2021/22. She did not have any capital losses for the tax year 2020/21.

Ordinary shares in Lima Ltd

On 24 July 2022, Hali sold 5,000 £1 ordinary shares in Lima Ltd, for £4.95 per share. Lima Ltd's shares have recently been selling for £5.30 per share, but Hali sold them at the lower price because he needed a quick sale.

Goma had originally subscribed for 30,000 ordinary shares in Lima Ltd at their par value of £1 per share on 28 July 2008. On 18 August 2017, she gave 8,000 ordinary shares to Hali. On that date, the market value for 8,000 shares was £23,200.

Hali and Goma will both dispose of their remaining shareholdings in Lima Ltd during the tax year 2023/24. However, they are unsure as to whether these disposals will qualify for business asset disposal relief.

Antique table

On 11 October 2022, an antique table owned by Hali was destroyed in a fire. The table had been purchased on 3 June 2010 for £44,000. Hali received insurance proceeds of £62,000 on 12 December 2022, and on 6 January 2023, he purchased a replacement antique table for £63,600. Hali will make a claim to roll over the gain arising from the receipt of the insurance proceeds.

Disposals by Goma during the tax year 2022/23

Goma disposed of the following assets during the tax year 2022/23, all of which resulted in gains:

(1) Qualifying corporate bonds sold for £38,300

(2) A car (suitable for private use) sold for £11,600

(3) An antique vase sold for £6,200

(4) A copyright (with an unexpired life of eight years when purchased) sold for £5,400

(5) Quoted shares held within an individual savings account (ISA) sold for £24,700

159 What amount of unused capital losses do Hali and Goma have brought forward to the tax year 2022/23?

Option	*Hali*	*Goma*
1	£23,000	£9,100
2	£23,000	£2,200
3	£35,300	£9,100
4	£35,300	£2,200

O Option 1

O Option 2

O Option 3

O Option 4 **(2 marks)**

---

160 What cost figure and what value per share (disposal value) will be used in calculating the chargeable gain on Hali's sale of 5,000 ordinary shares in Lima Ltd?

Option	*Cost figure*	*Value per share*
1	£5,000	£4.95
2	£14,500	£4.95
3	£14,500	£5.30
4	£5,000	£5.30

- O Option 1
- O Option 2
- O Option 3
- O Option 4 **(2 marks)**

---

161 In deciding whether Hali and Goma's future disposals of their shareholdings in Lima Ltd will qualify for business asset disposal relief, which ONE of the following statements is correct?

- O Hali and Goma must be directors of Lima Ltd
- O Lima Ltd must be a trading company
- O Hali and Goma must have shareholdings of at least 10% each in Lima Ltd
- O The qualifying conditions must be met for a period of three years prior to the date of disposal **(2 marks)**

---

162 What is the base cost of Hali's replacement antique table for capital gains tax (CGT) purposes?

- O £62,000
- O £63,600
- O £45,600
- O £44,000 **(2 marks)**

---

163 How many of the five assets disposed of by Goma during the tax year 2022/23 are exempt assets for the purposes of capital gains tax (CGT)?

- O Three
- O Five
- O Two
- O Four **(2 marks)**

(Total = 10 marks)

OT Case - Lily (March/June 2021) (18 mins)

The following scenario relates to the next five questions.

Lily disposed of various assets during the tax year 2022/23, resulting in chargeable gains.

Lily's disposals included the following:

A copyright sold on 30 June 2022

The copyright had been purchased on 1 July 2019 for £22,000 when it had an unexpired life of 15 years.

Four hectares of land sold on 12 August 2022

Lily had originally purchased six hectares of land on 30 May 2008 for £84,000. The four hectares of land were sold for £140,000, and the market value of the unsold two hectares of land at the time of sale was £60,000. Prior to the disposal, Lily spent £14,400 clearing and levelling the four hectares of land that were sold.

A house sold on 31 December 2022

The house had been purchased on 1 January 2009, and throughout the 168 months of ownership had been occupied by Lily as follows (periods shown chronologically):

	Months
Occupied	32
Unoccupied – travelling overseas	36
Unoccupied – required to work elsewhere in the United Kingdom	60
Occupied	20
Unoccupied – travelling overseas	20
	168

Throughout the period 1 January 2009 to 31 December 2022, Lily did not have any other main residence.

Cash received following takeover of Moon plc by Sun plc on 22 February 2023

Lily had originally purchased her £1 ordinary shares in Moon plc on 18 July 2011 for £27,280. Under the terms of the takeover, Lily received total cash of £19,800 and 22,000 £1 ordinary shares in Sun plc. Immediately after the takeover, Sun plc's £1 ordinary shares were quoted at £2.20.

Lily's sister

Lily's sister has chargeable gains for the year 2022/23 of £44,200 which qualify for business asset disposal relief and £107,400 of chargeable gains relating to the disposal of a residential property which is not her main residence.

Lily's sister does not have any taxable income for the tax year 2022/23.

164 What cost figure will have been used in calculating the chargeable gain on the disposal of Lily's copyright?

- O £22,000
- O £17,600
- O £4,400
- O £19,067

(2 marks)

---

165 What are the total deductions which will have been allowed in calculating the chargeable gain on the disposal of Lily's four hectares of land?

- O £68,880
- O £73,200
- O £70,400
- O £58,800

(2 marks)

---

166 What is the total period of occupation (both actual and deemed) for the purposes of calculating the private residence relief on the disposal of Lily's house?

- O 145 months
- O 157 months
- O 168 months
- O 136 months

(2 marks)

---

167 What is Lily's chargeable gain in respect of the cash received following the takeover of Moon plc by Sun plc?

- O £11,880
- O £6,878
- O £19,800
- O £8,640

(2 marks)

---

168 What is Lily's sister's capital gains tax liability for the tax year 2022/23?

- O £34,492
- O £27,278
- O £33,262
- O £31,048

(2 marks)

(Total = 10 marks)

Section C

169 Jorge (December 2011) (amended) (18 mins)

Jorge disposed of the following assets during the tax year 2022/23:

(1) On 30 June 2022 Jorge sold a house for £308,000. The house had been purchased on 1 January 2005 for £93,000. On 10 June 2011, Jorge had incurred legal fees of £5,000 in relation to a boundary dispute with his neighbour. Throughout the 210 months of ownership the house had been occupied by Jorge as follows:

Months	
34	Occupied
18	Unoccupied – Travelling overseas
24	Unoccupied – Required to work overseas by his employer
11	Occupied
30	Unoccupied – Required to work elsewhere in the United Kingdom by his employer
22	Unoccupied – Travelling overseas
26	Unoccupied – Required to work elsewhere in the United Kingdom by his employer
17	Occupied
12	Unoccupied – Required to work overseas by his employer
13	Unoccupied – Travelling overseas
3	Unoccupied – Lived with sister
210	

Jorge let the house out during all of the periods when he did not occupy it personally. Throughout the period 1 January 2005 to 30 June 2022 Jorge did not have any other main residence.

(2) On 30 September 2022 Jorge sold a copyright for £80,300. The copyright had been purchased on 1 October 2020 for £70,000 when it had an unexpired life of ten years.

(3) On 6 October 2022 Jorge sold a painting for £5,400. The painting had been purchased on 18 May 2013 for £2,200.

(4) On 29 October 2022 Jorge sold a car for £10,700. The car had been purchased on 21 December 2016 for £14,600.

Jorge has capital losses brought forward of £25,000.

Required

Calculate Jorge's taxable gains for the tax year 2022/23.

(Total = 10 marks)

170 Winston (June 2012) (amended) (18 mins)

(a) On 19 May 2022, Winston disposed of a painting, and this resulted in a chargeable gain of £47,560. For the tax year 2022/23, Winston has taxable income of £25,100 after the deduction of the personal allowance.

Winston is considering the sale of a business that he has run as a sole trader since 1 July 2009.

The business will be sold for £260,000, and this figure, along with the respective cost of each asset, is made up as follows:

	Sale proceeds	*Cost*
	£	£
Freehold shop	140,000	80,000
Freehold warehouse	88,000	102,000
Net current assets	32,000	32,000
	260,000	

The freehold warehouse has never been used by Winston for business purposes.

Required

(i) Assuming that Winston does not sell his sole trader business, calculate his capital gains tax liability for the tax year 2022/23.

(3 marks)

(ii) Calculate Winston's capital gains tax liability for the tax year 2022/23 if he sold his sole trader business on 25 March 2023. **(4 marks)**

(b) On 3 December 2022, Renaldo sold two hectares of land at auction for gross proceeds of £92,000. The auctioneers' commission was 5% of the sale price.

Renaldo's wife's father had originally purchased three hectares of land on 4 August 2002 for £19,500. He died on 17 June 2009, and the land was inherited by Renaldo's wife. On that date the three hectares of land were valued at £28,600.

Renaldo's wife transferred the land to Renaldo on 14 November 2012. On that date the three hectares of land were valued at £39,000. The market value of the unsold hectare of land as at 3 December 2022 was £38,000.

Compute Renaldo's chargeable gain in respect of the disposal on 3 December 2022.

(3 marks)

(Total = 10 marks)

171 Mick (June 2014) (amended) (18 mins)

Mick disposed of the following assets during the tax year 2022/23:

(1) On 19 May 2022, Mick sold a freehold warehouse for £522,000. The warehouse was purchased on 6 August 2003 for £258,000 and was extended at a cost of £99,000 during April 2005. In January 2009, the floor of the warehouse was damaged by flooding and had to be replaced at a cost of £63,000. The warehouse was sold because it was surplus to the business's requirements as a result of Mick purchasing a newly built warehouse during 2021. Both warehouses have always been used for business purposes in a wholesale business run by Mick as a sole trader.

(2) On 24 September 2022, Mick sold 700,000 £1 ordinary shares in Rolling Ltd, an unquoted trading company, for £3,675,000. He had originally purchased 500,000 shares in Rolling Ltd on 2 June 2007 for £960,000. On 1 December 2012, Rolling Ltd made a 3 for 2 bonus issue. Mick has been a director of Rolling Ltd since 1 January 2007.

Required

(a) Assuming that no reliefs are available, calculate the chargeable gain arising from each of Mick's asset disposals during the tax year 2022/23.

Note. You are not required to calculate the taxable gains or the amount of tax payable.

(4 marks)

(b) State which capital gains tax reliefs might be available to Mick in respect of each of his disposals during the tax year 2022/23, and what further information you would require in order to establish if the reliefs are actually available and to establish any restrictions as regards the amount of relief.

Note. For this part of the question, you are not expected to perform any calculations.

(6 marks)

(Total = 10 marks)

172 Ruby (September/December 2015) (amended) (18 mins)

You should assume that today's date is 1 March 2023.

(a) On 27 August 2022, Ruby disposed of a residential investment property and this resulted in a chargeable gain of £47,000.

For the tax year 2022/23 Ruby has taxable income of £23,515.

Required

Calculate Ruby's capital gains tax liability for the tax year 2022/23 if this is her only disposal in that tax year. **(2 marks)**

(b) In addition to the disposal already made on 27 August 2022, Ruby is going to make one further disposal during the tax year 2022/23. The disposal will be of either Ruby's holding of £1 ordinary shares in Pola Ltd, or her holding of 50p ordinary shares in Aplo plc.

Shareholding in Pola Ltd

Pola Ltd is an unlisted trading company. The shareholding was subscribed for by Ruby on 14 July 2019 for £23,700 and could be sold for £61,000. Ruby has never been an officer nor an employee of Pola Ltd.

Shareholding in Aplo plc

Aplo plc is a trading company listed on a recognised stock exchange in which Ruby has a shareholding of 40,000 50p ordinary shares. Ruby received the shareholding as a gift from her father on 27 May 2011. On that date, the shares were quoted on the stock exchange at £2.12–£2.18. The shareholding could be sold for £59,000.

No reliefs are available in respect of this disposal.

Required

Calculate Ruby's revised capital gains tax liability for the tax year 2022/23, if she also disposes of either (1) her shareholding in Pola Ltd; or alternatively (2) her shareholding in Aplo plc.

Note. The following mark allocation is provided as guidance for this requirement:

Pola Ltd (4½ marks)

Aplo plc (3½ marks) **(8 marks)**

(Total = 10 marks)

> **PART D: INHERITANCE TAX**
>
> Part D covers inheritance tax, the subject of Chapter 18 of the BPP Workbook for Taxation (TX – UK).

Section A

OTQ bank – Inheritance tax 1 (18 mins)

173 Gillian owned a 70% shareholding in Rose Ltd, an unquoted investment company. On 23 July 2022, she gave a 20% shareholding in Rose Ltd to her son. The values of shareholdings in Rose Ltd on 23 July 2022 were as follows:

	£
100% shareholding	600,000
70% shareholding	350,000
50% shareholding	200,000
20% shareholding	80,000

What is the diminution in value of Gillian's estate as a result of her gift on 23 July 2022?

£ ______ **(2 marks)**

---

174 Joel and Sunita were a married couple. Sunita died in July 2008 and 65% of her nil rate band of £312,000 (2008/09) was unused. Joel died in May 2022. He had made a potentially exempt transfer (after all available exemptions) of £75,000 in August 2018. Joel left his estate to his sister. Any relevant elections were made.

What is the nil rate band available to set against Joel's death estate?

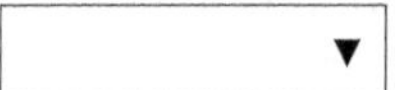

Pull down list

- £325,000
- £452,800
- £461,250
- £536,250

(2 marks)

---

175 On 7 July 2017, Paul made a gross chargeable transfer (after all exemptions) of £260,000. On 19 December 2022, he gave £190,000 to a trust. Paul agreed to pay any lifetime inheritance tax (IHT) due.

How much IHT will be payable by Paul on the December 2022 transfer of value?

- O £28,250
- O £31,250
- O £29,750
- O £23,800 **(2 marks)**

176 Donald made the following transactions in the tax year 2022/23:

(1) A gift of £2,000 to his granddaughter on the occasion of her marriage.

(2) A sale of a vase to his friend, Alan, for £1,000 which both Donald and Alan believed to be the market value of the vase. The vase was later valued by an auction house as worth £20,000 at the date of the sale.

Ignoring the annual exemption, what is the total value of potentially exempt transfers made by Donald as a result of these gifts?

- O £21,000
- O £0
- O £2,000
- O £19,000

(2 marks)

---

177 Kirstin made a gross chargeable transfer of £150,000 to a trust on 15 September 2013 and gifted shares worth £600,000 to her brother on 10 July 2019. The nil rate band in 2013/14 and 2019/20 was £325,000. Kirstin died on 23 October 2022.

Ignoring the annual exemption, what is the inheritance tax payable on Kirstin's death in relation to her lifetime transfers?

- O £170,000
- O £88,000
- O £136,000
- O £134,080

(2 marks)

(Total = 10 marks)

OTQ bank – Inheritance tax 2 (36 mins)

178 Mary made the following gifts in the tax year 2022/23:

(1) £1,000 on the first day of each month for nine months to her grandson to pay university living expenses. Mary used income surplus to her living requirements to make these payments and had made such payments to her grandson throughout his four-year university course.

(2) £100 to her grandnephew on his birthday and a further £250 to the same grandnephew as a Christmas gift.

Ignoring the annual exemption, what is the total value of potentially exempt transfers made by Mary as a result of these gifts?

- O £9,350
- O £100
- O £9,000
- O £350

(2 marks)

---

179 Daniel owned all 1,000 shares in Q Ltd, an unquoted investment company. On 10 October 2022, Daniel gave 300 of his shares in Q Ltd to his daughter.

The values of the shares on 10 October 2022 were as follows:

% shareholding	*Value per share*
	£
76–100	150
51–75	120
26–50	90
1–25	30

What is the diminution in value of Daniel's estate as a result of his gift on 10 October 2022?

[▼]

Pull down list

- £123,000
- £18,000
- £27,000
- £66,000

(2 marks)

---

180 Ken died on 15 January 2023 leaving a chargeable estate valued at £245,000. He had made gross chargeable lifetime transfers of £98,000 in October 2015 and £118,000 in June 2019.

How much inheritance tax (IHT) is payable in respect of Ken's chargeable estate of £245,000? ***(March/June 2021)***

£ [ ] **(2 marks)**

---

181 Rodney died on 13 August 2022. In his will he left £200 in cash to each of his five nephews, investments held in ISAs valued at £350,000 to his daughter, and the residue of his estate, which amounted to £520,000, to his wife.

What is the chargeable estate for inheritance tax purposes?

£ [ ] **(2 marks)**

---

182 Sandeep made a gift of £425,000 to a trust on 10 November 2022. No agreement has been made about who will pay the inheritance tax (IHT) in respect of this gift.

What is the due date for payment of the IHT and who is primarily liable for its payment? ***(June 2019)***

- O The trustees are liable to make the payment by 31 May 2023
- O The trustees are liable to make the payment by 30 April 2023
- O Sandeep is liable to make the payment by 31 May 2023
- O Sandeep is liable to make the payment by 30 April 2023 **(2 marks)**

---

183 Benjamin died on 30 November 2022 leaving an estate valued at £890,000. Inheritance tax of £276,000 was paid in respect of the estate.

Under the terms of his will, Benjamin left £260,000 to his wife, a specific legacy of £120,000 (free of tax) to his brother, and the residue of the estate to his grandchildren.

What is the amount of inheritance received by Benjamin's grandchildren?

▼

Pull down list

- £234,000
- £354,000
- £510,000
- £614,000

(2 marks)

---

184 Heng is a wealthy 45 year old who would like to reduce the potential inheritance tax liability on her estate when she dies.

Which of the following actions will or will not achieve Heng's aim of reducing the potential inheritance tax liability on her estate when she dies?

Changing the terms of her will so that the residue of her estate goes to her grandchildren rather than her children	**WILL ACHIEVE**	**WILL NOT ACHIEVE**
Making lifetime gifts to trusts up to the value of the nil rate band every seven years	**WILL ACHIEVE**	**WILL NOT ACHIEVE**
Changing the terms of her will so that the residue of her estate goes to her husband rather than her children	**WILL ACHIEVE**	**WILL NOT ACHIEVE**
Making lifetime gifts to her grandchildren early in life	**WILL ACHIEVE**	**WILL NOT ACHIEVE**

(2 marks)

---

185 Chan died on 8 December 2022, having made a lifetime cash gift of £500,000 to a trust on 16 October 2021. Chan paid the inheritance tax arising from this gift.

Match the due date payment of the additional inheritance tax arising from the gift made to the trustees and the persons who are responsible for paying this tax.

8 June 2023		Due date
30 June 2023		Persons responsible
The trustees		
The personal representatives of Chan's estate		

(2 marks)

---

186 Nadia died on 6 December 2022. Her death estate included her main residence which was valued at £360,000 on which there was secured an outstanding repayment mortgage of £140,000. Nadia will leave her entire estate to her three children.

Nadia is a widow. Her husband died in 2009 leaving his entire estate to Nadia.

What amount of residence nil rate band will be available in computing inheritance tax on Nadia's death estate?

- O £175,000
- O £220,000
- O £350,000
- O £360,000

(2 marks)

---

187 Rachel is aged 85 and in poor health. She is keen to minimise the inheritance tax due on her death estate which is likely to have a value of about £1.2 million. Her will currently leaves her main residence (valued at £300,000) to her brother and the residue of her estate to her son. Rachel has never been married.

Complete the following sentence by matching the correct response in each space.

The inheritance tax liability on Rachel's estate will (1) ▼ by (2) ▼ if she leaves her main residence to her son rather than her brother.

Pull down list 1

- Decrease
- Increase

Pull down list 2

- £175,000
- £70,000

(2 marks)

(Total = 20 marks)

Section B

OT case – Ning (June 2012) (amended) (18 mins)

The following scenario relates to the next five questions.

You should assume that today's date is 19 March 2023.

Ning owns the following assets:

(1) Two investment properties respectively valued at £674,000 and £442,000. The first property has an outstanding repayment mortgage of £160,000, and the second property is owned outright with no mortgage.

(2) Vintage cars valued at £172,000.

(3) Investments in Individual Savings Accounts valued at £47,000, National Savings & Investments savings certificates valued at £36,000, and government stocks (gilts) valued at £69,000.

Ning owes £22,400 in respect of a personal loan from a bank, and she has also verbally promised to pay legal fees of £4,600 incurred by her nephew. Her reasonable funeral expenses will amount to £5,500.

Ning's husband died on 12 March 2007, and 70% of his inheritance tax nil rate band was not used.

On 14 August 2011 Ning had made a gift of £90,000 to her daughter, and on 7 November 2021 she made a gift of her main residence, worth £220,000, to her son. These amounts are after taking account of any available exemptions.

The nil rate band for the tax year 2006/07 is £285,000.

188 What is the net value for the two properties in (1) which will be included in the calculation of Ning's chargeable estate were she to die on 20 March 2023?

- O £1,024,000
- O £956,000
- O £856,000
- O £864,000

(2 marks)

---

189 What is the value of the assets in (2) and (3) which will be included in the calculation of Ning's chargeable estate were she to die on 20 March 2023?

- O £172,000
- O £0
- O £324,000
- O £152,000

(2 marks)

---

190 What is the total amount of deductions (ignoring mortgage debts) which will be taken into account in the calculation of Ning's chargeable estate were she to die on 20 March 2023?

- O £5,500
- O £32,500
- O £10,100
- O £27,900

(2 marks)

---

191 What is the amount of Ning's own nil rate band for calculating the inheritance tax payable in respect of her estate were she to die on 20 March 2023?

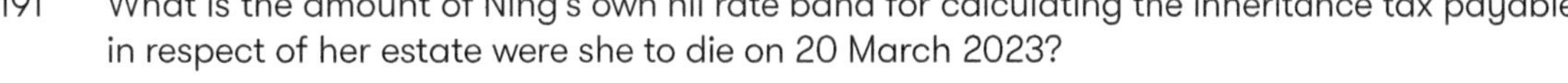

- O £325,000
- O £105,000
- O £15,000
- O £205,000

(2 marks)

---

192 What is the amount of Ning's husband's nil rate band that Ning's personal representatives could claim were she to die on 20 March 2023 and by when should the claim be made?

	Amount	*Claim*
O	£227,500	By 31 March 2025
O	£227,500	By 30 September 2023
O	£199,500	By 31 March 2025
O	£199,500	By 30 September 2023

(2 marks)

(Total = 10 marks)

OT case – Jimmy (June 2011) (amended) (18 mins)

The following scenario relates to the next five questions.

Jimmy died on 14 February 2023. He had used up his nil rate band at the date of his death by making the following gifts during his lifetime:

(1) On 2 August 2021 Jimmy made a cash gift of £10,000 to his grandson as a wedding gift when he got married.

(2) On 9 September 2021 Jimmy gave 200 shares valued at £5 each in J Ltd, an unquoted investment company, to his daughter. Before the gift, Jimmy owned 5,100 shares valued at £30 each in J Ltd. After the gift Jimmy owned 4,900 shares valued at £20 each in J Ltd.

(3) On 14 November 2021 Jimmy made a cash gift of £800,000 to a trust. Jimmy paid the inheritance tax arising from this gift. Additional inheritance tax was payable on this transfer as a result of Jimmy's death.

At the date of his death Jimmy owned assets valued at £980,000. He did not own a main residence at his death. Under the terms of his will Jimmy left £200,000 to his wife and the residue of his estate to his son.

The nil rate band for the tax year 2021/22 was £325,000.

193 What was the total amount of the exemptions that were deducted in computing the potentially exempt transfer made on 2 August 2021?

- O £3,000
- O £8,500
- O £6,000
- O £11,000

(2 marks)

---

194 What is the diminution in value in Jimmy's estate as a result of his gift on 9 September 2021?

[▼]

Pull down list

- £1,000
- £4,000
- £55,000
- £6,000

(2 marks)

---

195 What was the amount of the inheritance tax paid by Jimmy as a result of his gift made on 14 November 2021?

£ [ ] **(2 marks)**

---

196 Match the due date for payment of the additional inheritance tax on the gift made on 14 November 2021 as a result of Jimmy's death and by whom should it be paid.

Options		
14 August 2023		By whom paid
31 August 2023		Due date
Trustees of trust		
Executors of Jimmy's estate		

(2 marks)

---

197 What is the inheritance tax chargeable on Jimmy's death estate as a result of his death on 14 February 2023?

£ [ ] **(2 marks)**

(Total = 10 marks)

OT case – Zoe and Luke (June 2015) (amended) (18 mins)

The following scenario relates to the next five questions.

Zoe and Luke are brother and sister; they died within a few months of each other.

Zoe

Zoe died on 17 February 2023.

She had always used her annual exemption in April each year and had made the following additional gifts during her lifetime:

(1) On 21 March 2016, Zoe made a cash gift of £633,000 to a trust. Zoe paid the inheritance tax (IHT) arising from this gift. The nil rate band for the tax year 2015/16 is £325,000.

(2) On 17 August 2019, Zoe made a further cash gift of £200,000 to the trust. The trustees paid the IHT arising from the gift. The nil rate band for the tax year 2019/20 is £325,000.

Luke

Luke died on 10 October 2022. He was survived by two adult children, a son and a daughter. Luke's wife had died on 25 July 2008.

On 7 March 2021, Luke had made a cash gift of £270,000 to his daughter as a wedding gift when she got married.

Luke had also paid his son's university tuition fees in each of September 2020, 2021 and 2022, making the payments directly to the university. He was advised that these payments were exempt from inheritance tax under the normal expenditure out of income exemption.

On her death, Luke's wife had left £240,000 to their daughter and the remainder of her estate to Luke. She made no lifetime transfers. The nil rate band for the tax year 2008/09 was £312,000.

198 Which TWO of the following statements about Luke's payment of his son's university tuition fees are correct?

- ☐ The payments could be exempt without any cash limit under the normal expenditure out of income exemption.
- ☐ The payments could not be exempt under the normal expenditure out of income exemption because they were paid directly to the university and not to his son.
- ☐ The payments must have been reported each tax year to HM Revenue & Customs in Luke's income tax return to qualify for the normal expenditure out of income exemption.
- ☐ The payments must have left Luke with sufficient income to maintain his usual standard of living to qualify for the normal expenditure out of income exemption. **(2 marks)**

---

199 What is the amount of the gross chargeable transfer made by Zoe on 21 March 2016?

- O £702,500
- O £710,000
- O £694,600
- O £756,200

(2 marks)

---

200 What is the additional IHT which will be payable, as a result of Zoe's death, in respect of the transfer made on 17 August 2019, assuming that the nil rate band has been completely used by the gross chargeable transfer made by Zoe on 21 March 2016?

[▼]

Pull down list

- £24,000
- £40,000
- £64,000
- £80,000

(2 marks)

---

201 What is the value of the potentially exempt transfer made by Luke on 7 March 2021?

£ [ ]

(2 marks)

202 What is the amount of Luke's wife's nil rate band which could be transferred and used in calculating the IHT on Luke's death?

- O £75,000
- O £72,000
- O £312,000
- O £325,000

(2 marks)

(Total = 10 marks)

OT case – Marcus (Sept/Dec 2015) (amended) (18 mins)

The following scenario relates to the next five questions.

Marcus died on 10 March 2023. He had been married to his wife, Barbara, for many years. He had made the following gifts during his lifetime:

(1) On 14 January 2012, Marcus made a chargeable lifetime transfer of £328,000 to a trust. The trustees paid the lifetime inheritance tax which arose in respect of this gift.

(2) On 3 January 2019, Marcus made a chargeable lifetime transfer to another trust. In addition to the gift, Marcus paid the related lifetime inheritance tax on this gift. The gross chargeable lifetime transfer amounted to £491,250.

(3) On 17 March 2019, Marcus made a gift (a potentially exempt transfer) of 30,000 £1 ordinary shares in Scarum Ltd, an unquoted investment company, to his daughter.

Before the transfer, Marcus owned all of Scarum Ltd's issued share capital of 100,000 £1 ordinary shares. On 17 March 2019, Scarum Ltd's shares were worth £5 each for a holding of 30%, £9 each for a holding of 70%, and £12 each for a holding of 100%.

(4) On 29 June 2020, Marcus gave a plot of land worth £100,000 to Barbara. Marcus had bought the land in 2008 for £80,000.

The nil rate band for the tax years 2011/12 and 2018/19 was £325,000.

Under the terms of his will, Marcus left his entire estate to Barbara. Barbara has not made any gifts during her lifetime. She is intending to remarry. Ignore the inheritance tax annual exemption.

203 What was the amount of the lifetime inheritance tax paid by the trustees (if any) as a result of the gift made on 14 January 2012?

£ [ ]

(2 marks)

---

204 What was the amount of the lifetime inheritance tax paid by Marcus as a result of the gift made on 3 January 2019?

- O £122,812
- O £33,250
- O £98,250
- O £41,562

(2 marks)

---

205 What was the amount of the taper relief deductible from the additional inheritance tax due as a result of the death of Marcus on the gift made on 3 January 2019?

[▼]

Pull down list

- £117,900
- £26,600
- £39,900
- £78,600

(2 marks)

---

206 What was the amount of the potentially exempt transfer made by Marcus on 17 March 2019?

- O £360,000
- O £270,000
- O £150,000
- O £570,000

(2 marks)

---

207 Which TWO of the following statements about Marcus and Barbara for inheritance tax purposes are correct?

- ☐ There is no liability for inheritance tax on the transfer of Marcus's estate to Barbara because they are treated together as a single chargeable person for inheritance tax.
- ☐ If Barbara remarries, any unused nil rate band on her death can be transferred to her spouse if they survive her.
- ☐ The gift of the land on 29 June 2020 by Marcus to Barbara is a potentially exempt transfer of £80,000.
- ☐ The transfer of Marcus's estate to Barbara on his death is an exempt transfer.

(2 marks)

(Total = 10 marks)

OT case – Lebna and Lulu (March/June 2019) (18 mins)

The following scenario relates to the next five questions.

You should assume that today's date is 1 March 2023.

Lebna and Lulu were a married couple, but Lulu died on 24 January 2017.

Lulu

Lulu left an estate valued at £210,000 for inheritance tax (IHT) purposes. The estate did not include a main residence. Under the terms of her will, Lulu left a specific legacy of £40,000 to her brother, with the residue of the estate to her husband, Lebna. Lulu had made the following lifetime transfers:

Date	*Type of transfer*	*Amount*
		£
13 February 2009	Chargeable lifetime transfer	50,000
21 June 2015	Potentially exempt transfer	80,000

Both of these transfers are after taking account of all available exemptions.

The nil rate band for the tax year 2016/17 is £325,000.

Lebna's chargeable estate

Lebna has a chargeable estate valued at £980,000. His estate includes a main residence valued at £340,000 on which there is an outstanding interest-only mortgage of £152,000.

Under the terms of his will, Lebna has left his entire estate to his son.

Gift to son on 22 February 2018

On 22 February 2018, Lebna made a gift of 60,000 £1 ordinary shares in Blean Ltd, an unquoted investment company, to his son. Before the transfer, Lebna owned all of Blean Ltd's share capital of 100,000 ordinary shares. The market value of Blean Ltd's ordinary shares on 22 February 2018 was as follows:

Holding	Market value per share
40%	£4.20
60%	£6.30
100%	£7.10

Lebna had not made any previous lifetime gifts.

Gifts to friends during October 2022

Lebna made cash gifts of £85, £225, £190 and £490 to various friends during October 2022. The gifts of £85 and £190 were to the same friend.

208 If Lebna were to die today, 1 March 2023, how much of Lulu's nil rate band will the personal representatives of Lebna's estate be able to claim when calculating the IHT payable on his chargeable estate?

- O £155,000
- O £205,000
- O £35,000
- O £285,000 **(2 marks)**

209 If Lebna were to die today, 1 March 2023, what is the total amount of residence nil rate band which will be available when calculating the IHT payable on his chargeable estate?

- O £175,000
- O £350,000
- O £340,000
- O £188,000 **(2 marks)**

210 What is the amount of the potentially exempt transfer which Lebna has made to his son on 22 February 2018 (the gift of 60,000 shares in Blean Ltd) after deducting any available exemptions?

- O £542,000
- O £536,000
- O £372,000
- O £378,000 **(2 marks)**

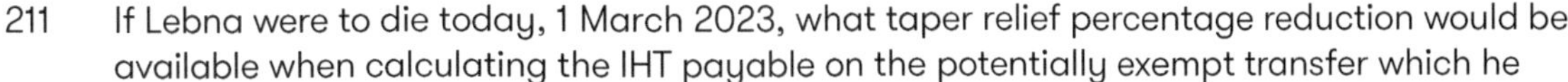

211 If Lebna were to die today, 1 March 2023, what taper relief percentage reduction would be available when calculating the IHT payable on the potentially exempt transfer which he

made to his son on 22 February 2018 (the gift of 60,000 shares in Blean Ltd), and when would this IHT be due?

Option	Taper relief reduction	Due date
1	60%	30 September 2023
2	60%	1 September 2023
3	40%	1 September 2023
4	40%	30 September 2023

- O Option 1
- O Option 2
- O Option 3
- O Option 4

(2 marks)

---

212 What amount of the cash gifts made by Lebna to his friends during October 2022 is covered by the small gifts exemption?

- O £500
- O £990
- O £225
- O £275

(2 marks)

(Total = 10 marks)

Section C

213 Pere and Phil (June 2013) (amended) (18 mins)

On 23 August 2016, Pere made a gift of a house valued at £420,000 to his son, Phil. This was a wedding gift when Phil got married. The nil rate band for the tax year 2016/17 is £325,000.

Pere

Pere died on 20 March 2023 at which time his estate was valued at £880,000. Under the terms of his will, Pere divided his estate equally, before inheritance tax, between his wife and his son, Phil. Pere had not made any gifts during his lifetime except for the gift of the house to Phil. Pere did not own a main residence.

Phil

Phil sold the house which he received as a wedding gift from Pere, his father, on 5 April 2023. The following information relates to the property:

	£
Net sale proceeds after costs of disposal	496,700
Cost of new boundary wall around the property (previously no boundary wall)	(5,200)
Cost of replacing the property's chimney	(2,800)

Phil has taxable income (after deduction of the personal allowance) of £14,150 in 2022/23. The house was never occupied by Phil.

Required

(a) Calculate the inheritance tax that will be payable as a result of Pere's death. **(6 marks)**

(b) Calculate Phil's capital gains tax liability for the tax year 2022/23. **(4 marks)**

(Total = 10 marks)

214 Afiya (December 2013) (amended) (18 mins)

Afiya died on 29 November 2022. She had made the following gifts during her lifetime:

(1) On 14 September 2021, Afiya made a gift of 6,500 £1 ordinary shares in Cassava Ltd, an unquoted investment company, to her daughter.

Before the transfer Afiya owned 8,000 shares out of Cassava Ltd's issued share capital of 10,000 £1 ordinary shares. On 14 September 2021, Cassava Ltd's shares were worth £3 each for a holding of 15%, £7 each for a holding of 65%, and £8 each for a holding of 80%.

(2) On 27 January 2022, Afiya made a cash gift of £400,000 to a trust. Afiya paid the inheritance tax arising from this gift.

On 29 November 2022, Afiya's estate was valued at £623,000 including her main residence which was valued at £90,000. Her executors paid funeral expenses of £3,000 on 12 January 2023. Under the terms of her will Afiya left £150,000 cash to her husband, a specific legacy of £40,000 to her sister, and the residue of the estate to her children.

The nil rate band for the tax year 2021/22 is £325,000.

Required

(a) Calculate the inheritance tax which will be payable as a result of Afiya's death. **(9 marks)**

(b) Calculate the amount of the inheritance which will be received by Afiya's children. **(1 mark)**

(Total = 10 marks)

215 Kendra (June 2014) (amended) (18 mins)

You should assume that today's date is 1 January 2023.

Kendra, aged 93, is in poor health with just a few months left to live. She has made no lifetime gifts.

Kendra owns the following assets:

(1) An investment residential property valued at £970,000. The property has never been occupied by Kendra, and if it were disposed of during the tax year 2022/23 the disposal would result in a chargeable gain of £174,000.

(2) Building society deposits of £387,000.

(3) Investments in Individual Savings Accounts (ISAs) valued at £39,000 and savings certificates from National Savings & Investments (NS&I) valued at £17,000.

(4) A life assurance policy on her own life. The policy has an open market value of £210,000 and proceeds of £225,000 will be received following Kendra's death.

None of the above valuations are expected to change in the near future. Kendra has income tax outstanding at her death of £12,800. She also has an outstanding unsecured loan of £1,200 which is due to be repaid on her death.

Under the terms of her will, Kendra has left her entire estate to her children.

The nil rate band of Kendra's husband was fully utilised when he died ten years ago.

For the tax year 2022/23, Kendra will pay income tax at the higher rate.

Required

(a) Calculate the inheritance tax which would be payable if Kendra were to die on 31 March 2023. **(5 marks)**

(b) Advise Kendra why it would not be beneficial to make an immediate lifetime gift of the property valued at £970,000 to her children.

Notes.

1 Your answer should take account of both the capital gains tax and the inheritance tax implications of making the gift.

2 For this part of the question, you should ignore the capital gains tax annual exempt amount and inheritance tax annual exemptions. **(3 marks)**

(c) Advise Kendra why it might be beneficial for inheritance tax purposes to change the terms of her will so that part of her estate was instead left to her grandchildren rather than her children. **(2 marks)**

(Total = 10 marks)

216 James (March/June 2016) (18 mins)

James died on 22 January 2023. He had made the following gifts during his lifetime:

(1) On 9 October 2015, a cash gift of £35,000 to a trust. No lifetime inheritance tax was payable in respect of this gift.

(2) On 14 May 2021, a cash gift of £420,000 to his daughter.

(3) On 2 August 2021, a gift of a property valued at £260,000 to a trust. No lifetime inheritance tax was payable in respect of this gift because it was covered by the nil rate band. By the time of James's death on 22 January 2023, the property had increased in value to £310,000.

On 22 January 2023, James's estate was valued at £870,000. James did not own a main residence. Under the terms of his will, James left his entire estate to his children.

The nil rate band of James's wife was fully utilised when she died ten years ago.

The nil rate band for the tax years 2015/16 and 2021/22 is £325,000.

Required

(a) Calculate the inheritance tax which will be payable as a result of James's death, and state who will be responsible for paying the tax. **(6 marks)**

(b) Explain why it might have been beneficial for inheritance tax purposes if James had left a portion of his estate to his grandchildren rather than to his children. **(2 marks)**

(c) Explain why it might be advantageous for inheritance tax purposes for a person to make lifetime gifts even when such gifts are made within seven years of death.

Notes.

1 Your answer should include a calculation of James's inheritance tax saving from making the gift of property to the trust on 2 August 2021 rather than retaining the property until his death.

2 You are not expected to consider lifetime exemptions in this part of the question.

(2 marks)

(Total = 10 marks)

217 Dembe (March/June 2019) (18 mins)

You should assume that today's date is 15 February 2023.

You are a trainee chartered certified accountant dealing with the tax affairs of Dembe and her husband Kato.

Personal pension contribution

Dembe is self-employed and her trading profit for the year ended 31 December 2022 is £130,000. She will not have any other income or outgoings for the tax year 2022/23.

Dembe is planning to make a personal pension contribution of £32,000 (net) before 5 April 2023 and would like to know the amount of income tax and national insurance contributions (NICs) which she will save as a result of making the pension contribution.

Sale of residential property

During March 2023, Dembe is going to sell a residential property, and this will result in a chargeable gain of £67,000 if she makes the disposal.

Dembe wants to know whether it would be beneficial to transfer the property to Kato, her husband, as a no gain/no loss transfer prior to it being sold during March 2023. The transfer from Dembe to Kato will cost £2,000 in additional legal fees, and this cost will reduce the chargeable gain to £65,000 if the disposal is made by Kato.

Dembe has already made other disposals during the tax year 2022/23 which have utilised her annual exempt amount. Kato, however, has not yet made any disposals.

Kato's taxable income for the tax year 2022/23 is £21,350.

Inheritance tax

Dembe, who knows nothing about inheritance tax (IHT), is concerned about the amount of IHT which will be payable when she and Kato die. The couple's combined chargeable estate is valued at £950,000 for IHT purposes. The estate includes a main residence valued at £360,000.

Under the terms of their wills, Dembe and Kato have initially left their entire estates to each other. Then when the second of them dies, the total estate of £950,000 will be left to the couple's children.

The couple are not sure whether to change the terms of their wills so that assets worth £325,000 are left to their children when the first of them dies.

Neither Dembe nor Kato have made any lifetime gifts.

Required

(a) Calculate the reduction in Dembe's income tax liability and NICs for the tax year 2022/23 if she makes the personal pension contribution of £32,000 (net) before 5 April 2023.

Note. You are not expected to prepare full tax computations. **(4 marks)**

(b) Calculate the couple's overall saving for the tax year 2022/23, after taking account of the additional legal fees of £2,000, if the residential property is transferred to Kato and sold by him, rather than the property being sold by Dembe. **(3 marks)**

(c) Calculate the amount of IHT payable, if any, were Dembe and Kato to both die in the near future and explain whether or not it might be beneficial to leave assets worth £325,000 to their children when the first of them dies.

Note. You should assume that the IHT rates and thresholds remain unchanged. **(3 marks)**

(Total = 10 marks)

PART E: CORPORATION TAX LIABILITIES
Part E covers corporation tax liabilities, the subject of Chapters 19 to 23 of the BPP Workbook for Taxation (TX – UK).

Section A

OTQ bank – Corporation tax liabilities (36 mins)

218 Jet Ltd has deducted some items in its statement of profit or loss for the year ended 31 December 2021.

Identify, by clicking on the relevant boxes in the table below, whether each of the following items of expenditure are allowable or not allowable for computing Jet Ltd's taxable trading profit.

Legal expenses relating to the acquisition of a new 40-year lease on its factory	ALLOWABLE	NOT ALLOWABLE
Cost of arranging a new bank loan to purchase machinery for trade	ALLOWABLE	NOT ALLOWABLE
Write off of an irrecoverable loan to a former employee	ALLOWABLE	NOT ALLOWABLE
Donation to local charity with mention of Jet Ltd's support in programme for fundraising concert (not a qualifying charitable donation)	ALLOWABLE	NOT ALLOWABLE

(2 marks)

---

219 Rat Ltd started trading on 1 December 2021 and prepared its first set of accounts to 31 March 2023.

What will Rat Ltd's accounting periods be for the period of account to 31 March 2023?

- O 4 months to 31 March 2022, 12 months to 31 March 2023
- O 4 months to 5 April 2022, nearly 12 months to 31 March 2023
- O 12 months to 30 November 2022, 4 months to 31 March 2023
- O 16 months to 31 March 2023 **(2 marks)**

---

220 Xeon Ltd purchases a newly-constructed office building from a developer for £1,875,000 on 1 March 2022 and starts using it on 1 April 2022. The purchase price includes acquisition costs of £75,000. Xeon Ltd has a 31 December year end.

What are the maximum SBAs available to Xeon Ltd in the year ended 31 December 2022?

£ [ ] **(2 marks)**

---

221 Kit Ltd was incorporated and started trading on 1 July 2022 and prepared its first set of accounts to 31 December 2022.

During the six-month accounting period to 31 December 2022, it purchased two vehicles:

		£
28 November 2022	Car [1] (CO_2 emissions 126 g/km)	15,400
2 December 2022	Car [2] (CO_2 emissions 41 g/km)	30,400

Car [1] is used 20% for private purposes by a director of Kit Ltd.

What are the capital allowances to which Kit Ltd is entitled for the period to 31 December 2022?

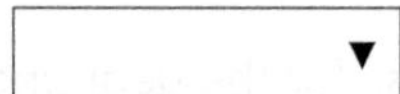

Pull down list

- £3,106
- £3,198
- £4,122
- £6,396

(2 marks)

---

222 Eminal Ltd purchased 50,000 shares in Vesterama Ltd for £3.50 a share on 6 June 2002. On 6 June 2022, Eminal Ltd sold 15,000 shares in Vesterama Ltd for £70,000. Eminal Ltd prepares accounts to 31 December each year. Indexation factor: June 2002 to December 2017 = 0.578.

What is Eminal Ltd's chargeable gain or capital loss for the year ended 31 December 2022? ***(June 2017)***

- O £12,845 loss
- O £105,000 loss
- O £0
- O £17,500 gain

(2 marks)

---

223 Crane plc started trading on 1 January 2022. In the year ended 31 December 2022, the company made an adjusted trading loss of £40,000. In the year ended 31 December 2023 the company will have trading income of £30,000, other taxable income of £6,000 and will make a qualifying charitable donation of £2,700. Crane plc wishes to use carry forward trading loss relief.

What is the most beneficial carry forward trading loss relief claim that Crane plc can make for the year ended 31 December 2023?

£ ____________ **(2 marks)**

---

224 Deal Ltd has the following results:

	12 months to 31 March 2022	*9 months to 31 December 2022*	*12 months to31 December 2023*
	£	£	£
Trading profits/(losses)	45,000	40,000	(160,000)
Property business profits	18,000	15,500	5,000

The company wishes to claim relief for its loss as early as possible.

What is the unused loss carried forward at 31 December 2023?

£ [ ] **(2 marks)**

---

225 Bab Ltd has owned 80% of the ordinary share capital of Boon Ltd for many years. The two companies' results for the year ended 31 December 2022 are as follows:

	Bab Ltd	*Boon Ltd*
	£	£
Trading profit/(loss)	(38,000)	36,000
Chargeable gains	7,000	4,000

What is the maximum amount of current period group relief which Boon Ltd can claim from Bab Ltd for the year ended 31 December 2022? ***(June 2018)***

- O £38,000
- O £31,000
- O £36,000
- O £32,000

(2 marks)

---

226 The Daffodil plc group of companies has the following structure:

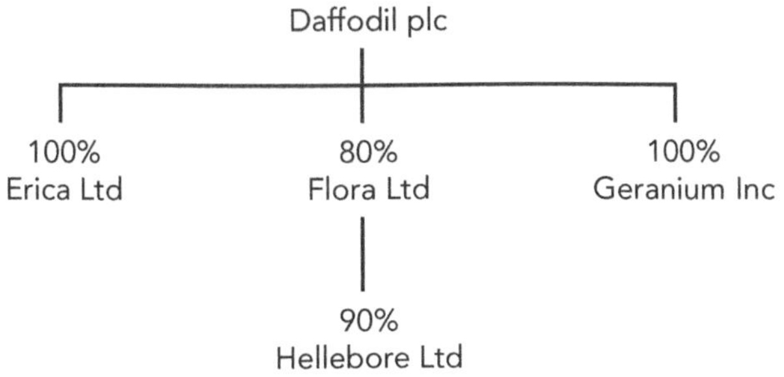

All companies are resident in the UK except Geranium Inc.

Identify, by clicking on the relevant boxes in the table below, the companies to which Erica Ltd could surrender a trading loss.

Daffodil plc	**YES**	**NO**
Geranium Inc	**YES**	**NO**
Flora Ltd	**YES**	**NO**
Hellebore Ltd	**YES**	**NO**

(2 marks)

227 The Pine plc group of companies has the following structure:

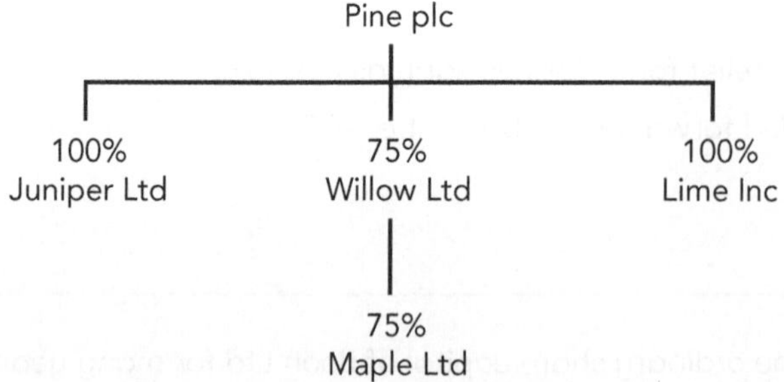

All companies are resident in the UK except Lime Inc.

Identify, by clicking on the relevant boxes in the table below, the companies to which Maple Ltd could transfer a capital loss.

Pine plc	**YES**	**NO**
Willow Ltd	**YES**	**NO**
Juniper Ltd	**YES**	**NO**
Lime Inc	**YES**	**NO**

(2 marks)

(Total = 20 marks)

Section B

OT case – Luna Ltd (June 2015) (amended) (18 mins)

The following scenario relates to the next five questions.

Luna Ltd had the following transactions in shares during the year ended 31 March 2023:

(1) On 29 November 2022, Luna Ltd sold its entire shareholding of £1 ordinary shares in Pluto plc for £53,400. Luna Ltd had originally purchased these shares in Pluto plc on 14 June 2008 for £36,800.

(2) On 30 November 2022, Luna Ltd sold 10,000 of its shares in Neptune plc for £26,000. Luna Ltd had originally purchased 16,000 shares in Neptune plc on 10 May 2010 for £32,000.

(3) On 10 December 2022, Luna Ltd acquired shares under a rights issue in Saturn plc. Luna Ltd had originally purchased 5,000 £1 ordinary shares in Saturn plc for £7,500 in August 2011. There was a 1 for 1 bonus issue in July 2013 when the shares were worth £1.75 each. The December 2022 rights issue was on a 1 for 4 basis and the cost of the rights issue shares was £2.25 per share.

(4) On 12 February 2023, Luna Ltd's shareholding in Asteroid plc was taken over by Comet plc. Luna Ltd had originally purchased 10,000 £1 ordinary shares in Asteroid plc and their indexed cost on 12 February 2023 was £33,000.

Under the terms of the takeover, for each of its £1 ordinary shares in Asteroid plc, Luna Ltd received £6.50 in cash plus one £1 ordinary share in Comet plc. Immediately after the takeover, Comet plc's £1 ordinary shares were quoted at £4.50.

Indexation factors are as follows:

June 2008–December 2017 = 0.283

May 2010–December 2017 = 0.244

228 Identify, by clicking on the relevant boxes in the table below, whether each of the following statements concerning the indexation allowance is true or false.

Indexation allowance can reduce a gain to nil but not create a loss	**TRUE**	**FALSE**
Indexation allowance can increase an unindexed loss	**TRUE**	**FALSE**

(2 marks)

229 What is Luna Ltd's chargeable gain on the sale of Pluto plc shares on 29 November 2022?

£ [ ] **(2 marks)**

230 What is the indexed cost of Luna Ltd's holding in Neptune Ltd immediately after the sale on 30 November 2022?

- O £12,000
- O £39,808
- O £24,880
- O £14,928

(2 marks)

231 What is the unindexed cost of Luna Ltd's holding in Saturn plc immediately after the rights issue on 10 December 2022?

- O £13,125
- O £11,875
- O £10,313
- O £21,875

(2 marks)

---

232 What is the cost that was used to compute Luna Ltd's chargeable gain on the takeover of Asteroid plc on 12 February 2023?

£ [ ]

(2 marks)

(Total = 10 marks)

OT case – Tay Ltd **(18 mins)**

The following scenario relates to the next five questions.

Tay Ltd prepares accounts to 31 March each year. In the year to 31 March 2023, it had the following events relating to chargeable assets:

(1) Received insurance proceeds of £180,000 in December 2022 as the result of the destruction of a freehold warehouse in a flood in that month. The warehouse originally cost £140,000 and had an indexed cost in December 2022 of £155,000. Tay Ltd purchased a new warehouse for £162,000 in March 2023.

(2) Received shares and cash on the takeover of Grey Ltd. Tay Ltd had acquired 20,000 shares in Grey Ltd. The shares had an indexed cost in September 2022 of £96,000 when Grey Ltd was taken over by Kline plc. On the takeover, Tay Ltd received one £1 ordinary share in Kline plc worth £4 per share and £2 in cash for each one share held in Grey Ltd.

(3) Sold a piece of machinery which it had used in its trade for £9,000 in July 2022. The machinery had an indexed base cost in July 2022 of £3,500. Capital allowances had been claimed on the machinery.

(4) Sold a plot of land, which it had held as an investment, for £45,000 in October 2022. The land had been acquired in June 2007 for £20,000. Tay Ltd had spent £2,000 on draining the land in January 2011. The indexation factor from June 2007 to December 2017 was 0.342, from January 2011 to December 2017 was 0.214.

In the year to 31 March 2024, Tay Ltd will dispose of an investment property which will realise a loss. The company wants to know how this loss can be relieved.

233 What is the base cost of the new warehouse purchased in March 2023, assuming any relevant claim was made?

- O £162,000
- O £155,000
- O £144,000
- O £140,000

(2 marks)

---

234 What was the chargeable gain or allowable loss arising on the takeover of Grey Ltd?

- O £8,000 gain
- O £24,000 gain
- O £16,000 gain
- O £(24,000) loss

(2 marks)

235 What was the chargeable gain (if any) arising on the disposal of the machinery?

O £0

O £5,500

O £2,500

O £5,000 **(2 marks)**

---

236 What was the chargeable gain arising on the disposal of the plot of land?

O £16,160

O £15,476

O £15,732

O £15,134 **(2 marks)**

---

237 Which TWO of the following statements about the use of the capital loss in the year ended 31 March 2024 are correct?

(1) The capital loss can be carried back against chargeable gains made in the year ended 31 March 2023.

(2) The capital loss can be set against chargeable gains made in the year ended 31 March 2024.

(3) The capital loss can be set against total profits in the year ended 31 March 2024.

(4) The capital loss can be carried forward and set against the first available chargeable gains.

O 1 and 2

O 1 and 3

O 2 and 4

O 3 and 4 **(2 marks)**

(Total = 10 marks)

OT case – Hyde plc group **(18 mins)**

The following scenario relates to the next five questions.

The Hyde plc group has the following structure:

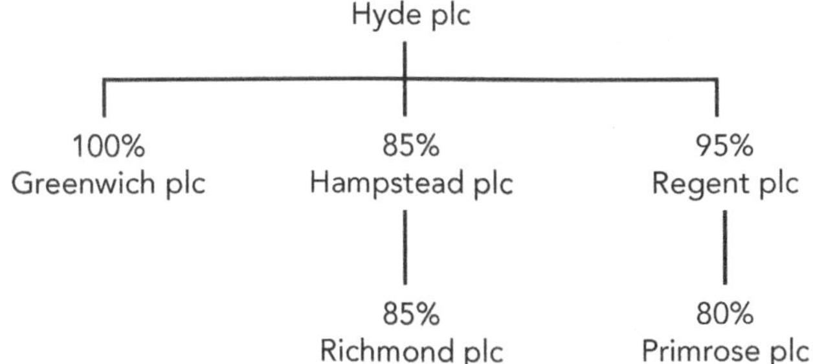

All the group companies prepared accounts to 31 March 2023. However, Greenwich plc intends to change its accounting reference date to 31 December and will prepare accounts to 31 December 2023.

Hyde plc and Greenwich plc are in a group relief group.

In the year ended 31 March 2023, Greenwich plc had the following results:

	£
Trading loss	(68,000)
Capital loss	(4,000)
Interest income	3,000
Qualifying charitable donations	(5,000)

Greenwich plc will surrender the maximum amount possible for the year ended 31 March 2023 to Hyde plc under current period group relief.

In the year ended 31 March 2023, Hyde plc had the following results:

	£
Trading loss	(8,000)
Chargeable gain	48,000
Interest income	12,000
Qualifying charitable donations	(1,500)

Greenwich plc will make a trading loss in the period ended 31 December 2023 and will surrender the maximum amount possible to Hyde plc under current period group relief.

Regent plc and Primrose plc are in a chargeable gains group. In the year to 31 March 2023, Regent plc sold a factory to Primrose plc for £250,000. The market value of the factory at that date was £300,000. Regent plc had acquired the factory for £100,000. The indexation factor between the date of acquisition and December 2017 is 0.200.

238 Identify, by clicking on the relevant boxes in the table below, which of the following companies are also members of the Hyde plc group for group relief purposes.

Hampstead plc	**YES**	**NO**
Regent plc	**YES**	**NO**
Richmond plc	**YES**	**NO**
Primrose plc	**YES**	**NO**

(2 marks)

239 What is the maximum amount that Greenwich plc could surrender as current period group relief of the year ended 31 March 2023?

- O £68,000
- O £70,000
- O £73,000
- O £77,000

(2 marks)

240 What are the maximum available taxable total profits of Hyde plc that could be current period group relieved for the year ended 31 March 2023?

Pull down list

- £2,500
- £50,500
- £52,000
- £58,500

(2 marks)

---

241 Which TWO of the following statements about current period group relief claims between Hyde plc and Greenwich plc are correct?

☐ A claim for current period group relief will be ineffective unless Greenwich plc gives a notice of consent.

☐ If Hyde plc pays Greenwich plc an amount up to the amount of the loss surrendered, the payment will be deducted from the current period group relief.

☐ A claim for current period group relief between Greenwich plc and Hyde plc will be available against the whole of the taxable total profits of Hyde plc for the year to 31 March 2024.

☐ The claim for current period group relief would be made on Hyde plc's corporation tax return. **(2 marks)**

---

242 What is base cost of the factory acquired by Primrose plc in the year ended 31 March 2023?

○ £100,000

○ £120,000

○ £250,000

○ £300,000 **(2 marks)**

(Total = 10 marks)

Section C

243 Problematic Ltd (June 2010) (amended) (18 mins)

Problematic Ltd sold the following assets during the year ended 31 March 2023:

(1) On 14 June 2022 16,000 £1 ordinary shares in Easy plc were sold for £54,400. Problematic Ltd had originally purchased 15,000 shares in Easy plc on 26 June 2005 for £12,600. On 28 September 2008 Easy plc made a 1 for 3 rights issue. Problematic Ltd took up its allocation under the rights issue in full, paying £2.20 for each new share issued. Indexation factors are as follows:

June 2005–September 2008 = 0.136

September 2008–December 2017 = 0.273

(2) On 28 January 2023 a freehold factory was sold for £171,000. The indexed cost of the factory on that date was £127,000. Problematic Ltd has made a claim to hold over the gain on the factory against the cost of a replacement leasehold factory under the rollover relief (replacement of business assets) rules. The leasehold factory has a lease period of 20 years and was purchased on 10 December 2022 for £154,800. The two factory buildings have always been used entirely for business purposes.

Required

(a) Calculate Problematic Ltd's chargeable gains for the year ended 31 March 2023. **(9 marks)**

(b) Advise Problematic Ltd of the carried forward indexed base cost of the leasehold factory. **(1 mark)**

(Total = 10 marks)

244 Volatile Ltd (December 2009) (amended) (18 mins)

Volatile Ltd commenced trading on 1 July 2021. The company's results for its first five periods of trading are as follows:

	p/e 31.12.21	*y/e 31.12.22*	*y/e 31.12.23*	*p/e 30.9.24*	*y/e 30.9.25*
	£	£	£	£	£
Trading profit/(loss)	44,000	(73,800)	86,500	78,700	(186,800)
Property business profit	9,400	6,600	6,500	–	–
Chargeable gain/(loss)	5,100	–	(2,000)	11,700	–
Qualifying charitable donations	(800)	(1,000)	(1,200)	–	–

Required

(a) State the factors that will influence a company's choice of loss relief claims.

Note. You are not expected to consider group relief. **(2 marks)**

(b) Assuming that Volatile Ltd claims relief for its trading losses as early as possible, calculate the company's taxable total profits for the six-month period ended 31 December 2021, each of the years ended 31 December 2022 and 2023 and the nine-month period ended 30 September 2024. Your answer should also clearly identify the amount of any unrelieved trading losses as at 30 September 2025. **(8 marks)**

(Total = 10 marks)

245 Maison Ltd (September/December 2019) (27 mins)

This scenario relates to one requirement.

You are a trainee Chartered Certified Accountant dealing with the tax affairs of Maison Ltd.

Your assistant has prepared a partly completed draft corporation tax computation for the year ended 31 March 2023. All of your assistant's workings for the figures provided are correct, but there are four uncompleted sections, all related to property, which your assistant does not know how to deal with.

The assistant's corporation tax computation, along with references to the uncompleted sections (with missing figures indicated by a question mark (?)), is shown below:

Maison Ltd – Corporation tax computation for the year ended 31 March 2023

	Uncompleted section	£
Operating profit		892,900
Non-deductible expenditure		22,340
Deduction for lease premium	1	?
Capital allowances	2	?
Trading profit		?
Property business income	3	?
Loan interest receivable		1,460
Chargeable gains	4	?
Taxable total profits		?
Corporation tax		?

Uncompleted section 1 – Deduction for lease premium

Your assistant has identified that on 1 January 2023, Maison Ltd acquired a leasehold office building, paying a premium of £44,000 for the grant of a 12-year lease. The office building was used for business purposes by Maison Ltd throughout the period 1 January to 31 March 2023.

Uncompleted section 2 – Capital allowances

Your assistant has correctly calculated that capital allowances of £12,037 are available on the main pool. However, she is unsure of the amount of capital allowance and structures and buildings allowance which are available in respect of the £140,000 spent by Maison Ltd during November 2022 constructing an extension which is adjacent to the company's existing freehold office building. The extension is used by the company's employees as a staff room and was ready for use on 1 December 2022. The total cost of £140,000 is made up of new purchases as follows:

	£
Integral to the building	
Building costs of extension	93,300
Ventilation system	6,700
Heating system	3,900
Not integral to the building	
Furniture and furnishings	33,500
Refrigerator and microwave cooker	2,600
Total cost	140,000

Uncompleted section 3 – Property business income

On 1 July 2022, Maison Ltd purchased a freehold warehouse. The warehouse is currently surplus to requirements, so it was let out from 1 November 2022. However, the warehouse was purchased in a dilapidated state and could not be let until repair work was carried out during August 2022. This fact was represented by a reduced purchase price. Your assistant has listed any income and expenditure that is potentially relevant:

Date received/(paid)		£
1 July 2022	Insurance for the period to 31 March 2023	(1,035)
August 2022	Initial repairs	(17,680)
28 September 2022	Advertising for tenants	(780)
1 November 2022	Security deposit of two months' rent	12,200
1 November 2022	Rent for the quarter ended 31 January 2023	18,300
1 February 2023	Rent for the quarter ended 30 April 2023	18,300

Uncompleted section 4 – Chargeable gains

Maison Ltd disposed of two investment properties during August 2022, both resulting in gains. Your assistant has correctly calculated the gains but is unsure of the amount of indexation allowance available. The assistant's workings are as follows:

	Date	1st property	2nd property
		£	£
Disposal proceeds	August 2022	237,000	143,000
Cost	April 2009	(101,000)	(117,000)
Enhancement expenditure	May 2018	(26,200)	0
Gain		109,800	26,000

Indexation factors are:

April 2009 to December 2017	0.315

No rollover relief claim is possible in respect of these gains.

Required

Prepare a completed version of Maison Ltd's corporation tax computation for the year ended 31 March 2023 after dealing with the sections uncompleted by your assistant.

Notes.

1 Your computation should commence with the operating profit figure of £892,900, and you should indicate by the use of zero (0) any items which are not included in your calculation.

2 In calculating the operating profit figure of £892,900, no deduction has been made for the lease premium (uncompleted section 1) or any capital allowances (uncompleted section 2). It also does not include any income or expenditure in relation to property business income (uncompleted section 3) or any chargeable gains in relation to the disposal of the two investment properties (uncompleted section 4).

(Total = 15 marks)

246 Black Ltd (December 2011) and Gastron Ltd (June 2009) (amended) (18 mins)

(a) Black Ltd owns 100% of the ordinary share capital of White Ltd and 80% of the ordinary shares of Grey Ltd. The results of Black Ltd, White Ltd and Grey Ltd for the year ended 31 March 2023 are as follows:

	Black Ltd	*White Ltd*	*Grey Ltd*
	£	£	£
Trading profit/(loss)	338,900	(351,300)	50,000
Property business profit	21,100	26,700	4,500
Qualifying charitable donations	(4,400)	(5,600)	0

At 1 April 2022, Grey Ltd had brought forward trading losses of £57,500 arising from the year ended 31 March 2022.

Required

Advise Black Ltd as to the maximum amount of group relief that it can set off in the year ended 31 March 2023 if claims are made both from White Ltd in respect of its losses for the year ended 31 March 2023 and from Grey Ltd in respect of its losses for the year ended 31 March 2022.

Note. You are not expected to calculate either company's corporation tax liability. **(5 marks)**

(b) Gastron Ltd is a manufacturing company. In the year to 31 March 2023 Gastron Ltd had taxable total profits of £600,000. The taxable total profits included a chargeable gain of £74,800 on the sale of a 1% shareholding. This figure is after taking account of indexation.

Gastron Ltd owns 100% of the ordinary share capital of Culinary Ltd. On 13 February 2023 Culinary Ltd sold a freehold factory and this resulted in a capital loss of £66,000. For the year ended 31 March 2023 Culinary Ltd made no other disposals.

Required

(i) Explain the group relationship that must exist in order for two or more companies to form a group for chargeable gains purposes. **(2 marks)**

(ii) Explain why it would be beneficial for Gastron Ltd and Culinary Ltd to make a joint election to transfer the whole of the capital gain on Gastron Ltd's disposal of shares to Culinary Ltd. **(1 mark)**

(iii) Explain what two other taxation consequences arise as a result of companies being in a chargeable gains group. **(2 marks)**

(Total = 10 marks)

247 Alimag Ltd (September/December 2017) (18 mins)

You should assume that today's date is 15 March 2022.

You are a trainee chartered certified accountant dealing with the tax affairs of Gamila, who is the managing director of, and (currently) 100% shareholder in, Alimag Ltd.

For the year ended 5 April 2023, Alimag Ltd's taxable total profits, before taking account of director's remuneration, are forecast to be £180,000.

Original basis of profit extraction

Gamila originally intended to withdraw £130,000 of the profits as director's remuneration, and you have calculated that this approach would result in the following tax liabilities and national insurance contributions (NICs):

	£
Alimag Ltd	
Corporation tax for the year ended 5 April 2023	6,043
Class 1 employer NICs for the tax year 2022/23	18,195
Gamila	
Income tax for the tax year 2022/23	44,460
Class 1 employee NICs for the tax year 2022/23	7,586
	76,284

Revised basis of profit extraction

After a meeting with Gamila, a more beneficial approach to withdrawing £130,000 of profits from Alimag Ltd has been agreed for the tax year 2022/23.

(1) Gamila will withdraw gross director's remuneration of £30,000.

(2) Gamila's husband, Magnus, will become a 30% shareholder in Alimag Ltd.

(3) Alimag Ltd will then pay dividends of £70,000 to Gamila and £30,000 to Magnus.

Neither Gamila nor Magnus will have any other income for the tax year 2022/23.

Required

Calculate the overall saving of taxes and NICs for the tax year 2022/23 if the revised basis of profit extraction is used instead of the original basis of profit extraction.

Notes.

1 You are expected to calculate the income tax payable by Gamila and Magnus, the class 1 NIC payable (if any) by Gamila, Magnus and Alimag Ltd, and the corporation tax liability of Alimag Ltd for the year ended 5 April 2023.

2 Alimag Ltd is not entitled to the NIC annual employment allowance.

3 You should assume that the rate of corporation tax remains unchanged.

(Total = 10 marks)

248 Hopi Ltd (March/June 2018) (18 mins)

You should assume that today's date is 25 March 2023.

Kaya is the managing director of, and 100% shareholder in, Hopi Ltd. Hopi Ltd has no other employees.

For the year ended 5 April 2023, Hopi Ltd's tax adjusted trading profit, after taking account of director's remuneration and employer's class 1 national insurance contributions (NICs), is forecast to be £80,000. Hopi Ltd has already paid Kaya gross director's remuneration of £30,000 and dividends of £45,000 for the tax year 2022/23. Kaya does not have any other income.

Based on these figures, the tax and NICs for Kaya and Hopi Ltd for the year ended 5 April 2023 will be:

	£
Kaya	
Income tax	13,431
Employee class 1 NICs	2,309
Hopi Ltd	
Employer class 1 NICs	3,145
Corporation tax	8,902

However, on 31 March 2023, Kaya is planning to pay herself a bonus of £25,000, but is unsure whether to take this as additional director's remuneration (the gross remuneration will be £25,000) or as an additional dividend.

Required

Calculate the revised tax and NICs for Kaya and Hopi Ltd for the year ended 5 April 2023 if, on 31 March 2023, Kaya pays herself the bonus of £25,000 (1) as additional director's remuneration or (2) as an additional dividend.

Notes.

1 You are expected to calculate the revised income tax liability and NICs for Kaya and the revised corporation tax liability and NICs for Hopi Ltd under each of options (1) and (2).

2 You should assume that the rate of corporation tax remains unchanged. **(10 marks)**

249 Kat (September/December 2018) (18 mins)

You should assume that today's date is 15 March 2022.

On 6 April 2022, Kat will purchase a residential freehold property which she will let out. However, Kat is unsure whether to purchase the property personally or via a limited company. The limited company would be incorporated for the sole purpose of purchasing and letting out the property, and Kat would hold all of the shares in the company.

Regardless of whether the property is purchased personally or via a limited company:

(1) The property will be let throughout the year ended 5 April 2023 at a monthly rent of £2,600 which will be paid when due.

(2) The purchase of the property will be partly financed with a repayment mortgage. Mortgage interest of £12,000 will be paid during the year ended 5 April 2023.

(3) The other expenditure on the property for the year ended 5 April 2023 will amount to £7,600, and this will all be allowable.

(4) Kat will also have employment income of £60,000 for the tax year 2022/23.

If the property is purchased via a limited company, then the company's corporation tax liability for the year ended 5 April 2023 will be £2,204 and Kat will withdraw dividends from the company totalling £6,000 during the tax year 2022/23.

Kat will not have any other income for the tax year 2022/23.

Required

(a) Determine if there will be an overall saving of tax for the year ended 5 April 2023 if Kat purchases the property via a limited company rather than purchasing it personally.

Notes.

1 Your answer should include a calculation of Kat's income tax liability if she purchases the property personally and if she purchases it via a limited company.

2 You should ignore national insurance contributions (NICs). **(9 marks)**

(b) Explain the ONE way in which the calculation of a future taxable gain on a property disposal made by the limited company would differ from the calculation of a taxable gain on a disposal made personally by Kat. **(1 mark)**

(Total = 10 marks)

250 Jogger Ltd (A) (December 2008) (amended) (27 mins)

Jogger Ltd is a manufacturing company. The company's summarised statement of profit or loss for the year ended 31 March 2023 is as follows:

	Note	£	£
Operating profit	1		1,052,482
Income from investments			
Bank interest	3	8,460	
Loan interest	4	24,600	
Income from property	5	144,000	
Dividends		45,000	
			222,060
Profit from sale of non-current assets			
Disposal of shares	6		102,340
Profit before taxation			1,376,882

Notes.

1 *Operating profit*

Depreciation of £58,840 has been deducted in arriving at the operating profit of £1,052,482.

2 *Plant and machinery*

On 1 April 2022 the tax written down values of plant and machinery were as follows:

	£
Main pool	26,600
Special rate pool	21,167

The following transactions took place during the year ended 31 March 2023:

		Cost/(proceeds)
		£
20 July 2022	Sold a special rate pool car	(11,700)
31 July 2022	Purchased car CO_2 emissions 40 g/km	11,800
15 August 2022	Purchased new car CO_2 emissions 0 g/km	9,000
30 September 2022	Purchased integral features	1,300,000
15 December 2022	Purchased second hand machinery	12,500
14 March 2023	Sold a lorry	(8,600)

The car sold on 20 July 2022 for £11,700 originally cost more than this amount. The machinery purchased on 15 December 2022 has a predicted working life of six years and any relevant election has been made. The lorry sold on 14 March 2023 for £8,600 originally cost £16,600.

3 *Bank interest received*

The bank interest was received on 31 March 2023. The bank deposits are held for non-trading purposes.

4 *Loan interest receivable*

The loan was made for non-trading purposes on 1 July 2022. Loan interest of £16,400 was received on 31 December 2022, and interest of £8,200 was accrued at 31 March 2023.

5 *Income from property*

Jogger Ltd lets out an unfurnished freehold office building that is surplus to requirements. The office building was let throughout the year ended 31 March 2023. On 1 April 2022 Jogger Ltd received a premium of £100,000 for the grant of a ten-year lease, and the annual rent of £44,000 which is payable in advance.

6 *Profit on disposal of shares*

The profit on disposal of shares is in respect of a shareholding that was sold in December 2022 for £150,000. The shares were acquired in August 2006 at a cost of £47,660. The relevant indexation factor is 0.396.

Required

(a) Calculate Jogger Ltd's tax adjusted trading loss for the year ended 31 March 2023.

Notes.

1 Your computation should start with the operating profit of £1,052,482.

2 You should assume that the company claims the maximum available capital allowances.

3 Ignore VAT. **(8 marks)**

(b) Assuming that Jogger Ltd claims relief for its trading loss against total profits, calculate the company's corporation tax liability for the year ended 31 March 2023. **(7 marks)**

(Total = 15 marks)

251 Mooncake Ltd (March/June 2021 amended) (27 mins)

Mooncake Ltd reported an operating loss of £93,820 in its statement of profit or loss for the year ended 31 March 2023 as follows:

	Note	£
Revenue		184,550
Operating expenses		
Depreciation		(7,230)
Leasing cost	1	(6,380)
Other expenses	2	(264,760)
Operating loss		(93,820)

Notes.

1 Leasing costs are as follows:

	£
Lease of office equipment	2,980
Lease of car with CO_2 emissions of 65 grams per kilometre	3,400
	6,380

2 Other expenses are as follows:

	£
Entertaining staff (cost of £160 per head)	4,320
Entertaining overseas customers	8,720
Qualifying charitable donations	1,600
Balance of expenditure (all allowable)	250,120
	264,760

Additional information

Plant and machinery

On 1 April 2022, the tax written down value of the main pool was £43,200.

The following vehicles were sold during the year ended 31 March 2023:

	Date of sale	Proceeds	Original cost
		£	£
Delivery van	12 April 2022	11,800	14,700
Car [1]	13 August 2022	8,400	8,100
Car [2]	9 March 2023	5,300	12,200

Property business loss

Mooncake Ltd has a property business loss of £4,400 for the year ended 31 March 2023.

Profit on disposal of shares

Mooncake Ltd made a profit on disposal of shares of £3,700 in respect of a 1% shareholding which was sold on 8 November 2022. This profit on disposal is calculated as disposal proceeds of £34,200 less cost of £30,500. The indexation allowance is £6,700.

Results for the year ended 31 March 2022

Mooncake Ltd's results for the year ended 31 March 2022 were:

	£
Trading profit	138,200
Property business income	23,700
Capital loss	(4,900)
Qualifying charitable donations	(1,400)

Required

(a) State the factors which will influence a company's choice of loss relief claims. **(2 marks)**

(b) Calculate Mooncake Ltd's tax adjusted trading loss for the year ended 31 March 2023.

Notes.

1 Your computation should commence with the operating loss figure of £93,820, and should indicate by the use of zero (0) any items which do not require adjustment.

2 You should assume that the company claims the maximum available capital allowances.

(7 marks)

(c) Assuming that Mooncake Ltd wishes to claim relief for its losses as early as possible:

(i) Calculate the company's corporation tax liabilities for each of the years ended 31 March 2022 and 31 March 2023. **(4 marks)**

(ii) Calculate the amount of unused losses or payments which Mooncake Ltd can carry forward to be utilised in the year ending 31 March 2024.

(2 marks)

(Total = 15 marks)

252 Retro Ltd (June 2015) (amended) (27 mins)

Retro Ltd's summarised statement of profit or loss for the year ended 31 March 2023 is as follows:

	Note	£	£
Gross profit			166,760
Operating expenses			
Gifts and donations	1	2,300	
Impairment loss	2	1,600	
Leasing costs	3	4,400	
Other expenses	4	232,400	
			(240,700)

	Note	£	£
Finance costs			
Interest payable	5		(6,400)
Loss before taxation			(80,340)

Notes.

1 *Gifts and donations*

Gifts and donations are as follows:

	£
Gifts to employees (food hampers costing £60 each)	720
Gifts to customers (calendars costing £8 each and displaying Retro Ltd's name)	480
Qualifying charitable donations	1,100
	2,300

2 *Impairment loss*

On 31 March 2023, Retro Ltd wrote off an impairment loss of £1,600 relating to a trade debt. This was in respect of an invoice which had been due for payment on 10 November 2022.

3 *Leasing costs*

The leasing costs of £4,400 are in respect of a car lease which commenced on 1 April 2022. The leased car has CO_2 emissions of 75 grams per kilometre.

4 *Other expenses*

The figure of £232,400 for other expenses includes a fine of £5,100 for a breach of health and safety regulations. The remaining expenses are all fully allowable.

5 *Interest payable*

The interest payable is in respect of the company's 5% loan notes which were repaid on 31 July 2022. Interest of £9,600 was paid on 31 July 2022, and an accrual of £3,200 had been provided for at 1 April 2022. The loan notes were issued in order to finance the company's trading activities.

Additional information

Plant and machinery

On 1 April 2022, the tax written down value of the plant and machinery main pool was £39,300.

The following new vehicles were purchased during the year ended 31 March 2023:

	Date of purchase	Cost	CO_2 emission rate
		£	
Car [1]	8 June 2022	14,700	44 grams per kilometre
Delivery van	3 August 2022	21,769	122 grams per kilometre
Car [2]	19 October 2022	12,400	0 grams per kilometre

New Offices

On 1 October 2022 Retro Ltd spent £850,000 on a new office block, including acquisition fees of £50,000. The offices were moved into immediately. Retro Ltd intends to claim the maximum SBAs on this expenditure.

Previous results

Retro Ltd commenced trading on 1 September 2020. The company's results for its two previous periods of trading are as follows:

	y/e 31 August 2021	p/e 31 March 2022
	£	£
Tax adjusted trading profit	56,600	47,900
Bank interest receivable	1,300	0
Qualifying charitable donations paid	(540)	(330)

Future results

Retro Ltd is expected to return to profitability in the year ended 31 March 2024 and to continue to be profitable in subsequent years.

Required

(a) Calculate Retro Ltd's tax adjusted trading loss for the year ended 31 March 2023.

Note. Your computation should commence with the loss before taxation figure of £80,340 and should also list all of the items referred to in notes (1) to (5), indicating by the use of zero (0) any items which do not require adjustment. **(9 marks)**

(b) Assuming that Retro Ltd claims relief for its trading loss as early as possible, calculate the company's taxable total profits for the year ended 31 August 2021 and for the seven-month period ended 31 March 2022. **(4 marks)**

(c) Identify the amount of unrelieved trading loss which Retro Ltd will have at 31 March 2023, and state how this can be relieved. **(2 marks)**

(Total = 15 marks)

253 Lucky Ltd (September/December 2015) (amended) (27 mins)

Lucky Ltd was incorporated on 20 July 2022 and commenced trading on 1 December 2022. The following information is available for the four-month period 1 December 2022 to 31 March 2023:

(1) The operating profit for the four-month period ended 31 March 2023 is £716,903. Advertising expenditure of £4,700 (incurred during September 2022), depreciation of £14,700, and amortisation of £9,000 have been deducted in arriving at this figure.

The amortisation relates to a premium which was paid on 1 December 2022 to acquire a leasehold warehouse on a 12-year lease. The amount of premium assessed on the landlord as income was £46,800. The warehouse was used for business purposes by Lucky Ltd throughout the period ended 31 March 2023.

(2) Lucky Ltd purchased the following new assets during the period 20 July 2022 to 31 March 2023:

		£
19 August 2022	Computer	6,300
22 January 2023	Integral features	291,200
31 January 2023	Office equipment	49,566
17 March 2023	Car	12,800

The integral features of £291,200 are in respect of expenditure on electrical systems, a ventilation system and lifts which are integral to a freehold office building owned by Lucky Ltd.

The car has a CO_2 emission rate of 42 grams per kilometre.

(3) Lucky Ltd made a loan to another company for non-trading purposes on 1 February 2023. Loan interest income of £700 was accrued at 31 March 2023.

Lucky Ltd will make a company car available to its chief executive officer. The car will be purchased, rather than leased, and will be made available to the chief executive officer in December 2023 onwards.

Required

(a) State when an accounting period starts for corporation tax purposes. **(2 marks)**

(b) Calculate Lucky Ltd's corporation tax liability for the four-month period ended 31 March 2023.

Note. Your computation should commence with the operating profit of £716,903 and should also indicate by the use of zero (0) any items referred to in the question for which no adjustment is required. **(9 marks)**

(c) Advise Lucky Ltd as to how long it must retain the records used in preparing its self-assessment corporation tax return for the four-month period ended 31 March 2023, and the potential consequences of not retaining the records for the required period. **(2 marks)**

(d) Advise Lucky Ltd on the effects of the company car on its taxable total profits for the year ended 31 March 2024. **(2 marks)**

(Total = 15 marks)

254 Jump Ltd (March/June 2016) (27 mins)

Jump Ltd's summarised statement of profit or loss for the three-month period ended 31 March 2023 is as follows:

	Note	£	£
Revenue			264,900
Operating expenses			
Depreciation		8,100	
Employee costs	1	189,700	
Lease of car	2	1,200	
Professional fees	3	7,800	
Other expenses	4	202,800	
			(409,600)
Loss before taxation			(144,700)

Notes.

1 *Employee costs*

Employee costs are as follows:

	£
Employee training courses	3,400
Employee pension contributions paid	11,6001
Cost of annual staff party (for eight employees)	1,500
Balance of expenditure (all allowable)	173,200
	189,700

2 *Lease of car*

The lease is in respect of a car with CO_2 emissions of 59 grams per kilometre.

3 *Professional fees*

Professional fees are as follows:

	£
Accountancy	2,200
Legal fees in connection with the issue of share capital	3,800
Legal fees in connection with the renewal of a 20-year property lease	1,800
	7,800

4 *Other expenses*

Other expenses are as follows:

	£
Entertaining UK customers	1,700
Entertaining overseas customers	790
Political donations	800
Balance of expenditure (all allowable)	199,510
	202,800

Additional information

Plant and machinery

On 1 January 2023, the tax written down values of Jump Ltd's plant and machinery were:

	£
Main pool	12,100
Special rate pool	5,700

The following cars were sold during the three-month period ended 31 March 2023:

	Date of sale	*Proceeds*	*Original cost*
		£	£
Car [1]	7 January 2023	9,700	9,300
Car [2]	29 March 2023	6,100	13,200

The original cost of car [1] was added to the special rate pool when it was purchased, and the original cost of car [2] was added to the main pool when it was purchased.

Previous results

Jump Ltd's results for its two previous periods of trading are as follows:

	Year ended 31 May 2022	*Period ended 31 December 2022*
	£	£
Tax adjusted trading profit	78,600	42,400
Bank interest receivable	1,200	0

Group companies

Jump Ltd owns 80% of the ordinary share capital of Hop Ltd and 60% of the ordinary share capital of Skip Ltd.

Hop Ltd commenced trading on 1 August 2022, and for the eight-month period ended 31 March 2023 has taxable total profits of £63,000.

Skip Ltd has been trading for several years and has taxable total profits of £56,000 for the year ended 31 March 2023.

Required

(a) Calculate Jump Ltd's tax adjusted trading loss for the three-month period ended 31 March 2023.

Notes.

1 Your computation should commence with the operating loss figure of £144,700, and should list all of the items referred to in notes (1) to (4), indicating by the use of zero (0) any items which do not require adjustment.

2 You should assume that the company claims the maximum available capital allowances.

(10 marks)

(b) (i) State the main factor which will influence Jump Ltd's choice of loss relief or group relief claims. **(1 mark)**

(ii) Advise Jump Ltd as to the maximum amount of its trading loss which can be relieved against its total profits for the year ended 31 May 2022 and the seven-month period ended 31 December 2022. **(2 marks)**

(iii) Advise Jump Ltd as to the maximum amount of its trading loss which can be surrendered as group relief. **(2 marks)**

(Total = 15 marks)

255 Online Ltd (March/June 2017) (27 mins)

The following information is available in respect of Online Ltd for the year ended 31 March 2023:

Operating profit

Online Ltd's operating profit for the year ended 31 March 2023 is £896,700. Depreciation of £21,660 and amortisation of leasehold property of £9,000 (see the leasehold property note below) have been deducted in arriving at this figure.

Leasehold property

On 1 April 2022, Online Ltd acquired a leasehold office building, paying a premium of £90,000 for the grant of a ten-year lease. The office building was used for business purposes by Online Ltd throughout the year ended 31 March 2023.

Plant and machinery

On 1 April 2022, the tax written down values of plant and machinery were as follows:

	£
Main pool	56,700
Special rate pool56	13,433

The following transactions took place during the year ended 31 March 2023:

		Costs/(proceeds)
		£
14 May 2022	Sold a car	(18,100)
18 July 2022	Sold all items included in the special rate pool	(9,300)
27 Jan 2023	Purchased a car	13,700

The car sold on 14 May 2022 for £18,100 was originally purchased during the year ended 31 March 2022 for £17,200. This expenditure was added to the main pool.

The car purchased on 27 January 2023 for £13,700 has a CO_2 emission rate of 48 grams per kilometre. The car is used as a pool car by the company's employees.

Qualifying charitable donations

During the year ended 31 March 2023, Online Ltd made qualifying charitable donations of £6,800. These were not included in arriving at the operating profit above.

Disposal of shareholding in Network plc

On 20 March 2023, Online Ltd sold its entire shareholding of £1 ordinary shares in Network plc for £90,600. Online Ltd had originally purchased 40,000 shares (less than a 1% shareholding) in Network plc on 24 June 2010 for £49,300. On 7 October 2013, Online Ltd sold 22,000 of the shares for £62,200.

Indexation factors are as follows:

June 2010 to October 2013	0.124
June 2010 to December 2017	0.241
October 2013 to December 2017	0.104

Brought forward losses

As at 1 April 2022, Online Ltd had the following brought forward amounts of unused losses:

	£
Capital loss	3,104
Property business loss	12,500

Planned acquisition

Online Ltd currently does not have any 51% group companies. However, Online Ltd is planning to acquire a 60% shareholding in Offline Ltd in the near future. Offline Ltd is profitable and will pay regular dividends to Online Ltd.

Required

(a) Calculate Online Ltd's taxable total profits for the year ended 31 March 2023. **(13 marks)**

(b) Briefly explain how the acquisition of Offline Ltd will affect the calculation and payment of Online Ltd's corporation tax liability in future years. **(2 marks)**

(Total = 15 marks)

256 Last-Orders Ltd (September/December 2017) (27 mins)

Last-Orders Ltd ceased trading on 31 January 2023, having traded profitably for the previous ten years. The ordinary share capital of Last-Orders Ltd is owned 80% by Gastro Ltd and 20% by Gourmet Ltd.

Last-Orders Ltd's summarised statement of profit or loss for the ten-month period ended 31 January 2023 is as follows:

	Note	£
Revenue		176,790
Operating expenses		
Depreciation		(9,460)
Employee costs	1	(142,400)
Lease of car	2	(1,600)
Other expenses	3	(299,810)
Operating loss		(276,480)
Other income		
Property business income	4	11,500
Profit on disposal of freehold office building	5	47,400
Loss before taxation		(217,580)

Notes.

1 *Employee costs*

Employee costs are as follows:

	£
Counselling services provided to employees who were made redundant	5,200
Pension contributions paid on behalf of employees	12,200
Employer class 1 national insurance contributions (NICs)	11,890
Employer class 1A NICs payable on benefits provided for employees	1,160
Employee bonuses declared but unpaid – these will not be paid during 2023	10,400
Balance of expenditure (all allowable)	101,550
	142,400

2 *Lease of car*

The lease is in respect of a car with CO_2 emissions of 40 grams per kilometre.

3 *Other expenses*

Other expenses are as follows:

	£
Entertaining UK suppliers	1,920
Entertaining overseas suppliers	440
Qualifying charitable donation	800
Balance of expenditure (all allowable)	296,650
	299,810

4 *Property business income*

During the ten-month period ended 31 January 2023, Last-Orders Ltd let out a freehold office building. The following income and expenditure was received or incurred during the final 12 months of trading:

Date received/(paid)		£
1 February 2022	Rent for the six months ended 31 July 2022	19,200
1 February 2022	Insurance for the 12 months ended 31 January 2023	(1,800)
1 August 2022	Rent for the six months ended 31 January 2023	19,200
21 November 2022	Repairs following a fire (not covered by insurance)	(7,700)

5 *Property business income*

The office building was sold on 31 January 2023. The profit has been calculated as disposal proceeds of £126,800 less cost of £79,400. The indexation allowance is £12,900. The office building was never used for business purposes.

Additional information

Plant and machinery – on 1 April 2022, the tax written down value of Last-Orders Ltd's main pool was £24,200. All of the items included in the main pool were sold for £13,600 on 31 January 2023, with none of the items sold for more than their original cost. Last-Orders Ltd has previously always made up its accounts to 31 March. Both Gastro Ltd and Gourmet Ltd are profitable and make up their accounts to 31 March.

Required

(a) Calculate Last-Orders Ltd's tax adjusted trading loss for the ten-month period ended 31 January 2023.

Notes.

1 Your computation should commence with the operating loss figure of £276,480, and should also list all of the items referred to in notes (1) to (3), indicating by the use of zero (0) any items which do not require adjustment.

2 You should assume that Last-Orders Ltd claims the maximum possible amount of capital allowances. **(6 marks)**

(b) Assuming Last-Orders Ltd claims relief for its trading loss against its taxable total profits for the ten-month period ended 31 January 2023, calculate the company's taxable total profits for this period.

Note. Your answer should show the amount of unused trading loss at 31 January 2023. **(5 marks)**

(c) Explain the alternative ways in which Last-Orders Ltd's unused trading loss for the ten-month period ended 31 January 2023 could be relieved. **(4 marks)**

(Total = 15 marks)

257 Solo Ltd (March/June 2018) (27 mins)

Solo Ltd's results for the previous two periods of trading are:

	Year ended 31 December 2021	*Three-month Period ended 31 March 2022*
	£	£
Trading profit	35,900	12,300
Property business income	12,100	4,200
Chargeable gains/(capital losses)	(3,300)	(2,100)
Qualifying charitable donations	(1,200)	(1,600)

The following information is available in respect of the year ended 31 March 2023:

Trading loss

The tax-adjusted trading loss based on the draft statement of profit or loss for the year ended 31 March 2023 is £151,300. This figure is before making any adjustments required for:

(1) A premium which was paid to acquire a leasehold office building on an eight-year lease

(2) Capital allowances

Premium paid to acquire leasehold office building

On 1 April 2022, Solo Ltd acquired a leasehold office building, paying a premium of £20,000 for the grant of an eight-year lease. The office building was used for business purposes by Solo Ltd throughout the year ended 31 March 2023.

Plant and machinery

The tax written down value of the plant and machinery main pool as at 1 April 2022 was £0. During the year ended 31 March 2023, Solo Ltd sold equipment for £4,300. The equipment was originally purchased during the year ended 31 March 2017 for £22,400, with this expenditure qualifying for the 100% annual investment allowance.

Property business income

Solo Ltd lets out a warehouse which is surplus to requirements. The building was empty from 1 April to 31 July 2022, but was let from 1 August 2022 onwards. The following income and expenditure was received or incurred during the year ended 31 March 2023:

Date received/paid

		£
1 April 2022	Insurance for the year ended 31 March 2023	(920)
1 August 2022	Rent for the six months ended 31 January 3	7,800
1 August 2022	Security deposit equal to two months' rent	2,600
1 March 2023	Rent for the six months ended 31 July 2023	7,800

Disposal of shareholding in Multiple plc

On 12 December 2022, Solo Ltd sold 6,500 £1 ordinary shares in Multiple plc for £31,200. Solo Ltd had originally purchased 20,000 shares (less than a 1% shareholding) in Multiple plc on 18 June 2006 for £27,000 and purchased a further 1,000 shares on 8 December 2022 for £4,600. Indexation factors are:

June 2006 to December 2017	0.401

Required

(a) Calculate Solo Ltd's revised tax-adjusted trading loss for the year ended 31 March 2023.

Note. You should assume that the company claims the maximum available capital allowances. **(3 marks)**

(b) On the basis that Solo Ltd claims relief for its trading loss against its total profits for the year ended 31 March 2023, prepare a corporation tax computation for this year showing taxable total profits. **(8 marks)**

(c) On the basis that Solo Ltd claims relief for the remainder of its trading loss as early as possible, calculate the company's taxable total profits for the year ended 31 December 2021 and the three-month period ended 31 March 2022. **(4 marks)**

(Total = 15 marks)

258 Ash Ltd, Beech Ltd and Cedar Ltd (September/December 2018) (27 mins)

You are a trainee chartered certified accountant assisting your manager with the tax affairs of three unconnected limited companies, Ash Ltd, Beech Ltd and Cedar Ltd.

Ash Ltd

Ash Ltd was incorporated in the UK on 1 December 2020 and immediately opened a non-interest bearing bank account. The company commenced trading on 1 February 2021, preparing its first accounts for the 14-month period ended 31 March 2022. Accounts were then prepared for the year ended 31 March 2023.

At the date of incorporation, all three of Ash Ltd's directors (who each own one-third of the company's ordinary share capital) were based in the UK. However, on 1 October 2022, two of the directors moved overseas. The directors have always held Ash Ltd's board meetings in the UK and will continue to do so despite two of them moving overseas.

Beech Ltd

Beech Ltd's summarised statement of profit or loss for the year ended 31 January 2023 is as follows:

	Note	£
Gross profit		566,175
Operating expenses		
Depreciation		(14,700)
Gifts and donations	1	(4,975)
Impairment loss	2	(3,700)
Leasing costs	3	(12,600)
Other expenses	4	(217,700)

	Note	£
Finance costs		
Interest payable	5	(7,000)
Profit before taxation		305,500

Notes.

1 *Gifts and donations*

Gifts and donations of £4,975 comprise:

	£
Gifts to customers (pens costing £70 each and displaying Beech Ltd's name)	3,500
Gifts to staff (decorative plaques costing £15 each to celebrate Beech Ltd's ten-year anniversary)	375
Qualifying charitable donations	1,100
	4,975

2 *Impairment loss*

On 31 January 2023, Beech Ltd wrote off an impairment loss of £3,700 relating to a trade debt. This was in respect of an invoice which had been due for payment on 15 October 2022.

3 *Leasing costs*

The leasing costs of £12,600 are in respect of four car leases which commenced on 1 February 2022. Each of the four leased cars has CO_2 emissions of 60 grams per kilometre.

4 *Other expenses*

The other expenses of £217,700 include a fine of £6,400 for a breach of data protection law, and legal fees of £5,700 in connection with the renewal of a 15-year property lease. The remaining expenses are all fully allowable.

5 *Interest payable*

The interest payable of £7,000 is in respect of the company's 4% loan notes which were issued on1 July 2022. Interest of £6,000 was paid on 31 December 2022, with an accrual of £1,000 provided for at 31 January 2023. The loan notes were issued in order to finance the company's trading activities.

Capital allowances

No capital allowances are available for the year ended 31 January 2023.

Cedar Ltd

Cedar Ltd is a 100% subsidiary company of Timber Ltd. The following information is available in respect of the two companies for the year ended 31 March 2023:

(1) For the year ended 31 March 2023, Cedar Ltd made a trading loss of £19,700.

(2) On 28 December 2022, Cedar Ltd sold its entire shareholding of 25,000 £1 ordinary shares in Forest plc for £6.00 per share. Cedar Ltd had originally purchased 20,000 shares in Forest plc on 1 July 2010 for £24,800. On 20 July 2010, Forest plc made a 1 for 4 rights issue. Cedar Ltd took up its allocation under the rights issue in full, paying £1.15 for each new share issued. The indexation factor from July 2010 to December 2017 is 0.244.

(3) For the year ended 31 March 2023, Timber Ltd made:

	£
Trading loss	20,800
Capital loss	8,800

There is no possibility of Cedar Ltd or Timber Ltd offsetting their trading losses against prior year profits. The group has a policy of utilising losses at the earliest opportunity.

Required

(a) (i) Identify Ash Ltd's accounting periods throughout the period 1 December 2020 to 31 March 2023.

(2 marks)

(ii) Explain Ash Ltd's residence status throughout the period 1 December 2020 to 31 March 2023. **(2 marks)**

(b) Calculate Beech Ltd's corporation tax liability for the year ended 31 January 2023.

Note. Your computation should commence with the profit before taxation figure of £305,500, and should also list all of the items referred to in notes (1) to (5), indicating by the use of zero (0) any items which do not require adjustment. **(6 marks)**

(c) On the basis that all available claims and elections are made, calculate Cedar Ltd's taxable total profits for the year ended 31 March 2023. **(5 marks)**

(Total = 15 marks)

259 Aoede Ltd, Bianca Ltd and Charon Ltd (March/June 2019) (27 mins)

You are a trainee chartered certified accountant dealing with the tax affairs of three unrelated limited companies, Aoede Ltd, Bianca Ltd and Charon Ltd.

Aoede Ltd

Aoede Ltd commenced trading on 1 April 2021. The company's results are:

	Year ended 31 March 2022	*Year ended 31 March 2023*
	£	£
Trading profit/(loss)	(111,300)	67,800
Property business income/(loss)	(26,400)	23,400
Chargeable gains	5,800	16,200
Qualifying charitable donations	(6,000)	(6,600)

Aoede Ltd owns 100% of the ordinary share capital of Moon Ltd. Moon Ltd commenced trading on 1 April 2022 and for the year ended 31 March 2023 made a trading profit of £19,700.

Bianca Ltd

Bianca Ltd commenced trading on 1 April 2022. The company's tax adjusted trading profit based on the statement of profit or loss for the year ended 31 March 2023 is £256,300. This figure is **before** making any adjustments required for:

(1) Advertising expenditure of £5,800 incurred during January 2021 to promote Bianca Ltd's new business. This expenditure has not been deducted in calculating the profit of £256,300.

(2) Leasing costs of £9,300 which have been deducted in arriving at the profit of £256,300. The leasing costs relate to two cars which have been leased since 1 April 2022. The first car has CO_2 emissions of 45 grams per kilometre and is leased at an annual cost of £4,200. The second car has CO_2 emissions of 65 grams per kilometre and is leased at an annual cost of £5,100.

(3) *Capital allowances*

On 1 April 2022, Bianca Ltd purchased four new laptop computers at a discounted cost of £1,000 per laptop. The original cost of each laptop was £1,800, but Bianca Ltd was given a discount because they were damaged.

Bianca Ltd also purchased two second-hand cars on 1 April 2022. Details are:

	Cost	*CO_2 emission rate*
	£	
Car [1]	12,400	35 grams per kilometre
Car [2]	13,900	120 grams per kilometre

Charon Ltd

During the year ended 31 March 2023, Charon Ltd disposed of two investment properties.

The first property was sold for £368,000 during January 2023. This property was purchased for £147,000 during October 1995 and was extended at a cost of £39,000 during June 2018.

The second property was sold for £167,000 during January 2023. This property was purchased for £172,000 during December 2017.

Indexation factors are:

October 1995 to December 2017	0.856

Required

(a) (i) On the basis that Aoede Ltd claims relief for its losses as early as possible, calculate the taxable total profits of Aoede Ltd for the years ended 31 March 2022 and 31 March 2023, and of Moon Ltd for the year ended 31 March 2023. **(5 marks)**

(ii) Explain which aspect of Aoede Ltd's loss relief claim made in part (i) is not beneficial for the company to make. **(1 mark)**

(b) Calculate Bianca Ltd's revised tax adjusted trading profit for the year ended 31 March 2023. **(5 marks)**

(c) Calculate Charon Ltd's chargeable gains and capital losses, if any, for the year ended 31 March 2023. **(4 marks)**

(Total = 15 marks)

PART F: VALUE ADDED TAX

Part F covers value added tax, the subject of Chapters 24 and 25 of the BPP Workbook for Taxation (TX – UK).

Section A

OTQ bank – Value added tax 1 (18 mins)

260 Jerome is a value added tax (VAT) registered trader who received an order for goods with a 10% deposit on 18 August. The goods were despatched on 26 August and an invoice was sent on 2 September. The balancing 90% of the payment was received on 10 September.

Match the tax points for the deposit and the balancing payment if Jerome does not use the cash accounting scheme.

18 August		Deposit
2 September		Balancing payment
26 August		
10 September		

(2 marks)

---

261 Frances commenced trading on 1 January 2022. An analysis of her taxable supplies for the first year of trading (spread evenly over the quarter) is as follows:

Quarter ended	£
31 March 2022	15,000
30 June 2022	20,000
30 September 2022	30,000
31 December 2022	33,000

Frances notifies HM Revenue and Customs (HMRC) of her liability to compulsorily register for value added tax (VAT) on time.

From what date will Frances be registered for VAT? ***(March/June 2021)***

- O 30 December 2022
- O 1 January 2023
- O 31 January 2023
- O 1 February 2023

(2 marks)

---

262 Light Ltd is registered for value added tax (VAT). On 1 January 2023, Light Ltd purchased a car costing £18,400 (inclusive of VAT) for use by the managing director for business and private purposes. The private use is estimated to be 40%.

The managing director is provided with free petrol for business and private mileage which cost Light Ltd £625 (exclusive of VAT). Light Ltd wishes to use the fuel scale charge: the relevant quarterly VAT inclusive scale charge is £377.

What is Light Ltd's VAT repayment in respect of the car and the fuel for the quarter ended 31 March 2023?

- O £50
- O £75
- O £62
- O £41

(2 marks)

---

263 Nora Ltd prepared a value added tax (VAT) return for the quarter ended 31 May 2022 which showed net VAT payable of £2,500.

By which dates should this return have been submitted to HM Revenue & Customs (HMRC) and the payment made to HMRC?

	Return submitted	*Payment*
O	30 June 2022	30 June 2022
O	7 July 2022	7 July 2022
O	7 July 2022	30 June 2022
O	30 June 2022	7 July 2022

(2 marks)

---

264 Mick is a value added tax (VAT) registered trader who prepares quarterly VAT returns to 31 March, 30 June, 30 September and 31 December each year. Mick's accounts are prepared annually to 30 September. Mick made a supply of goods amounting to £6,000 on 22 September 2022 with a due date of payment of 10 October 2022. The customer has defaulted on the payment and Mick has written the debt off in his accounts. He does not use the cash accounting scheme.

Which quarterly VAT return is the earliest in which relief for the impaired debt may be claimed?

- O VAT quarter ended 31 December 2022
- O VAT quarter ended 31 March 2023
- O VAT quarter ended 30 June 2023
- O VAT quarter ended 30 September 2023

(2 marks)

(Total = 10 marks)

OTQ bank – Value added tax 2 (36 mins)

265 Karen is a sole trader and is registered for value added tax (VAT). Karen sold goods for £8,000 exclusive of VAT. The sale was standard rated. Karen's invoice states that there is a discount of 8% on sales if invoices are paid within 21 days. The invoice for the supply was actually paid 25 days after it was issued.

How much VAT should Karen have added to the sale price of £8,000?

£ [ ] **(2 marks)**

---

266 Olive is a sole trader who is registered for value added tax (VAT). On 10 October 2022 she purchased a car for £12,000 (inclusive of VAT) to use for business and private purposes. The private use is estimated to be 30%. On 1 December 2022, the car was damaged in an accident and the repairs amounted to £2,000 (inclusive of VAT).

What is the input tax Olive can recover in relation to the car for the quarter ended 31 December 2022?

£ [ ] **(2 marks)**

---

267 Price Ltd incurred the following expenditure (inclusive of value added tax) in the quarter to 31 December:

	£
New car for salesman (20% private use)	14,040
New van	10,320
Entertaining UK customers	4,200
Entertaining overseas customers	3,600

How much input tax can be recovered by Price Ltd for the quarter to 31 December?

[▼]

Pull down list

- £2,320
- £3,020
- £4,192
- £5,360

(2 marks)

---

268 Ben has been in business for three years. Due to an upturn in trade, he applied to register for value added tax (VAT) with effect from 1 October 2022. Prior to registration, he had incurred the following VAT expenditure:

	£
Legal fees on an invoice dated 13 January 2022	500
Accountancy fees on an invoice dated 5 September 2022	30
Inventory of spare parts acquired in past two years and still held on 30 September 2022	240

What is the total pre-registration input tax that Ben can recover in respect of these items?

£ [ ] **(2 marks)**

---

269 In the first year of trading to 31 December 2021 Scott's taxable turnover was £5,000 per month.

For the first seven months of 2022 his turnover was as follows:

	£
January 2022	8,400
February 2022	8,600
March 2022	8,800
April 2022	9,600
May 2022	10,000
June 2022	10,200
July 2022	10,300

You have advised Scott that he is compulsorily required to be registered for value added tax (VAT).

From what date will Scott be registered for VAT under compulsory registration?

- O 30 July 2022
- O 1 August 2022
- O 30 June 2022
- O 1 July 2022

(2 marks)

---

270 During the quarter ended 31 December, Rachel makes purchases of office items for her business of £5,700 and spends £420 entertaining UK customers. Her sales for the period are £35,250. All figures are inclusive of value added tax (VAT) and standard rated.

What is Rachel's total VAT liability for the quarter ended 31 December?

£ [ ] **(2 marks)**

---

271 Charlie, a United Kingdom (UK) value added tax (VAT) registered trader, made a supply of goods in February 2023 to a customer in France who is VAT registered there.

What rate of VAT will Charlie charge on this sale?

- O 0%
- O 20%
- O 1/6
- O 5%

(2 marks)

---

272 Which TWO of the following are features of the value added tax (VAT) cash accounting scheme?

- ☐ Date of payment or receipt determines the VAT period in which the transaction is dealt with
- ☐ Only need to submit an annual VAT return
- ☐ Gives automatic impairment loss relief (bad debt relief)
- ☐ Payments on account of VAT are required throughout the quarter

(2 marks)

273 Alice is registered for value added tax (VAT) and calculates her VAT liability based on the flat rate scheme. The relevant flat rate percentage for Alice's business is 10%.

For the year ended 31 March 2023, Alice's sales (exclusive of VAT) were:

	£
Standard rated sales	50,000
Zero rated sales	20,000
Exempt sales	5,000

What amount of VAT is payable by Alice to HM Revenue and Customs (HMRC) in respect of the year ended 31 March 2023? ***(December 2018)***

- O £8,500
- O £8,000
- O £7,500
- O £6,000

(2 marks)

---

274 Match the thresholds for a business to join and to leave the value added tax (VAT) flat rate scheme.

Tax exclusive annual taxable turnover up to £150,000		Join scheme
Tax inclusive annual taxable turnover up to £150,000		Leave scheme
Tax exclusive annual turnover up to £230,000		
Tax inclusive annual turnover up to £230,000		

(2 marks)

(Total = 20 marks)

Section B

OT case – Anne (June 2009) (amended) (18 mins)

The following scenario relates to the next five questions.

Anne runs a retail clothing shop. She is registered for value added tax (VAT) and is in the process of completing her VAT return for the quarter ended 30 November 2022.

The following information is available (all figures are exclusive of VAT):

(1) Cash sales amounted to £42,000, of which £28,000 was in respect of sales of adult clothing (standard rated) and £14,000 was in respect of sales of children's clothing (zero rated).

(2) Sales invoices totalling £12,000 were issued in respect of credit sales. These sales were all standard rated. Anne states on her invoice that there is a 5% discount for payment within one month of the date of the sales invoice. 90% of the customers pay within this period. The sales figure of £12,000 is stated before any deduction for the 5% discount.

(3) Purchase and expense invoices totalling £19,200 were received from VAT registered suppliers. This figure is made up as follows:

	£
Standard rated purchases and expenses	11,200
Zero rated purchases	6,000
Exempt expenses	2,000
	19,200

Anne pays all of her purchase and expense invoices two months after receiving the invoice.

(4) On 30 November 2022 Anne wrote off two impairment losses that were in respect of standard rated credit sales. The first impairment loss was for £300 and was in respect of a sales invoice due for payment on 15 July 2022. The second impairment loss was for £800 and was in respect of a sales invoice due for payment on 10 April 2022.

Anne does not use the cash accounting scheme, but she is considering using the scheme.

275 What is the amount of output tax on cash sales payable by Anne for the quarter ended 30 November 2022?

£ ☐ **(2 marks)**

---

276 What is the amount of output tax on credit sales payable by Anne for the quarter ended 30 November 2022, taking into account impairment loss relief?

- O £2,052
- O £2,400
- O £2,280
- O £2,292 **(2 marks)**

---

277 What is the amount of input tax recoverable by Anne for the quarter ended 30 November 2022?

£ ☐ **(2 marks)**

278 Which TWO of the following statements about the cash accounting scheme are correct?

- ☐ Anne will be permitted to join the scheme if her expected taxable turnover for the next 12 months does not exceed £1,350,000.
- ☐ Anne must pay her 90% of the previous year's net VAT liability during the year by means of nine monthly payments commencing at the end of the fourth month of the year.
- ☐ Anne will be permitted to join the scheme if she is up to date with her VAT payments but not necessarily up to date with her VAT returns.
- ☐ If the value of Anne's taxable supplies exceeds £1,600,000 in the 12 months to the end of a VAT period, she must leave the scheme immediately. **(2 marks)**

---

279 Identify, by clicking on the relevant boxes in the table below, whether each of the following statements are the advantages of Anne using the cash accounting scheme.

Reduced amount of output VAT payable	**ADVANTAGE**	**NOT ADVANTAGE**
Automatic impairment loss relief (bad debt relief)	**ADVANTAGE**	**NOT ADVANTAGE**
Only one VAT return each year	**ADVANTAGE**	**NOT ADVANTAGE**
Output VAT on 10% of credit sales will be accounted for up to 1 month later than at present	**ADVANTAGE**	**NOT ADVANTAGE**

(2 marks)

(Total = 10 marks)

OT case – Auy and Bim (June 2010) (amended) (18 mins)

The following scenario relates to the next five questions.

Auy and Bim have been in partnership since 6 April 2006 and have been registered for value added tax (VAT) since that date. In the year ended 5 April 2023, the partnership's summarised statement of profit or loss shows sales revenue of £140,762, which is exclusive of output VAT of £25,600, and expenses of £60,200 which are exclusive of recoverable input VAT of £180 for motor expenses and £140 for other expenses.

The partnership has recently started invoicing for its services on new payment terms, and the partners are concerned about output VAT being accounted for at the appropriate time. The partnership is considering using the flat rate scheme. The relevant flat rate scheme percentage for the partnership's trade is 14%.

280 Which TWO of the following statements about the tax point are correct?

- ☐ The basic tax point for services is the date that services commence.
- ☐ If the VAT invoice is issued within 14 days after the basic tax point and payment has not been received before the basic tax point, the invoice date becomes the tax point.
- ☐ The tax point determines the VAT period in which output tax must be accounted for and credit for input tax will be allowed.
- ☐ If the VAT invoice is issued and payment is received before the basic tax point, the actual tax point is the later of those two dates.

(2 marks)

---

281 What is the total amount of VAT paid by the partnership to HM Revenue & Customs for the year ended 5 April 2023?

- O £25,600
- O £25,420
- O £25,280
- O £25,460

(2 marks)

---

282 Which TWO of the following statements about the flat rate scheme are correct?

- ☐ Businesses using the scheme must still issue VAT invoices to their VAT registered customers.
- ☐ Under the scheme, businesses calculate VAT by applying a fixed percentage to their standard rate income only.
- ☐ Businesses using the scheme cannot reclaim any input tax suffered.
- ☐ A 1% reduction off the flat rate percentage can always be made by businesses in the first year that they use the flat rate scheme.

(2 marks)

---

283 What are the conditions that the partnership must satisfy in order to join and continue to use the VAT flat rate scheme?

	Join	*Continue to use*
O	Expected taxable turnover (excluding VAT) for the next 12 months does not exceed £230,000.	Until its total turnover (including VAT) for the previous year exceeds £1,350,000
O	Expected taxable turnover (excluding VAT) for the next 12 months does not exceed £150,000.	Until its total turnover (including VAT) for the previous year exceeds £230,000
O	Expected taxable turnover (excluding VAT) for the next 12 months does not exceed £150,000.	Until its total turnover (including VAT) for the previous year exceeds £1,350,000
O	Expected taxable turnover (excluding VAT) for the next 12 months does not exceed £230,000.	Until its total turnover (including VAT) for the previous year exceeds £230,000

(2 marks)

---

284 What is the amount of VAT that would have been paid to HM Revenue & Customs if the partnership had used the flat rate scheme to calculate the amount of VAT payable for the year ended 5 April 2023?

- O £23,291
- O £19,707
- O £22,971
- O £28,152

(2 marks)

(Total = 10 marks)

OT case – Aston (June 2011) (amended) (18 mins)

The following scenario relates to the next five questions.

Aston commenced self-employment on 1 August 2022 providing consultancy services. His sales revenue has been as follows:

		Standard rated	*Zero rated*
		£	£
2022	August	6,300	–
	September	6,400	–
	October	21,900	4,800
	November	11,700	–
	December	17,100	–
2023	January	14,800	2,200
	February	4,200	–
	March	31,500	3,300
	April	44,600	6,600

Where applicable, the above figures are stated exclusive of value added tax (VAT). Aston only supplies services, and all of his supplies are to VAT registered businesses. He does not offer any discount for prompt payment.

Aston wants advice about when he will need to submit his VAT returns and pay the associated VAT due.

The following is a sample of the new sales invoice that Aston is going to issue to his customers:

SALES INVOICE

Aston

Address: 111 Long Road, London W1 9MG

Telephone: 0207 123 3456

Invoice date: 6 June 2023

Tax point: 6 June 2023

Description of services: Business advice

	£
Total price (excluding VAT)	12,000.00
Total price (including VAT)	14,400.00

Customer: Faster Motors plc

Address: 22 Short Lane, Manchester M1 8MB

You have advised Aston that he also needs to include the rate of VAT for each supply and the amount of VAT payable. Aston sometimes receives supplies of standard rated services from VAT registered businesses situated abroad. Aston wants to know how he should account for these services for VAT purposes. Because of the complexity of the VAT legislation, Aston is concerned that despite his best efforts he will incorrectly treat a standard rated supply as zero rated, thus understating the amount of VAT payable. He wants to know if such an error will result in a penalty, and if so, how much the penalty will be.

285 Match the dates on which Aston was liable to be registered for VAT and the date from which Aston's business should be registered for VAT.

28 February 2023		Liable for registration
28 February 2023		Date of registration
31 January 2023		
1 March 2023		

(2 marks)

---

286 When must Aston submit his VAT returns and pay the associated VAT?

	Submission	***Payment***
O	One month after the end of the VAT period	One month after the end of the VAT period
O	One month after the end of the VAT period	One month and seven days after the end of the VAT period
O	One month and seven days after the end of the VAT period	One month and seven days after the end of the VAT period
O	One month and seven days after the end of the VAT period	One month after the end of the VAT period

(2 marks)

---

287 Which TWO pieces of information must Aston show on his new sales invoices for them to be valid for VAT purposes in addition to those you have already advised him on?

- ☐ Date for payment
- ☐ Aston's VAT registration number
- ☐ HMRC reference number
- ☐ An identifying number (invoice number)

(2 marks)

---

288 Which TWO of the following statements about when and how Aston should account for VAT in respect of the supplies of services he receives from VAT registered businesses abroad are correct?

- ☐ The transaction is entered on Aston's VAT return as an output and an input.
- ☐ The tax point is the earlier of the 15th day of the month following that in which the service is completed and the date it is paid for.
- ☐ Supplies of services from VAT registered businesses situated abroad are always zero rated for the customer.
- ☐ The service is treated as being supplied in the UK since this is where Aston is situated.

(2 marks)

289 Assuming that Aston incorrectly treats a standard rated supply as zero rated with the result that the amount of VAT payable is understated, what is the maximum amount of penalty that is likely to be charged by HM Revenue & Customs and the minimum penalty that could be charged as a result of a subsequent unprompted disclosure?

	Maximum penalty	*Minimum penalty for unprompted disclosure*
O	70% of the VAT underpaid	15% of the VAT underpaid
O	70% of the VAT underpaid	0% of the VAT underpaid
O	30% of the VAT underpaid	15% of the VAT underpaid
O	30% of the VAT underpaid	0% of the VAT underpaid

(2 marks)

(Total = 10 marks)

OT case – Starfish Ltd (Dec 2011) (amended) (18 mins)

The following scenario relates to the next five questions.

Starfish Ltd, a retailing company, ceased trading on 31 March 2023 and deregistered from value added tax (VAT) on that date.

The following relates to the company's final VAT return for the quarter ended 31 March 2023:

(1) Cash sales revenue amounted to £41,160, of which £38,520 was in respect of standard rated sales and £2,640 was in respect of zero-rated sales.

(2) Sales invoices totalling £2,000 were issued in respect of credit sales revenue. This figure is exclusive of VAT, and the sales were all standard rated. Starfish Ltd states on its invoices that it offers all of its credit sale customers a 4% discount for payment within 14 days of the date of the sales invoice. 60% of the customers paid within this period.

(3) In addition to the above sales revenue, Starfish Ltd sold its remaining inventory on 31 March 2023 for £28,800.

(4) There were no purchases of inventory during the period.

(5) Standard rated expenses amounted to £69,960, of which £4,320 was in respect of entertaining UK customers.

(6) Starfish Ltd wrote off an impairment loss on 31 March 2023 in respect of a sales invoice (exclusive of VAT) that was due for payment on 8 August 2022. Output VAT of £384 was originally paid in respect of this sale.

(7) On 31 March 2023 the company sold all of its machinery for £31,200 and a car for £9,600. The car was used 30% privately by a director of Starfish Ltd.

Unless otherwise stated, all of the above figures are inclusive of VAT where applicable.

Starfish Ltd did not use the cash accounting scheme for VAT.

290 What is the amount of output tax on credit sales payable by Starfish Ltd for the quarter ended 31 March 2023?

O £384

O £480

O £390

O £325

(2 marks)

---

291 What is the amount of output tax, other than on credit sales, payable by Starfish Ltd for the quarter ended 31 March 2023?

- O £16,420
- O £11,620
- O £11,220
- O £10,000

(2 marks)

---

292 What is the amount of input tax recoverable by Starfish Ltd for the quarter ended 31 March 2023?

- O £12,744
- O £11,324
- O £10,940
- O £11,276

(2 marks)

---

293 From which date would default interest be payable if Starfish Ltd is late in paying the VAT for the quarter ended 31 March 2023?

- O 30 April 2023
- O 7 May 2023
- O 14 May 2023
- O 31 March 2023

(2 marks)

---

294 Which of the following would be the consequences for VAT if Starfish Ltd had instead sold its entire business as a going concern to a single VAT registered purchaser?

- O Output VAT would have been due on the sale of the inventory or the sale of the non-current assets but would be payable by the purchaser.
- O No output VAT would have been due on the sale of the inventory but would have been due on the sale of the non-current assets.
- O No output VAT would have been due on the sale of the non-current assets but would have been due on the sale of the inventory.
- O No output VAT would have been due on the sale of the inventory or the sale of the non-current assets.

(2 marks)

(Total = 10 marks)

OT case – Greenzone Ltd (June 2013) (18 mins)

The following scenario relates to the next five questions.

Greenzone Ltd owns 60% of Are Ltd, 40% of Be Ltd, 90% of Can Ltd and 70% of Doer Inc.

All the companies are UK resident except for Doer Inc which also does not have a fixed establishment in the UK.

The following information is available in respect of Greenzone Ltd's value added tax (VAT) for the quarter ended 31 March 2023:

(1) Output VAT of £38,210 was charged in respect of sales. This figure includes output VAT of £400 on a deposit received on 29 March 2023, which is in respect of a contract that is due to commence on 20 April 2023.

(2) In addition to the above, Greenzone Ltd charged output VAT of £4,330 on sales to Can Ltd. Greenzone Ltd does not have group registration.

(3) The managing director of Greenzone Ltd is provided with free fuel for his company car. The total cost of fuel for the car for the quarter is £500 and 60% of the total mileage is private mileage.

Greenzone Ltd wishes to use the fuel scale charge. The relevant quarterly scale charge is £334. Both these figures are inclusive of VAT.

(4) Input VAT of £12,770 was incurred in respect of expenses (excluding the fuel in (3)). This figure includes the following input VAT:

	£
Entertaining UK customers	210
Entertaining overseas customers	139
Repainting the exterior of the company's office building	1,678
Extending the office building in order to create a new reception area	3,300

295 What is the amount of output VAT charged on the sales in (1) and (2) for the quarter to 31 March 2023?

- O £42,540
- O £38,210
- O £42,140
- O £37,810

(2 marks)

---

296 What is the net amount of VAT payable or recoverable for the provision of the fuel for the managing director's company car in (3)?

- O £23 payable
- O £33 recoverable
- O £56 payable
- O £27 recoverable

(2 marks)

---

297 What is the amount of input VAT that can be recovered on the expenses in (4)?

£ [ ]

(2 marks)

---

298 Identify, by clicking on the relevant boxes in the table below, which of the following companies (apart from Can Ltd) could be registered in a VAT group with Greenzone Ltd.

ARE LTD	**YES**	**NO**

BE LTD	YES	NO
DOER INC	YES	NO

(2 marks)

---

299 Which TWO of the following statements about VAT group registration are correct?

- ☐ Each VAT group must appoint a representative member which accounts for the group's output tax and input tax.
- ☐ Each VAT group must appoint a representative member which is solely liable for paying the group VAT liability.
- ☐ All eligible companies must be part of the group registration.
- ☐ Any supply of goods or services by a member of the group to another member of the group is disregarded for VAT purposes.

(2 marks)

(Total = 10 marks)

OT case – Long Ltd group (B) (June 2014) (amended) (18 mins)

The following scenario relates to the next five questions.

Long Ltd owns 100% of the ordinary share capital of both Wind Ltd and Road Ltd. Long Ltd and Road Ltd run freight transport businesses, whilst Wind Ltd provides transport related insurance services.

Long Ltd, Wind Ltd and Road Ltd are not registered as a group for value added tax (VAT) purposes, but such a registration is being considered, with Long Ltd being the representative member.

The following VAT information is available for the quarter ended 31 March 2023:

Long Ltd

(1) All of Long Ltd's sales are standard rated for VAT.

(2) Output VAT of £52,640 was charged in respect of sales. This figure includes output VAT of £1,760 on a deposit received on 28 December 2022. The deposit was in respect of a contract which was completed on 6 January 2023, with a sales invoice being issued on 20 January 2023.

(3) In addition to the above, Long Ltd also charged output VAT of £1,940 on sales to Wind Ltd and output VAT of £960 on sales to Road Ltd.

(4) Input VAT of £14,720 was incurred in respect of expenses.

(5) In addition to the above, Long Ltd has discovered that it has not been claiming for the input VAT of £18 which it has paid each month since 1 January 2017 for the hire of a photocopier.

Wind Ltd

(1) All of Wind Ltd's sales are exempt from VAT.

(2) Input VAT of £7,330 was incurred in respect of expenses. This includes input VAT of £1,940 incurred on purchases from Long Ltd.

Road Ltd

(1) All of Road Ltd's sales are zero rated for VAT.

(2) Road Ltd registered for VAT on 1 January 2023 and this is the company's first VAT return.

(3) Input VAT of £3,120 was incurred in respect of expenses. This includes input VAT of £960 incurred on purchases from Long Ltd.

(4) In addition to the above, Road Ltd incurred input VAT in respect of advertising expenditure as follows:

	£
April 2022	640
November 2022	380
	1,020

300 What is the amount of output tax payable by Long Ltd for the quarter ended 31 March 2023?

£ [ ] **(2 marks)**

---

301 What is the amount of input tax recoverable by Long Ltd for the quarter ended 31 March 2023?

- O £14,720
- O £14,774
- O £14,882
- O £15,638

(2 marks)

---

302 What is the amount of input tax recoverable by Wind Ltd for the quarter ended 31 March 2023?

£ [ ] **(2 marks)**

---

303 What is the amount of input tax recoverable by Road Ltd for the quarter ended 31 March 2023?

[▼]

Pull down list

- £3,120
- £3,500
- £3,760
- £4,140

(2 marks)

---

304 Which TWO of the following statements about the Long Ltd group and VAT group registration are correct?

- ☐ If Wind Ltd and Road Ltd were both owned by the same individual, they would not be able to be included in a group registration.
- ☐ Supplies of goods or services to Road Ltd from outside the group will be treated as a supply to Long Ltd.

☐ Each company in the Long Ltd group must join the VAT group if group registration is applied for.

☐ The supplies by Long Ltd to Wind Ltd and Road Ltd would be disregarded for VAT purposes.

(2 marks)

(Total = 10 marks)

OT case – Zim (June 2015) (amended) (18 mins)

The following scenario relates to the next five questions.

Zim has been registered for value added tax (VAT) since 1 April 2007. The following information is available for the year ended 31 March 2023:

(1) Sales invoices totalling £126,000 were issued, of which £115,200 were in respect of standard rated sales and £10,800 were in respect of zero-rated sales. Zim's customers are all members of the general public.

(2) Purchase invoices totalling £49,200 were received, of which £43,200 were in respect of standard rated purchases and £6,000 were in respect of zero-rated purchases.

(3) On 31 March 2023, Zim wrote off two impairment losses which were in respect of standard rated sales.

The first impairment loss was for £780 and was in respect of a sales invoice which had been due for payment on 15 August 2022. The second impairment loss was for £660 and was in respect of a sales invoice which had been due for payment on 15 September 2022.

(4) During the year ended 31 March 2023, Zim spent £2,600 on mobile telephone calls, of which 40% related to private calls.

(5) During the year ended 31 March 2023, Zim spent £1,560 on entertaining customers, of which £240 was in respect of overseas customers.

All of the above figures are inclusive of VAT where applicable.

Zim does not use either the cash accounting scheme or the flat rate scheme. If he did use the flat rate scheme the relevant percentage for his business is 12%.

305 What is the net amount of VAT payable on the sales in (1) and the purchases in (2)?

£ ☐ **(2 marks)**

---

306 What is the amount of input VAT which can be recovered on the impairment losses in (3)?

O £0

O £110

O £130

O £240 **(2 marks)**

---

307 What is the amount of input VAT which can be recovered on the expenditure on the mobile phone calls in (4) and entertaining customers in (5)?

	Mobile phone	*Customers*
O	£0	£220
O	£0	£40

	Mobile phone	*Customers*
O	£260	£220
O	£260	£40

(2 marks)

---

308 Match the thresholds for Zim to be able to join and to be required to leave the flat rate scheme.

Taxable turnover excluding VAT not more than £150,000 in next 12 months		Join
Total turnover including VAT not more than £230,000 in next 12 months		Leave
Taxable turnover including VAT not more than £150,000 in next 12 months		
Total turnover excluding VAT more than £230,000 in previous 12 months		

(2 marks)

---

309 How much VAT would Zim have paid in the year to 31 March 2023 if he had been in the flat rate scheme for the whole of that year?

[▼]

Pull down list

- £13,824
- £13,860
- £15,120
- £9,216

(2 marks)

(Total = 10 marks)

OT case – Smart Ltd (Sept/Dec 2015) (amended) (18 mins)

The following scenario relates to the next five questions.

Smart Ltd commenced trading on 1 September 2022.

The company's sales for the first four months of trading were as follows:

2022	£
September	26,000
October	47,000
November	134,000
December	113,000

On 1 November 2022, the company signed a contract valued at £86,000 for completion during November 2022.

All of the above figures are stated exclusive of value added tax (VAT).

Smart Ltd only supplies services and all of the company's supplies are standard rated.

Smart Ltd allows its customers 60 days' credit when paying for services, and it is concerned that some customers will default on the payment of their debts.

The company pays its purchase invoices as soon as they are received.

Smart Ltd does not use either the VAT cash accounting scheme or the annual accounting scheme.

Smart Ltd is concerned about the penalties that could be charged if it makes a careless error in its VAT return resulting in underpaid VAT.

310 Match the dates from which Smart Ltd was required to register for VAT and by when it was required to notify HM Revenue & Customs (HMRC) of the registration.

1 November 2022		Register
30 December 2022		Notification
30 November 2022		
31 December 2022		

(2 marks)

---

311 Identify, by clicking on the relevant boxes in the table below, which of the following statements about how and when Smart Ltd will have to submit its quarterly VAT returns and pay any related VAT liability are true or false.

Smart Ltd can file its VAT returns by entering figures manually on HMRC's website.	**TRUE**	**FALSE**
Smart Ltd can choose whether to pay the VAT which is due electronically or by cheque.	**TRUE**	**FALSE**

The deadline for paying any VAT which is due is one month after the end of each quarter.	TRUE	FALSE
The deadline for filing the VAT return is one month and seven days after the end of each quarter.	TRUE	FALSE

(2 marks)

---

312 Which TWO of the following statements about the tax point for Smart Ltd's supplies of services are correct?

- ☐ The basic tax point is the date on which the invoice is issued.
- ☐ The basic tax point is the date on which services are completed.
- ☐ If a customer pays for services before the basic tax point, the payment date will be the tax point.
- ☐ If a customer pays for services after the basic tax point, the payment date will be the tax point.

(2 marks)

---

313 Which TWO of the following statements are advantages for Smart Ltd to use the VAT cash accounting scheme?

(1) The scheme will provide automatic relief for an impairment loss should a customer default on the payment of a debt.

(2) Only one VAT return will be required each year so there are fewer occasions to trigger a default surcharge.

(3) There will be reduced VAT administration as Smart Ltd will not be required to issue invoices to its customers.

(4) Output VAT will be accounted for 60 days later than at present, as the scheme will result in the tax point becoming the date when payment is received from customers.

- O 1 and 2
- O 2 and 3
- O 1 and 4
- O 2 and 4

(2 marks)

---

314 What is the maximum amount of penalty that could be charged by HMRC if Smart Ltd makes a careless error in its VAT return resulting in underpaid VAT and the minimum penalty that could be charged as a result of a subsequent prompted disclosure?

	Maximum penalty	*Minimum penalty for prompted disclosure*
O	70% of the VAT underpaid	15% of the VAT underpaid
O	70% of the VAT underpaid	0% of the VAT underpaid
O	30% of the VAT underpaid	15% of the VAT underpaid
O	30% of the VAT underpaid	0% of the VAT underpaid

(2 marks)

(Total = 10 marks)

OT case – Thidar (March/June 2019) (18 mins)

The following scenario relates to the next five questions.

You should assume that today's date is 25 April 2023.

Thidar commenced trading as a builder on 1 January 2022. She voluntarily registered for value added tax (VAT) on 1 January 2022.

Sales

Thidar's sales for the first 15 months of trading have been:

Month	*Standard rated*	*Zero rated*	*Month*	*Standard rated*	*Zero rated*
	£	£		£	£
1	3,400	0	9	8,800	6,300
2	0	1,900	10	2,900	7,300
3	5,700	2,100	11	0	0
4	6,800	0	12	0	2,600
5	9,500	1,200	13	2,800	900
6	7,900	2,200	14	3,200	1,700
7	0	3,700	15	22,200	3,600
8	12,100	0			

Pre-registration expenditure

Thidar paid for the following standard rated services prior to registering for VAT on 1 January 2022:

Date	*Cost of service*	*Description*
	£	
10 June 2021	1,800	Advertisement for the building business
8 Dec 2021	300	Advertisement for the building business

Both figures are exclusive of VAT. Thidar paid for the advertisement of £300 by cash, and she does not have any evidence of this transaction (such as a VAT invoice).

VAT return for the quarter ended 30 September 2022

Thidar's VAT return for the quarter ended 30 September 2022 was filed by the submission deadline of 7 November 2022 and the related VAT liability was paid on time.

However, on 15 February 2023, Thidar discovered that the amount of VAT paid was understated by £1,200 as a result of incorrectly treating a standard rated sale as zero rated. Given that the underpayment does not exceed £10,000, Thidar is permitted to correct this error on her VAT return for the quarter ended 31 March 2023, and this is what she will do. Thidar will file this VAT return by the submission deadline of 7 May 2023 and pay the related VAT liability (including the underpaid £1,200) on time.

VAT return for the quarter ended 31 March 2023

Thidar is currently completing her VAT return for the quarter ended 31 March 2023 and is unsure as to how much input VAT is non-deductible in respect of two items:

(1) During the quarter ended 31 March 2023, Thidar spent £800 on entertaining UK customers.

(2) During the quarter ended 31 March 2023, Thidar leased a car at a cost of £700. The car is used by Thidar and 75% of the mileage is for private journeys.

Both figures are exclusive of VAT.

315 In which month did Thidar exceed the VAT threshold for compulsory registration?

- O Month 14
- O Month 15
- O Month 13
- O Not yet exceeded **(2 marks)**

---

316 What amount of pre-registration input VAT was Thidar able to recover in respect of expenditure incurred prior to registering for VAT on 1 January 2022?

- O £360
- O £60
- O £420
- O £0

(2 marks)

---

317 Within what period must Thidar issue a VAT invoice after making a standard rated supply, and for how long must these VAT invoices then normally be retained by Thidar?

Option	VAT invoices	Retention
1	Within 14 days	Four years
2	Within 30 days	Six years
3	Within 30 days	Four years
4	Within 14 days	Six years

- O Option 1
- O Option 2
- O Option 3
- O Option 4 **(2 marks)**

---

318 Why will VAT default (or penalty) interest not be charged on Thidar's underpayment of VAT of £1,200 for the quarter ended 30 September 2022?

- O Because Thidar corrected the error within 12 months
- O Because the error was not deliberate
- O Because separate disclosure of the VAT underpayment was not required
- O Because Thidar paid the underpayment of £1,200 by the submission deadline of 7 May 2023 **(2 marks)**

---

319 For the quarter ended 31 March 2023, what is the amount of non-deductible input VAT in respect of entertaining UK customers and the leasing cost of the car?

Option	Entertaining UK customers	Leasing cost
1	£0	£105
2	£160	£105
3	£160	£70
4	£0	£70

- O Option 1
- O Option 2
- O Option 3
- O Option 4

(2 marks)

(Total = 10 marks)

Section C

320 Jogger Ltd (B) (December 2008) (amended) (18 mins)

Jogger Ltd is a manufacturing company and has been registered for value added tax (VAT) since 1 April 2014. From that date until 30 June 2021 the company's VAT returns were all submitted on time. Since 1 July 2021 the company's VAT returns have been submitted as follows:

Quarter ended	*VAT paid*	*Submitted*
	£	
30 September 2021	42,700	One month late
31 December 2021	41,200	On time
31 March 2022	38,900	One month late
30 June 2022	28,300	On time
30 September 2022	49,100	On time
31 December 2022	63,800	On time
31 March 2023	89,100	Two months late

Jogger Ltd always pays any VAT that is due at the same time as the related return is submitted.

Required

(a) State, giving appropriate reasons, the default surcharge consequences arising from Jogger Ltd's submission of its VAT returns for the quarter ended 30 September 2021 to the quarter ended 31 March 2023 inclusive, at the times stated. You may assume that Jogger Ltd is not a small business for the purposes of the default surcharge regime. **(6 marks)**

(b) Advise Jogger Ltd why it might be beneficial to use the VAT annual accounting scheme, and state the conditions that it will have to satisfy before being permitted to do so. **(4 marks)**

(Total = 10 marks)

321 Flick (June 2012) (amended) (18 mins)

On 1 January 2023, Flick commenced in partnership with Art running a small cinema.

The partnership voluntarily registered for value added tax (VAT) on 1 January 2023, and immediately began using the flat rate scheme to calculate the amount of VAT payable.

The relevant flat rate scheme percentage for the partnership's trade is 12%.

For the quarter ended 31 March 2023 the partnership had standard rated sales of £59,700, and these were all made to members of the general public. For the same period standard rated expenses amounted to £27,300. Both figures are stated inclusive of VAT.

The partnership has two private boxes in its cinema that can be booked on a special basis by privileged customers. Such customers can book the boxes up to two months in advance, at which time they have to pay a 25% deposit.

An invoice is then given to the customer on the day of the screening of the film, with payment of the balance of 75% required within seven days. For VAT purposes, the renting out of the cinema boxes is a supply of services.

Required

(a) Explain whether or not it was beneficial for the partnership to have used the VAT flat rate scheme for the quarter ended 31 March 2023.

Notes.

1 Your answer should be supported by appropriate calculations.

2 You should ignore the 1% reduction from the flat rate that is available during the first year of VAT registration. **(3 marks)**

(b) Explain whether or not it was financially beneficial for the partnership to have voluntarily registered for VAT from 1 January 2023.

Note. Your answer should be supported by appropriate calculations. **(3 marks)**

(c) Advise the partnership as to when it should account for output VAT on the renting out of its private boxes to privileged customers. **(4 marks)**

(Total = 10 marks)

322 Richard (December 2013) (amended) (18 mins)

On 6 April 2022, Richard commenced in self-employment, running a restaurant.

Richard's sales since the commencement of trading have been as follows:

April to July 2022	£10,500 per month
August to November 2022	£15,000 per month
December 2022 to March 2023	£21,500 per month

These figures are stated exclusive of value added tax (VAT). Richard's sales are all standard rated.

As a trainee Chartered Certified Accountant you have advised Richard in writing that he should be registered for VAT, but he has refused to register because he thinks his net profit is insufficient to cover the additional cost which would be incurred.

Required

(a) Explain from what date Richard was required to be compulsorily registered for VAT and the VAT implications of continuing to trade after this date without registering.

Note. You are not expected to explain the VAT penalties arising from late VAT registration. **(4 marks)**

(b) Briefly explain from an ethical viewpoint the issues you, as a trainee Chartered Certified Accountant, should consider in order for your firm to deal with Richard's refusal to register for VAT. **(2 marks)**

(c) State the circumstances in which a trader can issue a simplified (or less detailed) VAT invoice, when such an invoice should be issued, and FIVE pieces of information which such an invoice must show where the supply is entirely standard rated. **(4 marks)**

(Total = 10 marks)

323 Clueless Ltd (December 2012) (amended) (18 mins)

Clueless Ltd is a manufacturing company. It is registered for value added tax (VAT), but currently does not use any of the special VAT schemes. The company has annual standard rated sales of £1,200,000 and annual standard rated expenses of £550,000. Both these figures are exclusive of VAT and are likely to remain the same for the foreseeable future. Clueless Ltd is up to date with all of its tax returns, including those for corporation tax, PAYE and VAT. It is also up to date with its corporation tax, PAYE and VAT payments. However, the company often incurs considerable overtime costs due to its employees working late in order to meet tax return filing deadlines.

Clueless Ltd pays its expenses on a cash basis and allows customers two months' credit when paying for sales. The company does not have any impairment losses.

Clueless Ltd is planning to purchase some new machinery at a cost of £22,000 (exclusive of VAT). The machinery will be purchased from an overseas supplier. Clueless Ltd is not a regular importer and so is unsure of the VAT treatment for this purchase.

Required

(a) Explain why Clueless Ltd is entitled to use both the VAT cash accounting scheme and the VAT annual accounting scheme, and why it will probably be beneficial for the company to use both schemes. **(6 marks)**

(b) Explain when and how Clueless Ltd will have to account for VAT in respect of the new machinery:

(i) If they choose not to use postponed accounting

(ii) If they do choose to use postponed accounting **(4 marks)**

(Total = 10 marks)

324 Garfield (March/June 2016) (18 mins)

Garfield has been registered for valued added tax (VAT) since 1 April 2013. Garfield has previously completed his VAT returns himself, but for the quarter ended 31 March 2023 there are some items for which he is unsure of the correct VAT treatment.

Garfield's partly completed VAT computation for the quarter ended 31 March 2023 is shown below. All of the completed sections of the computation are correct, with the omissions marked as outstanding (O/S).

	Note	£
Output VAT		
Sales (all standard rated)		22,500
Discounted sale	1	O/S
Equipment	2	O/S
Fuel scale charge		414
Input VAT		
Purchases (all standard rated)		(11,200)
Car (purchased on 1 January 2023)		0
Equipment	2	O/S
Impairment losses	3	O/S

	Note	£
Entertaining – UK customers		0
– Overseas customers	4	O/S
Motor expenses	5	O/S
VAT payable		O/S

Unless otherwise stated, all of the figures in the following notes are stated exclusive of VAT.

Notes.

1 *Discounted sale*

On 10 February 2023, a sales invoice for £4,300 was issued by Garfield in respect of a standard rated supply. To encourage this previously late paying customer to pay promptly, Garfield offered a 10% discount for payment within 14 days of the date of the sales invoice. The customer paid within the 14-day period.

This invoice has not been taken into account in calculating the output VAT figure of £22,500, and this is the only sale for which Garfield has offered a prompt payment discount.

2 *Equipment*

During the quarter ended 31 March 2023, Garfield acquired some new equipment at a cost of £12,400 from an overseas supplier.

3 *Impairment losses*

On 31 March 2023, Garfield wrote off three impairment losses. Details are as follows:

Amount	Invoice date	Payment due date
£1,400	30 July 2022	29 August 2022
£2,700	12 September 2022	12 October 2022
£1,900	4 October 2022	3 November 2022

4 *Entertainment*

During the quarter ended 31 March 2023, Garfield spent £960 on entertaining overseas customers. This figure is inclusive of VAT.

5 *Motor expenses*

The car purchased on 1 January 2023 is used by Garfield 60% for business mileage. During the quarter ended 31 March 2023, Garfield spent £1,008 on repairs to the car and £660 on fuel for both his business and private mileage. Both of these figures are inclusive of VAT.

Additional information

Garfield does not use the cash accounting scheme, the annual accounting scheme or the flat rate scheme, but has read that the use of these schemes can be beneficial for small businesses such as his.

Garfield's VAT exclusive annual turnover is currently £450,000, and this is expected to steadily decrease over the coming years. He pays for most of his purchases and expenses on a cash basis, and allows many of his customers 30 days' credit when paying for sales.

Required

(a) Calculate the amount of value added tax (VAT) payable by Garfield for the quarter ended 31 March 2023. **(7 marks)**

(b) State which VAT schemes Garfield is currently permitted to use, and explain, with supporting reasons, which **ONE** of the available schemes would appear to be the most beneficial for him to use.

Notes.

1 Your answer should be confined to the information given in the question.

2 You are not expected to explain how any of the schemes operate. **(3 marks)**

(Total = 10 marks)

325 Zhi (March/June 2017) (18 mins)

You should assume that today's date is 15 December 2022.

Zhi has been self-employed since 2001, preparing accounts to 31 December. On 1 December 2022, Zhi purchased a new freehold warehouse for £164,000 for use in his business, but this purchase has resulted in Zhi having cash flow problems. He has various tax payments becoming due over the next two months and would like to reduce or postpone these payments as much as possible.

Income tax and national insurance contributions (NICs)

Zhi's income tax liabilities and class 4 NICs for the tax years 2020/21, 2021/22 and 2022/23 are, or are forecast to be:

	2020/21	*2021/22*	*2022/23*
	£	£	£
Income tax liability	25,200	27,600	18,000
Class 4 NICs	4,084	4,204	3,724

Zhi has not made any claims to reduce his payments on account.

Capital gains tax (CGT)

Zhi has a CGT liability of £12,740 becoming due for payment on 31 January 2023. This is in respect of a freehold office building which was sold for £210,000 on 10 December 2021, resulting in a chargeable gain of £76,000. The office building had always been used for business purposes by Zhi.

Zhi is a higher rate taxpayer. No claim has been made for rollover relief.

Value added tax (VAT)

Zhi has forecast that he will have to pay VAT of £20,200 on 7 February 2023 to HM Revenue & Customs (HMRC) in respect of the VAT quarter ended 31 December 2022.

On 12 December 2022, Zhi despatched goods relating to an exceptionally large credit sale of standard rated goods of £45,600 (inclusive of VAT). He has not yet issued a sales invoice for this sale.

Because the customer is unlikely to pay until 28 February 2023, Zhi is considering not issuing a sales invoice until 1 February 2023.

PAYE and NICs

Zhi will have to pay PAYE and NICs of £5,724 electronically on 22 January 2023 to HMRC in respect of his two employees for the tax month running from 6 December 2022 to 5 January 2023.

This includes amounts for bonuses which Zhi was planning to pay to his two employees on 1 January 2023, but could delay payment until 10 January 2023. The bonuses are in respect of the year ended 31 December 2022, and they will be treated as being received on whichever is the date of payment.

The first employee has a gross annual salary of £20,000 and is to be paid a bonus of £1,500. The second employee has a gross annual salary of £55,000 and is to be paid a bonus of £5,000.

Required

(a) Calculate the amount by which Zhi can claim to reduce his self-assessment income tax and NICs due for payment on 31 January 2023 without incurring interest or penalties. **(2 marks)**

(b) Calculate the amount by which Zhi's CGT liability due for payment on 31 January 2023 will be reduced if he makes a claim for rollover relief based on the warehouse purchased on 1 December 2022 for £164,000. **(3 marks)**

(c) Explain whether Zhi can reduce the amount of VAT payable on 7 February 2023 by not issuing a sales invoice for the credit sale of £45,600 until 1 February 2023, and, if so, by how much the payment will be reduced. **(2 marks)**

(d) Calculate the amount by which Zhi's PAYE and NICs due on 22 January 2023 will be reduced if he delays the payment of employee bonuses until 10 January 2023, and state when the postponed amount will be payable.

Note. Your calculations should be based on annual income tax and NIC thresholds.

(3 marks)

(Total = 10 marks)

OTQ bank - Mixed bank (18 mins)

326 In which of the following cases must an appeal be made directly to the Tribunal? ***(September 2019)***

- O A company appealing against a penalty for late filing of a corporation tax return
- O A company appealing against a penalty for late filing of employer year end returns
- O An individual appealing against a penalty for late registration for value added tax (VAT)
- O An individual appealing against a penalty for late payment of capital gains tax

(2 marks)

---

327 Giant Ltd is a large company, and therefore pays its corporation tax by instalments.

For the eight-month period ended 31 August 2022, the company estimated that its corporation tax liability would be £400,000.

What would Giant Ltd's first corporation tax instalment be in respect of the eight-month period ended 31 August 2022, and what is the due date of this instalment? ***(December 2019)***

- O £100,000 on 14 April 2022
- O £100,000 on 14 July 2022
- O £150,000 on 14 April 2022
- O £150,000 on 14 July 2022

(2 marks)

---

328 Daniel has had a 30% share in a manufacturing partnership since 2016. He intends to dispose of his entire interest in the partnership in the tax year 2022/23 by selling it to his son for less than its market value.

Daniel has also been a director and 10% shareholder in an unquoted investment company since 2012. He has decided to gift his shares to his daughter in the tax year 2022/23.

Which TWO of the following statements are true? **(March 2020)**

- ☐ Business asset disposal relief is available on the disposal of the interest in the partnership but not on the shares
- ☐ Business asset disposal relief is available on the disposal of the shares but not on the interest in the partnership
- ☐ Business asset disposal relief is available on both disposals
- ☐ Gift holdover relief is available on the disposal of the interest in the partnership but not on the shares
- ☐ Gift holdover relief is available on the disposal of the shares but not the interest in the partnership
- ☐ Gift holdover relief is available on both disposals **(2 marks)**

---

329 Oliver got married on 5 October 2022 and Oliver's mother and father each gave him £25,000 as a wedding present.

Oliver's parents have not made any previous gifts for the purposes of inheritance tax (IHT).

For the purposes of IHT, what is the total amount of exemptions that can be deducted from the gifts made to Oliver? **(June 2020)**

- O £17,000
- O £10,000
- O £11,000
- O £22,000 **(2 marks)**

---

330 On 1 October 2022, Sou granted a 25-year lease of a freehold property in return for a premium of £20,000.

What is Sou's assessable property income for the tax year 2022/23 in respect of this lease premium? **(September/December 2020)**

- O £10,400
- O £9,600
- O £5,200
- O £10,000 **(2 marks)**

---

331 Brett commenced trading on 1 February 2022.

His sales (exclusive of value added tax (VAT)) were £5,500 a month for the first three months of trading, £7,500 for the next four months and £10,000 a month after that.

From what date will Brett have to charge output VAT on his supplies? **(September/December 2020)**

- O 1 March 2023
- O 1 January 2023
- O 30 January 2023
- O 1 February 2023 **(2 marks)**

---

332 Which TWO of the following statements about allowable capital losses for an individual are true? ***(September/December 2020)***

☐ The annual exempt amount is deducted before any brought forward capital losses are utilised against current year gains

☐ Current year capital losses remaining after offset against current year chargeable gains can always be offset against current year income

☐ The annual exempt amount is deducted before any current year capital losses are utilised against current year gains

☐ Excess current year capital losses are carried forward indefinitely until future chargeable gains arise **(2 marks)**

---

333 Ella arrived in the UK to work as a nanny on 1 February 2022. She has never previously visited the UK. Ella lived with a family, for whom she worked full-time, until 31 August 2022.

On 1 September 2022 Ella left the UK to attend university in another country. As a result of this visit to the UK, Ella stayed in the UK for 65 days during the tax year 2021/22 and 148 days during the tax year 2022/23. For these two tax years, Ella was neither automatically not resident in the UK nor automatically resident.

What is Ella's UK residency status for each of the tax years 2021/22 and 2022/23? ***(September/December 2021)***

○ Resident in both years

○ Not resident in either year

○ Resident in 2021/22 but not in 2022/23

○ Resident in 2022/23 but not in 2021/22 **(2 marks)**

---

334 Gabe died on 22 November 2022. During his lifetime, Gabe had made the following potentially exempt transfers (PETs), after all available exemptions:

5 May 2014 Cash to his daughter	£200,000
12 July 2018 An antique painting to his son	£370,000

The inheritance tax (IHT) nil rate band for the tax years 2014/15 and 2018/19 is £325,000.

What is the amount of the nil rate band available in calculating the additional IHT due on the gift of the antique painting as a result of Gabe's death? ***(September/December 2021)***

£ [ ] **(2 marks)**

335 Naomi realised a chargeable gain of £30,000 in the tax year 2022/23. The gain related to the disposal of a residential property held for investment purposes and did not qualify for business asset disposal relief. In the tax year 2022/23, Naomi had taxable income of £29,500 and she contributed £2,000 (net) into her personal pension scheme.

What is Naomi's capital gains tax liability for the tax year 2022/23?

(September/December 2021)

- O £3,886
- O £7,330
- O £4,136
- O £7,580

(2 marks)

(Total = 20 marks)

Answers

Section A

OTQ bank – The UK tax system and its administration 1

1 The correct answers are:

- It is a progressive tax.
- It is a redistributive tax.

Inheritance tax is a progressive tax as the amount of tax payable as a proportion of the transfers increases as the transfers get bigger (the amount covered by the nil rate band is charged at 0% and the remainder at 20% or 40%). It is also a redistributive tax as it redistributes wealth.

Inheritance tax is a direct tax and it is not an environmental tax.

2 The correct answers are:

- A Statutory Instrument
- An Act of Parliament

Statutes (Acts of Parliament) and Statutory Instruments have legal force.

HMRC publications such as Revenue and Customs Briefs and Extra Statutory Concessions do not have legal force.

3 The correct answer is: By the Upper Tribunal

The Upper Tribunal deals with complex cases which either involve an important issue of tax law or a large financial sum.

4 The correct answer is:

Notification	**Payment**
5 October 2023	31 January 2024

The chargeable gain arises in the tax year 2022/23 and so Daren must notify HMRC of his chargeability within six months from the end of the tax year. The tax liability must be paid by 31 January following the end of the tax year.

5 The correct answer is: £742

Potential Lost Revenue is the tax payable of £2,120 (40% × £5,300).

The minimum penalty for a prompted, deliberate, but not concealed error is 35% × PLR which is £742.

The answer £1,484 uses 70% which is the maximum penalty for a deliberate, but not concealed error. The answer £424 uses 20% which is the minimum penalty for an unprompted deliberate, but not concealed error.

The answer £1,855 uses £5,300 as the Potential Lost Revenue.

6 The correct answer is: £1,801

Due date 1 April 2023, paid 31 July 2023 so four months late. Interest is:

4/12 × 3.25% × £166,250	£1,801

The answer £450 assumes the due date is 1 July 2023 so that one month's interest is due. The answer £2,701 assumes the due date is 31 January 2023 so that six months' interest is due. The answer £5,403 is one whole year of interest.

7 The correct answer is: Year ended 31 December 2025

The profit threshold for being a large company is £1,500,000/2 = £750,000 since there is one related 51% group company. This threshold is first exceeded in the year ended 31 December 2024 but a company is not required to pay its corporation tax by instalments in the first year that it is large unless its profits exceed £10,000,000, as reduced by related 51% group companies. Mammoth Ltd is also a large company in the year ended 31 December 2025 and so must pay its corporation tax liability by quarterly instalments for that year for the first time.

8 The correct answers are:

Value added tax	**NEITHER TYPE**		
Inheritance tax		**CAPITAL TAX**	
National insurance contributions			**REVENUE TAX**

9 £406,600

	£
Unconnected company	5,200
Group dividend	0
Non-51% group dividend	1,400
Taxable total profits	400,000
Profits	406,600

10 The correct answer is: £1,420

The tax return is submitted more than six but less than twelve months late. The penalties payable are therefore:

- £100 (initial penalty)
- £900 (daily penalties of £10 per day for a maximum of 90 days – this is applicable since the return is 3 months late and outstanding for the full 90 days)
- £420 (5% × £8,400 – this is applicable as the return is over 6 months late)

The alternative, incorrect options are as follows:

- £100 being the initial penalty only
- £1,000 being the initial penalty of £100 plus maximum daily penalties of £10 × 90
- £1,300 being the initial penalty of £100 plus maximum daily penalties of £10 × 90 plus minimum tax geared penalty of £300

OTQ bank – The UK tax system and its administration 2

11 The correct answers are:

31 January 2024	Submission
30 April 2025	Notification

As the return is filed after the due filing date, the notification must be made by the quarter day following the first anniversary of the actual filing date.

12 £5,164

	£
Income tax £(12,500 – 10,000 payments on account)	2,500
Class 2 NIC	164
Class 4 NIC £(2,500 – 2,000 payments on account)	500
Capital gains tax	2,000
Amount to pay on 31 January 2023	5,164

The answer £5,000 does not include the Class 2 NIC. The answer £4,005 assumes that payments on account are made also for Class 2 NIC and capital gains tax. The answer £4,164 assumes that payments on account are made also for capital gains tax.

13 £ 34

£10,000 is paid by the due date of 1 January 2024. The balance of £12,400 is one month late so the interest on late paid tax is £12,400 × 3.25% × 1/12 = £34.

14 The correct answer is: £50,000 due on 14 May 2023

The amount of each of the first three instalments is 3/10 × £500,000 = £150,000. The final instalment is the remaining liability of £500,000 – (3 × £150,000) = £50,000, and is due on the 14th day of the 4th month of the next accounting period.

15 £ 100

There is a £100 penalty for late return which is submitted within three months of the due date (here 12 months after the end of the period to which the return relates).

16 The correct answer is: Asset 1 only

Lying about a disposal date so that a gain is declared a year later amounts to tax evasion, which is illegal. Delaying a disposal until the next tax year is a legitimate example of tax planning.

17 10%

The due date for payment was 31 January 2023. The penalty date is 30 days after the due date for the tax. There is a penalty of 5% of the unpaid tax for failing to pay by the penalty date plus a further penalty of 5% of the unpaid tax as the payment is more than five months after the penalty date but not more than 11 months after the penalty date.

18 The correct answer is: 5 April 2043

ACCA Examining Team's Comments

This was a straightforward administration question, requiring candidates to identify the latest date by which HMRC can raise a discovery assessment where a taxpayer has made a deliberate error in their tax return. Where deliberate error is involved, the time limit for HMRC to raise a discovery assessment is 20 years from the end of the tax year, in this case 5 April 2043.

The majority of candidates selected 5 April 2024, suggesting that they had confused the deadline for a raising a discovery assessment with the deadline for notifying the taxpayer of a compliance check. 5 April 2027 is the basic deadline for issuing a discovery assessment, and 5 April 2029 is the deadline for issuing a discovery assessment where the taxpayer has made a careless error.

Candidates are reminded to devote sufficient attention to tax administration in their revision.

19 Make a determination

If notice has been served on a taxpayer to submit a return but the return is not submitted by the due filing date, an officer of HMRC may make a determination, to the best of their information and belief, of the amounts liable to income tax and CGT and of the tax due, within four years of the end of the relevant tax year.

ACCA Examining Team's Comments

This question tested candidates' knowledge of how HMRC can make a determination of the amount of tax that a taxpayer is liable to. Perhaps not surprisingly, more than 40% of candidates opted for 'start a compliance check enquiry into the return' – possibly because a compliance check was the most well-known of the options. However, the correct answer (a determination) was the second most popular choice. Although this style of question can be answered very quickly, it does not mean that it doesn't warrant any thought. Realising that a compliance check by its very nature involves a submitted return, could have easily ruled this option out.

20 The correct answer is: £62

ACCA Examining Team's Comments

This question tested candidates' ability to calculate late payment interest where an excessive claim has been made to reduce a payment on account. Answers were spread fairly evenly over the four choices, indicating that many candidates simply made an educated guess. Although not an easy question, taking a careful approach with amounts and dates would probably have achieved the correct answer. The most important point was the £6,000 payment on 30 September 2023, which was two months late. The final payment was made on time. Therefore, £7,800 was late for two months (31 July to 30 September 2023) and £1,800 (£7,800 – £6,000) was late for four months (1 October 2023 to 31 January 2024). The interest at 3.25% is £62, ie (£7,800 × 3.25% × 2/12) + (£1,800 × 3.25% × 4/12), making a total of £62. An alternative working would have been £6,000 late for two months and £1,800 late for six months. This question demonstrates just how much care needs to be taken with dates when calculating interest payable on late tax payments.

OTQ bank – The UK tax system and its administration 3

21 The correct answer is: The returns for the year ended 31 December 2022 and the period ended 31 March 2023 must both be filed by 31 March 2024.

ACCA Examining Team's Comments

This was a straightforward question on filing dates for corporation tax for a long period. The correct answer is the fourth option. Two tax returns are required, one for the year ended 31 December 2022 and one for the period ended 31 March 2023, however both of them have the same filing date and must be filed by 31 March 2024. Most candidates selected the third option, for each return being filed 12 months after the period end, and others selected the first option, using the payment dates rather than filing dates.

22 The correct answer is: 1 March 2023

ACCA Examining Team's Comments

This was another tax administration question on the date which a company must notify HMRC of its first accounting period. A company must notify HMRC of the beginning of its first accounting period within three months. The company was incorporated on 1 October 2022 but did not start to trade until 1 December 2022, and it is the date the

company started to trade that is relevant here, so the correct answer is the third option, 1 March 2023. Most candidates chose the second option, being three months after the company was incorporated, with the next most popular answer being the first option, the date that the company started to trade (or two months after the company was incorporated). The fourth option, being 12 months after the first accounts for the period to 30 June 2023, was also selected by more candidates than the correct answer. Tax administration is an important area of the syllabus, so future candidates should ensure they cover this area in their preparation.

23 The correct answer is: £1,700

ACCA Examining Team's Comments

If Dee Ltd files its tax return for the year ended 31 December 2022 on 31 August 2024, this would be eight months late, as it was due on 31 December 2023. As Dee Ltd had already been late filing its last two corporation tax returns, then the correct answer is £1,700, being a fixed penalty of £1,000 and a tax geared penalty of £700 (10% of £7,000). However, most candidates opted for the tax geared penalty of £700.

24 The correct answer is: 30 April 2024

ACCA Examining Team's Comments

If the taxpayer amends the return after the due filing date, as in the case of Petula, then the time limit for a compliance check is extended to the quarter day following the first anniversary of the date the amendment was filed. Since Petula amended her return on 29 March 2023, this is within the quarter ended 30 April 2023 and so the time limit for the compliance check is 30 April 2024.

31 January 2024 is the first anniversary of the due filing date.

20 September 2023 is the first anniversary of the actual filing date.

29 March 2024 is the first anniversary of the date that the amended return was filed.

Candidates' answers were mixed, with 30 April 2024 being the least popular answer, suggesting that most candidates weren't prepared for a question on this topic.

25 The correct answer is: Partnerships must file a separate return and account for each partner's tax through this return

ACCA Examining Team's Comments

The answer which is false is the second option. This is because each partner must include their share of partnership profits on their own personal tax return, not the partnership tax return. The third option was the most commonly chosen. This suggests that candidates' knowledge of tax administration could be improved.

Section B

OT case – Domingo and Fargo (June 2009) (amended)

26 The correct answer is:

Domingo	**Fargo**
31 October2023	31 January 2024

27 The correct answer is:

Domingo	***Fargo***
31 January 2025	31 January 2029

Domingo was not in business during 2022/23, so his records must be retained until one year after 31 January following the tax year, which is 31 January 2025.

Fargo was in business during 2022/23, so all of his records (both business and non-business) must be retained until five years after 31 January following the tax year, which is 31 January 2029.

28 The correct answer is: £3,000

29 The correct answer is:

Balancing payment 2022/23 and first POA 2023/24	**Second POA 2023/24**
31 January 2024	31 July 2024

30 The correct answer is: Interest £20, penalty £90

Interest £1,800 × 3.25% × 4/12 = £20

The answer £59 is the interest for a whole year.

Penalty £1,800 @ 5% = £90 (balancing payment not more than five months after the penalty date).

OT case – Ernest (June 2010) (amended)

Workbook references

Self-assessment for individuals is covered in Chapter 17. Ethics are covered in Chapter 1.

Top tips

If your firm ceases to act for a client, it must notify HMRC that it has ceased to act but not the reasons for doing so.

Easy marks

The definitions of tax evasion and tax avoidance should be well known.

31 The correct answers are:

Tax evasion is illegal.	**TRUE**	
Both tax evasion and tax avoidance are illegal.		**FALSE**
Tax avoidance is legal but may fail if challenged in the courts by HMRC.	**TRUE**	

Tax evasion always involves providing HM Revenue & Customs with false information.		**FALSE**

Tax evasion does not necessarily involve providing HM Revenue & Customs (HMRC) with false information. It could include this situation where Ernest is evading tax by not providing HMRC with information to which it is entitled.

32 The correct answers are:

- Ernest should be advised to disclose details of the capital gain to HMRC.
- If Ernest does not disclose the gain to HMRC, your firm would be obliged to report under the money laundering regulations.

Your firm should also consider ceasing to act for Ernest. If it does cease to act, your firm should notify HMRC that it no longer acts for him although your firm should not provide any reason for this.

33 The correct answer is: £12,600

The maximum penalty for an error which is deliberate but not concealed is 70% of potential lost revenue which is £18,000 × 70% = £12,600.

34 £6,300

The minimum penalty for prompted disclosure of an error which is deliberate but not concealed is 35% of potential lost revenue which is £18,000 × 35% = £6,300.

35 The correct answer is: £293

The due date for payment was 31 January 2023 so the payment is six months late. The interest payable is therefore £18,000 × 3.25% × 6/12 = £293.

OT case – Thai Curry Ltd

Workbook references

Chapter 23 deals with corporation tax administration. Chapter 17 contains material on the common penalty regime for errors.

Top tips

Remember that some elements of tax administration are the same for both individuals and companies such as penalties for errors. However, you need to watch out for circumstances where they are different such as the penalties for late filing.

Easy marks

Make sure you know due dates for returns and tax payments.

36 31 March 2024

The CT return must be submitted one year after the end of the period of account ie by 31 March 2024.

37 £3,462

As the return is more than three months late the fixed penalty is £200. As the return is more than six months late there is also a tax geared penalty of 10% × unpaid tax, ie £32,624 × 10% = £3,262. The total amount of penalties is therefore £(200 + 3,262) = £3,462.

38 The correct answer is: £32,624 on 1 January 2024

As the company is not large since its profits are below the profit threshold of £1,500,000 it must pay its corporation tax by nine months and one day after the accounting period, ie by 1 January 2024.

39 The correct answers are:

- An internal review is a less costly and more effective way to resolve disputes informally than a formal appeal.
- HMRC must usually carry out the review within 45 days.

An internal review is a less costly and more effective way to resolve disputes informally than a formal appeal and HMRC must usually carry out the review within 45 days. The internal review will be made by an objective HMRC review officer not previously connected with the case. After the review conclusion is notified, the company has 30 days to appeal to the Tax Tribunal.

40 The correct answers are:

Upper tier	Complex track
First tier	Standard track

Section C

41 John

Workbook references

Self-assessment for individuals is covered in Chapter 17. The UK tax system is the subject of Chapter 1.

Top tips

There are a number of penalties based on potential lost revenue, so you need to be able to explain what this is.

Easy marks

There were some easy marks for the date for notification and the date by which the compliance check needed to be started.

Marking guide			Marks	
(a)	(i)	Date for notification	1	
		Maximum penalty	1	
		Minimum penalty	1	
				3
	(ii)	Compliance check notification date	1	
		Random basis	1	
		Other reasons	1	
				3
(b)	(i)	Saving		
				1
	(ii)	Charitable support		
				1
	(iii)	Capital gains reliefs	1	
		Plant and machinery	1	
				2
Total				10

(a) (i) **Notification of chargeability**

John should have given notice to HM Revenue & Customs (HMRC) of his chargeability to income tax for 2021/22 by 5 October 2022.

The maximum penalty for careless late notification is 30% of the Potential Lost Revenue (PLR) to HMRC which will be John's tax payable on the return for 2021/22.

However, if John tells HMRC of his failure to notify within 12 months and John has no reason to believe HMRC has discovered, or is about to discover, the error (unprompted disclosure) as appears to be the case here, the penalty can be reduced by HMRC to 0%.

(ii) **Compliance check**

If HMRC intends to carry out a compliance check enquiry into John's 2021/22 tax return, it will have to notify him by the first anniversary of the actual filing date.

HMRC has the right to carry out a compliance check enquiry as regards the completeness and accuracy of any return, and some returns are selected for a compliance check enquiry at random.

Other returns are selected for a particular reason; for example, if HMRC believes that there has been an underpayment of tax due to the taxpayer's failure to comply with tax legislation.

(b) (i) Saving is encouraged by offering individuals tax incentives such as income tax and capital gains tax exemptions on individual savings accounts and income tax relief on pension contributions.

(ii) Charitable support is encouraged by giving individuals income tax relief on donations made through the gift aid scheme or by payroll deduction.

(iii) Entrepreneurs are encouraged to build their own businesses through various capital gains tax reliefs such as business asset disposal relief.

Investment in plant and machinery is encouraged through capital allowances.

42 Sugar plc

Workbook references

Chapter 19 deals with computing the corporation tax liability. Chapter 23 includes payment of tax by companies.

Top tips

The rules on related 51% group companies are highly examinable and could be tested as an objective test question or in a constructed response question.

Easy marks

The calculation of the corporation tax liability in part (c) was straightforward.

Marking guide		Marks
(a) Definition	1	
Honey plc	0.5	
Molasses plc	0.5	
Treacle plc	1	
		3
(b) Year ended 31 March 2023		
Profit limit	0.5	
Taxable total profits	0.5	
Dividends	1	
Profits, therefore large	0.5	
Year ended 31 March 2024		
Taxable total profits = profits, therefore large	0.5	
		3
(c) Year ended 31 March 2023		
Corporation tax	0.5	
Date payable	0.5	
Year ended 31 March 2024		
Corporation tax	0.5	

Marking guide	Marks	
Instalments	0.5	
Dates payable	2	
		4
Total		10

(a) Company B is a related 51% group company of another company A, if A is a 51% subsidiary of B (B owns more than 50% of A's ordinary shares directly or indirectly) or B is a 51% subsidiary of A or both A and B are 51% subsidiaries of another company. Honey plc is not a related 51% group company of Sugar plc because Sugar plc only directly owns 45% of the ordinary shares of Honey plc. Molasses plc is a related 51% group company of Sugar plc because Sugar plc directly owns 75% of the ordinary shares of Molasses plc. Treacle plc is a related 51% group company of Sugar plc because Sugar plc indirectly owns 75% × 70% = 52.5% of the ordinary shares of Treacle plc.

(b) *Year ended 31 March 2023*

Sugar plc has two related 51% group companies (Molasses plc and Treacle plc) at the end of the previous accounting period. The profit limit is therefore £1,500,000/3 = £500,000. Sugar plc's profits for the year to 31 March 2023 are:

	£
Taxable total profits	470,000
Dividends from non-group companies	50,000
Profits	520,000

Sugar plc is therefore a large company in the year to 31 March 2023.

Year ended 31 March 2024

The profit limit is the same and Sugar plc's taxable total profits of £600,000 are also its profits for these purposes. Sugar plc is therefore a large company in the year to 31 March 2024.

(c) Year ended 31 March 2023

	£
Corporation tax liability	
£470,000 × 19%	89,300

Since this is the first year that Sugar plc is a large company, its corporation tax liability will be due in one amount on 1 January 2024.

Year ended 31 March 2024

	£
Corporation tax liability	
£600,000 × 19%	114,000

This is payable in four equal instalments of £28,500. The instalments will be due on 14 October 2023, 14 January 2024, 14 April 2024 and 14 July 2024.

Section A

OTQ bank – Income tax and NIC liabilities 1

43 The correct answer is: 90

> **ACCA Examining Team's Comments**
>
> This question examines the third automatic non-UK residency test. For an individual to meet this test, and therefore be treated as automatically not resident in the UK for the tax year 2022/23, they would have to work full-time overseas and spend less than 91 days in the UK. Therefore, because Hana worked full-time in Egypt throughout 2022/23, he will be treated as automatically not resident in the UK for the tax year as long as he spends no more than 90 days in the UK.
>
> The correct answer is therefore 90, however, answer option 15 was most commonly chosen. This would be the correct answer using the sufficient ties tests. However, the sufficient ties tests are only used to determine residence status if none of the automatic non-UK residence tests (and none of the automatic UK residence tests) is met.
>
> This suggests that candidates may not have been familiar enough with the residence tests and the procedure to determine residence.

44 The correct answers are:

- Premium bond prizes
- Dividends on shares held in an Individual Savings Account

Interest on an NS&I Investment account and interest on UK government stocks ('gilts') are taxable as savings income.

45 The correct answer is: £2,500

	£
£3,000 @ 20%	600
£(5,000 – 3,000) = £2,000 @ 0% (starting rate band)	0
£1,000 @ 0% (savings income nil rate band)	0
£(12,500 – 2,000 – 1,000) = £9,500 @ 20%	1,900
Tax liability	2,500

The answer £2,900 does not apply the starting rate band. The answer £2,700 does not apply the savings income nil rate band. The answer £3,100 applies 20% to all income.

46 The correct answer is: £2,448

	£
Taxable income	13,500
Tax	
£13,500 ×20%	2,700
Less transferred personal allowance tax reducer £1,260 × 20%	(252)
Income tax liability	2,448

The answer £186 assumes that Delia can transfer her full personal allowance to Mike. The answer £1,440 deducts £1,260 as a tax reducer. The answer £2,700 is Mike's income tax liability with no transfer.

47 The correct answer is: £3,300

		£
Use: £3,600 × 20%		720
Gift: Current market value	£1,000	
or		
Original value	£3,600	
Less use:		
2021/22 £720 × 5/12	(300)	
2022/23	(720)	
	£2,580	
The greater amount is taken		2,580
Total benefits 2022/23		3,300

Note. That the value of the asset when first provided to any employee is used rather than the value when first provided to John.

The answer £2,880 assumes the first year of provision was taxed in full. The answer £1,720 uses the lower value for the gift rather than the higher value. The answer £1,833 uses the value of £2,000 when the asset was provided to John.

48 The correct answer is: £58,960

	£
£(37,700 + 10,000) = £47,700 @ 20%	9,540
£(150,000 + 10,000) = £(160,000 – 47,700) = £112,300 @ 40%	44,920
£(170,000 – 160,000) = £10,000 @ 45%	4,500
Tax liability	58,960

The answer £59,460 does not adjust the higher rate limit. The answer £61,460 does not adjust either the basic rate limit or the higher rate limit. The answer £53,432 deducts the personal allowance.

49 The correct answer is: £567

	£
Net income	57,000
Less personal pension contributions (gross)	(2,000)
Adjusted net income	55,000
Less threshold	(50,000)
Excess	5,000
÷ £100	50
Child benefit income tax charge: 1% × £1,134 × 50	567

The answer £1,134 assumes there is full recovery of child benefit. The answer £454 is the child benefit times 40%. The answer £794 does not adjust for pension contributions.

50 The correct answer is: £22,500

The bonus received on 30 September 2022 is taxable in 2022/23 as the receipts basis applies to employment income.

The gratuity received on 1 December 2022 is taxable as employment income in 2022/23 as it is a reward of the employment even though it was not received from the employer.

51 The correct answers are:

- Travel from employer's office to visit a client
- Travel from home to visit a trade fair relevant to the employer's business 100 miles away from permanent place of work

Travel from home to a workplace to which an employee has been seconded for 36 months does not qualify as travel to a temporary workplace as the secondment exceeds 24 months. Travel from home to a permanent place of work is not a qualifying travel expense.

52 The correct answer is: £6,000

ACCA Examining Team's Comments

The provision of job-related accommodation does not give rise to a taxable benefit in kind for the employee however, where ancillary services are also provided (ie the household bills and furniture) an assessable benefit in kind does arise. Where the accommodation is job-related, the assessable amount for these benefits is limited to 10% of net remuneration excluding the household costs, giving £6,000 (10% of £60,000) in this example. However, the answer £9,000 was most commonly chosen. This would be the correct answer if the accommodation was not job-related. It is calculated as the cost to the employer of the household bills, plus the use of furniture, calculated at 20% of the cost of the asset, giving £9,000 (£7,000 + (20% × £10,000)). This suggests that candidates may not have been aware of the rule to restrict the assessable amount where the accommodation is job-related.

OTQ bank – Income tax and NIC liabilities 2

53 The correct answers are:

£333	Marion
£167	Gerald

	£
Marion	
Accrued interest deemed received 31.12.22 taxable savings income	
£20,000 × 5% × 4/12	333
Gerald	
Interest received 31.12.22	
£20,000 × 5% × 6/12	500
Less relief for accrued interest (amount taxable on Marion)	
£20,000 × 5% × 4/12	(333)
Taxable savings income	167

54 The correct answer is: £5,800

CO_2 emission (rounded down)	100
Base figure	(55)
	45
Divided by 5	9
Starting percentage	16
Diesel addition	4
Final percentage	29
Benefit £20,000 (list price) × 29%	£5,800

The answer £4,500 uses actual cost (not list price) and there is no diesel addition. The answer £5,220 uses actual cost. The answer £5,000 does not use the diesel addition.

55 £55,000

	£
2022/23 annual allowance	40,000
2021/22 annual allowance £(40,000 – 25,000)	15,000
	55,000

The annual allowance for 2019/20 and 2020/21 are not available as Troy was not a member of a pension scheme in those years.

The answer £40,000 is the current year annual allowance. The answer £135,000 brings forward allowances from all three previous tax years. The answer £35,000 restricts the current year allowance to £10,000.

56 The correct answer is: £300

	£
Rental income £150 × 52	7,800
Less rent a room limit	(7,500)
	300

Luke should elect for the 'alternative basis' under rent a room relief, rather the normal basis which would give taxable property business income of £(150 – 20) = £130 × 52 = £6,760.

57 The correct answer is: £3,800

The replacement of an equivalent model of sofa is allowable as a deduction. It is restricted by the amount of proceeds realised by selling the first sofa.

£(4,000 – 200) = £3,800

The answer £5,500 allows the full cost of the enhancement of furniture. The answer £5,300 allows the cost of the enhancement of furniture less the proceeds of the first sofa. The answer £4,000 is the cost of the replacement sofa.

58 £2,470

	£
Rent received 3 × £900	2,700
Security deposit	0
Less: Insurance premium paid	(150)
Motoring expenses 178 × 45p	(80)
Taxable property business income 2022/23	2,470

The answer £1,932 uses the accruals basis for the rent and the insurance premium paid. The answer £2,970 includes the security deposit: this will only become a receipt when Amrul is legally entitled to retain some or all of it at the end of the tenancy.

The answer £2,505 uses the rate of 25p per mile for the motoring expenses.

59 £ 5,400

Depreciation and customer entertaining are not deductible and must be added back. The amount added back is therefore £(3,000 + 2,400) = £5,400.

Staff entertaining is fully deductible (the £150 limit applies to the taxable benefit for the employees).

60 £ 20,375

	£
Cash sales	41,000
Invoice sales £(4,000 – 1,500)	2,500
Less: Cash expenses	(20,200)
Motoring expenses 6,500 × 45p	(2,925)
Taxable trading income 2022/23	20,375

61 The correct answer is: £3,600

£(12,000 – 6,000) × 60% = £3,600

The answer £2,400 is the private use amount of £(12,000 – 6,000) × 40%.

The answer £648 uses the writing down allowance (WDA) and at the rate of 18% which does not apply to high emission cars.

The answer £216 uses the WDA at the rate of 6%.

ACCA Examining Team's Comments

This question required candidates to demonstrate their knowledge in respect of capital allowances on cars, where there was a disposal of a car during the year which was also used for private use by Olive.

As the car was disposed of during the year, candidates need to recognise that a balancing allowance arose on its disposal, and that the amount of capital allowance Olive could claim was restricted to the business use element (ie 60%).

Many candidates instead chose the fourth answer, continuing to write down the cost of the car, rather than calculating a balancing allowance. Candidates are reminded that cars which are used partly for private use by a sole trader are put into their own pool and on disposal a balancing charge or allowance may arise.

62 £417,667

	AIA	Main pool	Allowance
	£	£	£
p/e 5.4.23			
Plant	430,000		
AIA £1,000,000 × 5/12	(416,667)		416,667
Transfer to pool	13,333	13,333	
WDA @ 18% × 5/12		(1,000)	1,000
TWDV c/f	–	12,333	–
Allowances			417,667

The answer £339,133 time apportions from the date of acquisition rather than the length of the period of account. The answer £419,067 does not time apportion the WDA. The answer £430,000 is the unrestricted annual investment allowance.

OTQ bank – Income tax and NIC liabilities 3

63 The correct answer is: £400

	Main pool	Allowances
	£	£
y/e 5.4.23		
TWDV b/f	12,000	
Disposal (limit to cost)	(11,600)	
	400	
WDA – small pool	(400)	400
TWDV c/f	0	

64 The correct answers are:

6 April 2022	Start date
5 April 2023	End date

2022/23 is the second year of trading. There is no accounting date ending in this year so the actual basis applies.

65 £ 13,000

First tax year (2020/21): Actual basis 1.2.21 to 5.4.21

Second tax year (2021/22): First 12 months of trading 1.2.21 to 31.1.22

Third tax year (2022/23): Current year basis 1.12.21 to 30.11.22

Periods of overlap 1.2.21 to 5.4.21 and 1.12.21 to 31.1.22

	£
2/10 × £30,000	6,000
2/12 × £42,000	7,000
	13,000

66 £ 15,900

The seven-month period to 31 January 2023 ends in 2022/23 which is the final tax year. The penultimate tax year (2021/22) will be assessed on the current year basis; ie the accounting period ending in the tax year, being the year ended 30 June 2021.

Therefore, 2022/23 will catch the remaining untaxed profits less the overlap profits; being profits for the year ended 30 June 2022 of £11,200 plus profits of the final seven-month period of £7,300 less the overlap profits of £2,600 = £15,900.

67 The correct answers are:

£3,000	2021/22
£9,600	2022/23

	£
2021/22 Actual basis 1.1.22 to 5.4.22	
£9,000 × 3/9	3,000
2022/23 First 12 months 1.1.22 to 31.12.22	
£(9,000 – 3,000)	6,000
£14,400 × 3/12	3,600
	9,600

68 The correct answer is: 31 January 2025

ACCA Examining Team's Comments

This question examines knowledge of the deadline for an individual taxpayer to claim relief for a trading loss which they wish to offset in the tax year prior to the tax year in which the loss arose. The correct answer is the second option (31 January 2025), as a claim must be made within one year of 31 January following the end of the tax year in which the loss arose. Therefore, as the loss arose in the tax year 2022/23, a claim for relief must be made by 31 January 2025.

The second option was the most common answer selected but a significant number of candidates also chose each of the other answer options, suggesting that many candidates were not well prepared for a question on this topic.

The second most common answer was the first option (31 January 2024) which is the deadline for submitting a personal tax return online for the tax year 2022/23. Candidates may have selected this date as they are familiar with this deadline in relation to the tax year 2022/23 and assumed the deadline for claiming the loss would be the same.

Administration deadlines, both for individuals and companies, are an important part of the syllabus and future candidates are reminded of the importance of learning, and being able to distinguish between, the different deadlines as part of their studies.

69 £ 44,150

	£
1.8.21 to 31.8.21 1/12 × £96,000 × 1/2	4,000
1.9.21 to 31.7.22 Salary 11/12 × £9,000	8,250
1.9.21 to 31.7.22 Profit share ((11/12 × £96,000) – 8,250) × 2/5	31,900
	44,150

70 The correct answers are:

£48,000	Robin and Stuart each
£5,600	Tania

Robin and Stuart

CYB y/e 31.12.22 £96,000 × 1/2 = £48,000

Tania

Actual basis 1.1.23 – 5.4.23 £112,000 × 1/5 × 3/12 = £5,600

71 £ 139

	£
Class 2 contributions 14 × £3.15	44
Class 4 contributions £(13,500 – 12,570) × 10.25%	95
Total contributions	139

72 £ 218

	£
Class 4 contributions £([16,700 – 2,000] – 12,570) × 10.25%	218

OTQ bank - Income tax and NIC liabilities 4

73 £ 1,560

The emissions are between 1g and 50g per km so we need to use the electric range to determine the CO_2 percentage. The percentage for 39 miles is 12% and Katya had the car for six months. Therefore, the benefit is: £26,000 × 12% × 6/12 = £1,560

74 The correct answer is: £135

> **ACCA Examining Team's Comments**
>
> The correct answer was £135 (900 × 15.05%). This is because class 1A NIC is only charged on the gym membership and it is calculated based on the cost to the employer (not what the employee would have paid). A number of candidates selected £406 as the correct answer. This was calculated by including the employer contributions into Bee's private pension in the calculation (ie (900 + 1,800) × 15.05%), which is incorrect as these contributions are exempt from class 1A NIC.

ANSWERS

75 £ 500

The percentage for electric cars with zero CO_2 emissions is 2% (per tax tables).

	£
List price	30,000
Less capital contribution (maximum)	(5,000)
	25,000
Car benefit £25,000 × 2%	£500

76 The correct answer is: £75,000

ACCA Examining Team's Comments

The correct answer is £75,000. This is because, the annual allowance of £40,000 is reduced by £1 for every £2 by which the individual's adjusted income exceeds the threshold of £240,000, subject to a minimum annual allowance of £4,000. So, Niamhe's annual allowance for the tax year 2022/23 is £40,000 – ((£270,000 – £240,000)/2)), giving £25,000. The annual allowance charge is the amount by which Niamhe's gross personal pension scheme contributions exceed her annual allowance (£100,000 – £25,000), giving £75,000.

A number of candidates selected £25,000, which is the annual allowance, rather than the annual allowance charge.

77 The correct answers are:

- Zara's taxable income is £62,430.
- A child benefit charge of £1,885 will be added to Zara's income tax liability.

ACCA Examining Team's Comments

Zara's taxable income is £62,430, which is calculated as follows:

	£
Employment income	65,000
Property business income (£20,000 × 50%)	10,000
	75,000
Personal allowance	(12,570)
Taxable income	62,430

The first statement is therefore correct. Note that income generated from assets which are owned jointly is split 50:50 between spouses regardless of the actual ownership percentage. Therefore, the property income of £20,000 is split evenly between Dane and Zara. A child benefit income tax charge arises when an individual is in receipt of child benefit and either they or their spouse/civil partner (or person with whom they live as if they are married or in a civil partnership) has adjusted net income above £50,000.

Zara's adjusted net income is above £50,000, and so a child benefit income tax charge will arise. Since Zara's adjusted net income of £62,430 is above £60,000, the child benefit income tax charge is equal to the full amount of child benefit received by Dane, ie £1,885. Therefore, the fourth statement is correct.

The second statement is incorrect. It is not possible for Zara to claim the transferable personal allowance from Dane, as she is a higher rate taxpayer. In order to claim the transferable personal allowance neither spouse/civil partner can be a higher or additional rate taxpayer.

The third statement is also incorrect. It would not be beneficial to Zara to make a joint election to HMRC specifying their actual ownership share in the property. In doing so, Zara would be taxed on 75% of the property income, ie £15,000 (20,000 × 75%). This would increase Zara's tax liability for the tax year 2022/23 and it would also mean that more of the income would be taxed at the higher rate of 40%, than under the current 50:50 split.

Section B

OT case – Ann, Basil and Chloe (December 2008) (amended)

Workbook references

Pensions are covered in Chapter 5. The computation of taxable income and the income tax liability are dealt with in Chapter 2.

Top tips

Remember that higher rate tax relief for personal pension contributions made by higher rate taxpayers is given by increasing the basic rate limit.

Easy marks

There were some easy marks for working out a basic tax liability.

78 The correct answers are:

- Individuals can always make gross pension contributions of £3,600 in 2022/23 even if they do not have any relevant earnings in that tax year.
- Relevant earnings relate both to contributions to personal pension schemes and to occupational pension schemes.

Unused relevant earnings cannot be carried forward. Relevant earnings include trading income, employment income and income from furnished holiday lettings.

79 The correct answers are:

Employer contributions do not count towards the annual allowance.		**FALSE**
The annual allowance can be carried forward for three years to the extent that it is unused in the tax year.	**TRUE**	
The annual allowance is available even if the individual is not a member of a pension scheme in a tax year and so can be carried forward.		**FALSE**
If tax-relievable pension contributions exceed the annual allowance, there is a charge to income tax.	**TRUE**	

80 £ 15,200

The available annual allowance is £(40,000 + 20,000) = £60,000 and so there is no annual allowance charge for the tax year 2022/23. The basic rate band limit is £(37,700 + 49,000) = £86,700 so all of Ann's taxable income is within the basic rate band.

Tax £76,000 × 20%	£15,200

81 £ 6,750

The annual allowance must be tapered because Basil's adjusted income before any deduction for the pension contribution is more than £150,000. Basil is still an additional rate taxpayer because his higher rate limit is lifted by the gross pension contribution.

Annual allowance	£
£40,000 – [½ × £(250,000 – 240,000)]	35,000

Excess pension contribution over annual allowance	£
£(50,000 – 35,000) @ 45%	6,750

82 The correct answer is: £720

Maximum personal pension contribution is £3,600 since Chloe has no relevant earnings. The pension tax relief is therefore £3,600 × 20% = £720. This relief will have been given at source. The remaining £4,600 contribution is not given tax relief.

OT case – Ae, Bee, Cae, and Eu (December 2018) (amended)

Workbook references

Partnerships are covered in Chapter 11. Assessable trading income is dealt with in Chapter 9 and capital allowances are covered in Chapter 8.

Top tips

Remember that there is no annual investment allowance nor writing down allowance in the final period of account.

Easy marks

There were easy marks for working out the trading income assessment.

83 The correct answer is: £32,500

	£
2021/22	
Second year, short period of account (first 12 months trading)	
1 July 2020 to 30 April 2021	
£54,000 × ½	27,000
1 May 2021 to 30 June 2021	
£66,000 × ½ × 2/12	5,500
	32,500

84 The correct answer is: £21,750

	£
Y/e 30 April 2023 – Cae joined 1 July 2022	
1 July 2022 to 30 April 2023	
£87,000 × 10/12 = 72,500 × 1/3	24,167
First year	
Actual basis 1 July 2022 – 5 April 2023	
£24,167 × 9/10	21,750

ANSWERS

85 The correct answer is: £61,200

	£
2023/24	
CYB y/e 30.6.23 Trading income	62,775
Less CAs	(1,575)
	61,200

86 The correct answer is: £3,108

	£
p/e 30.9.24	
TWDV b/f	5,883
Addition – office furniture	2,400
Disposal at cessation	(5,175)
Balancing allowance (no AIA or WDA in the final period of account)	3,108

87 The correct answer is: £57,908

	£
2024/25	
y/e 30.6.24 £(57,600 – 1,292)	56,308
p/e 30.9.24 £(14,400 – 3,000)	11,400
Less overlap profits	(9,800)
	57,908

OT case – Rosie and Sam (December 2012) (amended)

Top Tips

Personal pensions are covered in Chapter 5. The income tax treatment of investments is covered in Chapter 2 and the capital gains tax implications of investments are dealt with in Chapter 13.

Top tips

Remember that there is useful information contained in the Tax Tables provided in the examination. For example, the annual allowance amounts were vital and could be found in the Tax Tables. The annual limit for ISAs is also in the Tax Tables.

Easy marks

There were easy marks for identifying the tax consequences of flexible access drawdown.

88 The correct answer is: £38,000

In 2022/23, Rosie's adjusted income is greater than £312,000 so her annual allowance is tapered to £4,000.

Rosie was not a member of a pension scheme in 2019/20, so no annual allowance is available to carry forward from that year.

In 2020/21, she had income of £130,000 so her annual allowance does not need to be tapered. She made a gross pension contribution of £26,000 during that year, and her employer made a contribution of £10,000 so she had £(40,000 – 26,000 – 10,000) £4,000 annual allowance available to carry forward.

In 2021/22, her income was also below the threshold so the annual allowance does not need to be tapered. She did not make any pension contributions, but her employer made a contribution of £10,000 leaving £30,000 available to carry forward.

Therefore, the available annual allowance for 2022/23 is:

	£
2022/23	4,000
2019/20	0
2020/21	4,000
2021/22	30,000
	38,000

The answer £74,000 does not restrict the 2022/23 annual allowance to the minimum amount. The answer £114,000 gives full allowances for the current year plus three years brought forward, after accounting for the contribution in 2020/21 and 2021/22. The answer £78,000 includes the £40,000 annual allowance for 2019/20 that would have been available if Rosie had been a pension scheme member in that year.

89 If Rosie makes pension contributions in excess of her available annual allowances, there will be a charge to income tax at [45] % on the excess contributions.

Charge at **45%** on excess contributions

The annual allowance charge is calculated by taxing the excess contribution as an extra amount of income received by Rosie and so is charged at her highest rate of income tax.

90 The correct answer is:

Lump sum	***Rest of pension fund***
Up to 25% of fund can be taken as tax-free lump sum	Taxable as pension income when received

91 [£19,000]

The ISA amount 2022/23 is £20,000. Sam has already invested £6,000 in the tax year, so can invest a further £(20,000 – 6,000) = £14,000.

He can also replace the £5,000 withdrawn in October 2022 so the total amount he can now invest is £(14,000 + 5,000) = £19,000.

92 The correct answers are:

Exempt from both income tax and capital gains tax	Premium bonds
Chargeable to income tax, exempt from capital gains tax	Government securities

ANSWERS

OT case – Fang and Hong (December 2013) (amended)

Workbook references

The basis of assessment for sole traders is covered in Chapter 9. Relief for pre-trading expenditure is described in Chapter 7 and capital allowances in Chapter 8. Trading losses are dealt with in Chapter 10.

Top tips

It is important to identify the relevant tax years when dealing with the basis of assessment.

Easy marks

The identification of relief for overlap profits in question 89 should have been easy marks.

93 The correct answers are:

£30,640	2020/21
£45,960	2021/22

Tax year	*Basis of assessment*	£
2020/21	Actual – 1 August 2020 to 5 April 2021	
	£45,960 × 8/12	30,640
2021/22	12 months to accounting date in tax year	
	y/e 31 July 2021	45,960

94 The correct answer is: Against trading income on cessation

95 The correct answer is:

Trading expenditure	***Computer equipment***
Treated as incurred on 1 August 2020	Addition for capital allowances purposes based on market value at 1 August 2020

96 £31,000

	£
Trading profit	29,700
Less trading loss brought forward	(2,600)
	27,100
Property business profit	3,900
	31,000
Less trading loss carried back	(31,000)
Net income	0

If your choice was £18,430, you restricted the loss relief to keep the personal allowance in charge which is not permitted.

97 The correct answers are:

- The trading loss is first set against general income of the tax year 2021/22 and only any excess loss is set against chargeable gains of that year.
- The amount of chargeable gains for the tax year 2021/22 is computed ignoring the annual exempt amount for the purposes of this relief.

Both capital losses of the tax year 2021/22 and brought forward losses are taken into account for the purposes of this relief. Hong cannot specify the amount to be set against chargeable gains, so her annual exempt amount for the tax year 2021/22 may be wasted.

OT case – Chi (June 2014) (amended)

Workbook references

Chapter 2 covers the computation of taxable income and the income tax liability. National insurance contributions are the subject of Chapter 12. The cash basis of assessment is dealt with in Chapter 7.

Top tips

If the cash basis is used there are no capital allowances on the office equipment but the expenditure is instead deducted in the same way as a revenue expense.

Easy marks

The computation of income tax in question 93 should have been easy marks. There were some easy marks in question 97 for identifying cash receipts and payments.

98 £ 8,632

	£
Trading income/net income	53,000
Less personal allowance	(12,570)
Taxable income	40,430
Tax	
£37,700 @ 20%	7,540
£2,730 (40,430 – 37,700) @ 40%	1,092
	8,632

99 £ 3,953

	£
£(50,270 – 12,570) = £37,700 @ 10.25%	3,864
£(53,000 – 50,270) = £2,730 @ 3.25%	89
Total Class 4 contributions	3,953

100 The correct answers are:

- The trader can deduct capital expenditure on plant and machinery (other than cars) as business expenses rather than using capital allowances.
- A trader can start to use the cash basis if his receipts for the tax year do not exceed £150,000.

Accounts can be prepared to any date in the tax year as for the normal basis of assessment. Cash basis traders cannot offset losses against other income or gains; they can only carry them forward against profits of the cash basis trade.

101 The correct answer is: £5,300

	£
10,000 miles @ 45p	4,500
3,200 miles @ 25p	800
	5,300

Capital allowances are not relevant since purchases of equipment are deducted as an expense. The running and capital costs of owning a car are replaced by the deduction based on approved mileage allowances.

102 The correct answer is: Revenue £70,900, other expenses £7,300

Revenue £(72,500 – 1,600) = £70,900

Section C

103 Kagan

Workbook references

Income tax computations are the subject of Chapter 2. Pensions are covered in Chapter 4. Basic capital gains and inheritance tax are dealt with in Chapters 13 and 18.

Top tips

It is important to realise that the first two requirements only score 1 mark each and therefore the answers must be very straightforward. There is no need for lengthy and time-consuming calculations.

Easy marks

There were some easy marks in part (b) ii for dealing with the exempt income and personal allowance.

Examining team's comments

This question involved Kagan who had inherited quoted ordinary shares valued at £510,000. Kagan was unsure whether to retain the shares or sell some of them in order to make four alternative investments.

Retain the inherited shares: Kagan would have received dividend income of £15,300 in addition to his employment income of £400,000 (for which the income tax liability was given) for the tax year 2022/23.

Four alternative investments: These consisted of:

(1) A personal pension contribution of £100,000, with Kagan having sufficient unused annual allowances to cover the pension contribution. He would immediately have withdrawn £25,000 of the pension fund tax-free.

(2) Investing £50,000 in premium bonds.

(3) Investing £20,000 in a cash individual savings account (ISA).

(4) Purchasing a freehold property for £295,000, with the property then let out unfurnished.

After making the four investments, Kagan would have been left with £65,000 of inherited shares, on which he would have received dividend income of £1,950 for the tax year 2022/23.

Part (a) for 1 mark required candidates to calculate Kagan's revised income tax liability for the tax year 2022/23 if he retained the inherited shares. Although fairly well answered, many candidates used valuable time doing full before and after-tax computations. Kagan was clearly an additional rate taxpayer, so all that was required was to calculate the additional rate tax due on the dividend income and then add it to the provided figure of tax on the employment income.

Part (b)(i) for 1 mark required an explanation as to why little or no capital gains tax would have been payable if Kagan had sold some of his inherited shares. This was because assets are inherited at the value at the time of the deceased's death. If these assets are sold soon after being inherited, there will generally be a minimal increase in value (this fact was stated in the question), so any gain is likely to be covered by the annual exempt amount. It was pleasing to see that this part was well answered by those candidates who appreciated the tax treatment.

Part (b)(ii) for 6 marks required a calculation of Kagan's revised income tax liability for the tax year 2022/23 if he sold some of his inherited shares and made the four alternative investments. This section was reasonably well answered, but several points should be noted:

- The question stated that a full tax computation was required, so exempt items (pension lump sum, premium bond prizes and the interest from the ISA) should simply have been listed within the main computation and indicated as such by the use of zero (0) – not by an explanation.

- The non-availability of the personal allowance should have been indicated in the same manner. There was no need to justify the non-availability given the level of Kagan's income.
- Although there might only be a ½ mark available for recognising an exemption, it is important to know the various exemptions so that time is not spent producing unnecessary, and more complicated workings – such as applying the savings income nil rate band where the interest from the ISA was included as savings income.

Part (c) for 2 marks required candidates to state for each of the four alternative investments whether the investment would reduce Kagan's potential inheritance tax liability compared to him retaining the inherited shares. Unfortunately, this section was not well answered. Candidates need to remember, that unlike other taxes, there are few exemptions from inheritance tax. Therefore, the replacement of the quoted shares with either premium bonds, an ISA or freehold property would not have changed the value of Kagan's chargeable estate. However, the investment in the pension fund (which is not withdrawn) would have been outside of Kagan's estate, thereby reducing his potential IHT liability.

Marking guide

		Marks
(a) Revised income tax liability		
		1
(b) (i) Base cost value inherited		
		1
(ii) Employment income	0.5	
Pension lump sum	0.5	
Premium bond prizes	0.5	
Interest from ISA	0.5	
Property income	0.5	
Dividend income	0.5	
Personal allowance	0.5	
Income tax liability	2.5	
		6
(c) Pension fund outside estate	0.5	
Other investments	1.5	
		2
Total		10

(a) Kagan's revised income tax liability for 2022/23 will be £170,234 (165,000 + ((15,300 – 2,000) at 39.35%)).

(b) (i) The base cost of the shares will be their value at the time of the aunt's death (£510,000), so the minimal increase in value is likely to be covered by Kagan's annual exempt amount of £12,300.

(ii) **Kagan – Income tax liability 2022/23**

	£
Employment income	400,000
Pension lump sum	0
Premium bond prizes	0
Interest from ISA	0

	£
Property income	9,600
Dividend income	1,950
	411,550
Personal allowance	0
Taxable income	411,550

Income tax

£37,700 at 20%	7,540
£100,000 at 20%	20,000
£112,300 at 40%	44,920
£159,600 £(411,550 – 1,950 – 100,000 – 150,000) at 45%	71,820
£1,950 at 0%	0
£411,550	—
Income tax liability	144,280

(c) Kagan's potential IHT liability:

(1) The amount invested in the pension fund (and not withdrawn) will be outside of Kagan's estate, reducing the potential IHT liability.

(2) The investments in premium bonds, the ISA and the freehold property will not affect Kagan's potential IHT liability because one asset is simply being replaced with another of equivalent value.

ANSWERS

104 Michael and Sean (June 2012) (amended)

Workbook references

Chapter 10 deals with trading losses.

Top tips

Remember that if a taxpayer claims loss relief against general income, the benefit of the personal allowance may be lost.

Easy marks

There were some easy marks for identifying the possible loss relief claims.

Marking guide	Marks	
Michael		
Early years relief against total income	1	
Claims	1	
Rate of tax saved – 2018/19	1	
Rates of tax saved – 2019/20	1	
Carry forward	0.5	
Sean		
Available loss	1	
Terminal loss relief	1	
Claims	1	
Rates of tax saved	1	
Relief against total income	1.5	
		10
Total		10

Michael

The loss of £26,230 for 2021/22 can be claimed against general income for the three preceding years, under early years loss relief, earliest year first, since the loss is incurred in one of the first four years of Michael's trade.

The loss relief claim will therefore be £20,365 in 2018/19 and £(26,230 – 20,365) = £5,865 in 2019/20.

For 2018/19, this will waste Michael's personal allowance, with the balance of the claim of £(20,365 – 12,570) = £7,795 saving income tax at the basic rate of 20%.

For 2019/20, Michael has income of £(57,095 – 12,570 – 37,700) = £6,825 subject to income tax at the higher rate of 40%, so the claim of £5,865 will save tax at the higher rate.

Alternatively, Michael could have carried the trading loss forward against future trading profits, but the trading profit of £9,665 for 2022/23 is covered by the personal allowance, and there is no information regarding future trading profits.

Tutorial note. A claim for loss relief against general income for 2021/22 and/or 2020/21 is not possible since Michael does not have any income for either of these years.

Sean

The unused overlap profits brought forward are added to the loss for the year ended 31 December 2022, so the total loss for 2022/23 is £(23,100 + 3,600) = £26,700.

The whole of the loss can be claimed as a terminal loss since it is for the final 12 months of trading. The claim is against trading income for the year of the loss (2022/23 – nil) and the three preceding years, latest first.

The terminal loss claim will therefore be £3,700 in 2021/22, £18,900 in 2020/21 and £(26,700 – 3,700 – 18,900) = £4,100 in 2019/20.

The property business profits are sufficient to utilise Sean's personal allowance for each year, so the loss relief claims will save income tax at the basic rate of 20%.

Alternatively, Sean could have initially claimed loss relief against his general income for 2022/23 and/or 2021/22, but this would have wasted his personal allowance in those years.

105 Paul and Palu Ltd (March/June 2021) (amended)

Marking guide	Marks	
Business run as limited company		
(1) Trading profit	0.5	
Director's remuneration	0.5	
Corporation tax at 19%	0.5	
(2) Income tax		
Director's remuneration	0.5	
Dividend income	0.5	
Personal allowance	0.5	
Income tax at 20%	0.5	
Income tax at 0% (dividend)	0.5	
Income tax at 8.75%	0.5	
Income tax at 33.75%	0.5	
(3) No Class 1 NIC as below threshold	0.5	
Business run as a sole trader	0.5	
(1) Taxable income		
Income tax at 20%	0.5	
Income tax at 40%	0.5	
Income tax at 45%	0.5	
(2) Class 2 NIC	0.5	
(3) Class 4 NIC	1	
Conclusion	1	
		10
Total		10

Business run as a limited company

(1) Palu Ltd's corporation tax liability for the year ended 5 April 2023 will be:

	£
Trading profit	175,000

	£
Director's remuneration	(8,000)
Taxable total profits	167,000
Corporation tax (167,000 at 19%)	31,730

Tutorial note. Equivalent marks will be awarded if the corporation tax liability is alternatively calculated as 175,000 - 8,000 - 135,270 = £31,730.

(2) Paul's income tax liability for 2022/23 will be:

	Non savings income	Dividend income	
	£	£	£
Director's remuneration	8,000		8,000
Dividend income		135,270	135,270
Net income	8,000	135,270	143,270
Personal allowance (income > £125,140)			0
Taxable income			143,270
£8,000 at 20%			1,600
£2,000 at 0%			0
£27,700 £(37,700 - 8,000 - 2,000) at 8.75%			2,424
£105,570 £(135,270 – 2,000 – 27,700) at 33.75%			35,630
£143,270			
Income tax liability			39,654

(3) There will be no class 1 NICs because the earnings of £8,000 are below the NIC lower thresholds.

Business run as a sole trader

(1) Paul's income tax liability for 2022/23 will be:

	£
Trading profit	175,000
Personal allowance	0
Taxable income	175,000
Income tax	
£37,700 at 20%	7,540
£112,300 at 40%	44,920
£25,000 at 45%	11,250
£175,000	
Income tax liability	63,710

(2) Class 2 national insurance contributions (NICs) for 2022/23 will be £164 (52 × 3.15).

(3) Class 4 NICs for 2022/23 will be:

	£
£37,700 £(50,270 - 12,570) at 10.25%	3,864
£124,730 £(175,000 - 50,270) at 3.25%	4,054
Class 4 NICs	7,918

Conclusion

If Paul runs his business as a sole trader, then overall tax and NIC will be £408 more than compared to running the business as a limited company:

	£
Limited company £(31,730 + 39,654)	71,384
Sole trader £(63,710 + 164 + 7,918)	(71,792)
Tax increase	(408)

106 Robinette (September/December 2019)

Workbook references

Chapter 9 deals with basis of assessment, and capital allowances are dealt with in Chapter 8. Employment income is covered in Chapter 4. Chapter 6 deals with property income.

Top tips

It is important to follow the requirements carefully to see that there was no need to calculate the income tax liability.

Easy marks

Some of the benefits were only worth half marks and were therefore very straight-forward. It was clear that Robinette's income is too high for a personal allowance, which can simply be indicated by a zero.

Examining team's comments

The income tax question involved Robinette.

- She had ceased self-employment on 30 June 2022, preparing accounts for the 14-month period from 1 May 2021 to 30 June 2022. The trading profit figure was given (before taking account of capital allowances).
- From 1 August 2022 to 31 January 2023, Robinette was employed by Bird plc, who provided her with living accommodation and a place in the company's workplace nursery for Robinette's son. Robinette used her private car for business purposes.
- Robinette commenced self-employment again, in a new business, on 1 February 2023. She prepared accounts for the five-month period from 1 February to 30 June 2023. The trading profit figure was again given (before taking account of capital allowances).
- In addition, Robinette received property income from letting out her main residence during the period she was employed by Bird plc.

Part (a) for 12 marks required candidates to calculate Robinette's taxable income for the tax year 2022/23. This section was generally very well answered.

However, candidates should always read the question carefully to ensure they understand what needs to be done before starting their answers. Where only taxable income is required, as in this part, candidates should never spend valuable time in also calculating the income tax liability. However, taxable income is after deducting the personal allowance, and this should have been shown by the use of zero (0) (Robinette's level of income meant that the personal allowance was reduced to nil).

Given that the question involved various changes in Robinette's sources of income, candidates needed to be very careful in regard to time-apportionment and basis periods. Common problems included:

- Time-apportioning profits for the period of cessation
- Not appreciating that WDAs, the AIA and FYAs are not given for the period of cessation.
- Time-apportioning the trading profits on commencement before capital allowances have been deducted.

With this type of question, candidates should think carefully about which workings can be included as one-line calculations within the main computation, and which need their own separate working. For example, the mileage allowance working of £5,200 at 10p (45p – 35p) = £520 should have been included within the main computation.

Part (b) for 3 marks required candidates to (1) state the period during which HM Revenue and Customs (HMRC) would have to notify Robinette if they intended to carry out a compliance check in respect of her self-assessment tax return for the tax year 2022/23, and the likely reason why such a check would be made, and (2) to advise Robinette as to how long she must retain the records used in preparing her self-assessment tax return for the tax year 2022/23. Although there were a number of good answers, in general this section was not so well answered as part (a). Candidates should note:

- The fact that the requirement was for a total of just three marks should have been a good indication that only a few brief points needed to be made, and not a much longer discussion.
- Where a question asks for dates, then these dates need to be precise - including the year relevant to the question.
- Answers should always be related to the information provided. The question made it clear that Robinette's self-assessment tax return was complete and accurate, so the likely reason for HMRC carrying out a compliance check was because her tax return was selected on a random basis.

Marking guide

		Marks	
(a)	Salary	0.5	
	Living accommodation	1	
	Running costs	0.5	
	Workplace nursery	0.5	
	Mileage allowance	1	
	Personal allowance	0.5	
	(W1) Trading profit old business	3.5	
	(W2) Trading profit new business	2.5	
	(W3) Property income	2	
			12
(b) (i)	(1) 12 months from receipt	1	
	(2) Random basis	1	
			2
(ii)	5 years from 31 January after tax year	1	
			1
Total			15

(a) Robinette – Taxable income 2022/23

		£
Employment income		
Salary (10,600 × 6)		63,600
Living accommodation – Rent paid (690 × 6)		4,140
Running costs		1,440
Workplace nursery		0
Mileage allowance (£5,200 at 10p (45p – 35p))		(520)
		68,660
Trading profit	– Old business (working 1)	75,350
	– New business (working 2)	11,800
		155,810
Property income (working 3)		6,288
		162,098
Personal allowance		(0)
Taxable income		162,098

Tutorial note. The fact that the requirement was for a total of just three marks should have been a good indication that only a few brief points needed to be made, and not a much longer discussion.

Tutorial note. Where a question asks for dates, then these dates need to be precise – including the year relevant to the question.

Tutorial note. Answers should always be related to the information provided. The question made it clear that Robinette's self-assessment tax return was complete and accurate, so the likely reason for HMRC carrying out a compliance check was because her tax return was selected on a random basis.

Tutorial note. The provision of a workplace nursery is an exempt benefit regardless of the cost to the employer.

Tutorial note. No personal allowance is available because Robinette's adjusted net income of £162,098 exceeds £125,140.

Workings

1 ***Trading profit (old business)***

	£
14-month period ended 30 June 2022	106,900
Balancing allowance	
(15,300 + 2,600 – 1,750 – 7,300)	(8,850)
	98,050
Relief for overlap profits	(22,700)
	75,350

ANSWERS

2 ***Trading profit (new business)***

		£
Five-month period ended 30 June 2023		55,700
Capital allowances (26,200 x 100% AIA)		(26,200)
		29,500
Assessed in 2022/23	29,500 × 2/5 =	11,800
1 February – 5 April 2023		

3 ***Property income***

	£
Rent receivable (1,100 × 6)	6,600
Insurance (624 × 6/12)	(312)
Property income	6,288

(b) (i) HMRC compliance check:

(1) If HMRC intend to carry out a compliance check into Robinette's self-assessment tax return for 2022/23, then they will have to notify her by 14 August 2024 (12 months after they received her tax return).

(2) If Robinette is confident that her return is complete and accurate, then the likely reason for HMRC carrying out a compliance check is because the return has been selected on a random basis.

(ii) Robinette was in business during 2022/23, so all of her records (both business and non-business) must be retained until five years after 31 January following the tax year, which is 31 January 2029.

107 Lucy

Workbook references

Chapter 2 deals with the income tax computation. Chapter 3 covers employment income and Chapter 7 covers trading income. National insurance contributions are dealt with in Chapter 12.

Top tips

Travel from home to work is not an allowable expense for tax purposes for an employee.

Easy marks

There were some easy marks for basic income tax and NIC computations for both the employment and self-employment work arrangements.

Marking guide	**Marks**
Employee	
Income tax payable	1.5
Class 1 NIC	1.5
Income	1
Self-employed	
Income tax payable	2

Marking guide	Marks	
Classes 2 and 4 NIC	2	
Income	1.5	
Determination of working pattern with higher disposable income	0.5	
		10
Total		10

Disposable income if Lucy is employee

Income tax	£
Employment income/net income	36,000
Less personal allowance	(12,570)
Taxable income	23,430
Income tax @ 20%	4,686

Class 1 NIC	£
Salary	36,000
Less employee's threshold	(12,570)
	23,430
Class 1 NIC @ 13.25%	3,104

Disposable income		£
Salary		36,000
Less:	Income tax	(4,686)
	Class 1 NIC	(3,104)
	Travel costs	(1,500)
		26,710

Disposable income if Lucy is self-employed

Income tax	£
Fees received	36,000
Less fixed rate mileage 4,600 @ 45p per mile	(2,070)
Trading income/net income	33,930
Less personal allowance	(12,570)
Taxable income	21,360
Income tax @ 20%	4,272

ANSWERS

Classes 2 and 4 NIC	£	£
Class 2 NIC £3.15 × 52		164
Class 4 NIC		
Trading income	33,930	
Less lower limit	(12,570)	
	21,360	
Class 4 NIC @ 10.25%		2,189
Total NICs		2,353

Disposable income	
Fees received	36,000
Less: Income tax	(4,272)
Classes 2 and 4 NICs	(2,353)
Travel costs 4,600 @ 40p	(1,840)
	27,535

Lucy will therefore have a higher disposable income by £(27,535 – 26,710) = £825 if she undertakes the self-employed work arrangement.

108 Daniel, Francine and Gregor (September/December 2015)

Workbook references

Partnerships are the subject of Chapter 11. Employment benefits are covered in Chapter 4. Trading losses are dealt with in Chapter 10.

Top tips

In part (a), it is important to realise that Daniel is treated as commencing a trade and therefore his trading income assessment for 2022/23 is on an actual basis. In part (c), remember that a trading loss can be relieved against total income in the tax year of the loss and the preceding tax year and can also be extended against chargeable gains.

Easy marks

There were some easy marks in part (b) for dealing with the interest paid by Francine on her loan.

Examining team's comments

This question had three separate scenarios, of which the first and third were fairly well answered and the second was less well answered.

The first scenario in part (a) involved three individuals who were in partnership, preparing accounts to 31 October annually. A fourth partner joined mid-way through an accounting period and the requirement was to calculate the new partner's trading income assessment for his first tax year as a partner. Although many candidates demonstrated satisfactory knowledge here, a large number wasted a significant amount of time by also performing calculations for the three existing partners, despite the requirement only concerning the new partner.

The second scenario in part (b) involved an employee who was provided with a beneficial loan part-way through the tax year. The loan was subsequently increased before the end of the tax year. The basic idea behind this question was that candidates had to calculate the benefit using the average method (they were instructed to use this method), with the interest actually

paid to the employer being calculated on a strict basis. However, many candidates failed to read the requirement carefully and thus ignored the instruction to use the average basis when calculating the taxable benefit. In addition, many candidates failed to use proper workings and accordingly became confused mid-way through their calculations.

The third scenario in part (c) involved a self-employed taxpayer who had made a trading loss in the tax year. On the assumption that the taxpayer relieved his trading loss as early as possible, the requirement was to calculate the amount of trading loss carried forward to the next tax year. Once again, many candidates' workings were not well laid out. Many candidates prepared tax computations for both years for which figures were provided, before realising that all that was required was a loss memorandum. The set off of the brought forward capital loss against the current year chargeable gain was also often overlooked.

Marking guide	Marks	
(a) 1 May 2022 to 31 October 2022	1.5	
1 November 2022 to 5 April 2023	1.5	
		3
(b) Average loan	1.5	
Interest paid	1.5	
		3
(c) 2021/22 claim against total income	1	
2022/23 claim against total income	1	
Claim against chargeable gain	1.5	
Loss carried forward	0.5	
		4
Total		10

(a) **Daniel – trading income assessment 2022/23**

	£
1 May 2022 to 31 October 2022	
£96,000 × ¼ × 6/12	12,000
1 November 2022 to 5 April 2023	
£180,000 × ¼ × 5/12	18,750
	30,750

Tutorial note. Daniel joined as a partner on 1 May 2022, so the commencement rules apply to him for 2022/23. The basis period is the 11-month period from 1 May 2022 to 5 April 2023.

(b) **Francine – beneficial loan 2022/23**

		£	£
$\frac{96{,}000 + (96{,}000 + 14{,}000)}{2} \times 2.0\% \times 8/12$			1, 373
Interest paid	£96,000 at 1.5% × 2/12	240	
	£110,000 at 1.5% × 6/12	825	

	£	£
		(1,065)
Taxable benefit		308

(c) **Gregor – trading loss carried forward**

		£
Trading loss		68,800
2021/22	– Claim against total income	
£(14,700 + 4,600 + 1,300)		(20,600)
2022/23	– Claim against total income	(900)
	– Claim against chargeable gain (working)	(14,500)
Loss carried forward to 2023/24		32,800

Working

Claim against chargeable gain

The loss relief claim against the chargeable gain is restricted to £14,500 (chargeable gain of £17,400 less the capital loss brought forward of £2,900).

Tutorial note. Gregor can claim loss relief against his total income and chargeable gains for 2021/22 and 2022/23.

109 George (March/June 2016)

Workbook references

Employment income is covered in Chapter 3. National insurance contributions are dealt with in Chapter 12.

Top tips

Use your tax tables for all the national insurance limits and rates.

Easy marks

There were some easy marks in part (a) for working out the income tax liability and in part (c) the comparison of the national insurance contributions gets some easy credit even if you have made errors in the main calculations.

Examining team's comments

In part (a), most candidates missed the fact that the taxpayer would not incur any significant expenses in respect of the contract and would not be taking any significant financial risk. Many candidates incorrectly gave the payment of tax under PAYE for the previous year as an indicator.

Part (b) was well answered, but many candidates produced extremely long answers for what should have been a simple set of workings. For example, the capital allowance was simply a 100% annual investment allowance on the purchase of a new asset and did not require a detailed capital allowances computation.

In part (c), as regards the payment aspect, most candidates just referred to PAYE without any further relevant detail. Very few appreciated that the due date under the self-employed basis was simply 31 January following the tax year – payments on account not being required because the previous year's tax liability was collected under PAYE.

Marking guide | **Marks**

(a)	Factors indicative of employment (½ mark each)		
			2
(b)	Income	0.5	
	Capital allowances	1	
	Personal allowance	0.5	
	Income tax	0.5	
	Class 2	0.5	
	Class 4	1	
			4
(c) (i)	PAYE	1	
	Self-assessment	1	
			2
(ii)	Class 1	1.5	
	Additional NIC	0.5	
			2
Total			10

(a) The contract is for a relatively long period of time.

George is required to do the work personally.

Xpee plc exercises control over George via the weekly meetings and instructions.

George will not incur any significant expenses in respect of the contract.

George will only be working for Xpee plc.

George is not taking any significant financial risk.

Note. Four items only required.

(b) **George – income tax liability 2022/23**

	£
Income	40,000
Capital allowances – annual investment allowance	(3,600)
Trading income	36,400
Less personal allowance	(12,570)
Taxable income	23,830
Income tax	
£23,830 × 20%	4,766

George – national insurance contributions 2022/23

Class 2 national insurance contributions will be £164 (52 × £3.15).

Class 4 national insurance contributions will be £2,443 [(36,400 – 12,570) = 23,830 × 10.25%)].

(c) (i) If George is treated as employed in respect of his contract with Xpee plc, the company will be required to deduct tax under PAYE every time that George is paid during 2022/23.

ANSWERS

If treated as self-employed, George's income tax liability for 2022/23 would not be payable until 31 January 2024.

(ii) If George is treated as employed in respect of his contract with Xpee plc, his Class 1 national insurance contributions for 2022/23 will be £3,634 (40,000 – 12,570) = £27,430 × 13.25%).

The additional amount of national insurance contributions which he will suffer for 2022/23 is therefore £1,027 (3,634 – 164 – 2,443).

> **Tutorial note.** For income tax purposes, capital allowances will reduce employment income in the same way that they are deducted in calculating the trading profit. However, there is no deduction for capital allowances when it comes to calculating Class 1 national insurance contributions.

110 Joe (December 2010) (amended)

Workbook references

Chapters 3 and 4 deal with employment income and employment benefits.

Top tips

Don't forget to show that you know if a benefit is exempt by including it in your computation with a zero.

Easy marks

There were some easy marks for basic employment benefit computations such as the living accommodation.

Marking guide	Marks	
Salary – Firstly plc	0.5	
Occupational pension scheme contributions	1.5	
Bonus	0.5	
Salary – Secondly plc	0.5	
Personal pension contributions	0.5	
Beneficial loan – Average method	1.5	
Beneficial loan – Strict method	1.5	
Van benefit	1	
Home entertainment system – Use	1.5	
Home entertainment system – Acquisition	1.5	
Living accommodation	2	
Furniture	1.5	
Working at home additional costs	1	
		15
Total		15

Joe – employment income 2022/23

	£
Salary – Firstly plc (6,360 × 9)	57,240
Pension contributions (57,240 × 6%) (N2)	(3,434)

		£
		53,806
Bonus (N1)		0
Salary – Secondly plc (6,565 × 3)		19,695
Beneficial loan (W1)		1,183
Company van (£3,600 × 9/12)		2,700
Home entertainment system	– Use (W2)	660
	– Acquisition (W2)	3,860
Living accommodation (W3)		6,750
Furniture (W3)		816
Working at home additional costs (N3)		0
Employment income		89,470

Working

(1) *Loan benefit*

The benefit of the beneficial loan using the average method is £1,267 ((120,000 + 70,000)/2 = 95,000 at 2.0% × 8/12).

Using the strict method, the benefit is £1,183 ((120,000 at 2.0% × 3/12) + (70,000 at 2.0% × 5/12)).

Joe will therefore elect to have the taxable benefit calculated according to the strict method.

(2) *Home entertainment system*

The benefit for the use of the home entertainment system is £660 (4,400 × 20% × 9/12).

The benefit for the acquisition of the home entertainment system is the market value of £3,860, as this is greater than £3,740 (4,400 – 660).

(3) *Living accommodation and furniture*

The benefit for the living accommodation is the higher of the annual value of £2,600 (10,400 × 3/12) and the rent paid of £6,750 (2,250 × 3).

The benefit for the use of the furniture is £816 (16,320 × 20% × 3/12).

Notes.

1 The bonus of £12,000 will have been treated as being received during 2021/22 as Joe became entitled to it during that tax year.

2 The personal pension contributions will increase Joe's basic rate tax limit and are therefore irrelevant as regards the calculation of employment income. Firstly, plc's employer contributions are an exempt benefit.

3 Additional home working costs up to £26 per month does not give rise to a taxable benefit.

111 Sammi (December 2010)

Workbook references

Chapter 4 deals with employment benefits. National insurance contributions are covered in Chapter 12. Computing taxable total profits and computing corporation tax are dealt with in Chapter 19.

Top tips

Use headings to show the examining team which of the two options you are dealing with.

Easy marks

There were easy marks for computing the car benefit and computing the national insurance contributions.

Marking guide		Marks
(a) Company car		
Car benefit	2	
Income tax	1	
NIC implications	0.5	
Additional director's remuneration		
Income tax	0.5	
Class 1 NIC	1	
		5
(b) Company car		
Class 1A NIC	1	
Allowable leasing costs	1	
Corporation tax saving	1	
Additional director's remuneration		
Class 1 NIC	1	
Corporation tax saving	1	
		5
(c) Sammi		
Director's remuneration – Net of tax income	1	
Director's remuneration – Overall result	1	
Conclusion	1	
Smark Ltd		
Director's remuneration	1	
Conclusion	1	
		5
Total		15

(a) **Sammi – company car**

The list price used in the car benefit calculation is £80,000. The relevant percentage is restricted to a maximum of 37% (16% + 26% (185 – 55 = 130/5) = 42%).

Sammi will therefore be taxed on a car benefit of £29,600 (80,000 × 37%).

Sammi's marginal rate of income tax is 45%, so her additional income tax liability for 2022/23 will be £13,320 (29,600 at 45%).

There are no national insurance contribution implications for Sammi.

Tutorial note. There is no fuel benefit as fuel is not provided for private journeys.

Sammi – additional director's remuneration

Sammi's additional income tax liability for 2022/23 will be £12,150 (27,000 at 45%).

The additional employee's Class 1 NIC liability will be £878 (27,000 at 3.25%).

Tutorial note. Sammi's director's remuneration exceeds the upper earnings limit of £50,270, so her additional Class 1 NIC liability is at the rate of 3.25%.

(b) **Smark Ltd – company car**

The employer's Class 1A NIC liability in respect of the car benefit will be £4,455 (29,600 at 15.05%).

The car has a CO_2 emission rate in excess of 50 grams per kilometre, so only £23,486 (27,630 less 15%) of the leasing costs are allowed for corporation tax purposes.

Smark Ltd's corporation tax liability will be reduced by £5,309 (23,486 + 4,455 = 27,941 at 19%).

Smark Ltd – additional director's remuneration

The employer's Class 1 NIC liability in respect of the additional director's remuneration will be £4,064 (27,000 at 15.05%).

Smark Ltd's corporation tax liability will be reduced by £5,902 (27,000 + 4,064 = 31,064 at 19%).

(c) **More beneficial alternative for Sammi**

Under the director's remuneration alternative, Sammi will receive additional net of tax income of £13,972 (27,000 – 12,150 – 878).

However, she will have to lease the car at a cost of £27,630, so the overall result is additional expenditure of £13,658 (27,630 – 13,972).

If Sammi is provided with a company car, she will have an additional tax liability of £13,320, so this is a slightly less costly alternative for her.

More beneficial alternative for Smark Ltd

The net of tax cost of paying additional director's remuneration is £25,162 (27,000 + 4,064 – 5,902).

This is more beneficial than the alternative of providing a company car since this has a net of tax cost of £26,776 (27,630 + 4,455 – 5,309).

112 Simon (December 2009)

Workbook references

The badges of trade are discussed in Chapter 7 which also deals with the computation of trading profit. Chapter 2 deals with the computation of taxable income and the income tax computation. National insurance contributions are the subject of Chapter 12.

Chapter 13 covers computation of chargeable gains for individuals.

Top tips

Think carefully about what costs are allowable as part of trading expenses in part (b) and, alternatively, as part of the cost of the asset in part (c).

Not all the expenses are allowable in both cases.

Easy marks

The question gave you the badges of trade in part (a) so it should have been easy marks to comment on them.

Marking guide	Marks
(a) Subject matter	0.5
Length of ownership	0.5

	Frequency of transactions	0.5	
	Work done	0.5	
	Circumstances of realisation	0.5	
	Profit motive	0.5	
			3
(b)	Income	0.5	
	Acquisition of house	0.5	
	Legal fees on acquisition	0.5	
	Renovation costs	0.5	
	Legal fees on sale	0.5	
	Loan interest	1	
	Personal allowance	0.5	
	Income tax liability	1	
	Class 4 NICs	1.5	
	Class 2 NICs	1.5	
			8
(c)	Sale proceeds	0.5	
	Legal fees on sale	0.5	
	Cost of house	0.5	
	Legal fees on acquisition	0.5	
	Enhancement expenditure	0.5	
	Loan interest – not allowable	0.5	
	Annual exempt amount	0.5	
	Capital gains tax liability	0.5	
			4
Total			15

(a) **Badges of trade**

Subject matter

Some assets are commonly held as investments for their intrinsic value, for example an individual may buy shares for dividend income produced by them or may buy a painting to enjoy it as a work of art. A subsequent disposal of an investment asset usually produces a capital gain. Where the subject matter of a transaction is not an investment asset, any profit on resale is usually a trading profit.

Length of ownership

If items purchased are sold soon afterwards, this indicates trading transactions.

Frequency of transactions

Transactions which may, in isolation, be of a capital nature will be interpreted as trading transactions where their frequency indicates the carrying on of a trade.

Work done

When work is done to make an asset more marketable, or steps are taken to find purchasers, this is likely to be indicative of trading.

Circumstances of realisation

A forced sale, for example to realise funds for an emergency, is not likely to be treated as trading.

Motive

The absence of a profit motive will not necessarily preclude a tax charge as trading income, but its presence is a strong indication that a person is trading.

(b) **Simon – Income tax and NICs for 2022/23 if trading**

		£	£
Income			260,000
Less:	Costs incurred		
	House	127,000	
	Legal fees on acquisition	1,800	
	Renovation	50,000	
	Legal fees on sale	2,600	
	Loan interest		
	£150,000 × 6% × 4/12	3,000	
			(184,400)
Trading income/Net income			75,600
Less personal allowance			(12,570)
Taxable income			63,030
Income tax			
£37,700 @ 20%			7,540
£25,330 @ 40%			10,132
Income tax liability			17,672
Class 4 NICs			
£(50,270 – 12,570) = £37,700@ 10.25%			3,864
£(75,600 – 50,270) = £25,330 @ 3.25%			823
Total Class 4 NICs			4,687
Class 2 NICs			
£3.15 × 19 weeks (N)			60

Note. Marks were awarded for any reasonable attempt at calculating the number of weeks. ½ mark was deducted if 52 weeks were used.

(c) **Simon – capital gains tax 2022/23 if not trading**

		£	£
Sale proceeds			260,000
Less legal fees on sale			(2,600)
Net proceeds of sale			257,400
Less:	Cost of house	127,000	
	Legal fees on acquisition	1,800	
	Renovation	50,000	
	Loan interest (N)	0	

	£	£
		(178,800)
Chargeable gain		78,600
Less annual exempt amount		(12,300)
Taxable gain		66,300
Capital gains tax		
£37,700 @ 18%		6,786
£(66,300 – 37,700) = 28,600 @ 28%		8,008
Capital gains tax liability		14,794

Note. The loan interest is a revenue expense and so is not allowable in computing the chargeable gain.

113 Alfred and Amaia (March/June 2021) (amended)

Marking guide		Marks
(a) Pre-trading expenditure	0.5	
Client entertaining	0.5	
Lease premium		
Premium paid	0.5	
Less £5,400	0.5	
Deduction	1.5	
Capital allowances		
Plant and machinery	0.5	
AIA	0.5	
Car WDA	1.5	
		6
(b) Salary	0.5	
Car	1.5	
Job related accommodation	1	
Personal allowance	0.5	
Income tax at 20%	0.5	
Income tax at 40%	0.5	
Interest relief	1	
PAYE	0.5	
Property income		
Rent received	1	
Insurance	1	
Mortgage interest	1	
		9
Total		15

(a) **Alfred – tax adjusted trading loss for the seven-month period ended 31 March 2023**

	£
Trading profit	63,000
Pre-trading expenditure	(5,000)
Deduction for lease premium (W1)	(1,435)
Client entertaining	0
Capital allowances (W2)	(118,520)
Trading loss	(61,955)

Workings

1 ***Deduction for lease premium***

	£
Premium paid	30,000
Less: 30,000 × 2% × (10 – 1)	(5,400)
Amount taxable on landlord	24,600
Deduction 24,600/10 × 7/12	1,435

2 ***Capital allowances***

		Main pool	Allowance
	£	£	£
Addition qualifying for AIA			
Plant and machinery	116,000		
AIA - 100%	(116,000)		116,000
Car		24,000	
WDA - 18% × 7/12		(2,520)	2,520
TWDV c/f		21,480	
Total allowances			118,520

Tutorial note. The cost of the marketing campaign is deductible because it was incurred in the seven years prior to the commencement of Alfred's trade and it would be deductible under general principles.

(b) **Amaia – income tax payable for the tax year 2022/23**

	£
Employment income	
Salary	80,000
Car (£25,000 × 15% × 3/12)	938
Job-related accommodation	0
Property income (working)	14,350
	95,288

	£
Personal allowance	(12,570)
Taxable income	82,718
£37,700 at 20%	7,540
£45,018 (82,718 - 37,700) at 40%	18,007
	25,547
Interest relief (£2,600 at 20%)	(520)
Income tax liability	25,027
PAYE	(19,240)
Income tax payable	5,787

Working

Property income

	£
Rent received (£1,200 × 13)	15,600
Mortgage interest	0
Insurance	(1,250)
Property income	14,350

114 John (June 2013) (amended)

Workbook references

Chapter 2 deals with the computation of taxable income and the income tax liability. Pensions are covered in Chapter 5. Employment income is dealt with in Chapters 3 and 4. Property income is the subject of Chapter 6.

Top tips

Make sure you distinguish between occupational pension contributions (which are given tax relief at all rates by being deducted in the computation of employment income) and personal pension contributions (which are given basic rate relief by the taxpayer making a net contribution and higher and additional rate relief by increasing the basic rate and higher rate limits).

Easy marks

The inclusion of salary, deduction of occupational pension contributions and calculation of the tax liability should have been straightforward in part (a).

Marking guide	Marks
(a) Remuneration	0.5
Occupational pension contributions	1
Beneficial loan	
Outstanding loan at end of tax year	1
Average loan	1

Interest paid	0.5	
Property business profit	0.5	
Letting agent fees	0.5	
Personal allowance – not available	0.5	
Personal pension contributions		
Unused allowances	1.5	
Available allowance 2022/23	1.5	
Increase in basic and higher rate limits	1	
Tax liability		
Basic rate	0.5	
Higher rate	0.5	
Additional rate	0.5	
Finance costs tax reducer	1	
		12
(b) One for each relevant point (maximum of three)		
		3
Total		15

(a) **John – income tax computation 2022/23**

	Non-savings income
	£
Employment income	
Remuneration	328,318
Less occupational pension contributions	(18,000)
	310,318
Beneficial loan (W1)	1,350
Property business income (W2)	12,980
Net income	324,648
Less personal allowance	(0)
Taxable income	324,648

Tutorial note. No personal allowance is available as John's adjusted net income of £(324,648 – 4,000 (W3)) = £320,648 exceeds £125,140.

Tax	£
£41,700 (W3) @ 20%	8,340
£112,300 (154,000 (W3) – 41,700) @ 40%	44,920
£170,648 (324,648 – 154,000) @ 45%	76,792
	130,052
Less: finance costs tax reducer £7,500 × 20%	(1,500)
Income tax liability	128,552

Workings

1 *Beneficial loan*

John repaid £(12,000 + 12,000) = £24,000 of the loan during 2022/23, so the outstanding balance at 5 April 2023 is £(84,000 – 24,000) = £60,000.

The benefit calculated using the average method (specified in the question) is as follows:

	£
$\frac{[84,000 + 60,000]}{2} \times 2.0\%$	1,440
Less interest paid	(90)
Taxable benefit	1,350

2 *Property business income*

	£
Profit before interest	14,855
Less: Letting agent fees	(1,875)
Property business income	12,980

3 *Effect of personal pension contributions on tax limits*

John has adjusted income which is higher than £240,000 in the tax year 2022/23 so his annual allowance is reduced (tapered) for 2022/23 by £1 for every £2 the adjusted income exceeds £240,000. However, the annual allowance is not reduced to less than £4,000.

Unused allowances can be carried forward for three years.

The maximum gross personal pension contribution possible in 2022/23 is as follows:

	£
2022/23 (tapered)	
Adjusted income = £(324,648 + 18,000 + 12,000) = £354,648 which is at least £312,000 so minimum annual allowance applies	4,000
2021/22	
No tapering required as adjusted income below £240,000	40,000
2020/21	
No tapering required as adjusted income below £240,000	40,000
2019/20	
No tapering required as adjusted income below £240,000	40,000
Occupational pension contributions already made £(18,000 + 12,000) × 4	(120,000)
Personal pension contribution allowable	4,000

John's basic and higher rate limits will be increased by this gross personal pension contribution to £(37,700 + 4,000) = £41,700 and £(150,000 + 4,000) = £154,000.

> **Tutorial note.** Adjusted income for an employee is net income plus employee pension contributions to occupational pension schemes under net pay arrangements plus employer contributions to occupational pension schemes and/or personal pension schemes.

(b) **Furnished holiday lettings**

Any three from:

(1) There is no restriction on finance costs.

(2) The cost of furniture purchased for use in the furnished holiday letting will be an allowable expense under the cash basis (or will qualify for capital allowances under the accruals basis) instead of replacement furniture relief.

(3) The profit from the furnished holiday letting will qualify as relevant earnings for pension tax relief purposes.

(4) Capital gains tax business asset disposal relief, relief for replacement of business assets and gift holdover relief for business assets will potentially be available on a disposal of the furnished holiday letting.

115 Ronald (June 2014) (amended)

Workbook references

Assessable trading income is covered in Chapter 9 and capital allowances in Chapter 8. Property business income is the subject of Chapter 6. The computation of taxable income and the income tax liability will be found in Chapter 2. Pensions are the subject of Chapter 5.

Top tips

You could work out the amount of dividend income by adding back the dividend nil rate band of £2,000 to the dividend included in the computation.

Easy marks

There were some easy marks in part (a) for working out the income tax liability as the question outlined the computation required and the rates of tax.

Marking guide		Marks	
(a)	Trading profit p/e 30 April 2022: Assessable trading profit	0.5	
	Trading profit p/e 30 April 2023: Capital allowances	1.5	
	Trading profit p/e 30 April 2023: Assessable trading profit	1	
	Property business income: Premium assessable	1	
	Property business income: Rent received	1	
	Property business income: Roof replacement	1	
	Property business income: Roof repairs	1	
	Property business income: Insurance paid	1	
	Dividends	1	
	Figures given	1	
	Tax @ 40%	1	
			11
(b)	No annual allowances for previous years	1	
	Annual allowance 2022/23	1	
	Basic rate relief	1	
	Higher rate relief	1	
			4
Total			15

(a) **Ronald – income tax computation 2022/23**

	Non-savings income	*Savings income*	*Dividend income*	*Total*
	£	£	£	£
Trading income (W1)	11,592			
Employment income	70,065*			
Property business income (W2)	8,240			
Building society interest		1,260*		

	Non-savings income	Savings income	Dividend income	Total
	£	£	£	£
Dividends £(800 + 2,000)	–	–	2,800	
Net income	89,897	1,260	2,800	93,957
Less personal allowance	(12,570)*	–	–	
Taxable income	77,327	1,260	2,800	81,387

	£
Income tax	
Non-savings income	
£37,700 @ 20%	7,540*
£39,627 (77,327 – 37,700) @ 40%	15,851
Savings income	
£500 @ 0%	0*
£760 (1,260 – 500) @ 40%	304
Dividend income	
£2,000 @ 0%	0*
£800 (2,800 – 2,000) @ 33.75%	270*
Income tax liability	23,965
Tax suffered at source	
PAYE	(11,513)*
Income tax payable	12,452

* Figures provided in question

Tutorial note. The amount of dividends are not given, but as the dividend nil rate band of £2,000 is available and only £800 is being taxed at the higher rate, the total dividends must be £(2,000 + 800) = £2,800.

Workings

1 *Trading profit*

	£	£
Period ended 30 April 2022		3,840
Period ended 30 April 2023	12,060	
Capital allowances £24,000 × 6% × 30%	(432)	
	11,628	
	× 8/12	7,752
		11,592

ANSWERS

2 *Property business income*

	£	£
Premium received		12,000
Less £12,000 × 2% × (30 – 1)		(6,960)
		5,040
Rents received £768 × 5		3,840
		8,880
SBA on roof replacement (£8,400 × 3% × 4/12)	84	
Roof repairs £(8,600 – 8,200)	400	
Insurance paid	156	
		(640)
Property business profit		8,240

Tutorial note. The rent received in the tax year is taxable under the cash basis rather than the rent receivable for the period.

Tutorial note. The initial replacement cost of the shop's roof is not deductible, being capital in nature, as the building was not in a usable state when purchased and this fact was reflected in the reduced purchase price. It will, however, qualify for SBAs as it is qualifying expenditure contracted for on or after 29 October 2018. The allowance can be claimed from the date the shop is let out.

Tutorial note. The whole of the insurance paid in the tax year is deductible under the cash basis.

(b) Ronald was not a member of a pension scheme prior to 2022/23, so the annual allowances for the three previous tax years are not available.

Although net relevant earnings are £(11,592 + 70,065) = £81,657, the maximum amount of tax relievable personal pension contribution is effectively restricted to the annual allowance of £40,000 for 2022/23.

Personal pension contributions are made net of basic rate tax, so Ronald would have paid £32,000 (£40,000 less 20%) to the pension company.

Higher rate tax relief would have been given by increasing Ronald's basic rate tax limit for 2022/23 by £40,000, being the gross amount of the pension contribution.

116 Wai (June 2015) (amended)

Workbook references

Employment income is covered in Chapters 3 and 4. The personal allowance is dealt with in Chapter 2.

Top tips

Make sure you are familiar with the tax rates and allowances which will be given to you in the exam. They include a lot of useful information such as mileage allowance, car benefit and the official rate of interest which will help you in answering this question.

Easy marks

There were some easy marks for calculation of basic employment benefits such as car benefit and living accommodation benefit.

Examining team's comments

Part (a) was generally very well answered. Surprisingly, the aspect that caused the biggest problem was the salary, because many candidates did not appreciate that it was necessary to calculate an annual figure. With calculations such as those for the mileage allowance, candidates are advised to study and replicate the layout followed in model answers rather than attempting their own style of short-cut. It is also a very poor approach to simply refer to a question note when answering, such as (5) instead of incidental expenses.

Many candidates found part (b) difficult, and often based their answers on self-assessment tax return information or PAYE form P45. One clue should have been that the question said "provided to Wai", so clearly a tax return could not be relevant.

Marking guide

		Marks	
(a)	Salary	0.5	
	Bonus	1	
	Mileage allowance		
	Reimbursement	0.5	
	Ordinary commuting	0.5	
	Travel to clients	0.5	
	Temporary workplace	0.5	
	Tax-free amount @ 45p	0.5	
	Tax-free amount @ 25p	0.5	
	Car benefit		
	Percentage	0.5	
	Benefit	1	
	Incidental expenses	0.5	
	Mobile telephone	1	
	Living accommodation		
	Annual value	0.5	
	Additional benefit		
	Cost	0.5	
	Improvements	1	
	Limit	1	
	Benefit	0.5	
	Personal allowance	1	
			12
(b)	Form P60 contents	1.5	
	Date	0.5	
	Form P11D contents	0.5	
	Date	0.5	
			3
Total			15

(a) **Wai – taxable income 2022/23**

	£
Employment income	
Salary (10,200 × 12)	122,400
Bonus	8,100
Mileage allowance (W1)	2,763
Car benefit (W2)	1,285
Incidental expenses (overseas, up to £10 per night – exempt)	0
Mobile telephone (400 × 20%)	80
Living accommodation – Annual value	4,828
– Additional benefit (W3)	1,824
	141,280
Less personal allowance	(0)
Taxable income	141,280

Tutorial note. The bonus of £4,600 will have been treated as being received during 2021/22 as Wai became entitled to it during that tax year. Similarly, the bonus of £2,900 will be treated as received during 2023/24.

Tutorial note. The exemption for mobile telephones does not apply to the second telephone.

Tutorial note. No personal allowance is available as Wai's adjusted net income of £141,280 exceeds £125,140.

Workings

1 *Mileage allowance*

	Miles	£
Reimbursement (13,860 at 55p)		7,623
Business mileage		
Ordinary commuting	0	
Travel to clients' premises	8,580	
Temporary workplace	2,860	
	11,440	
Tax-free amount		
10,000 miles at 45p		(4,500)
1,440 miles at 25p		(360)
Taxable benefit		2,763

Tutorial note. Travel to the temporary workplace qualifies as business mileage because the 24-month limit was not exceeded.

2 *Car benefit*

The relevant percentage for the car benefit is 22% because the car has CO_2 emissions from 85 to 89 grams per kilometre. The diesel addition does not apply because the car meets the RDE2 standard.

The car was available during the period 1 September 2022 to 5 April 2023, so the benefit for 2022/23 is £1,285 (10,013 × 22% × 7/12).

3 *Living accommodation additional benefit*

The benefit is based on the cost of the property plus subsequent improvements incurred before the start of the tax year.

	£
Cost	142,000
Improvements (prior to 6 April 2022 only)	24,200
	166,200
Limit	(75,000)
	91,200

The additional benefit is therefore £1,824 (91,200 at 2.0%).

(b) **Form P60**

Form P60 will show Wai's taxable earnings, income tax deducted, final tax code, national insurance contributions (NIC), and Qaz plc's name and address.

This form should have been provided to Wai by 31 May 2023.

Form P11D

Form P11D will detail the expenses and benefits provided to Wai.

This form should have been provided to Wai by 6 July 2023.

117 Samson and Delilah (September/December 2015) (amended)

Workbook references

The income tax computation is covered in Chapter 2. Chapters 3 and 4 deal with employment income and taxable and exempt benefits. Partnerships are the subject of Chapter 11.

Top tips

Trivial benefits (not exceeding £50) are exempt benefits.

Easy marks

There were some easy marks for dealing with the car benefit and computing income tax.

Examining team's comments

Part (a) of the question was a typical income tax liability calculation (for both the husband and wife), and it was generally very well answered.

Part (b) of the question involved income tax planning, requiring a calculation of the husband's income tax saving for the tax year if the building society deposit account had been in his wife's sole name instead of in joint names for the entire year. Given that the husband's personal allowance restriction would be reduced, the answer was simply the amount of interest (after deducting the savings income nil rate band of £500) at 60%. However, half page answers were quite common.

Once again, working at the margin (where appropriate) could have saved an enormous amount of time.

Marking guide	Marks	
(a) Samson		
Salary	0.5	
Building society interest	0.5	
Personal allowance	1	
Income tax	2	
Delilah		
Salary	0.5	
Payroll giving	1	
Car benefit	1	
Chauffeur	0.5	
Hamper	0.5	
Business travel	0.5	
Trading profit	1	
Building society interest	0.5	
Deductible interest	1	
Personal allowance not available	0.5	
Income tax	2	
		13
(b) Transfer part of account from Samson to Delilah		
		2
Total		15

(a) **Samson – Income tax computation 2022/23**

	Non-savings income	*Savings income*	*Total*
	£	£	£
Employment income – Salary	112,000		
Building society interest £9,600/2	–	4,800	
Net income	112,000	4,800	116,800
Less personal allowance (W)	(4,170)	–	
Taxable income	107,830	4,800	112,630

Income tax	£
£37,700 × 20%	7,540
£70,130 (107,830 – 37,700) × 40%	28,052
£500 × 0% (savings rate nil rate band)	0
£4,300 (4,800 – 500) × 40%	1,720
Income tax liability	37,312

Workings

1 Samson's adjusted net income exceeds £100,000, so his personal allowance of £12,570 is reduced to £4,170 (12,570 – 8,400 ((116,800 – 100,000)/2)).

Delilah – income tax computation 2022/23

	Non-savings income	*Savings income*	*Total*
	£	£	£
Employment income (W1)	213,248		
Trading profit £85,600 (93,600 – 8,000) × 40%	34,240		
Building society interest £9,600/2	–	4,800	
Total income	247,488	4,800	252,288
Less interest paid	(6,200)	–	
Net income/taxable income	241,288	4,800	246,088

2 *Employment income*

	£
Salary	184,000
Less charitable payroll deductions £250 × 12	(3,000)
	181,000
Car benefit (W2)	22,848
Chauffeur	9,400
Hamper	0
Reimbursement of travel to visit client	0
Employment income	213,248

3 *Car benefit*

The relevant percentage for the car benefit is 34% (16% + (145 – 55)/5).

The car was available throughout 2022/23 so the benefit is £22,848 (67,200 × 34%).

Income tax	£
£43,780 (W) × 20%	8,756
£112,300 (156,080 – 43,780) × 40%	44,920
£90,008 (246,088 – 156,080) × 45%	40,504
Income tax liability	94,180

4 Delilah's basic and higher rate tax limits are increased by:

$£4,864 \times \frac{100}{80} = £6,080$ to £43,780 (37,700 + 6,080) and £156,080 (150,000 + 6,080)

in respect of the charitable gift aid donations.

ANSWERS

Tutorial note. The car benefit does not cover the cost of a chauffeur, so this is an additional benefit.

Tutorial note. The hamper is a trivial benefit as it does not exceed £50.

Tutorial note. There is an automatic exemption for reimbursement of business expenses such as the train travel by Delilah (which would be a taxable benefit under general principles) provided that the expense would have been a deductible expense for the employee.

Tutorial note. The loan interest paid of £6,200 is deductible because the loan was used by Delilah for a qualifying purpose.

Tutorial note. No personal allowance is available as Delilah's adjusted net income of £240,008 (246,088 – 6,080) exceeds £125,140.

Tutorial note. No savings income nil rate band is available as Delilah is an additional rate taxpayer.

(b) If the building society deposit account had been in Delilah's sole name instead of in joint names for the entire year, this would have saved Samson income tax of £2,680 (£500 × 20% + £4,300 × 60%).

Tutorial note. Samson's effective marginal rate on the savings income covered by the savings income nil rate band (£500) is 20%. This is 40% of half of the £500 (ie 20% of the whole of the £500) of the savings income which was used to restrict the personal allowance. Samson's effective marginal rate of income tax on the savings income not covered by the savings income nil rate band (ie £4,800 – 500 = £4,300) is 60%. This is 40% (the higher rate) plus 40% of half (ie 20% of the whole) of the remaining £4,300 of savings income which was used to restrict the personal allowance.

118 Patience (March/June 2016)

Workbook references

Employment income is covered in Chapters 3 and 4 and national insurance contributions in Chapter 12. Assessable trading income is covered in Chapter 9 and capital allowances in Chapter 8. Property business income is the subject of Chapter 6. The computation of taxable income and the income tax liability will be found in Chapter 2. Pensions are the subject of Chapter 5.

Top tips

There are no writing down allowances or annual investment allowance in the final year of trading. Remember that gains on the disposal of residential property are taxed at 18% and 28% if they are not covered by the annual exempt amount and private residence relief.

Easy marks

Recognising the exempt benefits and mentioning them in your answer is important to get some easy marks.

Examining team's comments

Two aspects to this question caused particular difficulty. Firstly, many candidates treated the pension income (state pension, employer's occupational pension scheme and a private pension) as exempt income. Secondly, the format in which information was given for two properties caused a certain amount of confusion, with the information relevant for income tax and the capital gains tax details being shown within the one table; candidates being required to separate out the relevant information for income tax and capital gains tax purposes. Here figures were often duplicated with, for example, revenue expenditure being (correctly) deducted as an expense in calculating the property business profit, but then also (incorrectly) deducted in calculating chargeable gains.

Marking guide

	Marks	
Salary	1	
Pension contribution		
Patience	0.5	
Employer	0.5	
School place	1	
Long-service award	0.5	
Beneficial loan	0.5	
Trading income		
y/e 31.7.22	0.5	
y/e 31.12.22	0.5	
Overlap relief	1	
Capital allowances		
TWDV brought forward	0.5	
Laptop	0.5	
Disposal proceeds	1	
Balancing allowance	0.5	
Property business profit		
Rent received	0.5	
Expenditure	0.5	
Pension income	1	
Personal allowance	0.5	
Increase basic rate limit	1	
Income tax liability	1	
Capital gains		
Property one	0.5	
Property two	0.5	
Annual exempt amount	0.5	
CGT payable	0.5	
		15
Total		15

Patience – Income tax computation 2021/22

	£
Employment income	
Salary £3,750 × 9	33,750
Pension contributions – Patience £33,750 × 6%	(2,025)
– Employer	0
	31,725
School place	540
Long-service award	0
Beneficial loan	0

	£
Trading income (W1)	16,100
Pension income £(1,450 + 7,000 + 3,650)	12,100
Property business income (W3)	3,500
Net income	63,965
Less personal allowance	(12,570)
Taxable income	51,395
Income tax	
£42,200 (W4) × 20%	8,440
£9,195 (51,395 – 42,200) × 40%	3,678
Income tax liability	12,118

Tutorial note. An employer contribution to a pension scheme is not a taxable benefit.

Tutorial note. The taxable benefit on the provision of the school place is the additional marginal cost to the employer, not the normal fee payable.

Tutorial note. A non-cash long-service award is not a taxable benefit if it is for a period of service of at least 20 years, and the cost of the award does not exceed £50 per year of service.

Tutorial note. There is no taxable benefit if beneficial loans do not exceed £10,000 during the tax year.

Workings

1 *Trading income*

	£	£
Year ended 31 July 2022		14,800
Period ended 31 December 2022	6,900	
Balancing allowance (W2)	(1,900)	
		5,000
		19,800
Relief for overlap profits		(3,700)
		16,100

2 *Capital allowances*

	Main pool	Allowance
	£	£
WDV brought forward	2,200	
Addition – Laptop computer	1,700	
Proceeds £(1,200 + 800)	(2,000)	
Balancing allowance	(1,900)	1,900

3 *Property business income*

	£
Rent received £(3,600 + 7,200)	10,800
Expenditure paid £(4,700 + 2,600)	(7,300)
Property business income	3,500

4 *Basic rate limit*

Patience's basic rate tax limit is increased by £4,500 to £42,200 (37,700 + 4,500 (3,600 × 100/80)) in respect of the personal pension contributions.

Patience – Capital gains tax computation 2022/23	£	£
Property one – Disposal proceeds	122,000	
– Less cost	(81,000)	
		41,000
Property two – Disposal proceeds	98,000	
– Less cost	(103,700)	
		(5,700)
Net chargeable gains		35,300
Less annual exempt amount		(12,300)
Taxable gains		23,000
Capital gains tax		
£23,000 × 28%		6,440

119 Petula (March/June 2017)

Workbook references

Employment income is dealt with in Chapters 3 and 4. The income tax computation is covered in Chapter 2. Pensions are the subject of Chapter 5.

Top tips

Part (b) is quite challenging, and you need to adopt a logical approach by first working out the annual allowances that have been used and then working out the remaining allowances to be carried forward. Make sure you use the earliest available tax year brought forward allowance first. This maximises the amount that can be carried forward.

Easy marks

There were easy marks in part (a) for dealing with employment income benefits and expenses.

Examining team's comments

Part (a) was very well answered, and there were many perfect answers. However, the following points should be noted when answering this style of question:

(1) If a question requires just a calculation of taxable income, then that is where candidates should stop. Calculating the income tax liability wastes valuable time.

(2) As stated in the requirements, candidates should always clearly indicate (by the use of a zero) any items which are not taxable or deductible – such as the employer pension scheme contribution and the disallowable subscription.

(3) Candidates should think carefully about which workings can be included as one-line calculations within the main taxable income computation, and which need their own separate working. The only aspects which warranted separate workings here were the mileage allowance and property income. These workings should always have a heading or be obviously identifiable. Just referencing adjustments to the bullet list numbers used in the question is not good exam technique.

(4) The use of abbreviated numbers, such as 15.6k instead of 15,600 for the reimbursed mileage, should be avoided.

(5) With a computation containing both additions and deductions, candidates should be very careful to indicate which is which. A single column approach with deductions shown in brackets avoids any confusion.

(6) Where a result is obvious, such as no personal allowance being available (because the adjusted net income of £322,420 exceeded £125,140), all that is needed is a zero entry. There is no need for an explanation or a calculation of the reduction to nil.

(7) Candidates need to appreciate that each source of income is self-contained. It is not correct to show all the receipts from each source first (such as rent receivable), and then all the various expenses lumped together (such as property income deductions). With a separate working for property income, just the one figure for property income should then be included in the main taxable income computation.

Although most candidates scored some marks for part (b), few achieved full marks. The three marks available for this section should have been a good indication as to the complexity of the requirement.

Marking guide

		Marks	
(a)	Salary	0.5	
	Bonuses	1	
	Mileage allowance		
	Reimbursed	0.5	
	First 10,000 miles	0.5	
	Remaining miles	0.5	
	Pension contributions	0.5	
	Professional subscription	0.5	
	Golf club membership	0.5	
	Property income		
	Rent received	0.5	
	Washing machine	1	
	Dishwasher	1	
	Other expenses	0.5	
	Furnished room	1	
	Savings income	2	
	Interest paid	1	
	Personal allowance	0.5	
			12
(b)	2022/23 annual allowance used in 2022/23	1	
	2019/20 annual allowance used in 2022/23	0.5	

Marking guide		Marks
2020/21 annual allowance carried forward to 2023/24	0.5	
2021/22 annual allowance carried forward to 2023/24	1	
		3
Total		15

(a) **Petula – Taxable income 2022/23**

	£
Employment income	
Salary	260,000
Bonuses (18,600 + 22,400)	41,000
Mileage allowance (W1)	8,350
Pension contributions	0
	309,350
Less: Professional subscription	(630)
Less: Golf club membership	0
	308,720
Property income (W2)	11,340
Savings income (250,000 at 3% × 4/12)	2,500
Less: Interest paid	(140)
	322,420
Less: Personal allowance	(0)
Taxable income	322,420

Tutorial note. The bonus of £21,200 will have been treated as being received 2021/22 because Petula became entitled to it during that tax year.

Tutorial note. Under the accrued income scheme, Petula must include the accrued interest as savings income for 2022/23, even though she has not received any actual interest.

Tutorial note. No personal allowance is available because Petula's adjusted net income of £322,420 exceeds £125,140.

Workings

1 *Mileage allowance*

	£
Reimbursement (26,000 at 60p)	15,600
Tax free amount	
10,000 miles at 45p	(4,500)
11,000 miles at 25p	(2,750)
Taxable benefit	8,350

2 *Property income*

	£
Rent received	12,000
Replacement furniture relief	
Washing machine	(420)
Dishwasher	0
Other expenses paid	(1,640)
	9,940
Furnished room £(8,900 – 7,500)	1,400
Property income	11,340

Tutorial note. No relief is given for that part of the cost of the washer-dryer which represents an improvement over the original washing machine. Relief is therefore restricted to the cost of a similar washing machine.

Tutorial note. No relief is available for the cost of the dishwasher because this is an initial cost rather than the cost of a replacement.

Tutorial note. Claiming rent-a-room relief in respect of the furnished room is more beneficial than the normal basis of assessment £(8,900 – 2,890 = 6,010).

(b) *Annual allowances carried forward to 2023/24*

First work out the annual allowance used in 2022/23, remembering to use the current tax year allowance first and then the previous three tax years, earlier years first:

Used in 2022/23	£
Annual allowance 2022/23(N1)	4,000
Brought forward from 2019/20	
£(40,000 – 25,000)	15,000
Brought forward from 2020/21	
£(40,000 – 25,000)	β 6,000
Annual allowance used in 2022/23	25,000

Then work out the remaining annual allowances carried forward to 2023/24:

Carried forward from 2020/21	£
£(40,000 – 25,000 – 6,000)	9,000
Carried forward from 2021/22 (N2)	
£(40,000 – 25,000)	15,000
Annual allowance carried forward to 2023/24	24,000

Notes.

1 Petula's adjusted income for 2022/23 exceeds £312,000 so she is only entitled to the minimum annual allowance for this tax year.

2 Tapering of the annual allowance does not apply in 2019/20, 2020/21 and 2021/22 as Petula's adjusted income did not exceed £240,000 in those years.

120 Dill (September/December 2017) (amended)

Workbook references

Residence, exempt income and the restriction of the personal allowance are covered in Chapter 2. Employment income is the subject of Chapters 3 and 4.

Pensions are dealt with in Chapter 5. Trading losses are covered in Chapter 10.

Top tips

In part (a), keep your points brief and relevant to the facts given in the question.

Easy marks

In part (b) there were some easy marks for calculating taxable benefits and identifying exempt benefits.

Examining team's comments

Part (a) for 3 marks required candidates to explain why Dill was treated as not resident in the UK for the tax year 2021/22. Although reasonably well answered, very few candidates managed to pick up all the available marks for this section.

For example, most candidates simply stated that Dill had been in the UK for 60 days, rather than indicating that this fell in the 46- to 90-day band from the tax tables. A number of candidates wasted time by explaining the automatically resident and not resident tests, when it was obvious that these were not relevant. Then, when discussing UK ties, some candidates focused on those ties which were not met, rather than those which were. The three marks available should have been a clear indication that a long, detailed, explanation was not required.

Part (b) for 12 marks required candidates to calculate Dill's taxable income for the tax year 2022/23. This section was generally answered very well, with many candidates achieving high marks.

Common problems included:

- Not appreciating that the benefit of a workplace nursery is an exempt benefit.
- Treating subscriptions as benefits rather than as deductions.
- Omitting the personal allowance. Even when shown, it was obvious (given the level of Dill's income) that the personal allowance was not available, so all that was needed was a zero entry. There was no need for an explanation or a calculation of the reduction to nil.
- If a question requires just a calculation of taxable income, then that is where candidates should stop. Calculating the income tax liability just wastes valuable time.
- As stated in the requirements, candidates should always clearly indicate (by the use of a zero) any items which are not taxable or deductible – such as exempt benefits, non-deductible expenses and exempt income.
- Where a computation contains additions and deductions, candidates should be very careful to indicate which is which. A single column approach with deductions shown in brackets avoids any confusion.
- Candidates should think carefully about which workings can be included as one-line calculations within the main taxable income computation, and which need their own separate working. The only aspects which warranted a separate working here was the mileage allowance.
- The use of abbreviated numbers such as 45.5k instead of 45,500 for the bonuses should be avoided.

Marking guide

		Marks	
(a)	Sufficient ties test relevant	0.5	
	Number of sufficient ties needed	0.5	
	Identification of UK ties	1.5	
	Conclusion	0.5	
			3
(b)	Salary	0.5	
	Bonuses	1	
	Gym	0.5	
	Home entertainment system	1	
	Workplace nursery	0.5	
	Beneficial loan	1.5	
	Health club membership	0.5	
	Mileage allowance	1.5	
	Professional subscription	0.5	
	Golf club membership	0.5	
	Occupational pension contribution	1	
	Premium bond prize	0.5	
	Interest from savings certificate	0.5	
	Loss	1.5	
	Personal allowance	0.5	
			12
Total			15

(a) **Dill – residence status in the tax year 2021/22**

The sufficient ties test is relevant since Dill does not meet either of the automatic tests.

As Dill spends between 46 and 90 days in the UK in the tax year 2021/22 and was previously UK resident in at least one of the previous three tax years, she will be UK resident in that tax year if she has three or more UK ties.

Dill has two UK ties:

- Available UK accommodation in which she spent at least one night during the tax year; and
- More than 90 days spent in the UK in either or both of the previous two tax years.

On this basis, Dill is not UK resident in the tax 2021/22 as she has less than three UK ties.

> **Tutorial note.** Dill is not automatically non-UK resident in the tax year 2021/22 since she spends at least 16 days in the UK in that tax year and was resident in the UK for one or more of the three previous tax years, and does not work full-time overseas.
>
> **Tutorial note.** Dill is not automatically UK resident in the tax year 2021/22 since she does not spend at least 183 days in the UK in that tax year, has an overseas home as well as a UK home, and does not work full-time in the UK.
>
> **Tutorial note.** Dill might have a third UK tie which is that she was present in the UK at midnight for the same or more days in that tax year than in any other country. However, there is insufficient information to conclude on this point.

(b) **Dill – Taxable income 2022/23**

	£
Employment income	
Salary	430,000
Bonuses £(16,200 + 29,100)	45,300
Company gym	0
Home entertainment system £5,900 × 20%	1,180
Workplace nursery	0
Beneficial loan £96,000 × 2.0% × 10/12	1,600
Health club membership	990
Less: Mileage allowance (W)	(1,625)
Professional subscription	(560)
Golf club membership	(0)
Occupational pension scheme contribution	(4,000)
	472,885
Premium bond prize	0
Interest from savings certificates	0
Total income	472,885
Less loss relief against total income	(58,000)
Net income	414,885
Less personal allowance	(0)
Taxable income	414,885

Working

	£
10,000 miles @ 45p	4,500
4,500 miles @ 25p	1,125
	5,625
Less mileage allowance paid 16,000 @ 25p	(4,000)
Allowable deduction	1,625

Tutorial note. The bonuses are treated as received on the earlier of the time when payment is made and the time when Dill became entitled to the bonuses. These are 1 November 2022 for the first bonus and 1 March 2023 for the second bonus. Therefore, both bonuses are taxable in the tax year 2022/23.

Tutorial note. The use of the company gym is an exempt benefit as provision of sporting or recreational facilities available to employees generally and not to the general public.

Tutorial note. The golf club membership is not deductible as it is not incurred wholly, necessarily and exclusively for the purposes of Dill's employment.

Tutorial note. The maximum occupational pension scheme contribution that Dill can make without triggering an annual allowance charge is £4,000 since she has adjusted income of at least £312,000.

Tutorial note. The loss relief cap is the greater of £50,000 and 25% of Dill's adjusted total income of £472,885 which is £118,221. Therefore, Dill can relieve the whole of her trading loss of £58,000.

121 Danh (March/June 2018)

Workbook references

Residence, computing taxable income and the income tax liability are covered in Chapter 2. Property business income is dealt with in Chapter 6. Computing trading income is covered in Chapter 7, capital allowances in Chapter 8 and the basis of assessment in Chapter 9. Trading losses are covered in Chapter 10 and partnerships in Chapter 11.

Top tips

In part (a) you need to deal with Danh's residence position for both the tax years 2020/21 and 2021/22. Don't waste time dealing with ties that Danh does not satisfy, just state the ones which are relevant.

Easy marks

There are easy marks in part (b) for dealing with adjustment of profit. Watch out for the computation of the capital allowance on the car as you need to think about what rate of capital allowance will be given, private use and the length of the period of account.

Examining team's comments

Part (a) for 3 marks required candidates to explain whether Danh was treated as resident or not resident in the UK for each of the tax years 2020/21 and 2021/22. This section was reasonably well answered, although a number of candidates did not appreciate that there would be one additional UK tie for the tax year 2021/22. This is often the case where a question covers two tax years since for the second year a taxpayer will have the additional UK tie of being in the UK for more than 90 days during the previous tax year.

Where a question makes it clear that that the tests of automatic residence and automatic non-residence are not relevant, then there is nothing to be gained from explaining why this is the case. It should have been quite obvious from reading the question that only residence based on UK ties needed to be considered. The three marks available for this section was a good indication as to the length of answer required.

Part (b) for 12 marks required candidates to calculate Danh's income tax liability for the tax year 2022/23. This section was very well answered, and there were many perfect responses. However, the following points should be noted when answering this style of question:

- Candidates should think carefully about which workings can be included as one-line calculations within the main computation and which need their own separate working. For example, the partnership loss calculation of £12,600 × 7/12 × 20% = 1,470 was easily included within the main computation which would have saved candidates time. The only aspects which warranted separate workings here were the trading profit and property income.
- As mentioned above, the calculation for the partnership loss was fairly straightforward. There was no need to work out the loss allocations for the other partners and such workings simply used valuable time.
- Practice as many computations as possible. If this is done, basic mistakes such as applying the motor car benefit rules rather than claiming capital allowances should be avoided.
- As stated in the requirements, candidates should always clearly indicate (by the use of a zero) any items which do not require adjustment – the accountancy fees were deductible when calculating the trading profit, but this needed to be indicated.

- With computations containing both additions and deductions, candidates should be very careful to indicate which is which. A single column approach with deductions shown in brackets should avoid any confusion.
- Candidates need to appreciate that each source of income is self-contained. It is not technically correct to show all the receipts from each source first (such as rent receivable), and then the various deductions shown later in the main computation (such as property income deductions). With a separate working for property income, just the one figure for property income should then be included in the main taxable income computation.

Marking guide	Marks	
(a) 2020/21	2	
2021/22	1	
		3
(b) *Trading profit*		
Depreciation	0.5	
Motor expenses	1	
Accountancy	0.5	
Legal fees	0.5	
Use of office	1	
Capital allowances	2	
Property business income		
Rent received	0.5	
Other expenses	0.5	
Qualifying interest	1	
Partnership loss	2	
Personal allowance	0.5	
Income tax @ 20%	0.5	
Income tax @ 40%	0.5	
Tax reducer	1	
		12
Total		15

(a) **Danh – residence status in the tax years 2020/21 and 2021/22**

2020/21

Danh was not resident in the UK. Danh would be UK resident if he had three or more UK ties because he was in the UK between 91 and 120 days and was not UK resident in any of the previous three tax years. Danh had two ties which were available UK accommodation in which he spent at least one night during the tax year and substantive UK work.

2021/22

Danh was resident in the UK. Again, Danh would be UK resident if he had three or more UK ties. Danh had an additional tie which was that he spent more than 90 days in the UK in the previous tax year.

(b) **Danh – income tax liability 2022/23**

	£
Trading income (W1)	73,176
Property business income £14,400 – £3,980	10,420
Total income	83,596
Less: Qualifying interest	(875)
Partnership loss £12,600 × 7/12 × 20%	(1,470)
Net income	81,251
Less: Personal allowance	(12,570)
Taxable income	68,681
Tax	
£37,700 @ 20%	7,540
£(68,681 – 37,700) = £30,981 @ 40%	12,392
Less: Property finance costs tax reducer £10,000 × 20%	(2,000)
Income tax liability	17,932

Working

Trading profit for the eight-month period ended 5 April 2023

	£
Net profit	70,200
Add: Depreciation	2,300
Motor expenses private use £3,300 × 4,000/12,000	1,100
Accountancy	0
Legal fees in connection with grant of short new lease	1,460
Less: Use of office £4,200 × 1/6	(700)
Capital allowances £(14,800 × 18% × 8/12 × 8,000/12,000)	(1,184)
Trading profit	73,176

122 Martin (September/December 2018)

Workbook references

The income tax computation is the subject of Chapter 2. Employment income is covered in Chapters 3 and 4. Property income is the subject of Chapter 6. Assessable trading income is dealt with in Chapter 9 and partnerships in Chapter 11. Self-assessment for individuals is covered in Chapter 17.

Top tips

Make sure you indicate with a zero if a benefit or income received is exempt or a deduction is not allowable.

Easy marks

There were easy marks for recognising taxable and exempt benefits.

Examining team's comments

Part (a) was very well answered, and there were many perfect responses. However, the following points should be noted when answering this style of question:

- Candidates should think carefully about which workings can be included as one-line calculations within the main computation and which need their own separate working. For example, there were two car benefit calculations which were easily included within the main computation. The only aspect which warranted a separate working here was the partnership trading profit.
- When calculating Martin's share of the partnership's trading profit, it was only necessary to deal with his share. The allocations made to the other two partners were not relevant.
- Practice as many computations as possible. If this is done, basic mistakes such as claiming capital allowances rather than applying the car benefit rules can be avoided.
- As stated in the requirements, candidates should always clearly indicate (by the use of a zero) any items which do not require adjustment. The beneficial loan and the interest on the maturity of savings certificates were exempt, but this needed to be indicated.
- With computations containing both additions and deductions, candidates should be very careful to indicate which is which. A single column approach with deductions shown in brackets avoids any confusion.
- Candidates should appreciate that if expenses are paid privately by an employee, then they cannot possibly be taxable benefits – only a potential deduction against taxable income. In this case, Martin had paid a professional subscription (which was relevant to his employment with Global plc) and a membership fee to a health club (which he used to entertain Global plc's clients). It was clearly stated that Global plc did not reimburse Martin for either of these costs.
- Being aware of which benefits are exempt, such as the beneficial loan not exceeding £10,000, will avoid spending time on unnecessary calculations.
- Reading and understanding a question's requirements will avoid spending a lot of time calculating an income tax liability when it is not needed. The requirement was just to calculate Martin's taxable income.

Part (b)(i) was not answered particularly well. The deadline was 31 January 2025, but too many candidates gave a date of 12 months following the submission of Martin's self-assessment tax return.

Answers for TX-UK need to be precise, so the explanation how HMRC will calculate interest should have said that this will be from the original due date (31 January 2024) to the date that the additional tax is paid. A general discussion of how HMRC charges interest was not sufficient.

Although part (b)(ii) was better answered than part (b)(i), too many candidates wrote everything they knew on compliance checks rather than focusing on the information given – it being clearly stated that this was not a random check.

Candidates should note that detailed answers are not required where just a few marks are involved as was the case for both aspects of part (b).

Marking guide	**Marks**
(a) *Employment income*	
Salary	0.5
Bonuses	1
Car benefit 1st car	1
Car benefit 2nd car	1
Beneficial loan	0.5
Home entertainment system	1

Charitable payroll deductions	0.5	
Professional subscription	0.5	
Health club membership	0.5	
Trading profit		
January to September	1	
October to December	1	
Property income	1	
Dividend income	0.5	
Savings certificate income	0.5	
Personal allowance	0.5	
		11
(b) (i) Deadline for amending tax return	1	
Interest	1	
		2
(ii) Compliance check notice	1	
Reasons for check	1	
		2
Total		15

(a) **Martin – taxable income 2022/23**

	£
Employment income	
Salary	144,000
Bonuses (21,400 + 13,700)	35,100
Car benefit 18,450 × 16% × 9/12	2,214
Car benefit 24,905 × 19% × 3/12	1,183
Beneficial loan	0
Home entertainment system (7,400 × 20%)	1,480
Charitable payroll deductions	(1,000)
Professional subscription	(560)
Health club membership	0
	182,417
Trading profit (working)	20,930
Property income (9,200 – 7,500)	1,700
Dividend income	440
Interest from savings certificate	0
Net income	205,487
Less: Personal allowance	0
Taxable income	205,487

> **Tutorial note.** The bonus of £18,200 will have been treated as being received during 2021/22 because Martin became entitled to it during that tax year.
>
> **Tutorial note.** There is no taxable benefit in respect of the beneficial loan because it did not exceed £10,000 at any time during 2022/23.
>
> **Tutorial note.** No personal allowance is available because Martin's adjusted net income of £205,487 exceeds £125,140.

Working

Trading profit

	£
1 January to 30 September 2022 (54,600 × 9/12 × 40%)	16,380
1 October to 31 December 2022 (54,600 × 3/12 × 1/3)	4,550
	20,930

(b) (i) Martin's deadline for amending his self-assessment tax return for the tax year 2022/23 will be 31 January 2025 (12 months from the latest (electronic) filing date for the return of 31 January 2024).

Should additional tax become payable, then interest will be charged from 31 January 2024 to the day before the additional tax is paid.

(ii) If HMRC intend to carry out a compliance check into Martin's self-assessment tax return for 2022/23, then they will have to notify him by 26 December 2024 (12 months after they receive his tax return).

HMRC will carry out a compliance check because of a suspicion that income has been undeclared, or deductions have been incorrectly claimed.

123 Tonie (March/June 2019)

> **Workbook references**
>
> The income tax computation, including residence and the accrued income scheme, is covered in Chapter 2. Employment income is dealt with in Chapters 3 and 4. Property income is the subject of Chapter 6.
>
> **Top tips**
>
> In part (a) you only need to discuss the relevant UK ties which Tonie satisfied, not all of them. Be guided by the fact that there were only two marks for this part.
>
> **Easy marks**
>
> There were some easy ½ marks for showing that the premium bond prize and the interest from savings certificates were exempt income – but would you have got them by using a zero in your computation?
>
> **Examining team's comments**
>
> Part (a) was reasonably well answered, although candidates sometimes did not focus their answers on the information given. For example, there was no point mentioning the UK ties which were not met by Tonie. The section was for just two marks, so this should have been a good indication that only a few brief sentences were required and not a half page discussion on everything a candidate knew about the residence rules.
>
> Part (b) was well answered. However, candidates should avoid repetition by, for example, stating that Tonie (1) attended weekly meetings at Droid plc's offices, and (2) received instructions – these were both indications of control. When asked for a list it is easiest to answer using a list format.

With the exception of the accrued gilt income, part (c) was generally very well answered.

- Candidates should note that most of the workings for this style of question can be included within the main computation. For example, the mileage allowance deduction was easily included within the main computation. The only aspect which warranted a separate working here was property income.
- With computations containing both additions and deductions, candidates should be very careful to indicate which is which. A single column approach with deductions included as such on the spreadsheet avoids any confusion.
- Candidates should note that taxable income is after the personal allowance has been deducted.
- Reading and understanding a question's requirements will avoid spending time calculating an income tax liability when it is not needed. The requirement was just to calculate Tonie's taxable income.

Marking guide

	Marks	
(a) Three ties needed	0.5	
Two ties identified	1.5	
		2
(b) ½ mark for each factor		
		2
(c) Employment income		
Salary	0.5	
Mileage allowance	1	
Leasing costs	1	
Property income		
Rent received	0.5	
Mortgage interest – no relief	1	
Washing machine	1	
Dishwasher	1	
Other expenses	0.5	
Furnished room	1	
Accrued interest scheme income	2	
Premium bond prize	0.5	
Savings certificate interest	0.5	
Personal allowance	0.5	
		11
Total		15

(a) Tonie was previously resident and was in the UK between 46 and 90 days. She therefore needed three UK ties or more to be treated as UK resident. Tonie only had two UK ties, which were being in the UK for more than 90 days during the previous tax year, and spending more time in the UK than in any other country during 2021/22.

(b) The contract was for a relatively long period of time.

Tonie did not take any financial risk. Tonie only worked for Droid plc.

Tonie was required to do the work personally.

Droid plc exercised control over Tonie via the weekly meetings and instructions.

(c) **Tonie – taxable income 2022/23**

	£
Employment income	
Salary (6,200 × 12)	74,400
Mileage allowance (2,300 at 15p (60p – 45p))	345
Less leasing costs (180 × 12)	(2,160)
Property income (working)	7,570
Savings income (100,000 at 3% × 5/12)	1,250
Premium bond prize	0
Interest from savings certificate	0
	81,405
Less personal allowance	(12,570)
Taxable income	68,835

Tutorial note. Under the accrued income scheme, Tonie must include the accrued interest from the gilts as savings income for 2022/23, even though she has not received any actual interest.

Working

Property income

	£
Rent received	10,080
Less mortgage interest – relief as tax reducer	(0)
Less: Replacement furniture relief	
Washing machine	(380)
Dishwasher	(0)
Less other expenses	(3,210)
	6,490
Furnished room (8,580 – 7,500)	1,080
Property income	7,570

Tutorial note. No relief is given for that part of the cost of the washer-dryer which represents an improvement over the original washing machine. Relief is therefore restricted to the cost of a similar washing machine.

Tutorial note. No relief is available for the cost of the dishwasher because this is an initial cost rather than the cost of a replacement.

Tutorial note. Claiming rent-a-room relief in respect of the furnished room is more beneficial than the normal basis of assessment £(8,580 – 870 = 7,710).

PART C: CHARGEABLE GAINS FOR INDIVIDUALS

Section A

OTQ bank – Chargeable gains for individuals 1

124 The correct answer is: Gift of a motor boat valued at £10,000 (cost £5,000) to his aunt

The gift of the motor boat is exempt because this is a wasting chattel and is not plant and machinery eligible for capital allowances.

The gift of the unquoted shares is not a gift of tangible moveable property and so the chattels rules do not apply to it.

The gift of the antique jewellery is a gift of a non-wasting chattel but it would only be exempt if the proceeds (market value) were £6,000 or less. The gain cannot exceed 5/3 × (proceeds – £6,000).

The gift of the sculpture is a gift of a non-wasting chattel but results in a loss. The loss will be restricted by deeming the market value to be £6,000.

ACCA Examining Team's Comments

This question examines exempt gifts for capital gains tax purposes. The correct answer is gift of a motor boat valued at £10,000 (cost £5,000) to his aunt. This is an exempt gift because it is a wasting chattel (ie a tangible, movable asset with an expected life not exceeding 50 years). Wasting chattels (other than those eligible for capital allowances) are always treated as exempt disposals. The value and original cost are irrelevant.

Answer option gift of unquoted shares in a United Kingdom company valued at £2,500 (cost £1,800) to his brother was the most commonly chosen, suggesting that candidates may not have known the special rules regarding chattels well enough.

125 The correct answer is: £2,712

	£
Chargeable gain	26,300
Less annual exempt amount	(12,300)
Taxable gains	14,000
Tax	
£(37,700 – 25,620) = 12,080 × 18% (residential property)	2,174
£(14,000 – 12,080) = 1,920 × 28% (residential property)	538
Total capital gains tax	2,712

The answer £3,920 uses 28% throughout. The answer £6,156 does not deduct the annual exempt amount. The answer £1,592 uses the rates of 10% and 20%.

126 £12,600

The amount of the cost attributable to the part sold is:

$$\frac{£36,000}{£36,000 + £90,000} \times £80,000 = £22,857$$

	£
Proceeds £(36,000 – 1,000)	35,000
Less cost (see above)	(22,857)
Gain	12,143

The answer £12,600 uses the net proceeds in the part disposal fraction. The answer £13,143 ignores the cost of disposal. The answer £11,000 uses 3/10 as the part disposal fraction.

127 The correct answer is: £11,400

	2020/21	*2021/22*	*2022/23*
	£	£	£
Gains	2,000	4,000	14,900
CY losses	(14,000)	(2,000)	(2,000)
	(12,000)	2,000	12,900
AEA	(0)	(2,000)	(12,300)
	0	0	600
B/f losses			(600)
Losses c/f	12,000	12,000	11,400

Current year losses must be set against current year gains. Brought forward losses are set off after the annual exempt amount.

128 The correct answer is: £1,667

	£
Proceeds	7,000
Less cost	(1,500)
Gain	5,500

The maximum gain is 5/3 × £(7,000 × 6,000) = £1,667.

The chargeable gain is the lower of £5,500 and £1,667, so it is £1,667.

The answer £1,000 is the excess over £6,000. The answer £0 assumes the chattel is an exempt asset.

OTQ bank – Chargeable gains for individuals 2

129 £ 2,500

	£
Deemed proceeds	6,000
Less cost	(8,500)
Loss	(2,500)

ANSWERS

130 14 years

	Exempt years	*Chargeable years*	*Total years*
Actual occupation	3		3
Deemed occupation – any time employed overseas	5		5
Actual occupation	2		2
Deemed occupation – up to 3 years any reason	3		3
Unoccupied		1	
Occupied (including last 9 months of ownership)	1	–	1
Totals	14	1	15

131 12 August 2032

When a depreciating asset is purchased to replace a non-depreciating asset the gain on the sale is deferred until the earliest of:

The sale of the depreciating asset – 14 October 2032

Ceasing to use the depreciating asset in a business – not applicable here

The ten-year anniversary of the purchase of the depreciating asset – 12 August 2032

132 £ 1,160

Gains subject to business asset disposal relief are taxed at 10%. Other gains will be reduced by the annual exempt amount and then taxed, in this case at 20%, because Louise has taxable income in excess of the basic rate limit of £37,700. The capital gains tax (CGT) payable is therefore:

	£
£8,000 × 10%	800
£(14,100 – 12,300) = 1,800 × 20%	360
Total CGT	1,160

133 £ 13,650

	Number	*Cost*
		£
Purchase October 2004	1,000	1,500
Bonus issue November 2006		
1 for 2 bonus issue	500	0
	1,500	1,500
Rights issue July 2011		
3 for 1 rights issue @ £2.70	4,500	12,150
	6,000	13,650
Disposal February 2023	(6,000)	(13,650)

134 The correct answer is: £77,500

	£
Cost	73,000
Enhancement expenditure	41,700
Less insurance proceeds	(37,200)
Cost of restored property	77,500

135 The correct answer is: £16,200

	£
Proceeds	28,800
Less cost £21,000 × 9/15	(12,600)
Chargeable gain	16,200

A copyright is a wasting asset and so the cost is written down over its life on a straight-line basis.

136 £ 4,000

	£
Gain	24,400
Less current year loss	(10,000)
Net current year gain	14,400
Less annual exempt amount	(12,300)
	2,100
Less loss brought forward	(2,100)
Taxable gain	0
Loss carried forward £(6,100 – 2,100)	4,000

137 £ 143,000

The proceeds not reinvested in the new asset are £(184,000 – 143,000) = £41,000. Since this is greater than the gain of £38,600, no rollover relief is available. The cost of the replacement warehouse is therefore £143,000.

138 The correct answers are:

1 August 2021	Earliest date
31 July 2025	Latest date

ANSWERS

Section B

OT case – Nim (June 2009) (amended)

Workbook references

Transfers between spouses, exempt assets, the annual exempt amount and losses are covered in Chapter 13. The rules on chattels will be found in Chapter 14. The valuation of gifts of quoted shares is dealt with in Chapter 16.

Top tips

Questions may be set about spouses or civil partners. Transfers between these are on a no gain / no loss basis.

Easy marks

The valuation of the quoted shares should have been easy.

139 The correct answer is: £37,500

The shares in Kapook plc are valued at 3.70 + ½ × (3.80 – 3.70) = £3.75 so the deemed disposal proceeds are 10,000 × £3.75 = £37,500.

Make sure you learn this rule!

140 The correct answer is: £26,333

The disposal is first matched against the purchase on 24 July 2022 (this is within the following 30 days) and then against the shares in the share pool. The cost of the shares disposed of is, therefore, £26,333 (5,800 + 20,533).

Share pool	*No. of shares*	*Cost*
	£	£
Purchase 19 February 2004	8,000	16,200
Purchase 6 June 2009 1 for 2 @ £3.65 per share	4,000	14,600
	12,000	30,800
Disposal 20 July 2022 £30,800 × 8,000/12,000	(8,000)	(20,533)
Balance c/f	4,000	10,267

The answer £28,500 treats the rights issue as separate holding and disposes of it in priority to the 2004 shares. The answer £25,667 is a disposal of 10,000 shares from the pool only. The answer £20,533 is the pool disposal only.

141 The correct answers are:

- Nim will have deemed proceeds on the transfer of the Jooba Ltd shares to his wife so that neither a gain nor a loss will arise.
- Nim's wife will not be able to transfer her annual exempt amount to Nim.

Nim's wife will take the Jooba Ltd shares with a cost equal to the deemed proceeds ie the original cost to Nim. The spouse exemption applies for inheritance tax, not capital gains tax.

142 £3,500

	£
Net proceeds	8,700
Less cost	(5,200)
Gain	3,500

The maximum gain is 5/3 × £([8,700 + 300] × 6,000) = £5,000. The chargeable gain is the lower of £3,500 and £5,000, so it is £3,500.

143 £ 7,100

The set off of the brought forward capital losses is equal to the gain left in charge after the deduction of the annual exempt amount, £8,700 (21,000 – 12,300). Capital losses carried forward are therefore £(15,800 – 8,700) = £7,100.

OT case – Aloi, Bon and Dinah (June 2011) (amended)

Workbook references

Business asset disposal relief is dealt with in Chapter 15. Shares are covered in Chapter 16. Transfers on death, computing chargeable gains and the calculation of capital gains tax will be found in Chapter 13.

Top tips

Par value means the face value of the shares. Aloi therefore had a cost of £50,000 for her first 50,000 £1 shares in Alphabet Ltd.

Easy marks

The dates should have been well known.

144 The correct answers are:

- Bon was not an officer or employee of Alphabet Ltd for the requisite time before disposal.
- Alphabet Ltd was not Dinah's personal company for the requisite time before disposal.

Bon only became a director on 1 February 2021, so this qualifying condition was not met for two years prior to the date of disposal. Her shareholding of 25% (25,000/100,000 × 100) means that Alphabet Ltd is her personal company and she also satisfies the minimum two years for this condition to be met prior to the date of disposal.

Dinah was an employee for at least two years prior to the disposal but her shareholding of 3% (3,000/100,000 × 100) is less than the minimum required holding of 5% for Alphabet Ltd to be her personal company.

145 The correct answer is: £29,140

Gain qualifying for business asset disposal relief	£
Ordinary shares in Alphabet Ltd	
Proceeds of sale (60,000 × £6)	360,000
Less cost £(50,000 + 18,600)	(68,600)
Gain	291,400
CGT @ 10% on £291,400	29,140

ANSWERS

146 The correct answers are:

5 October 2023	Notification
31 January 2024	Payment

147 The correct answer is: £34,320

	£
Deemed proceeds of sale (10,000 × £7.12 (W1))	71,200
Less cost (W2)	(36,880)
Gain	34,320

Working

(1) The shares in XYZ plc are valued at 7.10 + ½ × (7.14 – 7.10) = £7.12.

(2) Following the takeover, Bon received 25,000 shares in XYZ plc. The cost of the original shareholding is passed on to the new shareholding so the cost attributable to the 10,000 shares sold is £36,880 (92,200 × 10,000/25,000).

148 The correct answer is: £0

There is no CGT liability on the sale of the XYZ plc shares as the gain of £5,000 (6,600 – (4,800 × 1,000/3,000)) is less than the annual exempt amount.

The transfer of the XYZ plc shares on Dinah's death is an exempt disposal.

OT case – Ginger, Innocent and Nigel (June 2013) (amended)

Workbook references

Chapter 13 covers the basics of computing chargeable gains. Chapter 15 deals with business reliefs.

Top tips

Think about why the disposals by Innocent and Nigel would give rise to different capital gains tax liabilities. Are there different rates of capital gains tax? When do those rates apply?

Easy marks

There were easy marks for working out the number of shares that could be sold without incurring a charge to CGT.

149 The correct answer is: £1.60

The disposal is at an undervalue, so only the gift element of the gain can be deferred under gift holdover relief. The consideration paid for each share will be immediately chargeable to capital gains tax to the extent that it exceeds the allowable cost. The chargeable amount is therefore £(4.00 – 2.40) = £1.60 per share.

150 The correct answer is: 8,506

Ginger's annual exempt amount for 2022/23 is £12,300 and she has a loss of £(800) brought forward from 2021/22. She can therefore sell (13,100/1.54) = 8,506 shares to her daughter without this resulting in any capital gains tax liability for 2022/23.

151 The correct answers are:

- There is a lifetime limit of £1,000,000 for business asset disposal relief.

- Business asset disposal relief is only available on shareholdings if they are held in a trading company.

The individual can be an officer (eg a director) or an employee of the company in which the shares are held. The conditions for business asset disposal relief must be satisfied for two years before the disposal.

152 £ 6,300

Innocent makes disposal

	£
Disposal proceeds	65,000
Less cost	(2,000)
Gain	63,000
CGT on £63,000 @ 10%	6,300

153 £ 6,840

Nigel makes disposal

	£
Disposal proceeds	65,000
Less cost (£46,200 × 2,000/3,000)	(30,800)
Gain	34,200
CGT on £34,200 @ 20%	6,840

OT case – Jerome (March/June 2016) (amended)

Workbook references

Computing chargeable gains is dealt with in Chapter 13. Chattels are covered in Chapter 14. Business reliefs are the subject of Chapter 15.

Top tips

If you are dealing with the disposal of a chattel, do not assume that the 5/3 rule always applies. Test it against the actual gain.

Easy marks

There were some easy marks for identifying the base cost of the house for Jerome's wife and for the administrative aspects of the election to hold over the gain on the Reward Ltd shares.

154 The correct answer is: £112,800

The disposal of the house does not give rise to a gain or a loss because it is a transfer between spouses. The base cost of the house for Jerome's wife is therefore Jerome's base cost which was the value of the house at the uncle's death.

155 £ 50,600

	£
Deemed proceeds	98,400
Less cost	(39,000)
Gain before gift holdover relief	59,400

Gift holdover relief is restricted to £50,600 (£59,400 × 460,000/540,000), being the proportion of chargeable business assets to chargeable assets.

156 The correct answers are:

5 April 2027	Latest date for election
Jerome and his son	Person(s) making election

157 £10,100

	£
Proceeds	12,200
Less cost	(2,100)
Chargeable gain	10,100

The maximum gain is 5/3 × £(12,200 × 6,000) = £10,333. The chargeable gain is the lower of £10,333 and £10,100, so it is £10,100.

If your choice was £3,900 make sure you don't confuse the rules on gains and the rules on losses – the deemed proceeds are only £6,000 for computing the restricted loss.

158 The correct answer is: £51,940

	£
Proceeds	78,400
Less cost (W)	(26,460)
Chargeable gain	51,940

Working

The amount of the cost attributable to the part sold is:

$$\frac{£78,400}{£78,400 + £33,600} \times £37,800 = £26,460$$

OT case – Hali and Goma (March/June 2019)

Workbook references

Capital gains tax (CGT) computation is covered in Chapter 13 and business reliefs in Chapter 15.

Top tips

Remember that current year losses are set against gains before the annual exempt amount (AEA), but brought forward losses are set against gains remaining after the AEA.

Easy marks

There were easy marks for knowledge of exempt assets for CGT.

159 The correct answer is: Option 4

Hali

	£
Gains	16,300
Less: AEA	(12,300)
	4,000
Less: Losses b/f	(4,000)
	0
Losses c/f £(39,300 – 4,000)	35,300

Goma

	£
Gains	6,900
Less: Current year losses	(9,100)
Losses c/f	(2,200)

For Hali, the answer £23,000 uses the carried forward loss against the gains first, before the annual exempt amount. For Goma, the answer £9,100 uses the annual exempt amount first so that there are no gains left to relieve.

160 The correct answer is: Option 1

The transfer of the shares between Goma and Hali was on a no gain/ no loss basis so Hali's cost is Goma's cost of £1 per share (par value). His cost of 5,000 shares is therefore 5,000 × £1 = £5,000.

The answer £14,500 is the value of 5,000 shares at the time of the transfer between Goma and Hali.

The value per share is £4.95.

The answer £5.30 could be the market value per share. This is used where there is a sale which is not at arm's length but not just because Hali wanted a quick sale.

161 The correct answer is: Lima Ltd must be a trading company

The first option is incorrect because the condition is that that they are either officers (could include company secretary, not just directors) or employees of the company.

The third option is incorrect because the condition is at least 5%.

The fourth option is incorrect because the qualifying period is two years.

162 The correct answer is: £45,600

	£
Proceeds (compensation received)	62,000
Less cost	(44,000)
Gain	18,000

ANSWERS

All proceeds reinvested so whole gain can be rolled over into the cost of the replacement asset.

The base cost of the replacement antique table is £(63,600 – 18,000) = £45,600.

The answer £62,000 is the compensation received. The answer £63,200 is the cost of the replacement antique table (ie no roll-over). The answer £44,000 is the cost of the original table.

163 The correct answer is: Three

Qualifying corporate bonds sold for £38,300

A car (suitable for private use) sold for £11,600

Quoted shares held within an individual savings account (ISA) sold for £24,700

The antique vase sold for £6,200 is a chargeable asset but the restriction applies of the gain to 5/3 × proceeds.

The copyright (with an unexpired life of eight years when purchased) sold for £5,400 is a chargeable asset but the cost will be written down on a straight-line basis so that only the remaining eight years of cost will be available.

OT Case - Lily (March/June 2021)

164 The correct answer is: £17,600

ACCA Examining Team's Comments

The copyright is a wasting asset; a useful life of 50 years or less, and the original value will depreciate over time.

£17,600 is the cost of £22,000 proportionate to the remaining life of the copyright. £22,000 × 12/15 = £17,600.

The alternative, incorrect options are:

£22,000 is the original cost.

£4,400 is the value by which the asset has depreciated: 3/15 × 22,000 = £4,400.

£19,067 is calculated using a remaining life of 13 years: 13/15 × 22,000 = £19,067.

165 The correct answer is: £73,200

ACCA Examining Team's Comments

The cost of the land originally purchased was for six acres but only four acres are sold. Unlike the copyright the land is not a wasting asset, therefore the original cost must be apportioned proportionate to the current market value.

The current market value is £200,000, being £140,000 (for the four acres sold) plus £60,000 (for the two acres not sold). Lily is also allowed to deduct any capital costs relating to the sale of this land; being the £14,400 for clearing and levelling those four acres.

The correct answer is the second option £73,200, being the proportion of the original cost £84,000 × (140,000/200,000) = £58,800 plus the costs of clearing and levelling of £14,400 = £73,200.

The alternative, incorrect answer options are:

The first option apportions the clearing and levelling costs across the six acres (84,000 + 14,400) × 140,000/200,000 = £68,880.

The third option apportions the cost by the number of acres and adds the capital cost (84,000 × 4/6) + 14,400 = £70,400.

The fourth option takes the correct proportion of the original cost but does not add the capital costs (84,000 × 140,000/200,000) = £58,800.

166 The correct answer is: 145 months

> **ACCA Examining Team's Comments**
>
> The months of actual occupation are shown clearly as 32 + 20 = 52. The deemed occupation must be preceded and succeeded by periods of occupation, so the first period of 36 months is covered as absence for any reason (up to three years) and the second period of working elsewhere in the UK is covered for 48 months. The final period of travelling is not covered as deemed occupation since there was no actual occupation afterwards. However, nine months of the final period of ownership are covered as deemed occupation, even if not actually occupied.
>
> The correct answer is the first option 145 being, 32 + 20 + 36 + 48 + 9 = 145.
>
> The alternative, incorrect answer options are:
>
> The second option 157 gives the full period of working in the UK (32 + 20 + 36 + 60 + 9) = 157.
>
> The third option 168 gives the full period of ownership.
>
> The fourth option 136 forgets the last nine months (32 +20 + 36 + 48) = 136.

167 The correct answer is: £11,880

> **ACCA Examining Team's Comments**
>
> The cash received on the takeover is treated as a part disposal and the original cost is apportioned according to current market value of £19,800 cash plus £48,400 (22,000 shares at £2.20) = £68,200. Applying this to the original cost of £27,780 gives £7,920 (£27,280 × £19,800/£68,200).
>
> The correct answer is £11,880, being proceeds of £19,800 cash, less apportioned cost of £7,920 = £11,880.
>
> The alternative, incorrect options are:
>
> £6,878 where the shares are valued at par and not current market value (19,800 – (27,280 × 19,800/(19,800 + 22,000)) = £6,878).
>
> £19,800 is the cash received.
>
> £8,640 apportions the cost by the market value of the shares only (19,800 – (27,280 × 19,800/(22,000 × 2.2) = £8,640).

168 The correct answer is: £31,048

> **ACCA Examining Team's Comments**
>
> Lily's sister has no taxable income for the year 2022/23 therefore her basic rate band is available. The chargeable gains (rather than taxable gains) are given and so the annual exempt amount (AEA) is also available of £12,300.
>
> It is more beneficial to set off the AEA against the residential gain; since residential property is subject to tax at 18% and 28%, whereas the other gain is taxed at 10% only.
>
> However, this gain qualifying for business asset disposal relief will use up the full basic rate band. So, this gain will be £44,200 which will be taxed at 10% = £4,420. The residential gain will be £107,400 less AEA of £12,300 = £95,100 which will be taxed at 28% = £26,628.
>
> The correct answer is £31,048, being £4,420 as above plus £26,628 as above = £31,048.

ANSWERS

The alternative, incorrect options are:

£34,492 forgets about AEA and correctly taxes the gain qualifying for business asset disposal relief (107,400 × 28% = £30,072 plus £4,420) = £34,492.

£27,278 applies 18% to the £37,700 of the gain on residential property forgetting that the other gain will use this basic rate band first (£107,400 - £12,300 = £95,100 taxed as £37,700 × 18% = £6,786 and remaining £57,400 × 28%= £16,072 plus the gain of £44,200 at 10% = £4,420) = a total of £27,278.

£33,262 applies the AEA against the gain qualifying for business asset disposal relief rather than against the residential gain. (£107,400 × 28% + ((£44,200 - £12,300) × 10%)) = £33,262.

Section C

169 Jorge (December 2011) (amended)

Workbook references

Chapter 13 deals with the basic computation of chargeable gains, including the annual exempt amount. Chapter 14 covers wasting assets, chattels, and the private residence exemption.

Top tips

Remember that deemed periods of occupation for private residence relief must usually be preceded by a period of actual occupation and followed by a period of actual occupation.

Easy marks

The painting and the car were easy half marks. Don't forget to deduct the annual exempt amount for another easy half mark.

Marking guide	Marks	
House		
Proceeds	0.5	
Cost	0.5	
Enhancement expenditure	0.5	
Period of exemption	3	
Private residence exemption	1	
Copyright		
Proceeds	0.5	
Cost	1.5	
Painting	0.5	
Car	0.5	
Annual exempt amount	0.5	
Capital loss bf	1	
		10
Total		10

Jorge – taxable gains computation 2022/23

	£
House (W1)	31,000
Copyright (W4)	24,300
Painting – exempt as proceeds and cost £6,000 or less	0
Car – exempt asset so loss not allowable	0
Chargeable gains	55,300
Less annual exempt amount	(12,300)
Less capital loss bf	(25,000)
Taxable gains	18,000

ANSWERS

Workings

1 *House*

	£
Proceeds	308,000
Less cost	(93,000)
Less enhancement expenditure (defending title to property)	(5,000)
Gain	210,000
Less private residence exemption (W2)	(179,000)
Gain after exemptions	31,000

2 *Private residence exemption*

	Exempt months	*Chargeable months*	*Total months*
Actual occupation	34		34
Deemed occupation – up to 3 years any reason	18		18
Deemed occupation – any time employed overseas	24		24
Actual occupation	11		11
Deemed occupation – up to 4 years working elsewhere in UK	30		30
Deemed occupation – up to 3 years any reason balance (36 – 18) = 18, (22 – 18) = 4 chargeable	18	4	22
Deemed occupation – up to 4 years working elsewhere in UK balance (48 – 30) = 18, (26 – 18) = 8 chargeable	18	8	26
Actual occupation	17		17
Working overseas – not followed by actual occupation		12	12
Unoccupied – travelling		7	7
Last 9 months – always treated as period of occupation	9		9
Totals	179	31	210

Private residence exemption £210,000 × 179/210	£179,000

Tutorial note. In calculating the private residence exemption, any periods of absence while working overseas, a maximum of four years' absence while working elsewhere in the UK, and a maximum of three years' absence for any reason are treated as deemed occupation, usually provided that they are preceded and followed by a period of actual occupation. The second period working overseas is therefore not a period of deemed occupation as it was not followed by a period of actual occupation.

No letting relief is available since Jorge let out the whole property while he was away, rather than sharing occupation.

3 *Alternative approach*

An alternative approach to calculate the chargeable months as follows:

	Months
Total period of ownership	210
Less actual occupation (34 + 11 + 17)	(62)
Deemed occupation:	
– any reason up to 3 years	(36)
– employed overseas without limit	(24)
– working in UK up to 4 years	(48)
Last 9 months – always treated as period of occupation	(9)
Chargeable months	31

4 *Copyright*

	£
Proceeds	80,300
Less cost £70,000 × 8/10 (N)	(56,000)
Gain	24,300

Tutorial note. The copyright is a wasting asset. The cost of £70,000 must therefore be depreciated based on an unexpired life of ten years at the date of acquisition and an unexpired life of eight years at the date of disposal.

170 Winston (June 2012) (amended)

Workbook references

Chapter 13 covers transfers on death, computing chargeable gains, transfers between spouses, part disposals and CGT liability. Chapter 15 includes business asset disposal relief.

Top tips

Losses on assets not qualifying for business asset disposal relief and the annual exempt amount should be deducted to produce the lowest CGT liability. This means that they should be deducted from gains taxed at 20% in priority to gains taxed at 10%.

Easy marks

The calculation of capital gains tax in part (a)(i) was straightforward.

Marking guide

			Marks	
(a)	(i)	Annual exempt amount	1	
		Unused basic rate band	0.5	
		Capital gains tax	1.5	
				3
	(ii)	Freehold shop	0.5	
		Painting	0.5	
		Capital loss	1	
		Annual exempt amount	0.5	
		Capital gains tax	1.5	
				4
(b)		Net proceeds	1	
		Cost – probate value taken over on transfer from spouse	1	
		Apportionment of cost	1	
				3
Total				10

(a) (i) **Winston – CGT liability 2022/23**

	£
Chargeable gain on painting	47,560
Less annual exempt amount	(12,300)
Taxable gain	35,260
CGT liability: £(37,700 – 25,100) = 12,600 @ 10%	1,260
£(35,260 – 12,600) = 22,660 @ 20%	4,532
	5,792

(ii) **Winston – revised CGT liability 2022/23**

	£
Gain qualifying for business asset disposal relief	
Gain on freehold shop £(140,000 – 80,000)	60,000
Gain not qualifying for business asset disposal relief	
Painting	47,560
Less allowable loss on warehouse £(102,000 – 88,000)	(14,000)
Net gain	33,560
Less annual exempt amount	(12,300)
Taxable gain	21,260
CGT liability: £60,000 @ 10%	6,000
£21,260 @ 20%	4,252
	10,252

Tutorial note. The capital loss on the sale of the freehold warehouse and the annual exempt amount are set against the chargeable gain from the sale of the painting as this saves CGT at the higher rate of 20%. Although the warehouse is being sold with the business, it was never actually used in the business, and so this aspect of the sale does not qualify for business asset disposal relief. If it had been used in the business, the loss of £14,000 would have been deducted from the gain on the shop to give a net gain on sale of the business of £46,000. CGT would then be charged on £46,000 at 10%.

Tutorial note. The unused basic rate tax band of £12,600 is effectively used by the gain qualifying for business asset disposal relief of £60,000 even though this has no effect on the 10% tax rate.

(b) **Renaldo – chargeable gain 3 December 2022**

	£
Gross proceeds	92,000
Less auctioneers' commission (cost of disposal) £92,000 × 5%	(4,600)
Net proceeds	87,400
Less cost $£28,600 \times \frac{92,000}{92,000 + 38,000}$	(20,240)
Chargeable gain	67,160

Tutorial note. The cost of the land is £28,600 which is the value when Renaldo's father-in-law died. Renaldo would have taken over this cost when his wife transferred the land to him.

Tutorial note. The gross proceeds of sale are used in the part-disposal fraction.

171 Mick (June 2014) (amended)

Workbook references

The computation of chargeable gains for individuals is covered in Chapter 13. Shares are the subject of Chapter 16. Business reliefs are dealt with in Chapter 15.

Top tips

In part (b) you need to think about how you would use replacement of business asset relief and business asset disposal relief to identify the missing information.

Easy marks

The share pool in part (a) should have scored easy marks.

Marking guide	Marks
(a) Warehouse	
Disposal proceeds	0.5
Cost	0.5
Extension	0.5
Floor	0.5
Shares in Rolling Ltd	

ANSWERS

Marking guide		Marks
Disposal proceeds	0.5	
Purchase	0.5	
Bonus issue	0.5	
Disposal cost	0.5	
		4
(b) Warehouse		
Replacement of business assets relief	1	
Acquisition date of new warehouse	1	
Cost of new warehouse	1	
Shares in Rolling Ltd		
Business asset disposal relief	1	
Rolling Ltd share capital	1	
Previous claims	1	
		6
Total		10

(a) **Mick – chargeable gains 2022/23**

Freehold warehouse

	£	£
Disposal proceeds		522,000
Less: Cost	258,000	
Enhancement expenditure: extension	99,000	
Enhancement expenditure: floor	0	
		(357,000)
Chargeable gain		165,000

Tutorial note. The cost of replacing the warehouse's floor is revenue expenditure as the floor is a subsidiary part of the property.

Shares in Rolling Ltd

	£
Disposal proceeds	3,675,000
Less cost (W)	(537,600)
Chargeable gain	3,137,400

Working

Share pool

	Number	Cost
		£
Purchase June 2007	500,000	960,000
Bonus issue December 2012		
500,000 × 3/2	750,000	0
Disposal September 2022	1,250,000	960,000
960,000 × 700,000/1,250,000	(700,000)	(537,600)
Balance carried forward	550,000	422,400

(b) **Freehold warehouse**

Replacement of business assets relief (rollover relief) may be available in respect of the chargeable gain arising on the disposal of the freehold warehouse.

The acquisition date of the replacement warehouse is required since relief will only be available if this is after 19 May 2021 (one year before the date of disposal).

The cost of the replacement warehouse is required since relief will be restricted if the sale proceeds of £522,000 have not been fully reinvested.

Shares in Rolling Ltd

Business asset disposal relief may be available in respect of the chargeable gain arising on the disposal of the shares in Rolling Ltd.

Details of Rolling Ltd's share capital are required, since relief will only be available if Mick had the minimum required holding of 5%.

Details of any previous business asset disposal relief claims made by Mick are required, since there is a lifetime limit of £1 million of gains.

172 Ruby (September/December 2015) (amended)

Workbook references

The computation of chargeable gains and capital gains tax is covered in Chapter 13. Business reliefs are the subject of Chapter 15 and shares are dealt with in Chapter 16.

Top tips

The annual exempt amount should be set against gains which do not qualify for investors' relief in priority to those which do qualify for the relief.

Easy marks

There were easy marks in part (a) for a basic computation of capital gains tax.

Examining team's comments

Part (a) of the question was well answered.

In part (b), the main problem was that candidates did not appreciate that both disposals would impact on the capital gains tax payable in respect of the disposal of the investment property. The disposal of the shares in the unquoted trading company (qualifying for investors' relief) would utilise the remaining basic rate tax band, meaning that the 28% rate was now applicable. The capital loss arising on the disposal of the shares in the quoted trading company would be offset against the chargeable gain on the investment property.

Another common problem was the 50p nominal value of the shares in the quoted trading company. This did not impact on the calculation of the capital loss, although many candidates incorrectly divided their cost figure by two.

Marking guide

		Marks	
(a)	Annual exempt amount	0.5	
	CGT at 18%	1	
	CGT at 28%	0.5	
			2
(b)	Pola Ltd		
	Disposal proceeds	0.5	
	Cost	0.5	
	Investment property	0.5	
	Annual exempt amount (best use)	1	
	CGT at 10%	1	
	CGT at 28%	1	
	Aplo plc		
	Disposal proceeds	0.5	
	Cost	1.5	
	Investment property	0.5	
	Annual exempt amount	0.5	
	CGT at 18%	0.5	
			8
Total			10

(a) **Ruby's CGT liability**

	£
Chargeable gain on investment property	47,000
Less annual exempt amount	(12,300)
	34,700
Capital gains tax	
£14,185 (37,700 – 23,515) @ 18% (residential property)	2,553
£20,515 (34,700 – 14,185) @ 28% (residential property)	5,744
	8,297

(b) **Choice of disposal**

Shareholding in Pola Ltd

	Investors' relief	*No reliefs*
	£	£
Pola Ltd shares £(61,000 – 23,700)	37,300	
Investment property (part (a))		47,000

	Investors' relief	No reliefs
	£	£
Less annual exempt amount (best use)	–	(12,300)
	37,300	34,700
Capital gains tax		
£37,300 @ 10%	3,730	
£34,700 @ 28%		9,716
Total CGT £(3,730 + 9,716)		13,446

Tutorial note. The shares in Pola Ltd qualify for investors' relief because they are shares in an unlisted trading company of which Ruby is neither an officer nor an employee, were subscribed for by Ruby on or after 17 March 2016 and held by her for at least 3 years before the disposal.

Shareholding in Aplo plc

	£
Aplo plc shares £59,000 – (40,000 × £2.15(W))	(27,000)
Investment property (part (a))	47,000
Less annual exempt amount	(12,300)
Taxable gain	7,700
Capital gains tax	
£7,700 @ 18%	1,386

Working

The Aplo plc shares are valued at £2.12 + ½ × (£2.18 – £2.12) = £2.15.

ANSWERS

PART D: INHERITANCE TAX

Section A

OTQ bank – Inheritance tax 1

173 £ 150,000

	£
Before the gift: 70% shareholding	350,000
After the gift: 50% shareholding	(200,000)
Transfer of value	150,000

174 £461,250

	£
Sunita's unused nil rate band £325,000 × 65%	211,250
Joel's nil rate band	325,000
	536,250
Less used against Joel's PET now chargeable	(75,000)
Available nil rate band to set against Joel's death estate	461,250

Sunita's nil rate band is increased pro-rata to that available at the time of Joel's death.

The answer £325,000 does not involve a spouse transfer and does not take account of the PET. The answer £452,800 transfers 65% of £312,000. The answer £536,250 does not deduct the PET.

175 The correct answer is: £29,750

	£
Gift	190,000
Less AE × 2 (current year + b/f)	(6,000)
	184,000
Less nil rate band available £(325,000 – 260,000)	(65,000)
	119,000
IHT @ $^{20}/_{80}$	29,750

The answer £28,250 deducts annual exemptions from the earlier transfer. The answer £31,250 does not deduct annual exemptions from the current transfer. The answer £23,800 does not gross up, ie uses a rate of 20%.

176 The correct answer is: £0

The gift to the granddaughter is covered by the marriage exemption of £2,500 by a remoter ancestor.

The sale of the vase is not a transfer of value because there is no gratuitous intent as Donald and Alan believed that the vase was worth what Alan paid for it.

177 The correct answer is: £136,000

	£
PET on 10.7.19 PET now chargeable	600,000
Less nil rate band available £(325,000 – 150,000)	(175,000)
	425,000
IHT @ 40%	170,000
Less taper relief (3 to 4 years) @ 20%	(34,000)
Death tax payable on lifetime transfer	136,000

The chargeable lifetime transfer on 15 September 2013 is cumulated with the later PET since it was made in the seven years before that transfer.

The answer £170,000 does not deduct taper relief. The answer £88,000 treats the earlier gift as exempt so the full nil rate band is available. The answer £134,080 deducts annual exemptions from the current transfer.

OTQ bank – Inheritance tax 2

178 The correct answer is: £350

The gifts to the grandson are exempt as normal expenditure out of income because they are part of the normal expenditure of the donor, made out of income and left the donor with sufficient income to maintain her usual standard of living.

The small gifts exemption only applies to gifts up to £250 per donee per tax year. If gifts total more than £250 the whole amount is chargeable. Since the gifts to the grandnephew totalled £(100 + 250) = £350 in the year, this exemption does not apply.

179 £66,000

	£
Before the gift: 100% shareholding 1,000 × £150	150,000
After the gift: 70% shareholding 700 × £120	(84,000)
Transfer of value	66,000

180 £ 15,200

ACCA Examining Team's Comments

Firstly, a review of the lifetime gifts at time of death shows that the chargeable lifetime transfer (CLT) in October 2015 is more than seven years before death so that falls out of consideration.

The CLT in June 2019 is within seven years of death so that will have to be reassessed on death. The NRB on death is £325,000, less the CLT in June 2019 of £118,000, gives a remaining NRB of £207,000.

Death liability on the estate is therefore the chargeable death estate of £245,000 less the remaining NRB after reviewing the lifetime transfers of £207,000, giving a taxable estate of £38,000 at the death rate of 40% = £15,200.

181 £ 351,000

	£
Cash to nephews £200 × 5	1,000
ISA investments	350,000
Chargeable estate	351,000

The small gifts exemption only applies to lifetime transfers. The ISA exemption only applies for income tax and capital gains tax. The residue to the wife is covered by the spouse exemption.

182 The correct answer is: Sandeep is liable to make the payment by 31 May 2023

ACCA Examining Team's Comments

This question tested candidates' knowledge of the payment of IHT on a chargeable lifetime transfer (CLT) to a trust.

The donor, Sandeep, is primarily liable for the tax due on a CLT and the due date is the later of the following:

- Six months after the end of the month of transfer
- 30 April after the end of the tax year of transfer

The later of these dates is therefore 31 May 2023 and so the correct answer was the third option. Many candidates were able to select the correct date but were less successful in determining who was primarily liable for payment.

Tax administration and the payment of tax are important aspects of the syllabus and candidates are reminded to devote sufficient attention to these topics when preparing for the TX – UK exam.

183 £234,000

	£
Estate	890,000
Less: IHT	(276,000)
Legacy to wife	(260,000)
Legacy to brother	(120,000)
Residue to grandchildren	234,000

184 The correct answers are:

Changing the terms of her will so that the residue of her estate goes to her grandchildren rather than her children		**WILL NOT ACHIEVE**
Making lifetime gifts to trusts up to the value of the nil rate band every seven years	**WILL ACHIEVE**	
Changing the terms of her will so that the residue of her estate goes to her husband rather than her children	**WILL ACHIEVE**	
Making lifetime gifts to her grandchildren early in life	**WILL ACHIEVE**	

There will be the same amount of inheritance tax on the residue of the estate if it is left to Heng's children or grandchildren. However, if the estate is left to her husband the spouse exemption will apply. Heng could reduce the potential inheritance tax liability on her estate

when she dies by making lifetime gifts to trusts up to the value of the nil rate band every seven years as these will reduce her assets and will not be cumulated if she survives seven years. She could also make lifetime gifts to her grandchildren early in life as these would be potentially exempt transfers and she is more likely to survive seven years the earlier in life she makes the gifts.

185 The correct answers are:

30 June 2023	Due date
The trustees	Persons responsible

ACCA Examining Team's Comments

This question tested knowledge of when IHT will be payable and by whom. The correct answer was the trustees on 30 June 2023, which is six months following the month of death. More candidates selected this option than any of the others, but 'The personal representatives of Chan's estate on 30 June 2023' and 'The trustees on 8 June 2023' were both popular choices. This is fairly basic knowledge, and it is the type of question which should represent a very easy (and quick) two marks.

186 The correct answer is: £220,000

Nadia is entitled to her husband's residence nil rate band (as it was unused at the date of his death). It is assumed to be £175,000. The maximum residence nil rate band is therefore £(175,000 + 175,000) = £350,000.

The residence nil rate band is the lower of the maximum residence nil rate band of £350,000 and the net value of the main residence of £(360,000 – 140,000) = £220,000, ie £220,000.

187 The inheritance tax liability on Rachel's estate will [decrease] by [£70,000] if she leaves her main residence to her son rather than her brother.

The residence nil rate band is the lower of the maximum residence nil rate band of £350,000 and the net value of the main residence of £(360,000 – 140,000) = £220,000, ie £220,000.

The inheritance tax liability on Rachel's estate will decrease by £70,000 if she leaves her main residence to her son rather than her brother.

This is because the residence nil rate band will apply since Rachel will be leaving her main residence to a direct descendent. The available residence nil rate band is the lower of £175,000 and £300,000 ie £175,000. This gives a decrease in the inheritance tax liability of £175,000 × 40% = £70,000.

ANSWERS

Section B

OT case – Ning (June 2012) (amended)

Workbook reference

Inheritance tax is covered in Chapter 18.

Top tips

If the nil rate band has increased since the death of the first spouse, the available nil rate band to be transferred on the death of the surviving spouse is calculated with reference to the increased nil rate band.

Easy marks

The second question was quite straightforward as long as you did not confuse the exemptions for income tax and capital gains tax on certain investments with the inheritance tax position.

188 The correct answer is: £956,000

	£
Property one	674,000
Less repayment mortgage	(160,000)
	514,000
Property two	442,000
	956,000

189 The correct answer is: £324,000

	£
Cars	172,000
Investments £(47,000 + 36,000 + 69,000)	152,000
	324,000

There are no exempt assets for inheritance tax.

190 The correct answer is: £27,900

	£
Bank loan	22,400
Nephew's legal fees	0
Funeral expenses	5,500
	27,900

The promise to pay the nephew's legal fees is not deductible as it is purely gratuitous (not made for valuable consideration).

191 The correct answer is: £105,000

The potentially exempt transfer on 14 August 2011 is exempt from inheritance tax as it was made more than seven years before 20 March 2023.

The potentially exempt transfer on 7 November 2021 will utilise £220,000 of the nil rate band, so only £(325,000 – 220,000) = £105,000 is available against the death estate. The residence nil rate band is not available as it cannot be used against lifetime gifts.

192 The correct answer is:

Amount	Claim
£227,500	By 31 March 2025

Ning's personal representatives could claim her deceased husband's unused nil rate band of £325,000 × 70% = £227,500. The time limit for the claim is two years from the end of the month of Ning's death ie by 31 March 2025.

OT case – Jimmy (June 2011) (amended)

Workbook references

Inheritance tax is dealt with in Chapter 18.

Top tips

Watch out for the spouse exemption – it applies both to lifetime gifts and on death.

Easy marks

There were easy marks in the fourth question for identifying the date of payment of additional tax on the lifetime gift as a result of Jimmy's death and that it was payable by the donee of the gift (the trustees of the trust).

193 The correct answer is: £8,500

	£
Marriage exemption	2,500
Annual exemption 2021/22	3,000
Annual exemption 2020/21 b/f	3,000
	8,500

The answer £3,000 is just the current year annual exemption. The answer £6,000 is the annual exemptions for the current year and the previous year. The answer £11,000 uses £5,000 as the marriage exemption.

194 £55,000

	£
Before the gift: 5,100 shares × £30	153,000
After the gift: 4,900 shares × £20	(98,000)
Diminution in value	55,000

The answer £4,000 is 200 shares at £20 each. The answer £6,000 is 200 shares at £30 each. The answer £1,000 is the actual value of the shares gifted which is 200 shares at £5 each.

195 £ 118,750

	£
Net transfer of value (Jimmy pays IHT)	800,000

ANSWERS

			£
IHT	£325,000	× 0% =	Nil
	£475,000	× 20/80 =	118,750
	£800,000		118,750

The annual exemptions have been used by the PET in August 2021.

196 The correct answers are:

Trustees of trust	By whom paid
31 August 2023	Due date

197 £ 312,000

	£
Death estate	980,000
Less spouse exemption	(200,000)
Chargeable death estate	780,000
£780,000 × 40%	312,000

The nil rate band has been used up by the lifetime transfers (stated in question) so the chargeable death estate is all taxed at 40%.

OT case – Zoe and Luke (June 2015) (amended)

Workbook reference

Inheritance tax is the subject of Chapter 18.

Top tips

Be careful to read the question thoroughly. You were told that Zoe always used her annual exemption in April each year.

Easy marks

There were some easy marks for working out the additional IHT due.

198 The correct answers are:

- The payments could be exempt without any cash limit under the normal expenditure out of income exemption.
- The payments must have left Luke with sufficient income to maintain his usual standard of living to qualify for the normal expenditure out of income exemption.

Payments can qualify for the normal expenditure out of income exemption even if they are not paid directly to the individual who benefits from them. The payments did not have been reported each tax year to HM Revenue & Customs in Luke's income tax return to qualify for the normal expenditure out of income exemption (they will be reported in the inheritance tax account submitted on Luke's death).

199 The correct answer is: £710,000

	£
Net chargeable transfer (AEs already used)	633,000
IHT	
£325,000 × 0%	0
£308,000 × 20/80	77,000
£633,000	77,000
Gross chargeable transfer £(633,000 + 77,000)	710,000

The answer £702,500 deducts two annual exemptions. The answer £694,600 treats the transfer as a gross chargeable transfer so uses the rate of 20%. The answer £756,200 uses the death rate of 40%.

200 £24,000

	£
Gross chargeable transfer	200,000
IHT on death (nil rate band already used)	
£200,000 × 40%	80,000
Less taper relief (3 to 4 years) £80,000 × 20%	(16,000)
	64,000
Less lifetime tax £200,000 × 20%	(40,000)
Additional IHT payable	24,000

The answer £40,000 does not deduct taper relief. The answer £80,000 is the death tax without deducting taper relief or lifetime tax. The answer £64,000 does not deduct lifetime tax.

201 £ 259,000

	£
Gift	270,000
Less	
Marriage exemption	(5,000)
Annual exemption current year	(3,000)
Annual exemption b/f	(3,000)
Potentially exempt transfer	259,000

202 The correct answer is: £75,000

	£
Unused nil rate band at wife's death £(312,000 – 240,000)	72,000
Amount to transfer £325,000 × 72,000/312,000	75,000

The answer £72,000 does not adjust for the change in the nil rate band between the death of Luke's wife and Luke. The answer £312,000 is the nil rate band at the date of Luke's wife's death. The answer £325,000 is the nil rate band at Luke's death.

OT case – Marcus (Sept/Dec 2015) (amended)

Workbook references

Inheritance tax is dealt with in Chapter 18.

Top tips

Don't mix up the rules for transfers between spouses for capital gains tax (no gain/no loss transfer) and inheritance tax (exempt transfer).

Easy marks

There were some easy marks for a basic inheritance tax computation provided that you remembered that the nil rate band at the date of the transfer should be used.

203 £ 600

			£
IHT	£325,000	× 0% =	Nil
	£3,000	×20% =	600
	£328,000		600

204 The correct answer is: £98,250

			£
IHT	£0	(325,000 – 328,000) × 0% =	Nil
	£491,250	× 20%	98,250
	£491,250		98,250

Although Marcus pays the inheritance tax due, since the gross chargeable transfer is given, to work out the tax he pays, this is 20% of the excess over the available nil rate band.

The answer £122,812 grosses up (ie uses 20/80). The answer £33,250 uses the full nil rate band. The answer £41,562 uses the full nil rate band and grosses up.

205 £78,600

			£
IHT	£0	× 0% =	Nil
	£491,250	× 40% =	196,500
	£491,250		196,500
Taper relief (4 to 5 years) £196,500 @ 40%			78,600

The answer £117,900 is the tax payable after taper relief. The answer £26,600 does not take account of the brought forward transfer. The answer £39,900 is does not take account of the brought forward transfer and is the tax payable after taper relief.

206 The correct answer is: £570,000

	£
Before: 100,000 × £12	1,200,000
After: 70,000 × £9	(630,000)
Potentially exempt transfer of value	570,000

The answer £360,000 is 30,000 shares at £12 each. The answer £270,000 is 30,000 shares at £9 each. The answer £150,000 is 30,000 shares at £5 each.

207 The correct answers are:

- If Barbara remarries, any unused nil rate band on her death can be transferred to her spouse if they survive her.
- The transfer of Marcus's estate to Barbara on his death is an exempt transfer.

Married couples (and registered civil partnerships) are not chargeable persons for inheritance tax (IHT) purposes, because each spouse (or civil partner) is taxed separately.

The gift of the land on 29 June 2020 by Marcus to Barbara is an exempt transfer.

OT case – Lebna and Lulu (March/June 2019)

Workbook references

Inheritance tax (IHT) is the subject of Chapter 18.

Top tips

Remember that IHT is charged on the diminution of the donor's estate, not on the value of the property transferred.

Easy marks

The taper relief percentage will be found in the Tax Rates and Allowances in the exam, and you should have known the payment date for IHT as a result of death.

208 The correct answer is: £205,000

	£
Nil rate band at Lulu's death	325,000
Less: Potentially exempt transfer (PET) now chargeable (within seven years of death)	(80,000)
Legacy to brother	(40,000)
Lulu's nil rate band for transfer to Lebna	205,000

Since the nil rate band at the date of both Lulu's and Lebna's death is the same (£325,000) there is no need to adjust the amount available to transfer.

The chargeable lifetime transfer (CLT) is more than seven years before Lulu's death and is therefore not cumulated on death. It would be cumulated to work out any inheritance tax on the PET (although in this case the cumulative amount would be within the nil rate band at Lulu's death and so no tax would be payable on the PET).

The answer £155,000 cumulates the CLT. The answer £35,000 deducts the PET twice, the legacy twice and the CLT once. The answer £285,000 only deducts the legacy.

209 The correct answer is: £188,000

	£	£
Lebna's available residence nil rate band (RNRB) is lower of:		
Value of house	340,000	
Less mortgage	(152,000)	
		188,000
Maximum RNRB at date of death = £175,000	175,000	
Lulu's RNRB	175,000	
Maximum RNRB		350,000
Available RNRB		188,000

The whole of Lulu's RNRB is available for transfer because she died before 6 April 2017 (so even if she had had a main residence at her death, it could not have been used since this was the date of introduction of the RNRB). It is not necessary that Lulu had a main residence at her death, the condition is that Lebnar has a main residence at his death which he leaves to a direct descendent (his son).

The answer £175,000 is just Lebna's RNRB. The answer £350,000 is the maximum RNRB. The answer £340,000 is the gross value of Lebna's main residence.

210 The correct answer is: £536,000

	£
Before transfer: 100,000 @ £7.10	710,000
Less After transfer: 40,000 @ £4.20	(168,000)
Transfer of value (diminution in value)	542,000
Less Current year and previous year annual exemptions £3,000 × 2	(6,000)
Potentially exempt transfer	536,000

The answer £542,000 does not deduct the annual exemptions (make sure you read the question carefully if you chose this answer!). The answer £372,000 is the value of the gifted holding (60,000 @ £6.30) less annual exemptions. The answer £378,000 is just the value of the gifted holding.

211 The correct answer is: Option 1

The period between the date of the PET (22 February 2018) and the date of Lebna's death (1 March 2023) is between five and six years so the taper relief reduction is 60% (in the Tax Rates and Allowance available in the exam).

The answer 40% is the amount of the transfer on which tax will be charged at the death rate.

The due date for payable of death tax on a PET is the end of six months following the month of death which is 30 September 2023.

The answer 1 September 2023 is exactly six months from the date of Lebna's death.

212 The correct answer is: £225

Only the gift of £225 is exempt under the small gifts exemption.

The limit of £250 applies per donee per tax year so the gifts of £(85 + 190) = £275 and £490 both exceed the limit.

The answer £500 exempts the gifts of £85, £225 and £190. The answer £990 exempts all the gifts. The answer £275 exempts the gifts of £85 and £190.

Section C

213 Pere and Phil (June 2013) (amended)

Workbook references

Inheritance tax is dealt with in Chapter 18. Chargeable gains and the computation of capital gains tax are in Chapter 13. The points on distinguishing between revenue and capital expenditure are covered in Chapter 7.

Top tips

You don't need to know names of tax cases in the Taxation (TX – UK) exam, but you are expected to know, and be able to apply, the principles decided, as in part (b) here.

Easy marks

There were some easy marks in part (a) for using the exemptions.

Marking guide	Marks	
(a) *Lifetime gift*		
Marriage exemption	1	
Annual exemption – current year	0.5	
Annual exemption – brought forward	0.5	
Potentially exempt transfer	0.5	
IHT @ 0%	0.5	
IHT @ 40%	0.5	
Taper relief	1	
Death estate		
Spouse exemption	1	
IHT @ 40%	0.5	
		6
(b) Disposal proceeds	0.5	
Cost	1	
Enhancement	1	
Annual exempt amount	0.5	
Capital gains tax @ 18%	0.5	
Capital gains tax @ 28%	0.5	
		4
Total		10

(a) **Pere – Inheritance tax (IHT) arising on death**

Lifetime transfer 23 August 2016

		£
Gift		420,000
Less:	Marriage exemption	(5,000)
	Annual exemption current year	(3,000)

	£
Annual exemption b/f	(3,000)
Potentially exempt transfer	409,000
IHT	
£325,000 @ 0%	0
£84,000 @ 40%	33,600
£409,000	
Less taper relief (6 to 7 years @ 80%)	(26,880)
IHT payable	6,720

Tutorial note. The potentially exempt transfer becomes chargeable as a result of Pere dying within seven years of making it.

Death estate

	£
Value of estate	880,000
Less spouse exemption £880,000/2	(440,000)
Chargeable estate	440,000
IHT on £440,000 @ 40%	176,000

(b) **Phil – capital gains tax computation 2022/23**

	£
Net disposal proceeds	496,700
Less: Cost	(420,000)
Enhancement expenditure	(5,200)
Gain	71,500
Less annual exempt amount	(12,300)
Taxable gain	59,200
CGT on £23,550 (37,700 – 14,150) @ 18%	4,239
CGT on £35,650 (59,200 – 23,550) @ 28%	9,982
	14,221

Tutorial note. The cost of replacing the property's chimney is revenue expenditure because the chimney is a part of the house and so this is a repair to the house. The cost of the new boundary wall is capital expenditure because the wall is a separate structure which is not part of the house.

Tutorial note. Because the house is residential property, the gain is taxed at 18% and 28% rather than 10% and 20%.

214 Afiya (December 2013) (amended)

Workbook references

Inheritance tax is covered in Chapter 18.

Top tips

A potentially exempt transfer is treated as if it were an exempt transfer during the lifetime of the donor, so it does not affect the computation of lifetime tax on subsequent chargeable lifetime transfers.

Easy marks

The calculation of the residue in part (b) was an easy mark.

Marking guide	Marks	
(a) *Lifetime transfers*		
Cassava Ltd shares		
Value of shares before transfer	1	
Value of shares after transfer	1	
Annual exemption current year	0.5	
Annual exemption brought forward	0.5	
Cash		
Nil rate band	0.5	
Balance @ 20/80	0.5	
Additional liabilities arising on death		
Cassava Ltd shares		
Potentially exempt transfer now chargeable	1	
Cash		
Gross chargeable transfer	0.5	
Nil rate band	0.5	
Balance @ 40%	0.5	
Lifetime tax already paid	0.5	
Death tax		
Value of estate	0.5	
Spouse exemption	0.5	
Residence nil rate band	0.5	
Charge @ 40%	0.5	
		9
(b) Residue of estate		
		1
Total		10

(a) **Afiya – Inheritance tax on death**

Lifetime transfers

14 September 2021

	£
Value of shares held before transfer 8,000 × £8	64,000
Less value of shares held after transfer 1,500 × £3	(4,500)
Transfer of value	59,500
Less: Annual exemption current year	(3,000)
Annual exemption b/f	(3,000)
Potentially exempt transfer	53,500

27 January 2022

	£
Net chargeable transfer	400,000
IHT	
325,000 × 0%	0
75,000 × 20/80 (donor pays tax)	18,750
400,000	18,750
Gross chargeable transfer £(400,000 + 18,750)	418,750

Additional tax on lifetime transfer on death of donor

14 September 2021

Potentially exempt transfer of £53,500 becomes chargeable as donor dies within seven years. Within nil rate band at death, no tax to pay.

27 January 2022

Nil rate band available £(325,000 – 53,500) = £271,500.

	£
Gross chargeable transfer	418,750
IHT	
271,500 × 0%	0
147,250 × 40%	58,900
418,750	58,900
No taper relief (death within three years of transfer)	
Less lifetime tax paid	(18,750)
Additional tax payable on death	40,150

Death estate

	£
Assets at death	623,000
Less funeral expenses	(3,000)
Value of estate for IHT purposes	620,000

	£
Less exempt legacy to spouse	(150,000)
Chargeable estate	470,000
Less residence nil rate band (lower of £90,000 and £175,000)	(90,000)
Taxable estate	380,000
IHT liability £380,000 × 40%	152,000

The nil rate band was used by lifetime transfers.

(b) Afiya's children will inherit the residue of £(620,000 – 150,000 – 40,000 – 152,000) = £278,000.

215 Kendra (June 2014) (amended)

Workbook references

Inheritance tax is covered in Chapter 18.

Top tips

Lifetime gifts may involve both inheritance tax and capital gains tax.

Sometimes it will be preferable for a gift to be made on death since there is no capital gains tax charge on death and the assets will pass to the beneficiary at death (probate) value.

Easy marks

The calculation of the death estate should have been easy marks.

Marking guide		Marks
(a) Property	0.5	
Building society deposits	0.5	
ISAs	0.5	
NS&I certificates	0.5	
Proceeds of life assurance policy	1	
Income tax	0.5	
Loan	0.5	
Inheritance tax	1	
		5
(b) No IHT benefit	1.5	
No CGT benefit	1.5	
		3
(c) Skip a generation	1	
Avoids double charge to IHT	1	
		2
Total		10

(a) **Kendra – inheritance tax on death**

	£
Property	970,000
Building society deposits	387,000
Individual savings accounts	39,000
NS&I certificates	17,000
Proceeds of life policy	225,000
Gross estate	1,638,000
Less: Income tax	(12,800)
Loan	(1,200)
Net estate	1,624,000
Inheritance tax	
£325,000 @ 0%	0
£1,299,000 @ 40%	519,600
Inheritance tax liability	519,600

(b) As the property is not expected to increase in value in the near future, there is no inheritance tax benefit in making a lifetime gift. Kendra would need to live for three more years for taper relief to be available.

Also, a lifetime gift would result in a capital gains tax liability of £48,720 (£174,000 at 28%) for 2022/23, whereas a transfer on death would be an exempt disposal.

(c) It can be beneficial to skip a generation so that gifts are made to grandchildren rather than children, particularly if the children already have significant assets.

This avoids a further charge to inheritance tax when the children die. Gifts will then only be taxed once before being inherited by the grandchildren, rather than twice.

216 James (March/June 2016)

Workbook references

Chapter 18 deals with inheritance tax.

Top tips

When working out the inheritance death tax on the lifetime transfer, remember to look back seven years from the date of the lifetime transfer (not the date of death) to see whether there are any previous transfers to cumulate.

Easy marks

The nil rate band is used up on the first gift so the calculation of the inheritance tax on the CLT and death estate are easy.

Marking guide	Marks
(a) Potentially exempt transfer (after annual exemptions)	1
Nil rate band available	1.5
Inheritance tax	0.5

Daughter to pay	0.5	
Chargeable lifetime transfer	0.5	
Inheritance tax	0.5	
Trustees to pay	0.5	
Death estate – IHT liability	0.5	
James's personal representatives to pay	0.5	
		6
(b) Avoidance of double taxation		
		2
(c) Taper relief	0.5	
Lifetime transfer values fixed	0.5	
IHT saving	1	
		2
Total		10

(a) **James – Inheritance tax arising on death**

Lifetime transfers within seven years of death

14 May 2021

		£
Gift		420,000
Less:	Annual exemption – current year	(3,000)
	Annual exemption – b/f	(3,000)
Potentially exempt transfer		414,000
Inheritance tax liability – £296,000 (W) @ 0%		0
	– £118,000 @ 40%	47,200
		47,200

James's daughter will be responsible for paying the inheritance tax of £47,200.

2 August 2021

Chargeable lifetime transfer	260,000
Inheritance tax liability £260,000 @ 40%	104,000

The trustees will be responsible for paying the inheritance tax of £104,000.

Death estate

Chargeable estate	870,000
Inheritance tax liability £870,000 @ 40%	348,000

The personal representatives of James's estate will be responsible for paying the inheritance tax of £348,000.

ANSWERS

Working

Available nil rate band

	£	£
Nil rate band at date of death		325,000
Gift 9 October 2015	35,000	
Less: Annual exemption – current year	(3,000)	
Annual exemption – b/f	(3,000)	(29,000)
Nil rate band available		296,000

(b) Skipping a generation avoids a further charge to inheritance tax when the children die. Gifts will then only be taxed once before being inherited by the grandchildren, rather than twice.

(c) Even if the donor does not survive for seven years, taper relief will reduce the amount of IHT payable after three years.

The value of potentially exempt transfers and chargeable lifetime transfers are fixed at the time they are made.

James therefore saved inheritance tax of £20,000 (£(310,000 – 260,000) @ 40%) by making the lifetime gift of property.

217 Dembe (March/June 2019)

Workbook references

The income tax computation is covered in Chapter 2 and pensions in Chapter 5. Chargeable gains computation is dealt with in Chapter 13. Inheritance tax is the subject of Chapter 18.

Top tips

In part (c) think about the nil rate bands available for each spouse. What happens if the first spouse dies without using up their nil rate bands?

Easy marks

There were some easy marks for basic computation of capital gains tax in part (b) but you should make sure that you clearly show which individual is making the disposal in each case.

Examining team's comments

Although there were some good answers to part (a), many candidates used up valuable time by producing full tax computations. The question stated that these were not required, indicating that workings were to be done at the margin.

Many candidates did not appreciate that the personal pension contribution would have no impact on NICs. This fact should have just been stated, without any need to perform calculations. Many candidates did not realise that the personal pension contribution would bring Dembe's adjusted net income down from in excess of £125,140, to less than £100,000. Therefore, the personal allowance would have been fully reinstated. This shows the importance of carefully considering the impact of all the information provided.

Part (b) was generally well answered provided the basic tax planning involved was understood. Transferring the property to Kato prior to its disposal meant a lower rate of capital gains tax (CGT) on part of the gain, plus Kato's annual exempt amount was available (Dembe's was not).

Somewhat surprisingly, quite a few candidates used the incorrect rates of CGT, despite the fact that these rates are provided in the tax rates and allowances. The £2,000 in additional legal fees were often not taken into account in the comparison.

Part (c) was not particularly well answered, with many candidates not appreciating how straightforward the answer actually was.

The couple's estate, with a value of £950,000, would have been fully covered by the available nil rate bands totalling £1,000,000 (two nil rate bands of £325,000, and two residence nil rate bands of £175,000). The IHT liability was therefore nil.

Even if IHT were payable (for example, if the value of the estate increased faster than the available nil rate bands), then there would be no advantage to leaving assets to children on the first death. This is because unused nil rate bands can be transferred to the surviving spouse. This very basic IHT planning was often overlooked.

Marking guide		**Marks**	
(a)	Extension of basic rate band	2	
	Reinstatement of personal allowance	1.5	
	National insurance contributions	0.5	
			4
(b)	Disposal by Dembe	0.5	
	Disposal by Kato		
	Taxable at basic rate	1	
	Taxable at higher rate	1	
	Overall saving	0.5	
			3
(c)	Spouse exemption	0.5	
	Residence nil rate bands	0.5	
	Nil rate bands	0.5	
	Chargeable at death rate	0.5	
	Transfer of unused nil rate band	1	
			3
Total			10

(a) Reduction in Dembe's income tax liability and NICs:

	£
Extension of basic rate tax band: 40,000 (32,000 × 100/80) at 20% (40% – 20%)	8,000
Reinstatement of personal allowance: 12,570 at 40%	5,028
Reduction in income tax liability	13,028
National insurance contributions (NICs)	0
Total tax reduction	13,028

Tutorial note. Before making the personal pension contribution, Dembe's adjusted net income of £130,000 exceeds £125,140, so no personal allowance is available.

The personal pension contribution will reduce Dembe's adjusted net income to less than £100,000 (130,000 – 40,000 = 90,000), so the personal allowance will be fully reinstated.

Tutorial note. Pension contributions have no impact on NICs.

(b) Overall saving for the tax year 2022/23:

	£	£
Disposal made by Dembe		
67,000 at 28%		18,760
Disposal made by Kato		
16,350 (37,700 – 21,350) at 18%	2,943	
36,350 (65,000 – 12,300 – 16,350) at 28%	10,178	(13,121)
Capital gains tax (CGT) saving		5,639
Additional legal fees		(2,000)
Overall saving		3,639

(c) On first death, there will be no inheritance tax (IHT) liability because of the spouse exemption.

There will also be no IHT liability on second death because the couple's residence nil rate bands and nil rate bands will exceed the value of the combined chargeable estate:

	£
Combined chargeable estate	950,000
Residence nil rate bands (175,000 × 2)	(350,000)
Nil rate bands (325,000 × 2)	(650,000)
Chargeable at 40%	0

Even if IHT were payable (for example, if the value of the estate increases faster than the available nil rate bands), then there is no advantage to leaving assets to children on the first death. This is because unused nil rate bands can be transferred to the surviving spouse.

Section A

OTQ bank – Corporation tax liabilities

218 The correct answers are:

Legal expenses relating to the acquisition of a new 40-year lease on its factory		**NOT ALLOWABLE**
Cost of arranging a new bank loan to purchase machinery for trade	**ALLOWABLE**	
Write off of an irrecoverable loan to a former employee		**NOT ALLOWABLE**
Donation to local charity with mention of Jet Ltd's support in programme for fundraising concert (not a qualifying charitable donation)	**ALLOWABLE**	

Legal expenses in respect of leases are only allowable if they relate to the **renewal** of a short lease. The cost of arranging a bank loan for trade purposes is allowable. A debt written off in respect of a former employee is accounted for under the non-trade loan relationship rules as it does not relate to the trade of the company. A small donation to a local charity with publicity would normally be allowable as being for the purposes of the trade.

219 The correct answer is: 12 months to 30 November 2022, 4 months to 31 March 2023

If the company has a long period of account, it is divided into one period of 12 months and one of the remainder.

220 £ 40,500

£1,800,000 × 3% × 9/12 = £40,500

The qualifying cost for SBAs excludes acquisition fees. The SBA must be time-apportioned in the year of acquisition from the date the building is brought into use.

221 £3,198

		Main pool	*Special rate pool*	*Allowances*
		£	£	£
Additions		30,400	15,400	
WDA	6% × 6/12		(462)	462
	18% × 6/12	(2,736)	–	2,736
TWDV c/f /Allowances		27,664	14,938	3,198

Do not forget to pro-rate writing down allowances in a short accounting period. No adjustment is made for private use by a director for a company.

The answer £4,122 uses 18% for both WDAs. The answer £6,396 is the full year's WDAs. The answer £3,106 adjusts for private use – this is a common mistake. Remember that there is never any private use by a company!

222 The correct answer is: £0

	£
Proceeds	70,000
Less cost 15,000 × £3.50	(52,500)
Unindexed gain	17,500
Less indexation allowance	
0.578 × £52,500 = £30,345 restricted to	(17,500)
Indexed gain	0

The answer £12,845 allows the indexation allowance to create a loss. The answer £105,000 loss uses the cost of all 50,000 of the shares. The answer £17,500 is the unindexed gain.

ACCA Examining Team's Comments

This was a straightforward chargeable gain computation on the disposal of shares. The correct answer is £0. However, the vast majority of candidates chose £12,845, suggesting they simply forgot that indexation cannot create a loss.

223 £ 33,300

Crane plc can make a carry forward loss relief claim against total profits but can leave sufficient profits to cover the qualifying charitable donation, thus maximising the unrelieved loss carried forward to the next accounting period. The most beneficial claim is therefore £(30,000 + 6,000 – 2,700) = £33,300. The remaining £(40,000 – 33,300) = £6,700 will be carried forward to the accounting period ending 31 December 2024.

224 £ 83,750

	£
Loss	160,000
Less loss relief y/e 31.12.23	(5,000)
Less loss relief p/e 31.12.22 (40,000 + 15,500)	(55,500)
Less loss relief y/e 31.3.22 3/12 × (45,000 + 18,000)	(15,750)
Loss c/f	83,750

225 The correct answer is: £38,000

ACCA Examining Team's Comments

This calculative question tested candidates' knowledge of group relief. The question asked candidates to calculate the maximum amount of group relief which Boon Ltd could claim from Bab Ltd. The correct answer was £38,000. Boon Ltd can claim group relief against its taxable total profits, in this case £40,000 (£36,000 + £4,000). Bab Ltd does not need to use its trading loss against its own profits first, so it can surrender the full amount of £38,000 to Boon Ltd.

Most candidates answered £31,000, indicating that they may have thought that Bab Ltd had to use the loss against its chargeable gains first. Many candidates answered £36,000, perhaps because they thought that group relief can only be set against trading income.

Group relief is an important aspect of the syllabus in respect of corporation tax, and candidates should ensure they are familiar with the rules and can apply them to a given scenario.

226 The correct answers are:

Daffodil plc	**YES**	
Geranium Inc		**NO**
Flora Ltd	**YES**	
Hellebore Ltd		**NO**

Group relief can be made to UK companies only, so not to Geranium Inc, and where there is a ≥75% direct and indirect holding by the controlling company. Daffodil plc only has a (80% × 90%) = 72% interest in Hellebore Ltd.

227 The correct answers are:

Pine plc	**YES**	
Willow Ltd	**YES**	
Juniper Ltd	**YES**	
Lime Inc		**NO**

Losses can only be transferred to UK companies where there is a ≥75% direct interest at each level and >50% indirect holding by the top company. Pine plc has a (75% × 75%) = 56.25% interest in Maple Ltd.

ANSWERS

Section B

OT case – Luna Ltd (June 2015) (amended)

Workbook references

Chargeable gains for companies are covered in Chapter 20.

Top tips

Learn the proforma for dealing with a pool of shares owned by a company. In this scenario you only needed to include the indexed cost column.

Easy marks

There were easy marks for identifying the correct statement about indexation allowance.

228 The correct answers are:

Indexation allowance can reduce a gain to nil but not create a loss	**TRUE**	
Indexation allowance can increase an unindexed loss		**FALSE**

Indexation allowance cannot increase or create a loss although it can reduce a gain to nil.

229 £ 6,186

	£
Proceeds	53,400
Less cost	(36,800)
	16,600
Less indexation allowance to December 2017 0.283 × £36,800	(10,414)
Gain	6,186

230 The correct answer is: £14,928

	No. of shares	*Indexed cost*
		£
Acquisition	16,000	32,000
Indexed rise to December 2017		
0.244 × £32,000		7,808
		39,808
Disposal	(10,000)	(24,880)
	6,000	14,928

The answer £12,000 is the unindexed pool of cost immediately after the sale. The answer £39,808 is the indexed cost of the pool immediately before the disposal. The answer £24,880 is the amount of indexed cost used on the disposal.

231 The correct answer is: £13,125

	No. of shares	Cost
		£
Acquisition	5,000	7,500
Bonus 1 for 1	5,000	0
	10,000	7,500
Rights 1 for 4 @ £2.25	2,500	5,625
	12,500	13,125

232 £ 19,500

$$£33{,}000 \times \frac{(£6.50 \times 10{,}000)}{(£6.50 \times 10{,}000) + (£4.50 \times 10{,}000)}$$ £19,500

OT case – Tay Ltd

Workbook references

Chargeable gains for companies is the subject of Chapter 20.

Top tips

The application of the rules on the destruction of assets in is similar to rollover relief for replacement of business assets.

Easy marks

The chattels rules should have been well known.

233 The correct answer is: £155,000

	£
Proceeds	180,000
Less indexed cost	(155,000)
Gain	25,000
Gain immediately chargeable £(180,000 – 162,000)	(18,000)
Deduction from base cost of new warehouse	7,000

The base cost of the new warehouse is £(162,000 – 7,000) = £155,000.

The answer £162,000 does not give any relief. The answer £144,000 deducts the gain immediately chargeable. The answer £140,000 uses the unindexed cost to work out the gain.

234 The correct answer is: £8,000 gain

	Market value	*Indexed cost*	*Gain*
	£	£	£
20,000 £1 ordinary shares @ £4 each	80,000	64,000	
£40,000 (20,000 × £2) cash	40,000	32,000	8,000
	120,000	96,000	

The answer £24,000 gain is the total gain if the acquisition of the shares was treated as a disposal. The answer £16,000 gain is the gain on the shares if the acquisition of the shares was treated as a disposal. The answer £(24,000) loss is the loss on cash if the nominal value of the shares of £1 is used for the apportionment.

235 The correct answer is: £5,000

Although the general rule is that wasting chattels are exempt, there is an exception for assets used for the purpose of a trade in respect of which capital allowances have been or could have been claimed. The usual chattel rules therefore apply as follows:

	£
Proceeds	9,000
Less indexed cost	(3,500)
Gain	5,500

The maximum gain is 5/3 × £(9,000 × 6,000) = £5,000.

The chargeable gain is the lower of £5,500 and £5,000, so it is £5,000.

236 The correct answer is: £15,732

		£
Proceeds		45,000
Less:	Cost	(20,000)
	Enhancement (drainage)	(2,000)
Unindexed gain		23,000
Less:	Indexation on cost £20,000 × 0.342	(6,840)
	Indexation on enhancement £2,000 × 0.214	(428)
Chargeable gain		15,732

The answer £16,160 does not index the enhancement. The answer £15,476 uses the indexation factor on cost for both cost and enhancement. The answer £15,134 indexes the unindexed gain using the indexation factor on cost.

237 The correct answer is: 2 and 4

The capital loss can be set against chargeable gains made in the year ended 31 March 2024 and the capital loss can be carried forward and set against the first available chargeable gains.

Capital losses cannot be carried back and cannot be set against profits other than chargeable gains.

OT case – Hyde plc group

> **Workbook references**
>
> Groups are the subject of Chapter 22.
>
> **Top tips**
>
> Make sure you know the difference between the rules for relationships between companies for group relief and those applying to chargeable gains groups.
>
> **Easy marks**
>
> The identification of the base cost of the factory should have been easy marks if you remembered that transfers between chargeable gains group companies are on a no gain, no loss basis.

238 The correct answers are:

Hampstead plc	**YES**	
Regent plc	**YES**	
Richmond plc		**NO**
Primrose plc	**YES**	

A company is in a group relief group where there is a ≥75% direct and indirect holding by the controlling company (Hyde plc). Hyde plc has a (95% × 80%) = 76% interest in Primrose Ltd but only has a (85% × 85%) = 72.25% interest in Richmond Ltd.

239 The correct answer is: £70,000

	£
Trading loss	68,000
Excess qualifying charitable donations £(5,000 – 3,000)	2,000
Maximum current period group relief	70,000

240 £50,500

	£
Chargeable gain	48,000
Interest income	12,000
Trading loss	(8,000)
Qualifying charitable donations	(1,500)
Available taxable total profits	50,500

Hyde plc is assumed to use its own current year losses in working out the taxable total profits against which it may claim current group relief, even if it does not in fact claim relief for current losses against total profits. Group relief is set against taxable total profits after all other reliefs for the current period such as qualifying charitable donations.

241 The correct answers are:

- A claim for current period group relief will be ineffective unless Greenwich plc gives a notice of consent.
- The claim for current period group relief would be made on Hyde plc's corporation tax return.

Any payment by Hyde plc for current period group relief, up to the amount of the loss surrendered, is ignored for all corporation tax purposes. A claim for current period group relief between Greenwich plc and Hyde plc will be available against 9/12ths of the taxable total profits of Hyde plc for the year to 31 March 2024, since surrendered losses must be set against taxable total profits of a corresponding accounting period (1 April 2023 to 31 December 2023).

242 The correct answer is: £120,000

	£
Cost	100,000
Indexation allowance to date of transfer £100,000 × 0.200	20,000
Base cost for Primrose plc	120,000

The transfer of assets within a chargeable gains group is on a no gain / no loss basis including indexation to the date of the transfer.

Section C

243 Problematic Ltd (June 2010) (amended)

Workbook references

Chargeable gains for companies are covered in Chapter 20.

Top tips

Make sure you use the three column proforma for the FA 1985 pool.

Easy marks

The base cost required in part (b) is easy provided you remember that the leasehold factory is a depreciating asset, and so do not reduce the base cost by rollover relief.

Marking guide

	Marks	
(a) Easy plc		
FA 1985 pool		
Purchase	0.5	
Rights issue	1	
Indexation	2	
Disposal	1	
Chargeable gain	1.5	
Freehold factory		
Disposal proceeds	0.5	
Indexed cost	0.5	
Rollover relief	2	
		9
(b) Leasehold factory	1	
		1
Total		10

(a) Easy plc shares

FA85 pool

	No. of shares	*Cost*	*Indexed cost*
		£	£
Purchase 26.6.05	15,000	12,600	12,600
Index to September 2008			
0.136 × £12,600			1,714
Rights issue 1 for 3 @ £2.20	5,000	11,000	11,000
c/f	20,000	23,600	25,314

	No. of shares	Cost	Indexed cost
		£	£
Index to December 2017			
0.273 × £25,314			6,911
			32,225
Sale	(16,000)	(18,880)	(25,780)
c/f	4,000	4,720	6,445

Gain	£
Proceeds	54,400
Less cost	(18,880)
	35,520
Less indexation £(25,780 – 18,880)	(6,900)
Chargeable gain	28,620

Freehold factory

	£
Proceeds	171,000
Less indexed cost	(127,000)
	44,000
Less gain deferred on purchase of leasehold factory £(44,000 – 16,200)	(27,800)
Chargeable gain (amount not reinvested £(171,000 – 154,800))	16,200

(b) The leasehold factory is a depreciating asset, so there is no adjustment to the base cost of £154,800.

Tutorial note. When a replacement asset is a depreciating asset then the gain is not rolled over by reducing the cost of the replacement asset. Instead, the gain is deferred until it crystallises on the earliest of:

- The disposal of the replacement asset
- The date the replacement asset is no longer used in the business
- Ten years after the acquisition of the replacement asset which in this case is 10 December 2032

244 Volatile Ltd (December 2009) (amended)

Workbook references

Corporation tax losses are covered in Chapter 21.

Top tips

Don't forget to set up a loss memorandum for each loss so that you can see how the loss is utilised.

Easy marks

You should have been able to state at least one of the principles of claiming loss relief in part (a).

Marking guide

		Marks	
(a)	Timing of relief	1	
	Loss of QCDs	1	
			2
(b)	Trading income	0.5	
	Property business income	0.5	
	Chargeable gains	1.5	
	Loss relief – y/e 31 December 2021	2	
	Loss relief – y/e 30 September 2025	2.5	
	Qualifying charitable donations	0.5	
	Unrelieved losses	0.5	
			8
Total			10

(a) **Choice of loss relief**

The two factors that will influence a company's choice of loss relief claims are:

(1) Timing of relief: both in terms of tax rate and cash flow (saving tax sooner is beneficial for cash flow)

(2) The extent to which relief for qualifying charitable donations might be lost so it may be beneficial to restrict carry forward loss relief claims to keep an amount of total profits in charge after loss relief to match donations.

(b) **Volatile Ltd**

	p/e 31.12.21	*y/e 31.12.22*	*y/e 31.12.23*	*p/e 30.9.24*
	£	£	£	£
Trading income	44,000	0	86,500	78,700
Property business income	9,400	6,600	6,500	0
Chargeable gains (11,700 – 2,000)	5,100	0	0	9,700
Total profits	58,500	6,600	93,000	88,400
Less current period loss relief	(0)	(6,600)	(0)	(0)
Less carry back loss relief	(58,500)		(23,250)	(88,400)
Less carry forward loss relief	(0)	(0)	(8,700)	(0)
Less qualifying charitable donations	(0)	(0)	(1,200)	(0)
Taxable total profits	0	0	59,850	0

ANSWERS

Loss memorandum

	£
Loss in y/e 31.12.22	73,800
Less used y/e 31.12.22	(6,600)
Less used p/e 31.12.21	(58,500)
Less used y/e 31.12.23	(8,700)
Loss remaining unrelieved	0
Loss in y/e 30.9.25	186,800
Less used y/e 31.12.23	(88,400)
	(23,250)
3 months to 31.12.23 £93,000 × 3/12	
Loss remaining unrelieved at 30.9.25	75,150

The loss of y/e 30.9.25 can be carried back against total profits of the previous 12 months ie against the 9-month period ending 30.9.24 and 3 months of the y/e 31.12.23.

245 Maison Ltd (September/December 2019)

Workbook references

Corporation tax computations are covered in Chapter 19, and gains for companies are covered in Chapter 20.

Top tips

Given that a draft layout was provided in the question, this should have been replicated in the answer.

Easy marks

There is a full mark for using figures given in the question in the TTP pro forma and two more half marks for picking up the gains figures provided.

Examining team's comments

The corporation tax question involved Maison Ltd, for which a partly completed draft corporation tax computation had been prepared for the year ended 31 March 2023. The figures provided were correct, but there were four uncompleted sections, all related to property. These were:

- A deduction for the payment of a lease premium
- Capital allowances in respect of the construction of an extension adjacent to the company's existing freehold office building
- Property business income from the letting of a warehouse which was purchased in a dilapidated state
- Chargeable gains on the disposal of two investment properties

The sole requirement for 15 marks was to prepare a completed version of Maison Ltd's corporation tax computation for the year ended 31 March 2023 after dealing with the uncompleted sections. The question was generally very well answered.

As regards layout, candidates should again include as many workings as possible within the main computation. Given that a draft layout was provided, then this layout should have been

followed by candidates in their answers, thereby allowing candidates to achieve as many of the available marks as possible.

Lease premium: A number of candidates did not appreciate that this was a deduction rather than an addition.

Capital allowances: This part of the question has been amended due to changes in the Finance Act so the examining team's comments are no longer relevant.

Property business income: Many candidates were not aware that the cost of initial repairs was disallowable capital expenditure because the property could not have been let out in its original state and this was reflected in the purchase price paid.

Chargeable gains: Figures for the two chargeable gains were given, so candidates should not have recalculated them. The reason for giving more information (proceeds and expenditure) was so that the indexation allowance could be calculated. Candidates should always deal with each gain separately, and not combine the figures.

Marking guide

	Marks	
(W1) Deduction for lease premium		
Premium paid	0.5	
Deduction	1	
Per annum and time apportioned	1	
(W2) Capital allowances		
Main pool	0.5	
AIA on integral features	1	
130% FYA on P&M	1	
SBA on building costs	1	
(W3) Property income		
Rent receivable	1	
Security deposit	0.5	
Insurance	1	
Initial repairs	1	
Advertising	0.5	
(W4) Chargeable gains		
First property		
Gain	0.5	
Indexation allowance	1	
Enhancement expenditure	0.5	
Second property		
Gain	0.5	
Indexation allowance	1	
Corporation Tax	0.5	
Figures provided in question	1	
		15
Total		15

ANSWERS

Maison Ltd – Corporation tax computation for the year ended 31 March 2023

	£
Operating profit	892,900*
Non-deductible expenditure	22,340*
Deduction for lease premium (working 1)	(715)
Capital allowances (working 2)	(70,500)
Trading profit	844,025
Property business income (working 3)	28,685
Loan interest receivable	1,460*
Chargeable gains (working 4)	77,985
Taxable total profits	952,155
Corporation tax (952,155 at 19%)	180,909

*Figures provided in question

Workings

1 ***Deduction for lease premium***

	£
Premium paid	44,000
Less: 44,000 × 2% × (12 – 1)	(9,680)
Amount assessed on the landlord as income	34,320
Deduction (34,320/12 years × 3/12)	715

2 ***Capital allowances***

	£	£
Main pool		12,037
Capital allowances		
Building costs	0	
Ventilation system - AIA preferable to 50% FYA	6,700	
Heating system - AIA preferable to 50% FYA	3,900	
Furniture and furnishings - 130% FYA (£33,500 × 130%)	43,550	
Refrigerator and microwave cooker- 130% FYA (£2,600 × 130%)	3,380	
		57,530
Structures and buildings allowance (£93,300 × 3% × 4/12)		933
Total allowances		70,500

3 ***Property business income***

	£
Rent receivable (18,300 + (18,300 ×2/3))	30,500
Security deposit	0

	£
Insurance	(1,035)
Initial repairs	0
Advertising	(780)
Property business income	28,685

Tutorial note. A security deposit, less the cost of making good any damage, is returned to the tenant on the cessation of a letting. It is therefore initially not treated as income.

Tutorial note. The cost of insurance for the period 1 July to 1 November 2022 is deductible as pre-trading expenditure.

Tutorial note. The cost of the initial repairs to the warehouse are disallowable capital expenditure as the warehouse could not be let out in its original state and this was reflected in the purchase price paid.

4 ***Chargeable gains***

	£
First property	
Gain	109,800
Indexation allowance	
Cost (101,000 × 0.315)	(31,815)
Enhancement expenditure	0
Chargeable gain	77,985
Second property	
Gain	26,000
Indexation allowance	
Cost (117,000 × 0.315) – Restricted	(26,000)
Chargeable gain	0

Tutorial note. There is no indexation allowance for the first property's enhancement expenditure of £26,200 because this was incurred after December 2017.

Tutorial note. For the second property, the indexation allowance cannot create a capital loss.

246 Black Ltd (December 2011) and Gastron Ltd (June 2009) (amended)

Workbook references

Groups are covered in Chapter 22.

Top tips

It is very important that you read the questions carefully and comply with any detailed instructions. For example, in part (a) you were given a note about what you were not expected to do.

Easy marks

You should have been able to outline the group structure in part (b)(i).

Marking guide		**Marks**
(a) Maximum potential claim by Black Ltd in relation to White Ltd		
Maximum claim	1	
Maximum surrender by White Ltd		
Current period trading loss – maximum claim	0.5	
Qualifying charitable donations	1	
Maximum group relief claim Black Ltd and White Ltd	0.5	
Maximum potential claim by Black Ltd in relation to Grey Ltd		
Maximum claim	0.5	
Maximum surrender by Grey Ltd		
Carried forward trading loss – maximum claim	1	
Maximum group relief claim Black Ltd and Grey Ltd	0.5	
		5
(b) (i) 75% shareholding	1	
50% effective interest	1	
		2
(ii) Set-off of capital loss		
		1
(iii) No gain no loss transfers	1	
Rollover relief	1	
		2
Total		10

(a) **Black Ltd – Group relief claims for year ended 31 March 2023**

Maximum potential claim by Black Ltd from White Ltd

Group relief is against taxable total profits after all other reliefs for the current period (for example qualifying charitable donations).

The maximum potential current period group relief claim by Black Ltd in relation to White Ltd is therefore £(338,900 + 21,100 – 4,400) = £355,600.

Maximum potential surrender by White Ltd to Black Ltd

White Ltd may surrender its current period trading losses of £351,300.

White Ltd may also surrender excess qualifying charitable donations (ie to the extent that they exceed total profits before taking account of any losses). Since the qualifying charitable donations of £5,600 do not exceed the total profits of £26,700, there is no excess.

The maximum potential surrender by White Ltd is therefore £351,300.

Maximum group relief claim by Black Ltd from White Ltd

The maximum current period group relief claim is the lower of the claim that can be made by Black Ltd and the surrender that can be made by White Ltd ie £351,300.

Maximum potential claim by Black Ltd from Grey Ltd

Current period group relief is taken before carry forward group relief. The maximum potential claim by Black Ltd in relation to Grey Ltd is therefore £(355,600 – 351,300) = £4,300.

Maximum potential surrender by Grey Ltd

Grey Ltd may surrender its carried forward trading losses after deducting the amount it can set against its own current period total profits ie £(57,500 – 50,000 – 4,500) = £3,000.

Maximum group relief claim by Black Ltd from Grey Ltd

The maximum carry forward group relief claim is the lower of the claim that can be made by Black Ltd and the surrender that can be made by Grey Ltd ie £3,000.

(b) (i) Companies form a chargeable gains group if at each level in the group structure there is a 75% shareholding.

However, the parent company must also have an effective interest of over 50% in each group company.

(ii) The election will enable the capital loss of £66,000 to be set against the capital gain of £74,800 and so save tax in the current year. Otherwise, the loss would have to be carried forward by Culinary Ltd and set against future gains.

> **Tutorial note.** Alternatively, an election could have been made to transfer the loss of Culinary Ltd to Gastron Ltd to set against the gain. The overall corporation tax effect for the chargeable gains group would have been the same.

(iii) Companies in a chargeable gains group make intra-group transfers of chargeable assets without a chargeable gain or an allowable loss arising.

If a member of a chargeable gains group disposes of an asset eligible for chargeable gains rollover relief, it may treat all of the group companies as a single unit for the purpose of claiming such relief.

247 Alimag Ltd (September/December 2017)

Workbook references

The income tax computation is covered in Chapter 2. National insurance contributions are the subject of Chapter 12. Corporation tax liability is dealt with in Chapter 19.

Top tips

Make sure that you use subheadings to identify your computations. This will help you extract the correct amounts for the overall tax and NICs savings.

Easy marks

There are plenty of easy marks in this question for basic computations, but you need to adopt a methodical approach to obtain these marks. Use the list in the question to make sure you don't miss any out!

Examining team's comments

The requirement for 10 marks was to calculate the overall saving of taxes and NICs if the revised basis of profit extraction was used instead of the original basis. There were many perfect answers to this question, although other candidates had difficulty with various aspects. This scenario is covered in the Higher Skills article which has been published, and candidates are advised to work carefully through the examples contained in the article. It is important that candidates appreciate the interactions involved in this type of higher skills question. For example, director's remuneration reduces a company's taxable total profits, but the payment of dividends does not. Most candidates forgot to deduct the employer's NICs when calculating Alimag Ltd's profits. Another fairly common mistake was to apply NICs to the dividends received.

As already mentioned, tax and NIC figures were provided for the original basis of profit extraction. Candidates should never attempt to recalculate these figures for themselves, since all this does is waste a lot of time. Where there are several computations forming part of the same question, then candidates should always use appropriate headings to indicate which aspect is being answered. The tax computations were relatively straightforward, so there was no need, for example, to have separate columns for director's remuneration and dividends. The same went for the NIC computations given that the 3.25% rate was not applicable. [**BPP note.** Despite this comment, we still prefer using separate columns for non-savings income and dividend income, as opposed to the examining team's approach of using a single column, since using separate columns ensures that the personal allowance is set off correctly and that a further deduction of the personal allowance against non-savings income does not need to be made when computing tax.]

The calculation of the overall tax and NICs saving was often omitted. This was a very easy one mark to obtain given that candidates simply had to use figures already calculated.

Marking guide	Marks	
Gamila income tax liability		
Director's remuneration	0.5	
Dividend income	0.5	
Personal allowance	0.5	
Income tax (½ mark for each amount)	2	
Magnus income tax liability		
Dividend income	0.5	
Personal allowance	0.5	
Income tax (½ mark for each amount)	1	
Gamila and Alimag Class 1 national insurance contributions	1	
Magnus Class 1 national insurance contributions	0.5	
Alimag Ltd corporation tax liability		
Trading profit	0.5	
Director's remuneration	0.5	
Employer's Class 1 NIC	0.5	
Corporation tax	0.5	
Overall tax and NICs savings	1	
		10
Total		10

Gamila – Income tax liability 2022/23

	Non-savings income	*Dividend income*
	£	£
Director's remuneration	30,000	
Dividend income	–	70,000
Net income	30,000	70,000
Less: Personal allowance	(12,570)	
Taxable income	17,430	70,000

	Non-savings income	Dividend income
	£	£
Tax		
£17,430 @ 20%		3,486
£2,000 @ 0% (dividend nil rate band)		0
£(37,700 – 17,430 – 2,000) = 18,270 @ 8.75%		1,599
£(70,000 – 2,000 – 18,270) = 49,730 @ 33.75%		16,784
Income tax liability		21,869

Magnus – Income tax liability 2022/23	*Dividend income*
	£
Dividend income/net income	30,000
Less: Personal allowance	(12,570)
Taxable income	17,430
Tax	
£2,000 @ 0%	0
£(17,430 – 2,000) = 15,430 @ 8.75%	1,350
Income tax liability	1,350

Gamila and Alimag Ltd – National insurance contributions 2022/23	£
Employee Class 1 £(30,000 – 12,570) = 17,430 @ 13.25%	2,309
Employer Class 1 £(30,000 – 9,100) = 20,900 @ 15.05%	3,145

Marcus – National insurance contributions 2022/23

There will be no employee or employer Class 1 contributions for Marcus as he does not have any earnings.

Alimag Ltd – Corporation tax liability for year ended 5 April 2023	£
Trading profit	180,000
Less: Director's remuneration	(30,000)
Employer's Class 1 NIC	(3,145)
Taxable total profits	146,855
Tax	
£146,855 @ 19%	27,902

Overall tax saving if revised basis of profit extraction used	£
Original basis	76,284
Revised basis (21,869 + 1,350 + 2,309 + 3,145 + 27,902)	(56,575)
Overall savings	19,709

248 Hopi Ltd (March/June 2018)

Workbook references

The income tax computation is covered in Chapter 2. National insurance contributions are the subject of Chapter 12. Corporation tax liability is dealt with in Chapter 19.

Top tips

When computing Kaya's income tax liability if she receives additional dividend income, simply calculate the additional tax on the dividend income rather than rework the whole income tax computation.

Easy marks

There were easy marks for stating that, if Kaya receives additional dividend income, there will be no change to the national insurance contributions for Kaya and Hopi Ltd and no change to Hopi Ltd's corporation tax liability.

Examining team's comments

The requirement for 10 marks was to calculate the revised tax and national insurance contributions (NICs) for Kaya and Hopi Ltd for the year ended 5 April 2023 if, on 31 March 2023, Kaya paid herself a bonus of £25,000 (1) as additional director's remuneration or (2) as an additional dividend.

Those candidates who understood basic tax rules had no difficulty answering this question.

As warned in previous reports, where tax figures are given for the original scenario, candidates should never attempt to recalculate these figures for themselves. All this does is lose valuable time with candidates producing three sets of workings rather than the expected two.

Candidates should always read the requirements very carefully. These types of questions often require a summary or a conclusion, but neither was necessary for this question – again those candidates who provided one lost a bit more time.

Where computations are required for two different scenarios, candidates should clearly indicate which scenario is being answered. It is much better to deal with one scenario first, then the second, rather than have a mix of computations dealing with one tax at a time, such as all the income tax and class 1 NIC computations for Kaya, then the corporation tax and class 1 NIC calculations for Hopi Ltd.

Although full marks are awarded for correct answers however the information is presented, dealing with one scenario at a time can help candidates to ensure they have covered all aspects in their answers.

Some of the calculations in this question required full computations (such as Kaya's income tax liability under the additional director's remuneration alternative), whereas others (such as Kaya's income tax liability under the additional dividend alternative) could be calculated by working at the margin. Appreciating where full computations can be avoided saves time as well as reducing the complexity of the workings. Also, under the additional dividend alternative, many candidates did not appreciate that the class 1 NICs and Hopi Ltd's corporation tax liability would not change from the original figures provided.

In summary, although many candidates correctly calculated most, if not all, of the revised tax and NICs, they often took a much longer route in reaching their answer than was necessary. Working through past examination questions will help candidates familiarise themselves with the best approach to be taken when answering these types of questions.

Also, it is important that candidates appreciate the interactions which can arise in these questions, and an article has been published covering many of the scenarios which could be examined.

Marking guide	Marks	
Revised liabilities if Kaya receives additional director's remuneration		
Kaya income tax liability		
Director's remuneration	0.5	
Dividend income	0.5	
Personal allowance	0.5	
Income tax (½ mark for each amount)	2	
Kaya Class 1 national insurance contributions	1.5	
Hopi Ltd Class 1 national insurance contributions	1	
Hopi Ltd corporation tax	1	
Revised liabilities if Kaya receives additional dividend income		
Kaya income tax liability	1.5	
Kaya and Hopi Ltd Class 1 national insurance contributions	1	
Hopi Ltd corporation tax	0.5	
		10
Total		10

Revised liabilities if Kaya receives additional director's remuneration

Kaya – Income tax liability 2022/23

	Non-savings income	*Dividend income*
	£	£
Director's remuneration £(30,000 + 25,000)	55,000	
Dividend income	–	45,000
Net income	55,000	45,000
Less: Personal allowance	(12,570)	
Taxable income	42,430	45,000

Tax	
£37,700 @ 20%	7,540
£(42,430 – 37,700) = £4,730 @ 40%	1,892
£2,000 @ 0% (dividend nil rate band)	0
£(45,000 – 2,000) = £43,000 @ 33.75%	14,513
Revised income tax liability	23,945

Kaya and Hopi Ltd – National insurance contributions 2022/23

	£
£(50,270 – 12,570) = 37,700 @ 13.25%	4,995
£(55,000 – 50,270) = 4,730 @ 3.25%	154
Revised employee Class 1 NICs	5,149
Revised employer Class 1 NICs £(55,000 – 9100) = £45,900 @ 15.05%	6,908

Hopi Ltd – Corporation tax liability for year ended 5 April 2023

	£
Trading profit before additional director's remuneration	80,000
Less: Additional director's remuneration	(25,000)
Additional employer's Class 1 NIC £(6,908 – 3,145)	(3,763)
Taxable total profits	51,237
Tax	
£51,237 @ 19%	9,735

Revised liabilities if Kaya receives additional dividend income

Kaya – Income tax liability 2022/23

	£
Original income tax	13,431
Add: tax on additional dividend income £25,000 @ 33.75%	8,438
	21,869

Kaya and Hopi Ltd – National insurance contributions 2022/23

There are no NICs payable on dividends so the Class 1 NICs for Kaya and Hopi Ltd will remain unchanged.

Hopi Ltd – Corporation tax liability for year ended 5 April 2023

Hopi Ltd's corporation tax liability will remain unchanged.

249 Kat (September/December 2018)

Workbook references

The income tax computation is the subject of Chapter 2. Property income is dealt with in Chapter 6. Corporation tax computation is covered in Chapter 19. The computation of chargeable gains for individuals is covered in Chapter 13 and for companies in Chapter 20.

Top tips

When you are given a figure for a tax liability in the question don't waste time proving that the figure is correct – just use it!

Easy marks

There were some easy marks for basic income tax and corporation tax computations, but you needed to keep them separate and then compare them at the end of your answer.

Examining team's comments

In part (a), those candidates who made sure that they understood the scenario and worked carefully through each calculation had no difficulty answering this section.

As warned in previous reports, where a tax figure is given for one of the scenarios (in this case, the corporation tax figure), candidates should never attempt to recalculate the figure for themselves. All this does is use up valuable time. As regards the conclusion, this should have just been a calculation of the tax difference between the two scenarios. There was no need for a detailed explanation.

Where computations are required for two different scenarios, candidates should clearly indicate which scenario is being answered. This is particularly important where some of the same information is used in both scenarios. In this case employment income and the personal allowance were common across both scenarios. Some candidates attempted to answer this question with just the one computation; impossible given that property income formed part of the first computation, with dividend income included in the second.

It should have been quite clear from the information provided that full computations were necessary for both scenarios. Those candidates who calculated the tax liability for a personal purchase and then attempted to adjust the figures for a corporate purchase invariably ended up with a very confused answer.

The personal purchase required candidates to apply the restriction whereby relief for property income finance costs is restricted to the basic rate.

Candidates should be particularly aware of recent tax changes, and this is why an annual Finance Act update article is published.

Working through past examination questions will help candidates familiarise themselves with the best approach to be taken when answering questions which examine more than one tax. Also, it is important that candidates appreciate the interactions that can arise in such questions, and an article has been published covering many of the scenarios which could be examined.

Although there were many good answers to part (b), some candidates discussed the finance costs restriction when this has nothing to do with taxable gains. All that was required was a brief mention (not a detailed answer) of the annual exempt amount.

Marking guide

	Marks	
(a) *Property purchased personally*		
Employment income	0.5	
Property income		
Rent received	1	
Other expenses	0.5	
Personal allowance	0.5	
Income tax at basic rate	0.5	
Income tax at higher rate	0.5	
Finance costs tax reducer	1	
Property purchased via limited company		
Employment income	0.5	
Dividend income	0.5	
Personal allowance	0.5	
Income tax on non-savings income at basic rate	0.5	
Income tax on non-savings income at higher rate	0.5	
Dividend nil rate band	0.5	
Income tax on dividend income at higher rate	0.5	
Conclusion	1	
		9
(b) Annual exempt amount		
		1
Total		10

(a) **Property purchased personally**

	Non-savings income
	£
Employment income	60,000
Property income (W)	23,600
Net income	83,600
Less: Personal allowance	(12,570)
Taxable income	71,030
Income tax	
£37,700 at 20%	7,540
£33,330 at 40%	13,332
£71,030	—
	20,872
Interest relief (12,000 at 20%)	(2,400)
Income tax liability	18,472

Working – Property income

	£
Rent receivable (2,600 × 12)	31,200
Other expenses	(7,600)
Property income	23,600

Property purchased via a limited company

	Non-savings income	Dividend income
	£	£
Employment income	60,000	
Dividends	—	6,000
Net income	60,000	6,000
Less: Personal allowance	(12,570)	—
Taxable income	47,430	6,000
Income tax		
Non-savings income		
£37,700 at 20%	7,540	
£9,730 at 40%	3,892	
£47,430		

	Non-savings income	Dividend income
	£	£
Dividend income		
£2,000 at 0%	0	
£4,000 at 33.75%	1,350	
£6,000		
Income tax liability	12,782	

Conclusion

If Kat purchases the property via a limited company, then the overall tax saving will be £3,486 compared to purchasing the property personally:

	£
Property purchased personally	18,472
Property purchased via a limited company (2,204 + 12,782)	(14,986)
Tax saving	3,486

Tutorial note. The comparison ignores the fact that not all of the profits are withdrawn under the company purchase option. However, profits might typically be retained within a company to repay the mortgage borrowing or to fund a future property purchase.

(b) Annual exempt amount of £12,300 not available if gain occurs within limited company.

250 Jogger Ltd (A) (December 2008) (amended)

Workbook references

Computing taxable total profits, including capital allowances, and the corporation tax liability are dealt with in Chapter 19. Losses are covered in Chapter 21.

Top tips

Make sure you use the capital allowances proforma in part (a).

Easy marks

There were easy marks in part (b) for the corporation tax computation.

Marking guide	Marks	
(a) Operating loss	0.5	
Depreciation	0.5	
P&M		
AIA set against integral features in priority to SLA	1	
FYA @ 50%	1	
FYA @ 100%	1	
Main pool	1.5	
Special rate pool	1	
Short life asset	1.5	
		8

ANSWERS

Marking guide	Marks
(b) Bank interest	0.5
Loan interest	1
Property business profit	2
Chargeable gain	2
Loss relief	1
Corporation tax	0.5
	7
Total	15

(a) **Jogger Ltd – Trading loss y/e 31 March 2023**

	£
Operating profit	1,052,482
Add depreciation	58,840
	1,111,322
Less capital allowances (W)	(1,167,182)
Adjusted trading loss	(55,860)

Working

Plant and machinery

	AIA/FYA	*Main pool*	*Special rate pool*	*SLA*	*Allowances*
	£	£	£	£	£
TWDV b/f		26,600	21,167		
30.9.22 Integral features	1,300,000				
AIA	1,000,000				1,000,000
	300,000				
50% FYA	(150,000)				150,000
15.12.22 Second hand machinery				12,500	
15.8.22 Car	9,000				
100% FYA	(9,000)				9,000
31.7.22 Car		11,800			
Disposal					
20.7.22 Car			(11,700)		
			9,467		
14.3.23 Lorry		(8,600)			
		29,800			
WDA @ 18%		(5,364)		(2,250)	7,614

	AIA/FYA	Main pool	Special rate pool	SLA	Allowances
	£	£	£	£	£
WDA @ 6%			(568)		568
Transfer balance of 50% FYA addition	(150,000)		150,000		
TWDV c/f		24,436	158,899	10,250	
Allowances					1,167,182

Tutorial note. 50% FYA is available on the new integral features but it is more beneficial to claim AIA.

The super deduction is not available on the plant and machinery because it is not new.

(b) **Jogger Ltd – Corporation tax liability y/e 31 March 2023**

	£
Interest income (W1)	33,060
Property income (W2)	126,000
Chargeable gain (W3)	83,467
Total profits	242,527
Less loss relief	(55,860)
Taxable total profits	186,667
£186,667 × 19%	35,467

Workings

1 *Interest income*

		£
Bank interest receivable		8,460
Loan interest	– received 31.12.22	16,400
	– accrued 31.3.23	8,200
		33,060

2 *Property income*

	£
Premium received	100,000
Less 2% × (10 – 1) × £100,000	(18,000)
Taxable as property income	82,000
Add rental income accrued	44,000
	126,000

ANSWERS

3 *Chargeable gain*

	£
Disposal proceeds	150,000
Less cost	(47,660)
	102,340
Less indexation allowance £47,660 × 0.396	(18,873)
Gain	83,467

251 Mooncake Ltd (March/June 2021 amended)

Marking guide	Marks	
(a) Timing	1	
Qualifying charitable donations	1	
		2
(b) Depreciation	0.5	
Lease of office equipment	0.5	
Lease of car	1	
Entertaining staff	0.5	
Entertaining overseas customers	0.5	
QCDs	0.5	
Capital allowances	0.5	
WDV b/f	0.5	
Proceeds - van	1	
Proceeds - motor car	1	
Proceeds - motor car	0.5	
WDA	0.5	
		7
(c) (i) Trading profit	0.5	
Property business income	0.5	
Chargeable gain	1	
Trading loss	0.5	
QCDs	0.5	
Corporation tax	0.5	
		4
(ii) Trading loss	0.5	
Property business loss	0.5	
Capital loss	0.5	
QCDs	0.5	
		2
Total		15

(a) Factors which will influence a company's choice of loss relief claim:

(1) The timing and cash flow in relation to the relief obtained, with an earlier claim generally being preferable.

(2) The extent to which relief for qualifying charitable donations will be lost.

(b) **Mooncake Ltd – Trading loss for the year ended 31 March 2023**

	£
Operating loss	(93,820)
Depreciation	7,230
Lease of office equipment	0
Lease of car (3,400 × 15%)	510
Entertaining staff	0
Entertaining overseas customers	8,720
Qualifying charitable donations	1,600
Capital allowances (working)	(3,240)
Trading loss	(79,000)

Working

Capital allowances

	Main pool	Allowances
	£	£
WDV b/f	43,200	
Proceeds		
Delivery van	(11,800)	
Car [1]	(8,100)	
Car [2]	(5,300)	
WDA - 18%	18,000	
WDA c/f	(3,240)	3,240
Total allowances	14,760	—
		3,240

(c) (i) **Corporation tax liabilities for the years ended 31 March 2022 and 2023**

	Year ended 31 March 2022	Year ended 31 March 2023
	£	£
Trading profit	138,200	0
Property business income	23,700	0
Chargeable gain	0	0
	161,900	0
Trading loss	(79,000)	0
Qualifying charitable donations	(1,400)	0
Taxable total profits	81,500	0
Corporation tax at 19%	15,485	0

> **Tutorial note.** There is no chargeable gain for the year ended 31 March 2023 because the indexation allowance of £6,700 exceeds the gain of £3,700.

(ii) **Carry forward to the year ending 31 March 2024**

	£
Trading loss	0
Property business loss	4,400
Capital loss	4,900
Qualifying charitable donations	0

> **Tutorial note.** Indexation allowance cannot be used to create a capital loss.

252 Retro Ltd (June 2015) (amended)

Workbook references

The computation of taxable total profits is covered in Chapter 19. Losses are dealt with in Chapter 21.

Top tips

For part (a) you might want to start this question by computing the capital allowances. You can then just slot this into the adjustment of profit proforma at the appropriate place.

Easy marks

There were some easy marks for standard adjustments to profit in part (a).

Examining team's comments

Most candidates had little difficulty with part (a). One poor practice was the use of notes and explanations. It was a simple matter, as per the model answer, to just list all the items of expenditure (and show whether or not an adjustment was required), so the use of notes (such as for the gifts and donations) was completely unnecessary and against the guidance given in the note to the requirement. Since the requirement was for a calculation, explanations are not required, and result in wasted time. As regards the capital allowances, many candidates did not appreciate that the delivery van qualified for the 100% annual investment allowance – instead including it in the special rate pool.

There were many perfect answers to part (b), although disappointingly a few candidates tried to time-apportion profits using the opening year rules.

Part (c) caused few problems.

Marking guide	**Marks**
(a) Adjustment to profit	
Gifts to employees	0.5
Gift to customers	0.5
Qualifying charitable donations	0.5
Impairment loo	0.5
Lease of car	1
Health and safety fine	0.5
Interest payable	0.5

ANSWERS

		Marks	
	Capital allowances		
	WDV b/f	0.5	
	Delivery van	0.5	
	FYA @ 130%	0.5	
	Car [1]	0.5	
	WDA	0.5	
	Car [2]	0.5	
	FYI @100%	0.5	
	Structures and Buildings allowance		
	Exclude cost of land	0.5	
	@3%	0.5	
	Time-apportion	0.5	
			9
(b)	Trading profit	0.5	
	Bank interest	0.5	
	Carry back loss relief p/e 31 March 2022	1	
	Carry back loss relief in y/e 31 August 2021	1	
	Qualifying charitable donations	1	
			4
(c)	Unrelieved trading loss amount	1	
	Carry forward loss relief	1	
			2
Total			15

(a) Trading loss for the year ended 31 March 2023

	£
Loss before taxation	(80,340)
Gifts to employees	0
Gifts to customers	0
Qualifying charitable donations	1,100
Impairment loss	660
Health and safety fine	5,100
Interest payable	0
Capital allowances (working 1)	(50,420)
Structures and Buildings allowance (working 2)	(12,000)
Trading loss	(135,900)

Tutorial note. Gifts to customers are an allowable deduction if they cost less than £50 per recipient per year, are not of food, drink, tobacco or vouchers for exchangeable goods and carry a conspicuous advertisement for the company making the gift. Gifts to employees are an allowable deduction because the gifts will potentially be assessed on the employees as benefits.

Tutorial note. Interest on a loan used for trading purposes is deductible on an accruals basis.

Workings

1 ***Capital allowances***

	FYA	Main pool	Allowances
	£	£	£
WDV brought forward		39,300	
Delivery van (£21,769 × 130%)	28,300		
FYA – 130%	(28,300)		28,300
Addition – Car [1]		14,700	
		54,000	
WDA – 18%		(9,720)	9,720
Car [2]	12,400		
FYA – 100%	(12,400)		12,400
		0	
WDV carried forward		44,280	—
Total allowances			50,420

2 ***Structures and Buildings allowance***

(£850,000 – £50,000) × 3% × 6/12 = £12,000

Tutorial note. Car [1] has CO_2 emissions between 1 and 50 grams per kilometre, and therefore qualifies for writing down allowances at the rate of 18%.

Tutorial note. Motor car [2] has zero CO_2 emissions and is new, and therefore qualifies for the 100% first year allowance.

	Year ended 31 August 2021	*Period ended 31 March 2022*
	£	£
Trading profit	56,600	47,900
Bank interest	1,300	0
	57,900	47,900
Loss against total profits (working)	(24,125)	(47,900)
	33,775	0
Qualifying charitable donations	(540)	—
Taxable total profits	33,235	0

Working

Trading loss

For the year ended 31 August 2021, loss relief is restricted to £24,125 (57,900 × 5/12).

(c) The amount of unrelieved trading loss at 31 March 2023 is £63,875 (135,900 – 47,900 – 24,125).

ANSWERS

The unrelieved trading loss will be carried forward automatically and a claim can be made to set it, wholly or partly, against total profits of the next accounting period and then against total profits of future accounting periods until it is completely relieved.

253 Lucky Ltd (September/December 2015) (amended)

Workbook references

The computation of taxable total profits and the computation of the corporation tax liability are covered in Chapter 19. The adjustment to trading profits is dealt with in Chapter 7 and capital allowances in Chapter 8. National insurance contributions are covered in Chapter 12.

Top tips.

Administrative aspects of corporation tax are very likely to be examined so don't omit them from your revision.

Easy marks

There were some easy marks for the adjustment to trading profit and computation of corporation tax in part (b).

Examining team's comments

In part (a), most candidates appreciated that an accounting period starts when a company commences to trade, but many could not provide any other circumstances. For example, an accounting period will also start when a company otherwise becomes liable to corporation tax.

In part (b), the aspect of this question which appeared to cause candidates the most difficulties was the lease premium deduction and the difficulties were largely due to a failure to read the question carefully. Candidates were given the amount of the premium assessed on the landlord as income. However, a lot of candidates misread this figure as being the total premium paid.

Part (c) of the question was reasonably well answered.

[**BPP note.** Part (d) has been added to this question and there are no relevant examining team's comments.]

Marking guide	Marks	
(a) After end of previous period	1	
Other situations	1	
		2
(b) Trading profit		
Advertising	0.5	
Depreciation	0.5	
Amortisation	0.5	
Lease premium deduction	1.5	
Capital allowances		
Integral feature addition	0.5	
AIA in preference to 50% FY	0.5	
Computer addition	0.5	
Office equipment addition	0.5	
FYA @ 130%	1	
WDA	1	

Marking guide		Marks
Car addition	0.5	
FYA	0.5	
Interest income	0.5	
Corporation tax	0.5	
		9
(c) Date for retention	1	
Penalty	1	
		2
(d) Capital allowances	1	
National insurance contributions	1	
		2
Total		15

(a) An accounting period will normally start immediately after the end of the preceding accounting period.

An accounting period will also start when a company commences to trade, or otherwise becomes liable to corporation tax.

(b) Lucky Ltd – Corporation tax computation for the four-month period ended 31 March 2023

	£
Operating profit	716,903
Advertising	0
Depreciation	14,700
Amortisation	9,000
Deduction for lease premium £46,800/12 × 4/12	(1,300)
Capital allowances (W1)	(364,594)
Trading profit	374,709
Interest income	700
Taxable total profits	375,409
Corporation tax £375,409 @ 19%	71,328

Tutorial note. The advertising expenditure incurred during September 2022 is pre-trading and is treated as incurred on 1 December 2022. It is therefore deductible, and no adjustment is required.

Workings

1 *Capital allowances*

	AIA/FYA	*Main pool*	*Allowances*
	£	£	£
Integral features	291,200		
AIA (W2)	(291,200)		291,200

ANSWERS

	AIA/FYA	Main pool	Allowances
	£	£	£
Computer (6,300 x 130%)	8,190		
Office equipment (49,566 x 130%)	64,436		
	72,626		
FYA @ 130%	(72,626)		72,626
Car		12,800	
WDA 18% × 4/12		(768)	768
TWDV carried forward		12,032	—
Total allowances			364,594

2 *Annual investment allowances*

The annual investment allowance is reduced to £333,333 (£1,000,000 × 4/12) because Lucky Ltd's accounting period is four months long.

> **Tutorial note.** It is beneficial to claim the annual investment allowance against the integral features expenditure, as it would otherwise only qualify for first year allowance of 50%, with the balance going into the special rate pool.
>
> **Tutorial note.** The computer purchased on 19 August 2022 is pre-trading and is treated as incurred on 1 December 2022.
>
> **Tutorial note.** The car has CO_2 emissions up to 50 grams per kilometre and therefore qualifies for the 18% WDA in the main pool.

(c) Lucky Ltd must retain the records used in preparing its self-assessment corporation tax return until six years after the end of the accounting period, which is 31 March 2029.

A failure to retain records could result in a penalty of up to £3,000 per accounting period. However, the maximum penalty will only be charged in serious cases.

(d) The cost of the car will be included in Lucky Ltd's capital allowance computation and written down at the appropriate rate each year depending on the car's CO_2 emissions.

Lucky Ltd will also have to pay Class 1A national insurance contributions on the company car. Class 1A is deductible from taxable trading profits.

254 Jump Ltd (March/June 2016)

> **Workbook references**
>
> The computation of taxable total profits and the corporation tax liability are covered in Chapter 19.
>
> Groups of companies are covered in Chapter 22.
>
> **Top tips**
>
> In part (a), remember to include a zero when an item needs no adjustment; otherwise, you will not be credited for this knowledge.
>
> **Easy marks**
>
> Most of the adjustments to profit appear regularly in corporation tax questions.

Marking guide		Marks
(a) Trading loss		
Depreciation	0.5	
Employee training courses	0.5	
Employee pension contributions0	0.5	
Staff party	0.5	
Car lease	1	
Accountancy	0.5	
Legal fees – share capital	0.5	
Legal fees – renewal of short lease	0.5	
Entertaining UK customers	0.5	
Entertaining overseas customers	0.5	
Political donations	0.5	
Balancing charge adjustment	0.5	
Capital allowances		
Tax written down values b/f	0.5	
Car 1	1	
Car 2	0.5	
Balancing charge	0.5	
Writing down allowance	1	
		10
(b) (i) Choice of relief		
		1
(ii) Maximum relief claim – 7 m/e 31.12.22	0.5	
Maximum relief claim – y/e 31.5.22	1.5	
		2
(iii) Maximum surrender	1.5	
Skip Ltd	0.5	
		2
Total		15

(a) Jump Ltd – Trading loss for the three-month period ended 31 March 2023

	£
Loss before taxation	(144,700)
Depreciation	8,100
Employee training courses	0
Employee pension contributions	0
Staff party	0
Lease of car £1,200 × 15%	180
Accountancy	0

ANSWERS

		£
Legal fees	– Issue of share capital	3,800
	– Renewal of short lease	0
Entertaining UK customers		1,700
Entertaining overseas customers		790
Political donations		800
Balancing charge (W)		3,330
Trading loss		(126,000)

Working

Capital allowances

	Main pool	Special rate pool	Allowances
	£	£	£
TWDV brought forward	12,100	5,700	
Proceeds – Car [1]		(9,300)	
Proceeds – Car [2]	(6,100)	–	
Balancing charge		3,600	(3,600)
	6,000		
WDA – 18% × 3/12	(270)		270
TWDV carried forward	5,730		
			–
Net balancing charge			(3,330)

Tutorial note. The proceeds for car [1] are restricted to the original cost figure of £9,300.

(b) (i) The main factor which will influence Jump Ltd's choice of loss relief or group relief claims is the timing of the relief obtained, with an earlier claim generally being preferable in terms of cash flow (saving tax sooner is beneficial for cash flow).

Tutorial note. The other possible factor is the extent to which relief for qualifying charitable donations will be lost. However, this is not relevant given that Jump Ltd has not made any charitable donations.

(ii) The maximum loss relief claim for the seven-month period to 31 December 2022 is £42,400, being the total profits for this period.

The loss relief claim for the year ended 31 May 2022 is restricted to £33,250 ((78,600 + 1,200) × 5/12).

(iii) The maximum amount of trading loss which can be surrendered to Hop Ltd is £23,625, being the lower of £23,625 (63,000 × 3/8) and £126,000.

Skip Ltd is not a 75% subsidiary of Jump Ltd, so no group relief claim is possible.

255 Online Ltd (March/June 2017)

Workbook references

Computing taxable total profits is covered in Chapter 19. Chargeable gains for companies is the subject of Chapter 20. The use of losses is dealt with in Chapter 21. Payment of tax by companies is covered in Chapter 22.

Top tips

Don't forget to answer both parts of the question. In part (b) you only needed to make a couple of points in order to gain the marks.

Easy marks

There should have been easy marks for well-known adjustments such as depreciation and amortisation. The capital allowances computation was quite straightforward.

Examining team's comments

Part (a) was well answered. Surprisingly, the one aspect which consistently caused difficulty was the qualifying charitable donation. Many candidates added this back prior to deducting it, with others grossing up the deduction. Also, it is important that candidates know basic tax rules. Even though all of the items included in the capital allowances special rate pool had been sold, there was no balancing allowance because Online Ltd's trade did not cease. This was another computation where candidates needed to think carefully about where to show workings. In this case, the deduction for the lease premium, capital allowances and the chargeable gain warranted separate workings. It was not a good idea for candidates to attempt a short-cut approach to any of these workings. As regards the chargeable gain, quite a few candidates included the gain from the disposal made three years previously. This shows just how much care needs to be taken over dates.

In part (b) many candidates appreciated that acquiring a 51% group company would mean that the profit threshold for establishing whether Online Ltd is a large company would be reduced to £750,000. It would therefore be likely that the company's corporation tax would in future be payable by quarterly instalments. Having established this point, there was no need to then go on and explain quarterly instalments in detail. If such detail was needed, then this would have been made clear in the requirement. For some candidates, this was another example of where they wanted to answer the question that would have preferred had been set – in this case, explaining why the reliefs available with a 75% group relationship were not available with just a 60% shareholding. Few candidates correctly stated that the dividends received from Offline Ltd, being group dividends, would not form part of Online Ltd's profits when establishing its large company status.

Marking guide	Marks
(a) Depreciation	0.5
Amortisation	0.5
Property loss brought forward	1
Qualifying charitable donations	0.5
Lease premium	
Amount assessed on landlord	1
Deduction	1
Capital allowances	
Tax written down values b/f	0.5
Disposal – car	1
Disposal – pool	0.5

Marking guide	Marks	
WDA @ 18%	0.5	
WDA @ 6%	1	
Chargeable gain		
Disposal proceeds	0.5	
Share pool – original cost	0.5	
Share pool – indexation to October 2013	0.5	
Share pool – disposal October 2013	1	
Share pool – indexation to December 2017	0.5	
Share pool – disposal March 2022	0.5	
Capital loss brought forward	0.5	
		13
(b) Profit threshold reduced	1.5	
Group dividends	0.5	
		2
Total		15

(a) Online Ltd – Corporation tax computation for the year ended 31 March 2023

	£
Operating profit	896,700
Depreciation	21,660
Amortisation	9,000
Deduction for lease premium (W1)	(7,380)
Capital allowances (W2)	(9,824)
Trading profit	910,156
Chargeable gain (W3)	59,967
	970,123
Property business loss brought forward	(12,500)
Qualifying charitable donations	(6,800)
Taxable total profits	950,823

Workings

1 *Deduction for lease premium*

	£
Premium paid	90,000
Less: 90,000 × 2% × (10 – 1)	(16,200)
Amount assessed on the landlord	73,800
Deduction (73,800/10)	7,380

2 *Capital allowances*

	Main pool	Special rate pool	Allowances
	£	£	£
WDV brought forward	56,700	13,433	
Addition – Car	13,700		
Disposals – Car	(17,200)		
Disposals – Pool	–	(9,300)	
	53,200	4,133	
WDA – 18%	(9,576)		9,576
WDA – 6%	–	(248)	248
WDV carried forward	43,624	3,885	–
Total allowances			9,824

Tutorial note. The car purchased has CO_2 emissions between 1 and 50 grams per kilometre, and therefore qualifies for writing down allowances at the rate of 18%.

Tutorial note. The proceeds for the car which was sold are restricted to the original cost figure of £17,200.

Tutorial note. Although all of the items included in the special rate pool have been sold, there is no balancing allowance because the business has not ceased.

3 *Chargeable gain*

	£
Disposal proceeds	90,600
Less: Indexed cost (W4)	(27,529)
	63,071
Less: Capital loss brought forward	(3,104)
Chargeable gain	59,967

4 *Share pool*

	Number	Indexed cost
	£	£
Purchase June 2010	40,000	49,300
Indexation to October 2013 (49,300 × 0.124)		6,113
		55,413
Disposal October 2013 (55,413 × 22,000/40,000)	(22,000)	(30,477)
	18,000	24,936
Indexation to December 2017 (24,936 × 0.104)		2,593
		27,529
Disposal March 2023	(18,000)	(27,529)

ANSWERS

(b) The profit threshold for establishing whether Online Ltd is a large company will be reduced to £750,000 (1,500,000/2), so it is likely that the company's corporation tax will have to be paid by quarterly instalments.

The dividends received from Offline Ltd, being group dividends, will not form part of Online Ltd's profits.

256 Last-Orders Ltd (September/December 2017)

Workbook references

The computation of taxable total profits is covered in Chapter 19. Chargeable gains for companies are covered in Chapter 20. Corporate losses are the subject of Chapter 21 and group relief is dealt with in Chapter 22.

Top tips

When a company ceases to trade, no writing down allowances are given in the final accounting period but there will be a balancing adjustment.

Easy marks

In part (a) there were plenty of easy marks for adjustment to profit items but be careful to identify the effect of each of the adjustments on the trading loss. An item added back, such as depreciation, will reduce the loss, but an item deducted, such as capital allowances, will increase the loss.

Examining team's comments

Although section (a) was very well answered by many candidates, it caused problems for others. The section did not require any detailed workings, with any adjustments easily contained within the single computation. When commencing with a loss figure, candidates should be particularly careful to indicate which adjustments are deductions and which are additions. A single column approach with deductions shown in brackets avoids any confusion. Many candidates did not show those items not requiring any adjustment, despite being instructed specifically to do so – easy marks thereby being lost. Also, candidates should appreciate that there is no need to adjust for items of income which occur in the statement of profit or loss **after** the figure used to commence the loss adjustment. Last-Orders Ltd had ceased trading, so this meant that there was a balancing allowance. Many candidates missed this point, instead calculating capital allowances for the period.

Section (b) was generally well answered, with a number of perfect answers. However, candidates do not impress if they make basic mistakes such as deducting the annual exempt amount when calculating a corporate chargeable gain. Also, candidates should always be careful to follow the requirements – an easy half-mark was sometimes missed by not showing a figure for the amount of unused trading loss despite this being specifically requested.

In section (c), given that the company had ceased trading, candidates should really have realised that the loss could not be carried forward. Vague answers such as 'claim terminal loss relief' are not sufficient. Instead, candidates should have stated that relief was against total profits, for the previous three years and on a latest year first (LIFO) basis.

Marking guide		Marks
(a)	Depreciation	0.5
	Counselling services	0.5
	Employee pension contributions	0.5
	Employer Class 1 NICs	0.5
	Employer Class 1A NICs	0.5
	Unpaid bonuses	0.5

Lease of car	0.5	
Entertaining UK suppliers	0.5	
Entertaining overseas customers	0.5	
Qualifying charitable donations	0.5	
Balancing allowance	1	
		6
(b) *Property business income*		
Rent receivable	1	
Insurance	1	
Repairs	0.5	
Chargeable gain	1	
Trading loss	0.5	
Qualifying charitable donation	0.5	
Unused trading loss	0.5	
		5
(c) Terminal loss relief	1.5	
Group relief to Gastro Ltd	2	
No group relief to Gourmet Ltd	0.5	
		4
Total		15

(a) **Last-Orders Ltd – Trading loss for the ten-month period ended 31 January 2023**

	£
Operating loss	(276,480)
Add	
Depreciation	9,460
Counselling services	0
Employee pension contributions	0
Employer Class 1 NICs	0
Employer Class 1A NICs	0
Unpaid bonuses	10,400
Lease of car	0
Entertaining UK suppliers	1,920
Entertaining overseas customers	440
Employer Class 1A NICs	0
Employer Class 1A NICs	0
Qualifying charitable donations	800
Less: Balancing allowance £(24,200 – 13,600)	(10,600)
Trading loss	(264,060)

Tutorial note. No deduction is permitted where earnings are not paid within nine months of the end of the period of account.

Tutorial note. No adjustment is required where the CO_2 emissions of a leased car do not exceed 50 grams per kilometre.

Tutorial note. All business entertaining is disallowable. The distinction between UK and overseas is only relevant for value added tax (VAT) purposes.

(b) **Last-Orders Ltd – Taxable total profits for the ten-month period ended 31 January 2023**

		£
Property business income (W)		22,800
Chargeable gain £(126,800 – 79,400 – 12,900)		34,500
Total profits		57,300
Less	Trading loss	(57,300)
	Qualifying charitable donations	(0)
Taxable total profits		0
Unused trading loss £(264,060 – 57,300)		206,760

Working

		£
Rent receivable £19,200 × 2 × 10/12		32,000
Less	Insurance £1,800 × 10/12	(1,500)
	Repairs	(7,700)
Property business income		22,800

Tutorial note. The accruals basis is always used by companies in computing property business income.

(c) The trading loss can be relieved against Last-Orders Ltd's total profits for the previous three years, later years first, because it is a terminal loss.

The trading loss can be surrendered to Gastro Ltd because there is a 75% group relationship. The amount surrendered will be restricted to 10/12ths of Gastro Ltd's taxable total profits for the year ended 31 March 2023.

There is not a 75% group relationship with Gourmet Ltd, so no group relief claim is possible.

257 Solo Ltd (March/June 2018)

Workbook references

The computation of taxable total profits is covered in Chapter 19. Chargeable gains for companies are covered in Chapter 20. Corporate losses are the subject of Chapter 21.

Top tips

Think about why you are given capital losses for the two previous accounting periods. How can capital losses be relieved?

Easy marks

You should have gained two easy marks for dealing with the deduction for the lease premium in part (a) as this topic is regularly examined and a further two easy marks in part (b) for the calculation of property business income.

Examining team's comments

Part (a) for 3 marks required candidates to calculate Solo Ltd's revised tax-adjusted trading loss for the year ended 31 March 2023. This section was quite well answered. However, when dealing with a trading loss, candidates need to be very careful that adjustments are correctly added or deducted. Treating the loss as a negative means that there is no need to change the approach from that used for a trading profit. A number of candidates did not appreciate that there was a balancing charge because the disposal proceeds for the plant and machinery main pool exceeded the written down value brought forward.

Part (b) for 8 marks asked candidates to prepare a corporation tax computation for the year ended 31 March 2023 showing taxable total profits. This was on the basis that Solo Ltd claimed relief for its trading loss against its total profits. The requirement meant that candidates had to calculate property business income, calculate a chargeable gain on a share disposal, deduct brought forward capital losses from the gain, and then deduct the trading loss so that taxable total profits were nil. This section was again well answered. One aspect which consistently caused difficulty was candidates not preparing a separate gain calculation for the share purchase made during the preceding nine days. A number of candidates incorrectly restricted the insurance deduction in the property business income calculation to 8/12ths because the building was unoccupied from 1 April to 31 July 2022.

Information was provided in date order, and candidates often tried to use the details provided for the year ended 31 December 2021 and the period ended 31 March 2022 in this section of the question. The only details which were relevant were the capital losses, and these were often omitted in any case.

Part (c) for 4 marks required candidates to calculate Solo Ltd's taxable total profits for the year ended 31 December 2021 and the three-month period ended 31 March 2022. This was on the basis that the company claimed relief for the remainder of its trading loss as early as possible. This section was very well answered, and it was pleasing to see most candidates correctly restricting the trading loss set off for the year ended 31 December 2021 to 9/12ths of the total profits. Candidates should note that where two accounting periods are involved, then a two-column approach avoids the need to type out descriptions twice.

Marking guide

	Marks	
(a) Deduction for lease premium		
Premium received	0.5	
Amount treated as capital	1	
Trading income deduction	0.5	
Balancing charge	1	
		3
(b) *Property business income*		
Rent receivable	1	
Security deposit	0.5	
Insurance	1	
Chargeable gain		
Disposal proceeds on shares purchased in previous 9 days	0.5	
Cost of shares purchased in previous 9 days	0.5	
Disposal proceeds on shares from share pool	0.5	

Marking guide		Marks
Share pool		
Original purchase	0.5	
Indexation to December 2017	1	
Disposal	1	
Capital losses relieved	1	
Trading loss relieved	0.5	
		8
(c) Trading profits	0.5	
Property business income	0.5	
Chargeable gains	0.5	
Trading loss relieved	1.5	
Qualifying charitable donations	1	
		4
Total		15

(a) **Solo Ltd – Trading loss for the year ended 31 March 2023**

	£
Trading loss	(151,300)
Less: Deduction for lease premium (W)	(2,150)
Add: Balancing charge	4,300
Trading loss	(149,150)

Working

	£
Premium received	20,000
Less: £20,000 × 2% × (8 – 1)	(2,800)
Amount assessable on landlord	17,200
Trading income deduction £17,200/8	2,150

(b) **Solo Ltd – Corporation tax computation for the year ended 31 March 2023**

	£
Property business income (W1)	9,480
Net chargeable gains £(16,198(W2) – 3,300 – 2,100)	10,798
Total profits	20,278
Less: Trading loss	(20,278)
Taxable total profits	0

Workings

1 *Property business income*

	£
Rent receivable £(7,800 + (7,800 × 2/6))	10,400
Security deposit	0
Less: Insurance	(920)
Property business income	9,480

Tutorial note. The accruals basis is always used by companies in computing property business income.

Tutorial note. A security deposit is not treated as income when received.

It will be treated as income if the landlord uses it, for example to cover unpaid rent at the end of the tenancy.

Any amount repaid to the tenant is not treated as an expense.

2 *Chargeable gains*

	£	£
Purchase 8 December 2022		
Disposal proceeds £31,200 × 1,000/6,500	4,800	
Less: Cost	(4,600)	
		200
Share pool		
Disposal proceeds £31,200 × 5,500/6,500	26,400	
Less: Cost (W3)	(10,402)	
		15,998
Chargeable gains		16,198

3 *Share pool*

	No.	Cost
		£
Purchase June 2006	20,000	27,000
Indexation to December 2017 £27,000 × 0.401		10,827
		37,827
Disposal December 2022 £37,827 × 5,500/20,000	(5,500)	(10,402)
c/f	14,500	27,425

Tutorial note. The disposal is first matched with the shares purchased in the nine days before the disposal and then against the share pool.

Tutorial note. Indexation is frozen at December 2017.

(c) **Solo Ltd – Taxable total profits for the periods ended 31 December 2021 and 31 March 2022**

		y/e 31 December 2021	*p/e 31 March 2022*
		£	£
Trading profit		35,900	12,300
Property business income		12,100	4,200
Chargeable gain		0	0
Total profits		48,000	16,500
Less	Trading loss relief	(W) (36,000)	(16,500)
	Qualifying charitable donations	(1,200)	Wasted
Taxable total profits		10,800	0

Working

	£
Year ended 31 December 2021 £48,000 × 9/12	36,000

258 Ash Ltd, Beech Ltd and Cedar Ltd (September/December 2018)

Workbook references

Computing taxable total profits (including residence of companies and accounting periods) and the corporation tax liability are covered in Chapter 19. Chargeable gains for companies is the subject of Chapter 20. Losses for a single company are dealt with in Chapter 21 and group relief in Chapter 22.

Top tips

Take care you answer all three parts of the question.

Easy marks

These were available for basic adjustments to profits in part (b).

Examining team's comments

Part (a)(i) was quite well answered. However, when considering accounting periods, it is very important not to confuse the corporate and unincorporated business rules. Applying the unincorporated business opening year rules to a limited company will obviously not achieve many marks.

If asked to identify a company's accounting periods throughout a given period, then candidates should make sure that all relevant periods are stated. It does not create a good impression if there are gaps between the accounting periods stated by a candidate, or if a stated period ends before it has started.

In part (a)(ii), again candidates should be careful not to confuse the rules for companies with those applicable to individuals. If a limited company is incorporated in the UK, then nothing else is relevant. So, as regards the majority of Ash Ltd's director/shareholders moving overseas, candidates should just have stated that this did not have any impact on the company's residence status.

Part (b) was very well answered. When making adjustments to a trading profit, candidates need to be very careful that adjustments are correctly added and not deducted.

Part (c) was again well answered. When calculating chargeable gains for a corporate share disposal, then carefully check the dates that have been given. There was a rights issue which had taken place in the month of purchase, so there was no need to index prior to adding the new shares into the share pool.

Marking guide		Marks	
(a) (i)	First accounting period	1	
	Second accounting period	0.5	
	Third accounting period	0.5	
			2
(ii)	Incorporated in UK	1	
	Move overseas by director/shareholders	1	
			2
(b)	Depreciation	0.5	
	Gifts to customers	0.5	
	Gifts to staff	0.5	
	Qualifying charitable donations added back	0.5	
	Impairment loss	0.5	
	Lease of cars	1	
	Fine	0.5	
	Legal fees	0.5	
	Interest payable	0.5	
	Qualifying charitable donations deducted from total profits	0.5	
	Corporation tax liability	0.5	
			6
(c)	Disposal proceeds	0.5	
	Indexed cost		
	Purchase	0.5	
	Rights issue	1	
	Indexation allowance	1	
	Capital loss	1	
	Loss relief	0.5	
	Group relief	0.5	
			5
Total			15

(a) **Ash Ltd**

(i) *Accounting periods*

1 February 2021 to 31 January 2022

1 February 2022 to 31 March 2022

Year ended 31 March 2023

> **Tutorial note.** The bank account opened by Ash Ltd on 1 December 2020 is not a source of income, and therefore does not trigger the start of an accounting period.

> **Tutorial note.** An accounting period cannot be longer than 12 months, so the period of account ended 31 March 2022 must be split into two accounting periods.
>
> **Tutorial note.** The move overseas of a majority of Ash Ltd's director/shareholders on 1 October 2022 has no impact on the company's accounting periods.

(ii) *Residence status*

(1) Ash Ltd was incorporated in the UK, so the company is therefore resident in the UK throughout the period 1 December 2020 to 31 March 2023.

(2) The move overseas of a majority of Ash Ltd's director/shareholders on 1 October 2022 does not have any impact on the company's residence status.

(b) **Beech Ltd**

Corporation tax computation for the year ended 31 January 2023

	£
Profit before taxation	305,500
Depreciation	14,700
Gifts to customers	3,500
Gifts to staff	0
Qualifying charitable donations	1,100
Impairment loss	0
Lease of cars (12,600 ×15%)	1,890
Data protection fine	6,400
Legal fees – Renewal of short lease	0
Interest payable	0
Trading profit/Total profits	333,090
Less Qualifying charitable donations	(1,100)
Taxable total profits	331,990
Corporation tax	
331,990 at 19%	63,078

> **Tutorial note.** Gifts to customers are only an allowable deduction if they cost less than £50 per recipient per year, are not of food, drink, tobacco or vouchers for exchangeable goods and carry a conspicuous advertisement for the company making the gift. Gifts to staff are allowable.

(c) **Cedar Ltd**

Corporation tax computation for the year ended 31 March 2023

	£
Disposal proceeds (25,000 × 6.00)	150,000
Indexed cost (W)	(38,004)
Chargeable gain	111,996
Capital loss	(8,800)
Loss relief	(19,700)

	£
Group relief	(20,800)
Taxable total profits	62,696

Working

Indexed cost

Share pool

	Number	*Indexed cost*
	£	£
Purchase July 2010	20,000	24,800
Rights issue July 2010		
20,000 × 1/4 × £1.15	5,000	5,750
	25,000	30,550
Indexation to December 2017 (frozen)		
30,550 × 0.244		7,454
		38,004
Disposal December 2022	(25,000)	(38,004)

Tutorial note. A joint election can be made so that Cedar Ltd is treated as having incurred Timber Ltd's capital loss.

Tutorial note. Indexation allowance is frozen at December 2017.

259 Aoede Ltd, Bianca Ltd and Charon Ltd (March/June 2019)

Workbook references

Computing taxable total profits is covered in Chapter 19, losses for a single company in Chapter 21 and group relief in Chapter 22. Chargeable gains for companies is the subject of Chapter 20.

Top tips

It is important that you attempt all three parts of this question in order to gain reasonable marks.

Easy marks

There were easy marks for straightforward adjustments to profits in part (b).

Examining team's comments

Although Moon Ltd was often overlooked, part (a)(i) was generally well answered.

For the year ended 31 March 2022, many candidates did not appreciate that loss relief was claimed against Aoede Ltd's chargeable gain in priority to offsetting the qualifying charitable donations.

Part (a)(ii) was often not answered. The answer was simply that it was not beneficial for Aoede Ltd to make the loss relief claim against total income for the year ended 31 March 2022 because the income would have otherwise been covered by qualifying charitable donations.

Part (b) was very well answered. Candidates should note that when dealing with straightforward capital allowance computations such as those involved here, it is quicker to include them in the main computation rather than producing a full capital allowances working.

Part (c) was also well answered. However, a few candidates combined the two computations.

Where a question involves more than one disposal, then the gain or loss for each disposal must be calculated separately.

Marking guide

		Marks	
(a)	(i) *Aoede Ltd y/e 31.3.22*		
	Total profits	0.5	
	Current period loss relief	1	
	Qualifying charitable donation unrelieved	0.5	
	Aoede Ltd y/e 31.3.23		
	Total profits	0.5	
	Carry forward loss relief	1	
	Qualifying charitable donation	0.5	
	Moon Ltd y/e 31.3.23		
	Trading profit	0.5	
	Group relief	0.5	
			5
	(ii) Loss relief claim not beneficial		
			1
(b)	Advertising expenditure	0.5	
	Lease of cars	1.5	
	Laptops	1	
	Car [1]	1	
	Car [2]	1	
			5
(c)	*First property*		
	Disposal proceeds	0.5	
	Cost	0.5	
	Enhancement expenditure	0.5	
	Indexation allowance	1	
	Second property		
	Disposal proceeds	0.5	
	Cost	0.5	
	Indexation allowance	0.5	
			4
Total			15

(a) (i) Aoede Ltd - Taxable total profits

	y/e 31.3.22	y/e 31.3.23
	£	£
Trading profit	0	67,800
Property business income	0	23,400
Chargeable gain	5,800	16,200
Total profits	5,800	107,400
Less: Current period trading loss relief	(5,800)	(0)
Carry forward trading loss relief	(0)	(100,800)
Qualifying charitable donation	(0)	(6,600)
Taxable total profits	0	0

(ii) Moon Ltd – Taxable total profits

	y/e 31.3.23
	£
Trading profit	19,700
Less: Trading loss carry forward group relief	(4,700)
Property business loss carry forward group relief	(15,000)
Taxable total profits	0

Tutorial note. *Loss memorandum*

	Trading loss	Property business loss
	£	£
y/e 31.3.22	111,300	26,400
Used in y/e 31.3.22 against own profits	(5,800)	(0)
Used in y/e 31.3.23 against own profits	(100,800)	(0)
Used in y/e 31.3.23 s group relief	(4,700)	(15,000)
Losses c/f	0	11,400

Tutorial note. There are independent claims for Aoede Ltd's trading loss and property business loss. We have used the trading loss in priority to the property business loss but it would be possible to use the property business loss first – the result for these two accounting periods would be the same.

Tutorial note. Aoede Ltd's current period loss relief claim must be taken against total profits as far as possible. It is not possible to restrict it to preserve relief on the qualifying charitable donation of £6,000.

Tutorial note. Aoede Ltd will automatically carry forward its unused losses to y/e 31 March 2023 but can make a partial relief claim to keep sufficient total profits in charge to cover the qualifying charitable donation of £6,600.

Tutorial note. Aoede Ltd must use it's carried forward losses itself before surrendering losses under carry forward group relief.

ANSWERS

> **Tutorial note.** It is not beneficial for Aoede Ltd to make the loss relief claim against total income for the year ended 31 March 2022 because the income would have otherwise been covered by the qualifying charitable donations of £6,000.

(b) **Bianca Ltd – Tax adjusted trading profit for the year ended 31 March 2023**

	£
Trading profit	256,300
Less: Advertising expenditure	(5,800)
Add: Lease of cars (5,100 × 15%)	765
Less Capital allowances	
Laptops (1,000 × 4 × 130%)	(5,200)
Car [1] (12,400 × 18%)	(2,232)
Car [2] (13,900 × 6%)	(834)
Revised trading profit	242,999

> **Tutorial note.** The advertising expenditure incurred during January 2021 is pre-trading and is therefore treated as incurred on 1 April 2022.
>
> **Tutorial note.** The original cost of the laptops is irrelevant.
>
> **Tutorial note.** Car [2] has CO_2 emissions over 50 grams per kilometre and therefore qualifies for writing down allowances at the rate of 6%.

(c) **Charon Ltd – Chargeable gains and capital losses for the year ended 31 March 2023**

First property

	£
Disposal proceeds	368,000
Less: Cost	(147,000)
Less: Enhancement expenditure	(39,000)
	182,000
Indexation allowance	
147,000 × 0.856	(125,832)
Chargeable gain	56,168

Second property

	£
Disposal proceeds	167,000
Less: Cost	(172,000)
Indexation allowance	0
Less: Capital loss	(5,000)

> **Tutorial note.** There is no indexation allowance for the first property's enhancement expenditure of £39,000 because this was incurred after December 2017.

PART F: VALUE ADDED TAX

Section A

OTQ bank – Value added tax 1

260 The correct answers are:

18 August	Deposit
2 September	Balancing payment

The basic tax point is the date the goods were supplied (26 August). Where payment is received before the basic tax point, then this date becomes the actual tax point. The tax point for the 10% deposit is therefore the date that it is received (18 August). The actual tax point for the balancing payment is the date the invoice was issued (2 September) as this was within 14 days of the basic tax point.

261 The correct answer is: 1 January 2023

ACCA Examining Team's Comments

Frances' taxable turnover exceeds £85,000 on 30 November 2022 (15,000 + 20,000 + 30,000 + 2/3 × 33,000) = £87,000. She has 30 days to notify MH Revenue and Customs and is registered from 1 January 2023.

The alternative, incorrect answer options are as follows:

30 December 2022 being 30 days after historic test exceeded

31 January 2023 being one month after quarter end when historic test exceeded

1 February 2023 which would be correct if the historic test was met on 31 December 2022

262 The correct answer is: £62

	£
Output VAT: £377 × 1/6	63
Less input VAT: £625 × 20%	(125)
VAT due	(62)

Input VAT on the car is not recoverable because there is private use. The answer £50 treats the scale charge as VAT-exclusive but recovers the correct amount on the petrol. The answer £75 treats the scale charge as VAT-exclusive and fails to recover the VAT on the actual petrol purchase. The answer £41 treats petrol as inclusive, instead of exclusive, of VAT.

263 The correct answer is:

Return submitted	*Payment*
7 July 2022	7 July 2022

The time limit for submission of the return and payment is one month plus seven days after the end of the VAT period.

264 The correct answer is: VAT quarter ended 30 June 2023

The value added tax (VAT) on an impaired debt may only be reclaimed once the debt has been outstanding for six months from the due date. The due date in this instance is 10 October 2022, therefore the VAT can be reclaimed in the quarter ended 30 June 2023.

OTQ bank – Value added tax 2

265 £ 1,600

The VAT will be calculated on the actual amount received so is £8,000 × 20% = £1,600.

266 £ 333

Input tax on the car is not recoverable because there is private use. However, since there is some use of the car for business purposes, then any VAT charged on repairs and maintenance costs can be treated as input tax without apportionment for private use. The input VAT recoverable is therefore £2,000 × 1/6 = £333.

267 £2,320

	£
New car for salesman	0
New van £10,320 × 1/6	1,720
Entertaining UK customers	0
Entertaining overseas customers £3,600 × 1/6	600
Total input tax recoverable	2,320

The answer £5,360 allows full input tax recovery. The answer £4,192 allows business use recovery of input tax on the car. The answer £3,020 allows recovery of input tax on the entertaining of UK customers.

268 £ 270

The following rules apply to pre-registration input tax:

Goods: if acquired within four years prior to registration and still held on registration date (so the VAT on the inventory of spare parts is recoverable).

Services: if supplied within six months prior to registration (so the VAT on the accountancy fees is recoverable but not that on the legal fees).

269 The correct answer is: 1 August 2022

Scott is required to notify HMRC within 30 days of exceeding the £85,000 registration threshold, ie 30 July 2022 (30 days after the year to 30 June 2022). He will then be registered from 1 August 2022.

270 £ 4,925

	£
Output VAT: £35,250 × 1/6	5,875
Less input VAT: £5,700 × 1/6 (UK customer entertaining not recoverable)	(950)
VAT due	4,925

271 The correct answer is: 0%

Charlie will charge VAT at zero rate because exports of goods to anywhere in the world are zero rated.

272 The correct answers are:

- Date of payment or receipt determines the VAT period in which the transaction is dealt with
- Gives automatic impairment loss relief (bad debt relief)

273 The correct answer is: £8,500

	£
Standard rated sales (£50,000 × 120%)	60,000
Zero rated sales	20,000
Exempt sales	5,000
Total VAT inclusive sales	85,000
Value added tax £85,000 × 10%	8,500

ACCA Examining Team's Comments

This question on value added tax (VAT) required candidates to calculate the amount of VAT payable by an individual taxpayer who calculates their liability based on the flat rate scheme. The taxpayer made standard rated, zero rated and exempt sales so it was crucial for candidates to know that the flat rate percentage is applied to total VAT-inclusive turnover under the flat rate scheme in order to answer this question correctly.

The correct answer was the first option (£8,500).

The most common answer was the third option (£7,500) which is the answer arrived at if VAT at the standard rate is not included on the standard rated sales ((£50,000 + £20,000 + £5,000) × 10%). This demonstrates that many candidates did not appreciate the need to calculate VAT using VAT inclusive figures, or had not realised that the figures provided excluded VAT.

Candidates are reminded of the importance of the VAT special schemes for the TX-UK exam and also of the importance of reading questions carefully before calculating and selecting an answer.

274 The correct answers are:

Tax inclusive annual taxable turnover up to £150,000	Join scheme
Tax inclusive annual turnover up to £230,000	Leave scheme

ANSWERS

Section B

OT case – Anne (June 2009) (amended)

> **Workbook references**
>
> Value added tax liability is covered in Chapter 24. Special schemes are dealt with in Chapter 25.
>
> **Top tips**
>
> Make sure that you read all the information given in the question – you are given this information by the examining team for a reason so you must make use of it when answering the question.
>
> **Easy marks**
>
> The output tax on cash sales should have been easy to deal with.

275 £ 5,600

Cash sales £28,000 (adult clothes standard rated) × 20% = £5,600

276 The correct answer is: £2,292

	£
Credit sales with discount £12,000 × 95% × 90% × 20%	2,052
Credit sales without discount £12,000 × 10% × 20%	240
	2,292

The calculation of output VAT on the credit sales only takes into account the discount for prompt payment for the 90% of customers that took it.

The answer £2,052 is just the output VAT on the discounted sales. The answer £2,280 is the output tax if all sales are treated as discounted. The answer £2,400 is the answer if no sales are treated as discounted.

277 £ 2,400

	£
Purchases and expenses £11,200 × 20%	2,240
Impairment loss £800 × 20%	160
	2,400

Relief for an impairment loss is not given until six months from the time that payment is due. Therefore, relief can only be claimed in respect of the invoice due for payment on 10 April 2022. Obviously, the customer did not take up the discount for prompt payment.

278 The correct answers are:

- Anne will be permitted to join the scheme if her expected taxable turnover for the next 12 months does not exceed £1,350,000.
- If the value of Anne's taxable supplies exceeds £1,600,000 in the 12 months to the end of a VAT period, she must leave the scheme immediately.

Anne will be permitted to join the scheme if she is up to date with both her VAT payments and her VAT returns. Payment in nine monthly instalments is a feature of the annual accounting scheme.

279 The correct answers are:

Reduced amount of output VAT payable		NOT ADVANTAGE
Automatic impairment loss relief (bad debt relief)	ADVANTAGE	
Only one VAT return each year		NOT ADVANTAGE
Output VAT on 10% of credit sales will be accounted for up to 1 month later than at present	ADVANTAGE	

The output VAT payable will remain the same and accounting for VAT will also remain the same.

OT case – Auy and Bim (June 2010) (amended)

Workbook references

The tax point and VAT liability are covered in Chapter 24. Special schemes are dealt with in Chapter 25.

Top tips

Learn the rules about the tax point – they are often examined! For the basic tax point, you need to distinguish between supplies of goods (date goods are removed or made available to the customer) and services (date on which services are completed).

Easy marks

There were easy marks for the computation of the VAT paid or payable by the partnership.

280 The correct answers are:

- If the VAT invoice is issued within 14 days after the basic tax point and payment has not been received before the basic tax point, the invoice date becomes the tax point.
- The tax point determines the VAT period in which output tax must be accounted for and credit for input tax will be allowed.

The basic tax point for services is the date that services are completed. If the VAT invoice is issued and payment is received before the basic tax point, the actual tax point is the earlier of those two dates.

281 The correct answer is: £25,280

The partnership's output VAT for the year ended 5 April 2023 is £25,600 and its total input VAT for the year is £(180 + 140) = £320.

Therefore, VAT of £25,280 (25,600 – 320) will have been paid to HM Revenue & Customs for the year ended 5 April 2023.

282 The correct answers are:

- Businesses using the scheme must still issue VAT invoices to their VAT registered customers.
- Businesses using the scheme cannot reclaim any input tax suffered.

Under the scheme, businesses calculate VAT by applying a fixed percentage to all their income (ie, including reduced rate, zero rated and exempt income). A 1% reduction off the flat rate percentage can be made by businesses in the first year that they use the flat rate scheme only if it is also the first year of registration.

283 The correct answer is:

Join	*Continue to use*
Expected taxable turnover (excluding VAT) for the next 12 months does not exceed £150,000.	Until its total turnover (including VAT) for the previous year exceeds £230,000

284 The correct answer is: £23,291

If the partnership had used the flat rate scheme throughout the year ended 5 April 2023, then it would have paid VAT of £(140,762 + 25,600) = £166,362 @ 14% = £23,291.

OT case – Aston (June 2011) (amended)

Workbook references

Registration for value added tax is covered in Chapter 24. VAT invoices, penalties and overseas aspects are dealt with in Chapter 25.

Top tips

Remember that the common penalty regime for errors applies to a number of taxes, including VAT.

Easy marks

There were easy marks for dealing with the registration of Aston.

285 The correct answers are:

31 January 2023	Liable for registration
1 March 2023	Date of registration

Aston would have been liable to compulsory value added tax (VAT) registration when his taxable supplies during any 12-month period (or the period from commencement of trade, if less) exceeded £85,000.

This happened on 31 January 2023 when taxable supplies amounted to £85,200 (6,300 + 6,400 + 21,900 + 4,800 + 11,700 + 17,100 + 14,800 + 2,200).

Registration is required from the end of the month following the month in which the limit is exceeded, so Aston will have been registered from 1 March 2023 or from an agreed earlier date.

286 The correct answer is:

Submission	*Payment*
One month and seven days after the end of the VAT period	One month and seven days after the end of the VAT period

287 The correct answers are:

- Aston's VAT registration number
- An identifying number (invoice number)

288 The correct answers are:

- The transaction is entered on Aston's VAT return as an output and an input.
- The service is treated as being supplied in the UK since this is where Aston is situated.

The tax point for a supply of such services is the earlier of the time the service is completed and the time the service is paid for. Supplies of services from VAT registered businesses situated abroad are categorised in the same way as UK supplies and so are not necessarily zero rated.

289 The correct answer is:

Maximum penalty	***Minimum penalty for unprompted disclosure***
30% of the VAT underpaid	0% of the VAT underpaid

HM Revenue & Customs (HMRC) will not charge a penalty if Aston has taken reasonable care, provided he informs them of any errors upon subsequent discovery.

However, applying the incorrect rate of VAT is more likely to be treated as careless, since Aston would be expected to check the VAT classification of his supplies.

The maximum amount of penalty will therefore be 30% of the VAT underpaid, but this penalty could be reduced to 0% as a result of a subsequent unprompted disclosure to HMRC.

OT case – Starfish Ltd (Dec 2011) (amended)

Workbook references

Calculation of value added tax (VAT) and transfer of a business as a going concern are covered in Chapter 24. Default interest is dealt with in Chapter 25.

Top tips

In the last question, you need to identify the supplies which will not be subject to VAT as a result of the transfer of going concern rules.

Easy marks

There were some easy marks available in the computation of VAT in the second question.

290 The correct answer is: £390

	£
Credit sales revenue discount taken up £2,000 × (100 – 4)% × 60% × 20%	230
Credit sales revenue discount not taken up £2,000 × 40% × 20%	160
	390

291 The correct answer is: £16,420

	£
Cash sales revenue £38,520 × 20/120	6,420
Sale of inventory on cessation £28,800 × 20/120	4,800
Sale of non-current assets £31,200 × 20/120	5,200
	16,420

There is no VAT charged on the sale of the car, as none was recovered on purchase (owing to private usage).

292 The correct answer is: £11,324

	£
Expenses £([69,960 – 4,320] = £65,640) × 20/120	10,940
Impairment loss	384
	11,324

Input VAT on business entertainment for UK customers is not recoverable.

Relief for the impairment loss is available because the claim is made more than six months from the time that payment was due, and the debt has been written off in the company's books.

293 The correct answer is: 7 May 2023

Default interest will be payable from the reckonable date (7 May) to the date of payment.

294 The correct answer is: No output VAT would have been due on the sale of the inventory or the sale of the non-current assets.

A sale of a business as a going concern is outside the scope of VAT, and therefore output VAT would not have been due on either the sale of the inventory or the sale of the non-current assets.

OT case – Greenzone Ltd (June 2013)

Workbook references

All the VAT aspects in this question are dealt with in Chapter 24.

Top tips

Watch out for the difference between entertaining UK customers and overseas customers.

Easy marks

There were easy marks for working out the output VAT.

295 The correct answer is: £42,540

Output VAT	£
Sales	38,210
Group sales	4,330
Output VAT	42,540

The tax point for the deposit is the date of payment, so no adjustment is required to the output VAT figure of £38,210.

The answer £38,210 does not include group sales. The answer £42,140 does not include the deposit. The answer £37,810 does not include either group sales or the deposit.

296 The correct answer is: £27 recoverable

Output VAT	£
Fuel scale charge £334 × 20/120	56
Input VAT	
Fuel purchased £500 × 20/120	(83)
VAT recoverable	(27)

The answer £23 payable adjusts the input tax for private mileage, so the input VAT is £500 × 20/120 = £33. The answer £33 recoverable treats the amounts as VAT exclusive. The answer £56 payable is just the fuel scale charge.

297 £ 12,560

	£
Total input VAT	12,770
Entertaining UK customers	(210)
Entertaining overseas customers	0
Repainting office building	0
New reception area	0
	12,560

Input VAT on business entertaining is not recoverable unless it relates to the cost of entertaining overseas customers.

There is no distinction between capital and revenue expenditure for VAT so input tax is recoverable on both the repainting of the office building (revenue) and the building of the new reception area (capital).

298 The correct answers are:

ARE LTD	**YES**	
BE LTD		**NO**
DOER INC		**NO**

Are Ltd can register with Greenzone Ltd as a group for VAT purposes as it is UK resident and controlled by Greenzone Ltd.

Be Ltd is not controlled by Greenzone Ltd and Doer Inc is not UK resident and does not have a fixed establishment in the UK.

299 The correct answers are:

- Each VAT group must appoint a representative member which accounts for the group's output tax and input tax.
- Any supply of goods or services by a member of the group to another member of the group is disregarded for VAT purposes.

All members of the group are jointly and severally liable for any VAT due from the representative member. It is not necessary for each company, which is eligible for group registration, to join a particular VAT group.

OT case – Long Ltd group (B) (June 2014) (amended)

Workbook references

Value added tax (VAT) calculation and group registration will be found in Chapter 24.

Top tips

It is vital to understand the difference between making exempt supplies and zero-rated supplies – think about whether input VAT can be recovered in either case.

Easy marks

There were some easy marks for dealing with input VAT.

300 £ 53,780

	£
Sales £(52,640 – 1,760)	50,880
Group sales £(1,940 + 960)	2,900
	53,780

The tax point for the deposit is the date of payment, so this will have been included in output VAT for the quarter ended 31 December 2022.

301 The correct answer is: £15,638

	£
Expenses	14,720
Hire of photocopier £18 × [(4 years × 12 = 48 months) + 3 months]	918
	15,638

Refunds of VAT are subject to a four-year time limit so, in addition to the input VAT for the hire of the photocopier incurred during the quarter ended 31 March 2023, Long Ltd can claim for the input VAT incurred during the period 1 January 2019 to 31 December 2022.

The answer £14,720 does not include the hire of the photocopies. The answer £14,774 includes only three months of the hire of the photocopier. The answer £14,882 includes an additional six months of hire of the photocopier giving nine months in total – this is a confusion between the rules for recovery of goods and of services.

302 £ 0

Wind Ltd's sales are exempt from VAT, so the company cannot be registered for VAT and thus cannot recover input tax.

303 £3,500

	£
Expenses	3,120
Advertising	380
	3,500

Input VAT on services incurred prior to registration is subject to a 6-month time limit, so the input VAT of £640 in respect of the advertising expenditure incurred during April 2022 cannot be recovered.

The answer £3,120 does not include the advertising at all. The answer £4,140 includes all the advertising. The answer £3,540 includes only the £640 of advertising expenditure.

304 The correct answers are:

- Supplies of goods or services to Road Ltd from outside the group will be treated as a supply to Long Ltd.
- The supplies by Long Ltd to Wind Ltd and Road Ltd would be disregarded for VAT purposes.

Two or more companies are eligible to be treated as members of a group if one of them controls each of the others, or one person (which could be an individual or a holding company) controls all of them, or two or more persons carrying on a business in partnership control all of them.

The controlling entity therefore does not need to be a company. It is not necessary for each company, which meets the requirements, to join a particular VAT group.

OT case – Zim (June 2015) (amended)

Workbook references

Value added tax is dealt with in Chapters 24 and 25.

Top tips

You must make sure you know the thresholds for entering and leaving the flat rate scheme as they are not given in the rates and allowances available in the examination.

Easy marks

There are easy marks for working out the net VAT payable.

305 £ 12,000

		£	£
Sales	– Standard rated £115,200 × 20/120		19,200
	– Zero rated		0
Purchases	– Standard rated £43,200 × 20/120	7,200	
	– Zero rated	0	
			(7,200)
Net VAT payable			12,000

306 The correct answer is: £240

Impairment losses £(780 + 660) = 1,440 × 20/120 = £240

Relief for impairment losses is given once six months have expired from the time when payment was due, so relief can be claimed in respect of both impairment losses.

The answer £0 assumes no relief for impairment losses is available. The answer £130 gives relief only on the loss of £780. The answer £110 gives relief only on the loss of £660.

307 The correct answer is:

Mobile phone	***Customers***
£260	£40

Mobile phone £2,600 × 60% (100% – 40%) × 20/120 = £260

An apportionment is made where a service such as the use of a telephone is partly for business purposes and partly for private purposes.

Customer entertainment £240 × 20/120 = £40

Input VAT on business entertainment is not recoverable unless it relates to the cost of entertaining overseas customers.

308 The correct answers are:

Taxable turnover including VAT not more than £150,000 in next 12 months	Join

ANSWERS

Total turnover excluding VAT more than £230,000 in previous 12 months	Leave

309 £15,120

Using the flat rate scheme to calculate his VAT liability, Zim would have paid VAT of £126,000 × 12% = £15,120 for the year ended 31 March 2023.

The answer £13,860 assumes that the 1% reduction is available – be careful of this rule as it only applies in the first year of VAT registration. The answer £13,824 only charges standard rated sales. The answer £9,216 charges the flat rate on sales less expenses.

OT case – Smart Ltd (Sept/Dec 2015) (amended)

Workbook references

VAT registration, accounting for VAT and the tax point will be found in Chapter 24. Penalties and special schemes are dealt with in Chapter 25.

Top tips

There is a common penalty regime for errors which can apply to VAT errors as well as, for example, income tax or corporation tax errors.

Easy marks

There were some easy marks for identifying the date of registration and the date of notification.

310 The correct answers are:

1 November 2022	Register
30 November 2022	Notification

Smart Ltd was liable to register for VAT from 1 November 2022 because this is the date when it signed the contract valued at £86,000. The company would therefore have known that its taxable supplies for the following 30-day period would have exceeded £85,000. Registration is required from the start of the 30-day period.

Smart Ltd would have had to notify HM Revenue & Customs by 30 November 2022, being the end of the 30-day period.

311 The correct answers are:

Smart Ltd can file its VAT returns by entering figures manually on HMRC's website.		**FALSE**
Smart Ltd can choose whether to pay the VAT which is due electronically or by cheque.		**FALSE**
The deadline for paying any VAT which is due is one month after the end of each quarter.		**FALSE**
The deadline for filing the VAT return is one month and seven days after the end of each quarter.	**TRUE**	

Smart Ltd must use the Making Tax Digital software to directly submit its VAT returns to HMRC.

Smart Ltd must pay the VAT which is due electronically. The deadline for paying any VAT which is due is one month and seven days after the end of each quarter.

312 The correct answers are:

- The basic tax point is the date on which services are completed.
- If a customer pays for services before the basic tax point, the payment date will be the tax point.

313 The correct answer is: 1 and 4

The scheme will provide automatic relief for an impairment loss should a customer default on the payment of a debt. Output VAT will be accounted for 60 days later than at present, because the scheme will result in the tax point becoming the date when payment is received from customers.

314 The correct answer is:

Maximum penalty	*Minimum penalty for prompted disclosure*
30% of the VAT underpaid	15% of the VAT underpaid

OT case – Thidar (March/June 2019)

Workbook references

Value added tax (VAT) is covered in Chapters 24 and 25.

Top tips

In the first question, make sure you only have 12-months of sales when testing against the registration limit.

Easy marks

The rules on invoices should have been easy marks if you had studied the required knowledge of VAT.

315 The correct answer is: Month 14

	£	£
Months 1 to 12 Standard rated and zero-rated		84,400
Month 13 Standard rated and zero-rated	3,700	
Less: Month 1 Standard rated and zero-rated	(3,400)	
		300
		84,700
Month 14 Standard rated and zero-rated	4,900	
Less: Month 2 Standard rated and zero-rated	(1,900)	
		3,000
		87,700

VAT registration threshold of £85,000 exceeded at the end of Month 14.

The answer Month 15 ignores the month where no supplies are made as one of the 12 months. The answer Month 13 uses the first 13-months of trading (ie does not take out Month 1). The answer Not yet exceeded only uses the standard rated supplies.

ANSWERS

316 The correct answer is: £0

Pre-registration input tax suffered on the supply of services within six months prior to registration can be reclaimed. The supply on 10 June 2021 is earlier than six months before registration on 1 January 2022. The input tax on the supply on 8 December 2021, whilst it is within six months before registration, cannot be reclaimed as Thidar does not have evidence for the supply.

The answer £360 allows reclaim for the 10 June 2021 supply only. The answer £60 allows reclaim for the 8 December 2021 supply only. The answer £420 allows reclaim for both supplies.

317 The correct answer is: Option 2

VAT invoices must be issued within 30 days. VAT records (including invoices) must be retained for six years.

318 The correct answer is: Because separate disclosure of the VAT underpayment was not required

Default interest on unpaid VAT as a result of an error is only charged where the limit is exceeded for the error to be corrected on the next VAT return (here £10,000) such that it must be separately disclosed to HM Revenue & Customs.

The 12-month period is not relevant for penalties for errors (it applies to penalties for failure to notify chargeability). There can be a penalty for a careless (ie not deliberate) error. Default interest runs from the date the VAT should have been paid if the error had not been made.

319 The correct answer is: Option 3

The input tax of £800 × 20% = £160 on entertaining UK customers is non-deductible (but would be deductible for entertaining overseas customers). The answer £0 permits deduction of input tax on entertaining UK customers.

50% of the input tax is deductible on leased cars where there is some private use so the remaining 50% × £700 × 20% = £70 is non-deductible. The answer £105 is 75% × £700 × 20% = £105 (ie based on the amount of private use).

Section C

320 Jogger Ltd (B) (December 2008) (amended)

> **Workbook references**
>
> Value added tax default surcharges and special schemes are covered in Chapter 25.
>
> **Top tips**
>
> In part (b), make sure that you make four points to get the available marks.
>
> **Easy marks**
>
> The conditions for Jogger Ltd to join the annual accounting scheme in part (b) should have been easy marks.

Marking guide		Marks	
(a)	Quarter ended 30 September 2021	2	
	Quarter ended 31 March 2022	2	
	Quarter ended 31 March 2023	2	
			6
(b)	One VAT return	1	
	Payments on account	1	
	Limit	1	
	VAT payments up to date	1	
			4
Total			10

(a) The late submission of the VAT return for the quarter ended 30 September 2021 will have resulted in HM Revenue & Customs (HMRC) issuing a surcharge liability notice specifying a surcharge period running to 30 September 2022.

The late payment of VAT for the quarter ended 31 March 2022 will have resulted in a surcharge of £778 (£38,900 × 2%) because this is the first default in the surcharge period. The surcharge period will also have been extended to 31 March 2023.

The late payment of VAT for the quarter ended 31 March 2023 will therefore have resulted in a surcharge of £4,455 (£89,100 × 5%) because this is the second default in the surcharge period. The surcharge period will also have been extended to 31 March 2024.

(b) The reduced administration from only having to submit one VAT return each year should mean that default surcharges are avoided in respect of the late submission of VAT returns.

In addition, making payments on account based on the previous year's VAT liability will improve both budgeting and possibly cash flow if Jogger Ltd's business is expanding.

Jogger Ltd can apply to use the annual accounting scheme if its expected taxable turnover for the next 12 months does not exceed £1,350,000 exclusive of VAT.

However, the company must be up to date with its VAT payments before it is allowed to use the scheme.

321 Flick (June 2012) (amended)

Workbook references

The flat rate scheme is dealt with in Chapter 25. Registration is covered in Chapter 24 as is the tax point.

Top tips

In a multiple part question such as this, it is really important to attempt all the parts.

Easy marks

Part (c) might have looked a little unusual but was really a basic question on the tax point.

Marking guide

		Marks	
(a)	Flat rate scheme	1	
	Normal basis	1	
	Conclusion	1	
			3
(b)	No recovery of VAT by customers	1	
	Possible need to absorb VAT	1	
	Conclusion	1	
			3
(c)	VAT period	1	
	Basic tax point	1	
	Deposit	1	
	Balance	1	
			4
Total			10

(a) Using the flat rate scheme to calculate its VAT liability the partnership will have paid VAT of £(59,700 × 12%) = £7,164 for the quarter ended 31 March 2023.

If the partnership had used the normal basis, it would have paid VAT of £(59,700 – 27,300 = 32,400 × 20/120) = £5,400.

It was therefore not beneficial to use the flat rate scheme as the additional cost of £(7,164 – 5,400) = £1,764 for the quarter would appear to outweigh the advantage of simplified VAT administration.

(b) The partnership's sales are all to members of the general public, who cannot recover the input VAT.

It may not therefore be possible to pass the output VAT on to customers in the prices charged. To the extent this is not possible the partnership would have had to absorb all or some of this amount itself as a cost.

It was therefore not beneficial for the partnership to have voluntarily registered for VAT from 1 January 2023. For the quarter ended 31 March 2023 voluntary registration reduced the partnership's profits by a maximum of £7,164 (£5,400 if the normal basis had been used).

(c) Output VAT must be accounted for according to the VAT period in which the supply is treated as being made. This is determined by the tax point.

The basic tax point is the date when the service is completed, which will be the date that a film is screened.

Where payment is received before the basic tax point, then this date becomes the actual tax point. The tax point for each 25% deposit is therefore the date that it is received.

Invoices are issued on the same day as the basic tax point, so this is the tax point for the balance of 75%.

322 Richard (December 2013) (amended)

Workbook references

Registration for VAT is covered in Chapter 24 as is VAT administration. VAT invoices are dealt with in Chapter 25. Ethical considerations are covered in Chapter 1.

Top tips

Ethical considerations are an important part of the Taxation (TX – UK) syllabus and you might be asked about them in relation to any tax.

Easy marks

The calculation of the date for registration for VAT in part (a) was straightforward.

Marking guide		Marks	
(a)	Compulsory registration limit	0.5	
	Date registration required	1.5	
	Date registration effective	1	
	Consequences of non-registration	1	
			4
(b)	Honesty and integrity	0.5	
	Cease to act and inform HMRC	1	
	Money laundering notification	0.5	
			2
(c)	Simplified invoice	1	
	Request for invoice	0.5	
	Details on invoice: 0.5 mark per item to maximum	2.5	
			4
Total			10

(a) Richard would have been liable to compulsory VAT registration when his taxable supplies during any 12-month period (or from the commencement of trade, if less) exceeded £85,000.

This happened on 31 October 2022 when taxable supplies were £([10,500 × 4] + [15,000 × 3]) = £87,000.

Registration is required from the end of the month following the month in which the limit is exceeded, so Richard should have been registered from 1 December 2022.

If Richard continued to trade after 1 December 2022 without registering for VAT, he would still have to pay the VAT due from the time he should have been registered.

(b) The matter is one of professional judgement and a trainee Chartered Certified Accountant would be expected to act honestly and with integrity.

If Richard refuses to register for VAT, you should cease to act for him. You must notify HM Revenue & Customs (HMRC) that you no longer act for Richard although you should not provide any reason for this.

You would also be obliged to make a report under the money laundering regulations.

(c) A simplified (or less detailed) VAT invoice can be issued by a trader where the VAT inclusive total of the invoice is less than £250.

Such an invoice should be issued when a customer requests a VAT invoice.

A simplified VAT invoice must show the following information:

- The supplier's name and address
- The supplier's registration number
- The date of the supply
- A description of the goods or services supplied
- The rate of VAT chargeable
- The total amount chargeable including VAT

323 Clueless Ltd (December 2012) (amended)

Workbook references

Special schemes for VAT and overseas aspects of VAT are in Chapter 25.

Top tips

The question stated that the company incurred considerable overtime costs due to its employees working late in order to meet tax return filing deadlines which should have alerted you to one of the advantages of the annual accounting scheme.

Easy marks

There were some easy marks in part (a) for the conditions for the cash accounting and annual accounting schemes.

Marking guide		Marks	
(a)	Eligible for both schemes on turnover	1.5	
	Up to date with payments for both schemes	1	
	Up to date with returns for cash accounting scheme	0.5	
	Output tax under cash accounting scheme	1	
	Input tax under cash accounting scheme	1	
	Annual accounting scheme – one return	1	
			6
(b)	(i) Payment on importation	1	
	Input tax recovery	1	
	(ii) Output tax on date of acquisition	1	
	Input tax reclaimed on same return	1	
			4
Total			10

(a) **Clueless Ltd can use both schemes because its expected taxable turnover for the next 12 months does not exceed £1,350,000 exclusive of VAT.**

In addition, for both schemes the company is up to date with its VAT payments, and for the cash accounting scheme it is up to date with its VAT returns.

With the cash accounting scheme, output VAT will be accounted for two months later than at present as the date of the cash receipt determines the return in which the transaction is dealt with rather than the invoice date.

The recovery of input VAT on expenses will not be affected as these are dealt with on a cash basis. With the annual accounting scheme, the reduced administration in only having to file one VAT return each year should save on overtime costs.

(b) (i) **Import without postponed accounting**

Clueless Ltd will have to pay VAT of £22,000 @ 20% = £4,400 to HM Revenue & Customs at the time of importation. This will then be reclaimed as input VAT on the VAT return for the period during which the machinery is imported.

(ii) **Import with postponed accounting**

Import VAT is declared as output VAT on the VAT return covering the date that the machinery is imported. It is reclaimed as input VAT on the same VAT return, so there is no VAT cost.

324 Garfield (March/June 2016)

Workbook references

Computation of value added tax (VAT), including deduction of input tax and relief for impairment losses, is dealt with in Chapter 24. Overseas trade and special schemes for VAT are covered in Chapter 25.

Top tips

Remember the input VAT on entertaining UK customers is not recoverable but that suffered on entertaining overseas customers is recoverable.

Easy marks

Most of the content of this question has appeared a number of times in previous questions and so there were easy marks in part (a) for computing VAT payable.

Marking guide		Marks
(a) *Output VAT*		
Discounted sale	1	
Equipment	1	
Input VAT		
Equipment	0.5	
Impairment losses	1	
Entertaining	1	
Motor expenses	1.5	
VAT payable (including figures provided in question)	1	
		7
(b) Possible schemes	1	
Identify cash accounting scheme as beneficial	0.5	
Benefits of cash accounting scheme (½ mark each)	1.5	
		3
Total		10

(a) **Garfield – Value added tax (VAT) return for the quarter ended 31 March 2023**

	£
Output VAT	
Sales	22,500*
Discounted sale £4,300 × 90% × 20%	774
Equipment £12,400 × 20%	2,480
Fuel scale charge	414*
Input VAT	
Purchases	(11,200)*
Car	0*
Equipment	(2,480)
Impairment losses £1,400 × 20%	(280)
Entertaining – UK customers	0*
– Overseas customers £960 × 20/120	(160)
Motor expenses £1,668 (1,008 + 660) × 20/120	(278)
VAT payable	11,770

*Figures provided in question

Tutorial note. Relief for an impairment loss is only available if the claim is made more than six months from the time when payment was due.

Therefore, relief can only be claimed in respect of the invoice due for payment on 29 August 2022.

Tutorial note. Input VAT on business entertainment is recoverable if it relates to the cost of entertaining overseas customers.

(b) Given Garfield's current annual turnover of £450,000, he can use the cash accounting scheme and the annual accounting scheme, but not the flat rate scheme.

The cash accounting scheme would appear to be the most beneficial scheme for Garfield to use.

The scheme will provide automatic VAT relief for the impairment losses which Garfield is incurring.

Where credit is given to customers, output VAT could be accounted for later than at present.

The recovery of input VAT on most purchases and expenses will not be affected as Garfield pays for these on a cash basis.

Tutorial note. The annual turnover limit for both the annual accounting scheme and the cash accounting scheme is £1,350,000, but for the flat rate scheme it is £150,000.

Tutorial note. Although the annual accounting scheme would mean only having to submit one VAT return each year (reducing the risk of late return penalties), payments on account are based on the VAT payable for the previous year. From a cash flow viewpoint, this is not beneficial where turnover is decreasing.

325 Zhi (March/June 2017)

Workbook references

Self-assessment and payment of tax by individuals is covered in Chapter 17. Capital gains tax business reliefs are the subject of Chapter 15. The VAT tax point is dealt with in Chapter 24. Computation of income tax is covered in Chapter 2 and national insurance contributions in Chapter 12. The PAYE system is dealt with in Chapter 4.

Top tips

If you are asked to calculate a reduction in tax, don't waste time setting out a full tax computation. Just work out the reduction using the marginal rate of tax.

This is a similar process to working out additional tax covered in Chapter 2 of the Workbook.

Easy marks

There were some easy marks in part (c) for applying the rules on the tax point.

Examining team's comments

This 10-mark question had a focus on higher skills.

Part (a) was not very well answered and was not attempted by some candidates. Essentially, all that candidates had to do was select the two relevant tax years (out of the three provided), deduct one set of figures from the other, and divide by two.

Part (b) was the only part of the question which was consistently well answered. One particular issue, however, was that some candidates worked out the current capital gains tax liability (prior to the rollover relief claim) despite this being provided. Carefully noting which information has been provided in the question will avoid time being wasted in this manner.

Whether or not candidates did well in part (c) depended on them realising that 1 February 2023 was more than 14 days after 12 December 2022. This being the case, postponing the sales invoice would not affect the basic tax point.

Candidates should appreciate that a suggested tax planning strategy might not necessarily be effective, and they need to have the courage to base their answer on this conclusion if led there following the application of basic principles. However, some candidates either did not read the question carefully or chose to answer a question they would have preferred to have been asked and based their answer on the amount of VAT which could be postponed.

There were some good answers to part (d). However, only a few candidates appreciated that by far the quickest and easiest way to calculate the tax reductions was to work at the margin – rather than producing full before and after-tax computations.

Of course, it was also important to realise that the first employee was a basic rate taxpayer, subject to employee national insurance contributions at 13.25%, whereas the second employee was a higher rate taxpayer and only subject to employee national insurance contributions at 3.25%.

Marking guide	Marks	
(a) No reduction in balancing payment	0.5	
Reduction in payment on account	1.5	
		2
(b) Current CGT liability	0.5	
Proceeds not reinvested	1	
Annual exempt amount	1	
CGT computation	0.5	
		3

Marking guide		Marks
(c) Basic tax point	0.5	
Invoice does not displace	1	
Cannot reduce VAT payable	0.5	
		2
(d) *First employee*		
PAYE	0.5	
NIC – employee	0.5	
NIC – employer	0.5	
Second employee		
PAYE	0.5	
NIC – employee	0.5	
NIC – employer	0.5	
Payment date	0.5	
		3
Total		10

(a) The balancing payment for 2021/22 due on 31 January 2023 cannot be reduced.

A claim can be made to reduce the payment on account for 2021/22 due on 31 January 2023 by £5,040:

	£
Current POA (27,600 + 4,204) × 50%	15,902
Revised POA (18,000 + 3,724) × 50%	(10,862)
Reduction	5,040

(b) CGT liability due:

	£	£
Current CGT liability		12,740
Revised CGT liability		
Proceeds not reinvested (210,000 – 164,000)	46,000	
Annual exempt amount	(12,300)	
	33,700	
CGT: 33,700 at 20%		(6,740)
Reduction		6,000

> **Tutorial note.** Equivalent marks will be awarded if the reduction is alternatively calculated as 30,000 (76,000 – (210,000 – 164,000)) at 20% = £6,000.

(c) The basic tax point for goods is the date when they are made available to the customer, which in the case of Zhi's sale is 12 December 2022. An invoice date of 1 February 2023 will not affect this because the invoice will not have been issued within 14 days of the basic tax point.

Zhi therefore cannot reduce the amount of VAT payable on 7 February 2023.

(d) PAYE and NICs:

	£
First employee	
PAYE (1,500 at 20%)	300
NIC – Employee (1,500 at 13.25%)	199
– Employer (1,500 at 15.05%)	226
Second employee	
PAYE (5,000 at 40%)	2,000
NIC – Employee (5,000 at 3.25%)	163
– Employer (5,000 at 15.05%)	753
Reduction	3,641

The postponed PAYE and NICs of £3,641 will be payable one month later on 22 February 2023.

OTQ bank - Mixed bank

326 The correct answer is: An individual appealing against a penalty for late registration for value added tax (VAT)

> **ACCA Examining Team's Comments**
>
> The correct answer is the third option, because appeals relating to indirect taxes must be made directly to the Tribunal. Many candidates selected the first option, which is not correct because for direct taxes, appeals must first be made to HMRC.
>
> This is a challenging question on tax administration, an area which candidates often appear to struggle with. Candidates are reminded of the importance of being prepared for questions on all aspects of the syllabus, including tax administration, which is an important aspect of TX – UK.

327 The correct answer is: £150,000 on 14 July 2022

> **ACCA Examining Team's Comments**
>
> The correct answer is £150,000 on 14 July 2022. This is because the period ended 31 August 2022 is a short period of less than 12 months, meaning that only three instalment payments will be made. The first instalment is due six months and 14 days (ie in month 7) following the start of the period commencing on 1 January 2022, ie by 14 July 2022, and is calculated as £400,000 × 3/8, giving £150,000.
>
> A number of candidates selected £100,000 on 14 July 2022, which is the correct due date however the instalment amount (calculated as £400,000 × 3/12, giving £100,000) is incorrect because £100,000 would be the amount payable if the period had been 12 months (rather than eight months) long.

328 The correct answers are:

- Business asset disposal relief is available on the disposal of the interest in the partnership but not on the shares
- Gift holdover relief is available on the disposal of the interest in the partnership but not on the shares

ACCA Examining Team's Comments

Business asset disposal relief (BADR) is available where there is a material disposal of business assets. This includes the disposal of the whole or part of a business carried on by an individual either alone or in partnership which has been owned by the individual throughout the period of two years ending with the date of disposal. Therefore, BADR is available on the disposal of the interest in the partnership. BADR is also available in respect of a disposal of shares and securities in a trading company (or the holding company of a trading group) where the company is the individual's personal company, the individual is an officer or employee of the company and these conditions are met for throughout the period of two years ending with the date of disposal. BADR is therefore not available in respect of the disposal of the shares, because the shares are in an unquoted investment company, not a trading company.

Gift holdover relief is available where there is a gift (or sale at undervalue) by an individual of a qualifying business asset. Qualifying business assets for gift holdover relief include assets used in a trade, profession or vocation carried on by the donor and shares and securities in trading companies. Therefore, gift holdover relief is available in respect of the disposal of the interest in the partnership to his son for less than market value, however it is not available in respect of the gift of shares to his daughter, since the company is not a trading company.

329 The correct answer is: £22,000

ACCA Examining Team's Comments

The correct answer is £22,000. This amount is comprised of two annual exemptions of £3,000 for the tax years 2022/23 and 2021/22 for each parent (total £12,000) plus the exemption for a gift in consideration of marriage given by a parent of £5,000, also from each parent (total £10,000).

Many candidates chose £10,000 which did not include the annual exemptions which each parent had available (since they had made no other lifetime gifts). Also, a number of candidates selected £11,000, which was the total amount of exemptions available for one parent only.

330 The correct answer is: £10,400

ACCA Examining Team's Comments

The premium received is on a short lease therefore a proportion of it is treated as income. £20,000 less (2%((25–1) × £20,000)) = £10,400 being the correct income portion of the premium.

£9,600: Calculates the capital portion of the premium 2%((25–1) × 20,000) = 9,600

£5,200: Calculates the correct part of the premium but it is unnecessarily time apportioned (since Sou is the lessor and is taxed to income on receipt of the premium) 10,400 × 6/12 = 5,200

£10,000: 20,000 less (2%((25) × 20,000)) = 10,000 – this does not deduct one year from 'n', the number of years on the lease

331 The correct answer is: 1 February 2023

ACCA Examining Team's Comments

The VAT registration threshold of £85,000 is breached in December 2022 ((Feb, Mar, Apr 3 × 5,500) + (May, Jun, Jul, Aug 4 × 7,500) + (Sep, Oct, Nov, Dec 4 × 10,000) = £86,500). So, registration will be from 30 January 2023 and Brett must charge VAT from 1 February 2023.

332 The correct answers are:

- The annual exempt amount is deducted before any brought forward capital losses are utilised against current year gains
- Excess current year capital losses are carried forward indefinitely until future chargeable gains arise

ACCA Examining Team's Comments

Brought forward capital losses are deducted after the annual exempt amount (AEA) is deducted, thus ensuring that no AEA is wasted. Capital losses are generally not set against income but can be carried forward to be set off against future chargeable gains.

333 The correct answer is: Resident in 2022/23 but not in 2021/22

ACCA Examining Team's Comments

As Ella has not previously been resident in the UK then she will need to have four UK ties to be UK resident in 2021/22 and will need two UK ties to be UK resident in 2022/23. These details are given in the Tax Tables available in the exam.

Ella has two UK ties, substantive work in the UK (she works full-time) and available accommodation in the UK (she lives with the family) and is therefore UK resident in 2022/23 but not 2021/22.

334 £ 325,000

ACCA Examining Team's Comments

As with all IHT questions, we must first consider what gifts were made during an individual's lifetime and then consider the situation at death. During Gabe's lifetime he gave two PETs, ie gifts to individuals which will become exempt from IHT if Gabe lives for seven years following the date of the gift. On death (on 22 November 2022) we look back seven years, to 22 November 2015, and any gifts made before then are excluded but any gifts after that date are reviewed again. The first PET (cash to daughter) is before this date and so that will never become chargeable to IHT (it is now actually exempt). However, the second PET (painting to son made on 12 July 2018) is within this period of seven years and so we have to review that again. The second PET which we are now reviewing on death had a value of £370,000; the nil rate band (NRB) at the time of death is £325,000 and we need to establish how much of that is available to set against this PET. In order to do this, we need to check if any of that NRB has been used up in the seven years before this PET. So now we are looking back to 12 July 2011 to see if any gifts after that date have used the NRB. The only previous gift was that PET to Gabe's daughter which did not use any NRB in lifetime (being a PET) and did not use any NRB at death (since it is now actually exempt). [Note that if this first gift had been a chargeable lifetime transfer (CLT), it would have used some NRB.] This means that the NRB available to this second PET on Gabe's death is the full £325,000.

335 The correct answer is: £3,886

ACCA Examining Team's Comments

Because the asset being disposed of is a residential property, Naomi's chargeable gain will be taxed at 18%/28%, depending on how much of the basic rate band (BRB) is available. Naomi has taxable income (ie total income after personal allowance) of £29,500. The BRB is £37,700 but this is extended by the gross pension contribution of £2,500 (£2,000 × 100/80) to £40,200. Her taxable income therefore uses up £29,500 of this £40,200 leaving £10,700 BRB.

The chargeable gain (ie before annual exempt amount (AEA)) is £30,000 against which the AEA of £12,300 can be deducted leaving a taxable gain of £17,700. Of this £17,700, £10,700 is within the remaining BRB and is taxable at 18% (tax of £1,926) and £7,000 is taxable at 28% (tax of £1,960) giving a total capital gains tax liability of £3,886.

£7,330 forgets to deduct the AEA from the chargeable gain

£4,136 forgets to extend the BRB by the gross pension contribution, and

£7,580 does not deduct the AEA or extend the BRB

Mock Exams

ACCA

Taxation (TX - UK)

Mock Exam 1

September 2016 exam updated to FA 2022

Questions	
Time allowed	3 Hours
This exam is divided into three sections: Section A - All 15 questions are compulsory and MUST be attempted Section B - All 15 questions are compulsory and MUST be attempted Section C - All THREE questions are compulsory and MUST be attempted	

DO NOT OPEN THIS EXAM UNTIL YOU ARE READY TO START UNDER EXAMINATION CONDITIONS

Section A

ALL 15 questions are compulsory and MUST be attempted

1 On 1 July 2021, Sameer made a cash gift of £2,500 to his sister.

On 1 May 2022, he made a cash gift of £2,000 to a friend.

On 1 June 2022, he made a cash gift of £50,000 to a trust.

Sameer has not made any other lifetime gifts.

In respect of Sameer's cash gift of £50,000 to the trust, what is the lifetime transfer of value for inheritance tax purposes after taking account of all available exemptions?

- O £48,500
- O £44,000
- O £46,000
- O £46,500

(2 marks)

2 On 31 March 2023, Angus sold a house, which he had bought on 31 March 2009.

Angus occupied the house as his main residence until 31 March 2014, when he left for employment abroad.

Angus returned to the UK on 1 April 2016 and lived in the house until 31 March 2017, when he bought a flat in a neighbouring town and made that his private residence.

What is Angus' total number of qualifying months of occupation for private residence relief on the sale of the house?

- O 72 months
- O 141 months
- O 105 months
- O 96 months

(2 marks)

3 Abena has made the following gross contributions to her personal pension scheme over the past three tax years:

Tax Year	£
2019/20	42,000
2020/21	27,000
2021/22	28,000

Abena is entitled to an annual allowance of £40,000 in all tax years from 2019/20 to 2022/23.

What is the maximum gross contribution which Abena can make to her personal pension scheme for the tax year 2022/23 without giving rise to an annual allowance charge?

- O £63,000
- O £40,000
- O £65,000
- O £35,000

(2 marks)

4 Triangle Ltd is registered for value added tax (VAT) and uses the annual accounting scheme.

For the year ended 31 December 2022, the net VAT payable by Triangle Ltd was £73,500.

For the year ended 31 December 2021, the net VAT payable by Triangle Ltd was £47,700.

Match the number and amount of the monthly payments on account of VAT which Triangle Ltd must make in respect of the year ended 31 December 2022 prior to submitting its VAT return for that year.

Options		
Nine		Number of monthly payments
Ten		Monthly payment amount
£4,770		
£7,350		

(2 marks)

5 Lili Ltd commenced trading on 1 January 2022. The company incurred the following expenditure prior to 1 January 2023:

		£
30 November 2014	Initial market research	15,000
6 June 2017	Research into competitors	12,000
31 July 2021	Entertaining potential customers and suppliers	8,000
15 December 2021	Donation to local school fair in exchange for advertising	2,000

What is the amount of Lili Ltd's deductible pre-trading expenditure in respect of the year ended 31 December 2022?

£ ____ **(2 marks)**

6 Paloma has been trading for a number of years. Her tax adjusted trading profit for the year ended 31 May 2022 was £53,150 and for the year ended 31 May 2023 was £50,350.

What is the amount of class 4 national insurance contributions (NIC) payable by Paloma for the tax year 2022/23?

- O £3,882
- O £4,160
- O £3,864
- O £3,958

(2 marks)

7 Identify, by clicking on the relevant boxes in the table, whether the following are true or false.

Corporation tax is a direct tax on the turnover of companies.	**TRUE**	**FALSE**
National insurance is a direct tax suffered by employees, employers and the self-employed on earnings.	**TRUE**	**FALSE**

Inheritance tax is a direct tax on transfers of income by individuals.	**TRUE**	**FALSE**
Value added tax is a direct tax on the supply of goods and services by businesses.	**TRUE**	**FALSE**

(2 marks)

8 Which of the following statements concerning self-assessment tax returns for individuals is TRUE?

- O Individuals with tax payable of less than £1,000 for a tax year are not required to file a tax return.
- O Individuals are only required to file a tax return for a tax year if they receive a notice to deliver from HM Revenue & Customs (HMRC).
- O All individuals who submit a tax return on time are able to have their tax payable calculated by HMRC.
- O The tax return for an individual covers income tax, class 1, class 2 and class 4 national insurance contributions and capital gains tax liabilities. **(2 marks)**

9 In certain circumstances, an individual is automatically not resident in the UK.

Indicate, by clicking on the relevant boxes in the table below, whether the following two individuals satisfy or do not satisfy the tests to be treated as automatically not resident in the UK for the tax year 2022/23.

Eric, who has never previously been resident in the UK. In the tax year 2022/23, he was in the UK for 40 days.

Fran, who was resident in the UK for the two tax years prior to the tax year 2022/23. In the tax year 2022/23, she was in the UK for 18 days.

Eric	**SATISFIES**	**DOES NOT SATISFY**
Fran	**SATISFIES**	**DOES NOT SATISFY**

(2 marks)

10 Max is employed by Star Ltd. On 6 April 2021, Star Ltd provided Max with a camera for his personal use.

The camera had a market value of £2,000 on 6 April 2021.

On 6 April 2022, Star Ltd gave the camera to Max for free.

The camera had a market value of £1,400 on 6 April 2022.

What is Max's taxable benefit in respect of the camera for the tax year 2022/23?

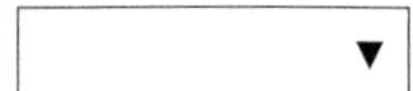

Pull down list

- £1,000
- £1,400
- £1,600
- £2,000

(2 marks)

11 Cora made a cash gift of £300,000 to her niece on 30 April 2017.

She then made a cash gift of £500,000 to her nephew on 31 May 2018.

Both of these amounts are stated after deducting available exemptions.

Cora subsequently died on 31 October 2022.

What amount of inheritance tax was payable as a result of Cora's death in respect of the cash gift of £500,000 to her nephew?

- O £190,000
- O £110,000
- O £114,000
- O £105,000

(2 marks)

12 Rajesh is a sole trader. He correctly calculated his self-assessment payments on account for the tax year 2022/23 and paid these on the due dates.

Rajesh paid the correct balancing payment of £1,200 for the tax year 2022/23 on 30 June 2024.

Indicate, by clicking on the relevant boxes in the table below, what penalties and interest Rajesh may be charged as a result of his late balancing payment for the tax year 2022/23.

£0		Penalty
£60		Interest
£16		
£39		

(2 marks)

13 Oblong Ltd has had the following results:

	Year ended 31 March 2022	*Year ended 31 March 2023*
	£	£
Trading profit/(loss)	79,400	(102,800)
Property business income	6,800	10,100
Qualifying charitable donations	(1,600)	(1,300)

If Oblong Ltd makes a claim to relieve its trading loss of £102,800 for the year ended 31 March 2023 against total profits for the year ended 31 March 2022, how much of this loss will remain unrelieved?

- O £6,500
- O £16,600
- O £9,400
- O £23,400

(2 marks)

14 Putting an asset into joint names with a spouse (or a partner in a registered civil partnership) prior to the asset's disposal can be sensible capital gains tax (CGT) planning.

Which of the following CANNOT be achieved as a direct result of using this type of tax planning?

Pull down list

- Deferring the CGT due date
- Making the best use of annual exempt amounts
- Making the best use of capital losses
- Reducing the amount of CGT payable

(2 marks)

15 Eva's income tax liability and class 4 national insurance contributions (NIC) for the tax year 2022/23 are £4,840. Her income tax liability and class 4 NICs for the tax year 2021/22 were £6,360.

What is the lowest amount to which Eva could make a claim to reduce each of her payments on account for the tax year 2022/23 without being charged interest?

£ [ ] **(2 marks)**

Section B

ALL 15 questions are compulsory and MUST be attempted

Adana

The following scenario relates to Questions 16 to 20.

Adana died on 17 March 2023, and inheritance tax (IHT) of £566,000 is payable in respect of her chargeable estate. Under the terms of her will, Adana left her entire estate to her children.

At the date of her death, Adana did not own a main residence. She had these debts and liabilities:

(1) An outstanding interest-only mortgage of £220,000

(2) Income tax of £43,700 payable in respect of the tax year 2022/23

(3) Legal fees of £4,600 incurred by Adana's sister which Adana had verbally promised to pay

Adana's husband had died on 28 May 2006, and only 20% of his inheritance tax nil rate band was used on his death. The nil rate band for the tax year 2006/07 was £285,000.

On 22 April 2010, Adana had made a chargeable lifetime transfer of shares valued at £500,000 to a trust. Adana paid the lifetime IHT of £52,250 arising from this gift. If Adana had not made this gift, her chargeable estate at the time of her death would have been £650,000 higher than it otherwise was. This was because of the subsequent increase in the value of the gifted shares.

16 What is the maximum nil rate band which will have been available when calculating the IHT of £566,000 payable in respect of Adana's chargeable estate?

[▼]

Pull down list

- £325,000
- £390,000
- £553,000
- £585,000

(2 marks)

---

17 What is the total amount of deductions which would have been permitted in calculating Adana's chargeable estate for IHT purposes?

£ [ ]

(2 marks)

---

18 Match who will be responsible for paying the IHT of £566,000 in respect of Adana's chargeable estate, and what is the due date for the payment of this liability.

Options	Answer	Category
Beneficiaries of Adana's estate (her children)		Responsible persons
Personal representatives of Adana's estate		Due date for payment

17 September 2023

30 September 2023

(2 marks)

---

19 How much of the IHT payable in respect of Adana's estate would have been saved if, under the terms of her will, Adana had made specific gifts of £400,000 to a trust and £200,000 to her grandchildren, instead of leaving her entire estate to her children?

- O £240,000
- O £160,000
- O £0
- O £80,000

(2 marks)

---

20 How much IHT did Adana save by making the chargeable lifetime transfer of £500,000 to a trust on 22 April 2010, rather than retaining the gifted investments until her death?

- O £260,000
- O £207,750
- O £147,750
- O £200,000

(2 marks)

(Total = 10 marks)

Kat Ltd and Kitten

The following scenario relates to Questions 21 to 25.

Kitten is the controlling shareholder in Kat Ltd, an unquoted trading company.

Kat Ltd

Kat Ltd sold a freehold factory on 31 May 2023 for £364,000, which resulted in a chargeable gain of £120,700. The factory was purchased on 1 October 2005 for £138,600, and further capital improvements were immediately made at a cost of £23,400 during the month of purchase. Further improvements to the factory were made during the month of disposal. The relevant indexation factor is 0.439.

Kat Ltd is unsure how to reinvest the proceeds from the sale of the factory. The company is considering either purchasing a freehold warehouse for £272,000 or acquiring a leasehold office building on a 40-year lease for a premium of £370,000. If either reinvestment is made, it will take place on 30 September 2023.

All of the above buildings have been, or will be, used for the purposes of Kat Ltd's trade.

Kitten

Kitten sold 20,000 £1 ordinary shares in Kat Ltd on 5 October 2022, which resulted in a chargeable gain of £142,200. This disposal qualified for business asset disposal relief.

Kitten had originally subscribed for 90,000 shares in Kat Ltd on 7 July 2010 at their par value. On 22 September 2013, Kat Ltd made a 2 for 3 rights issue. Kitten took up her allocation under the rights issue in full, paying £6.40 for each new share issued.

Kitten also sold an antique vase on 16 January 2023, which resulted in a chargeable gain of £28,900.

For the tax year 2022/23, Kitten had taxable income of £12,000.

21 What amount of indexation allowance will have been deducted in calculating the chargeable gain of £120,700 on the disposal of Kat Ltd's factory?

£ [ ]

(2 marks)

---

22 If Kat Ltd decides to purchase the freehold warehouse and makes a claim to roll over the chargeable gain on the factory under the rollover relief rules, what will be the base cost of the warehouse for chargeable gains purposes?

- O £243,300
- O £272,000
- O £180,000
- O £151,300

(2 marks)

---

23 If Kat Ltd decides to acquire the leasehold office building and makes a claim to hold over the chargeable gain on the factory under the rollover relief rules, what is the latest date by which the held-over gain will crystallise?

[▼]

Pull down list

- 10 years from 30 September 2023
- 10 years from 31 May 2023
- 40 years from 30 September 2023
- The date when the office building is sold

(2 marks)

---

24 What cost figure will have been used in calculating the chargeable gain on Kitten's disposal of 20,000 ordinary shares in Kat Ltd?

- O £12,000
- O £63,200
- O £84,800
- O £20,000

(2 marks)

---

25 What is Kitten's capital gains tax (CGT) liability for the tax year 2022/23?

- O £15,880
- O £20,000
- O £18,770
- O £17,540

(2 marks)

(Total = 10 marks)

Alisa

The following scenario relates to Questions 26 to 30.

Alisa commenced trading on 1 January 2022. Her sales since commencement have been as follows:

January to April 2022	£7,500 per month
May to August 2022	£10,000 per month
September to December 2022	£15,500 per month

The above figures are stated exclusive of value added tax (VAT). Alisa only supplies services, and these are all standard rated for VAT purposes. Alisa notified her liability to compulsorily register for VAT by the appropriate deadline.

For each of the eight months prior to the date on which she registered for VAT, Alisa paid £240 per month (inclusive of VAT) for website design services and £180 per month (exclusive of VAT) for advertising. Both of these supplies are standard rated for VAT purposes and relate to Alisa's business activity after the date from when she registered for VAT.

After registering for VAT, Alisa purchased a car on 1 January 2023. The car is used 60% for business mileage. During the quarter ended 31 March 2023, Alisa spent £456 on repairs to the car and £624 on fuel for both her business and private mileage. The relevant quarterly scale charge is £290. All of these figures are inclusive of VAT.

All of Alisa's customers are registered for VAT, so she appreciates that she has to issue VAT invoices when services are supplied.

26 From what date would Alisa have been required to be compulsorily registered for VAT and therefore have had to charge output VAT on her supplies of services?

Pull down list

- 1 November 2022
- 1 October 2022
- 30 October 2022
- 30 September 2022 **(2 marks)**

---

27 What amount of pre-registration input VAT would Alisa have been able to recover in respect of inputs incurred prior to the date on which she registered for VAT?

- O £468
- O £608
- O £536
- O £456 **(2 marks)**

---

28 What is the maximum amount of input VAT which Alisa can reclaim in respect of her motor expenses for the quarter ended 31 March 2023?

- O £108
- O £138
- O £180
- O £125 **(2 marks)**

---

29 Complete the following sentence by matching the correct due date and payment method into the relevant target area.

Alisa has to pay any VAT liability for the quarter ended 31 March 2023 by

(1) ▼ using (2) ▼ method.

Pull down list 1

- 30 April 2023
- 7 May 2023

Pull down list 2

- An electronic payment
- Any payment

(2 marks)

---

30 Which of the following items of information is NOT required to be included by Alisa on a valid VAT invoice?

- O The customer's VAT registration number
- O The customer's address
- O An invoice number
- O A description of the services provided

(2 marks)

(Total = 10 marks)

Section C

ALL three questions are compulsory and MUST be attempted

31 Joe

Joe is the managing director and 100% shareholder of OK-Joe Ltd. He has always withdrawn the entire profits of the company as director's remuneration but given a recent increase in profitability he wants to know whether this basis of extracting the profits is beneficial.

For the year ended 5 April 2023, OK-Joe Ltd's taxable total profits, before taking account of director's remuneration, are £65,000. After allowing for employer's class 1 national insurance contributions (NIC) of £7,312 Joe's gross director's remuneration is £57,688.

The figure for employer's NIC of £7,312 does not deduct the £5,000 employment allowance as this is not available since Joe is the only employee of OK-Joe Ltd.

Required

Calculate the overall saving of tax and NIC for the year ended 5 April 2023 if Joe had instead paid himself gross director's remuneration of £8,000 and dividends of £46,170.

Notes.

1 You are expected to calculate the income tax payable by Joe, the class 1 NIC payable by both Joe and OK-Joe Ltd, and the corporation tax liability of OK-Joe Ltd for the year ended 5 April 2023.

2 You should assume that the rate of corporation tax remains unchanged. **(10 marks)**

32 Ashura

Ashura has been employed by Rift plc since 1 January 2020. She has also been self-employed since 1 July 2022, preparing her first accounts for the nine-month period ended 5 April 2023. The following information is available for the tax year 2022/23:

Employment

(1) During the tax year 2022/23, Ashura was paid a gross annual salary of £56,600.

(2) On 1 January 2023, Ashura personally paid two subscriptions. The first was a professional subscription of £320 paid to a professional body. The second was a subscription of £680 to a health club which Ashura regularly uses to meet Rift plc's clients. Ashura was not reimbursed for the costs of either of these subscriptions by Rift plc.

(3) During the tax year 2022/23, Ashura used her private car for business purposes. She drove 3,400 miles in the performance of her duties for Rift plc, for which the company paid her an allowance of 55 pence per mile.

(4) During the tax year 2022/23, Ashura contributed £2,800 into Rift plc's occupational pension scheme and £3,400 (gross) into a personal pension scheme.

Self-employment

(1) Ashura's tax adjusted trading loss based on her draft accounts for the nine-month period ended 5 April 2023 is £3,300. This figure is before making any adjustments required for:

   (i) Advertising expenditure of £800 incurred during January 2022. This expenditure has not been deducted in calculating the loss of £3,300.

   (ii) The cost of Ashura's office (see note (2) below).

   (iii) Capital allowances.

(2) Ashura runs her business using one of the five rooms in her private house as an office. The total running costs of the house for the nine-month period ended 5 April 2023 were £4,350. No deduction has been made for the cost of the office in calculating the loss of £3,300.

(3) On 10 June 2022, Ashura purchased a laptop computer for £2,600.

On 1 July 2022, Ashura purchased a car for £25,600. The car has a CO_2 emission rate of 117 grams per kilometre. During the nine-month period ended 5 April 2023, Ashura drove a total of 8,000 miles, of which 2,500 were for self-employed business journeys.

Other information

Ashura's total income for the previous four tax years is as follows:

Tax year	*Total income*
	£
2018/19	11,100
2019/20	10,800
2020/21	48,800
2021/22	54,300

Required

(a) State **TWO** advantages for Ashura of choosing 5 April as her accounting date rather than a date early in the tax year such as 30 April. **(2 marks)**

(b) Calculate Ashura's revised tax adjusted trading loss for the nine-month period ended 5 April 2023. **(6 marks)**

(c) Explain why it would not be beneficial for Ashura to claim loss relief under the provisions giving relief to a loss incurred in the early years of trade.

Note. You should assume that the tax rates and allowances for the tax year 2022/23 also applied in all previous tax years. **(2 marks)**

(d) Assuming that Ashura claims loss relief against her total income for the tax year 2022/23, calculate her taxable income for this tax year. **(5 marks)**

(Total = 15 marks)

33 Mable

Mable is a serial entrepreneur, regularly starting and disposing of businesses. On 31 July 2022, Tenth Ltd, a company owned by Mable, ceased trading. On 1 October 2022, Eleventh Ltd, another company owned by Mable, commenced trading. The following information is available:

Tenth Ltd

(1) For the final four-month period of trading ended 31 July 2022, Tenth Ltd had a tax adjusted trading profit of £52,400. This figure is **before** taking account of capital allowances.

(2) On 1 April 2022, the tax written down value of the company's main pool was £12,400. On 3 June 2022, Tenth Ltd purchased a laptop computer for £1,800.

On 31 July 2022, the company sold all of the items included in the main pool at the start of the period for £28,200 and the laptop computer for £1,300. None of the items included in the main pool was sold for more than its original cost.

(3) On 31 July 2022, Tenth Ltd sold the company's freehold office building for £180,300. The building was purchased on 3 May 2014 for £151,334, and its indexed cost to December 2017 was £164,500.

(4) During the four-month period ended 31 July 2022, Tenth Ltd let out one floor of its freehold office building which was always surplus to requirements. The floor was rented at £1,200 per month, but the tenant left owing the rent for July 2022 which Tenth Ltd was unable to recover. The total running costs of the office building for the four-month period ended 31 July 2022 were £6,300, of which one-third related to the let floor. The other two-thirds of the

running costs have been deducted in calculating Tenth Ltd's tax-adjusted trading profit of £52,400.

(5) During the four-month period ended 31 July 2022, Tenth Ltd made qualifying charitable donations of £800.

Eleventh Ltd

(1) Eleventh Ltd's operating profit for the six-month period ended 31 March 2023 is £122,900. Depreciation of £2,580 and amortisation of leasehold property of £2,000 (see note (2) below) have been deducted in arriving at this figure.

(2) On 1 October 2022, Eleventh Ltd acquired a leasehold office building, paying a premium of £60,000 for the grant of a 15-year lease. The office building was used for business purposes by Eleventh Ltd throughout the six-month period ended 31 March 2023.

(3) On 1 October 2022, Eleventh Ltd purchased two new cars. The first car cost £12,600 and has a CO_2 emission rate of 40 grams per kilometre. This car is used as a pool car by the company's employees. The second car cost £13,200 and has a zero CO_2 emission rate per kilometre. This car is used by Mable, and 45% of the mileage is for private journeys.

(4) On 1 October 2022, Mable made a loan of £100,000 to Eleventh Ltd at an annual interest rate of 5%. This is a commercial rate of interest, and no loan repayments were made during the period ended 31 March 2023. The loan was used to finance the company's trading activities.

Required

(a) Calculate Tenth Ltd's taxable total profits for the four-month period ended 31 July 2022. **(7 marks)**

(b) Calculate Eleventh Ltd's tax adjusted trading profit for the six-month period ended 31 March 2023. **(8 marks)**

(Total = 15 marks)

Answers

DO NOT TURN THIS PAGE UNTIL YOU HAVE COMPLETED THE MOCK EXAM

Mock exam 1

Plan of Attack

If this were the real Taxation (TX – UK) exam and you had been told to turn over and begin, what would be going through your mind?

Perhaps you're having a panic. You've spent most of your study time on income tax and corporation tax computations (because that's what your tutor/BPP Workbook told you to do), plus a selection of other topics, and you're really not sure that you know enough. So calm down. Spend the first few moments or so **looking at the exam** and develop a **plan of attack**.

Looking through the exam.

Section A contains **15 Objective Test (OT) questions** each worth **2 marks**. These will cover all sections of the syllabus. Some you may find easy and some more difficult. In Question 8, where you are asked to identify the true statement about self-assessment tax returns for individuals, read the possible answers at least twice before you decide which one to select. Don't spend a lot of time on anything you really don't know. For multiple choice questions you are not penalised for wrong answers, so you should answer all of them. If all else fails – guess!

Section B contains **three OT Case** scenarios. These each have **five questions** each worth **2 marks**. Make sure you read the scenario carefully before you start to answer the OTQs.

- **Questions 16 to 20** test your knowledge of inheritance tax (IHT). Question 18 is a quick question as you only need to select two answers, one is the persons responsible for payment of tax and the other is the date for payment.
- **Questions 21 to 25** concern chargeable gains for a company and for an individual. Make sure to double check your calculations to avoid losing marks for simple mistakes. This is particularly applicable to Question 25.
- **Questions 26 to 30** are about value added tax (VAT). Read the questions carefully to make sure you answer the question set. For example, in Question 26 you need to identify the date from which Alisa would have been required to be compulsorily registered, not the date on which the registration limit was exceeded.

In **Section C** you have **three constructed response (long) questions**:

- **Question 31** for **10 marks** is about whether there is an overall tax saving by taking a mixture of dividends and remuneration from a company rather than just remuneration. You need to work out the individual's income tax, the national insurance contributions for an employee and corporation tax.
- **Question 32** for **15 marks** is an income tax computation and also deals with choice of accounting date.
- **Question 33** for **15 marks** is a corporation tax question dealing with a company ceasing to trade and one commencing to trade.

Allocating your time

BPP's advice is always allocate your time **according to the marks for the question** in total and for the parts of the question. But **use common sense**. If you're confronted by an OTQ on a topic of which you know nothing, pick an answer and move on. Use the time to pick up marks elsewhere.

After the exam...**Forget about it**!

And don't worry if you found the exam difficult. More than likely other candidates will too. If this were the real thing you would need to **forget** the exam the minute you left the exam hall and **think about the next one**. Or, if it's the last one, **celebrate**!

Section A

1 The correct answer is: £48,500

		£
Gift 1 June 2022		50,000
Less:	AE 2022/23 £(3,000 – 2,000 PET 1 May 2022)	(1,000)
	AE 2021/22 b/f £(3,000 – 2,500 PET 1 July 2021)	(500)
Chargeable lifetime transfer		48,500

Note that the current tax year annual exemption is used first (against the PET on 1 May 2022 and then against the CLT on 1 June 2022) and then the balance brought forward from the previous tax year.

2 The correct answer is: 105 months

Qualifying period		*Months*
31.3.09–31.3.14	Actual occupation	60
1.4.14–31.3.16	Employed abroad (any length with reoccupation)	24
1.4.16–31.3.17	Actual occupation	12
1.7.22–31.3.23	Last 9 months ownership	9
Qualifying months		105

Check: non-qualifying months 1.4.17–30.6.22 = 63 months, total period of ownership 31.3.09–31.3.23 = 168 months = (105 + 63) months.

3 The correct answer is: £65,000

	£
2022/23	40,000
2019/20 £(40,000 – 42,000) = £(2,000) excess	0
2020/21 £(40,000 – 27,000)	13,000
2021/22 £(40,000 – 28,000)	12,000
Available annual allowance	65,000

Use the current tax year allowance first and then start working forwards from the earliest available tax year (maximum three tax years before current year).

4 The correct answers are:

Nine	Number of monthly payments
£4,770	Monthly payment amount

$$\frac{90\% \times £47{,}700 \text{ (previous year VAT payable)}}{9} = £4{,}770$$

5 £ 14,000

	£
30.11.14: More than seven years before commencement	0
6.6.17: Research deductible	12,000
31.7.21: Entertaining not deductible under general rules	0
15.12.21: Donation for trade purposes deductible	2,000
Deductible pre-trading expenditure	14,000

6 The correct answer is: £3,958

	£
£(53,150 – 50,270) = 2,880 @ 3.25%	94
£(50,270 – 12,570) = 37,700 @ 10.25%	3,864
Class 4 NIC payable	3,958

The answer £3,882 uses the accruals basis rather than the profits for the year ended 31 May 2022. The answer £4,160 uses a rate of 10.25% throughout. The answer £3,864 is just the amount chargeable at 10.25%.

7 The correct answers are:

Corporation tax is a direct tax on the turnover of companies.		**FALSE**
National insurance is a direct tax suffered by employees, employers and the self-employed on earnings.	**TRUE**	
Inheritance tax is a direct tax on transfers of income by individuals.		**FALSE**
Value added tax is a direct tax on the supply of goods and services by businesses.		**FALSE**

Corporation tax is a direct tax on profits (not turnover).

National insurance is a direct tax (collected directly from taxpayer either through PAYE or by self-assessment) suffered by employees (Class 1 employee's), employers (Class 1 employer's) and the self-employed (Classes 2 and 4).

Inheritance tax is a direct tax on transfers of capital (not income) by individuals.

Value added tax is an indirect tax (collected by businesses not customers) on the supply of goods and services by businesses.

8 The correct answer is: All individuals who submit a tax return on time are able to have their tax payable calculated by HMRC.

ACCA Examining Team's Comments

This question tested candidates' knowledge of various aspects of the income tax self-assessment system. The majority of candidates appreciated that there can be a requirement to file a tax return despite not receiving a notice to do so from HMRC. However, a significant number of candidates chose the last option, despite class 1 national insurance contributions (NIC) not being part of the self-assessment system.

Many candidates chose the first option, not remembering that the de minimis limit of £1,000 instead relates to payments on account. All individuals who submit a tax return on time (either a paper return or electronically) are able to have the tax payable calculated by HMRC therefore the third option was the correct answer.

This should have been a fairly straightforward question and it demonstrates the need to carefully read and consider each alternative – not just quickly jump to the first one that seems to fit.

9 The correct answers are:

Eric	**SATISFIES**	
Fran		**DOES NOT SATISFY**

Eric was not previously UK resident and was present in the UK for between 16 and 45 days (see table in Tax Rates and Allowances). He is therefore automatically not UK resident in the tax year 2022/23.

Fran was previously UK resident and was present in the UK for between 16 and 45 days (again, see table in Tax Rates and Allowances). Her residence status is therefore determined by the number of her UK ties, so she is not automatically UK resident in the tax year 2022/23.

10 £1,600

		£	£
2021/22	Use benefit £2,000 × 20%	400	
2022/23	Gift		
	Greater of:		
	(1) Market value at gift	1,400	
	(2) Original cost	2,000	
	Less: Use benefit	(400)	
		1,600	
			1,600

11 The correct answer is: £114,000

	£	£
31.5.18 PET now chargeable		500,000
Nil rate band at death	325,000	
Less: 30.4.17 PET now chargeable	(300,000)	
		(25,000)
Transfer chargeable to IHT @ 40%		475,000
£475,000 @ 40%		190,000
Less: Taper relief (4 to 5 years) @ 40%		(76,000)
IHT payable as a result of Cora's death		114,000

12 The correct answers are:

£60	Penalty
£16	Interest

The due date for payment of the balancing payment was 31 January 2024.

Interest is due for the period February 2024 to June 2024 (working in whole months) so is £1,200 × 3.25% × 5/12 = £16. The answer £39 is the interest for a 12-month period.

The penalty date was 30 days after the due date and so payment was less than five months after the penalty date. The penalty due is £1,200 × 5% = £60.

13 The correct answer is: £6,500

	y/e 31.3.22	y/e 31.3.23
	£	£
Trading income	79,400	0
Property business income	6,800	10,100
Total profits	86,200	10,100
Less: loss against total profits	(86,200)	(10,100)
Taxable trading profits	0	0

Loss memorandum

	£
Trading loss incurred in y/e 31.3.23	102,800
Less: used in y/e 31.3.23	(10,100)
used in y/e 31.3.22	(86,200)
Loss unrelieved	6,500

The qualifying charitable donations are unrelieved.

14 Deferring the CGT due date

The CGT due date will be 31 January following the end of the tax year of the disposal for both spouses/civil partners.

Note the three ways in which tax planning for spouses can be used: making the best use of annual exempt amounts; reducing the amount of CGT payable (eg if one spouse has unused basic rate band); and making best use of capital losses.

15 £ 2,420

2022/23 Relevant amount = £4,840 / 2 = £2,420

Section B

Adana

Workbook references

Inheritance tax (IHT) is the subject of Chapter 18.

Top Tips

In Question 20, you need to think about the lifetime IHT paid as well as the death tax on the estate.

Easy Marks

There were easy marks in Questions 16 and 17 for basic IHT knowledge.

Examining team's comments

The first two questions (involving the available nil rate band and the amount of deductions permitted in calculating the taxpayer's chargeable estate) were well answered.

One of the questions asked who was responsible for paying the IHT liability in respect of the taxpayer's chargeable estate, and also the due date. The due date was not a problem, but many candidates opted for the beneficiaries of the taxpayer's estate as responsible rather than the personal representatives of the estate.

A further question asked for how much of the IHT payable in respect of taxpayer's estate would have been saved if specific gifts had been made to a trust and to the taxpayer's grandchildren (instead of the entire estate being left to the taxpayer's children). Although most candidates chose the correct answer (that there was no tax saving), a significant number opted for either of the gifts resulting in an IHT saving at 40%.

There was also a question that asked for how much IHT was saved as a result of the taxpayer making a chargeable lifetime transfer (CLT) rather than retaining the gifted assets until death. Again, the correct answer (based on the value at death less the amount of lifetime IHT paid) was most popular, but a significant number of candidates instead based their answer on the initial value of the CLT.

These three, less well answered questions, demonstrate the need for a good grasp of how a tax such as IHT is applied, rather than just rote learning the basic mechanics of tax calculation. These questions show how tax planning can feature within a case question.

16 £585,000

	£
Adana: own nil rate band (lifetime transfer more than 7 years before death)	325,000
Adana's husband: 80% × £325,000 (use 2022/23 nil rate band)	260,000
Maximum nil rate band available	585,000

17 £ 263,700

	£
Mortgage (debt incurred for consideration)	220,000
Income tax (statutory debt)	43,700
Total deductions	263,700

The legal fees are not deductible as the agreement to pay them is not legally enforceable because no consideration is received.

18 The correct answers are:

Personal representatives of Adana's estate	Responsible persons
30 September 2023	Due date for payment

The beneficiaries of Adana's estate will bear the IHT, as it will reduce the amount due to them from the estate, but it is her personal representatives (the executors of her will) who are responsible for making the payment. The IHT on a death estate is due by the end of six months from the end of the month of death.

19 The correct answer is: £0

There would be no IHT saving by making either of these gifts as both are chargeable in the same way as gifting the entire estate to Adana's children. The only exempt transfer in relation to the death estate for Taxation (TX – UK) purposes is a gift to a spouse/civil partner.

20 The correct answer is: £207,750

	£
Extra IHT on death estate: £650,000 × 40%	260,000
Less: lifetime IHT paid	(52,250)
IHT saving	207,750

Kat Ltd and Kitten

Workbook references

Chargeable gains for companies are dealt with in Chapter 20. Computation of CGT is covered in Chapter 13 and business reliefs in Chapter 15.

Top tips

Double check your computations! Just because your answer is one of those given, it does not necessarily mean that it is correct.

Easy marks

The indexation allowance in Question 21 was made easier by both the cost and the enhancement expenditure being incurred in the same month.

Examining team's report

Questions involving the indexation allowance, the crystallisation date for a heldover gain and the base cost of shares following a rights issue were well answered.

One of the questions asked for the base cost of an asset against which a rollover relief claim had been made. Although the correct answer was the most popular (with candidates appreciating that the amount of proceeds not reinvested could not be rolled over), a significant number of candidates ignored the amount of proceeds not reinvested and rolled over the full amount of gain.

Another question asked for the taxpayer's CGT liability. Again, the correct answer (the disposal qualifying for business asset disposal relief utilised the available basic rate tax band, with the other gain therefore taxed at 20%) was marginally the most popular. However, many candidates ignored the impact of business asset disposal relief on the basic rate band or did not deduct the annual exempt amount.

These two less well answered questions demonstrate the need to be very careful with all aspects of a calculation. One simple mistake means the loss of the two marks available.

21 £ 71,118

	£
0.439 × £162,000 (138,600 + 23,400)	71,118

22 The correct answer is: £243,300

	£
Gain	120,700
Immediately chargeable = amount not reinvested £(364,000 – 272,000)	(92,000)
Deduction from base cost of new warehouse	28,700

The base cost of the new warehouse is £(272,000 – 28,700) = £243,300.

23 10 years from 30 September 2023

The gain will become chargeable on the latest of: the date of disposal of the replacement asset; the date it ceases to be used in the trade; and ten years from its acquisition.

24 The correct answer is: £63,200

Date	*Transaction*	*No. of shares*	*Cost*
			£
7 July 2010	Acquisition at par £1 cost for each £1 share bought	90,000	90,000
22 Sept 2013	Rights issue 2 new shares for every 3 original shares held @ £6.40	60,000	384,000
		150,000	474,000
5 October 2022	Sale	(20,000)	(63,200)
c/f		130,000	410,800

25 The correct answer is: £17,540

	BADR gain	*Non-BADR gain*
	£	£
Gains	142,200	28,900
Less: annual exempt amount (best use)	–	(12,300)
Taxable gains	142,200	16,600
Tax @ 10%/20%	14,220	3,320
Total CGT payable		£17,540

The basic rate band is treated as being used first by the gain qualifying for business asset disposal relief. This means that the band is entirely used up and so the tax on the gain not qualifying for business asset disposal relief is taxable at 20%.

The answer £15,880 uses the basic rate of 10% on the gain not qualifying for business asset disposal relief. The answer £20,000 does not deduct the annual exempt amount. The answer £18,770 sets the annual exempt amount against the gain qualifying for business asset disposal relief.

Alisa

Workbook references

Value added tax is covered in Chapters 24 and 25.

Top tips

For Question 28 note that the fuel scale charge is the basis for **output** tax charged in relation to private use fuel. You were asked to identify the **input** tax which could be reclaimed.

Easy marks

There were easy marks in Question 26 for identifying the date from which the trader would have been required to be compulsorily registered for VAT. However, it was important to read the question carefully to see exactly what was being asked – it was **not** the date on which the registration threshold was reached.

Examining team's comment

Generally, this case question was not as well answered as the previous two. However, candidates made reasonable attempts at questions on the recovery of pre-registration input VAT, how and by when the VAT liability would be paid, and the information included on a valid VAT invoice.

A further question asked for the date of compulsory VAT registration. Although the correct answer was the most popular, many candidates opted for the end of the month in which the registration limit was exceeded.

One of the questions asked for the maximum amount of input VAT which could be reclaimed in respect of motor expenses. The correct answer (ignoring private use) was by a long way the most popular, but a significant number of candidates either adjusted for private use or used the fuel scale charge instead of the actual fuel figure.

26 1 November 2022

	£
January to April: 4 × £7,500	30,000
May to August: 4 × £10,000	40,000
September	15,500
	85,500

The registration threshold of £85,000 is met by 30 September 2022. Alisa should therefore have notified HMRC by 30 October 2022, with registration effective from 1 November 2022.

27 The correct answer is: £456

	£
Website design service: £240 × 6 × 1/6	240
Advertising: £180 × 6 × 20%	216
Input tax reclaimable	456

Pre-registration input tax is recoverable on services which are supplied within six months prior to registration. Note the different calculations for VAT-inclusive and VAT-exclusive amounts.

28 The correct answer is: £180

	£
Repairs	456
Fuel	624
	1,080
Input tax reclaimable £1,080 × 1/6	180

Full input tax can be reclaimed on the repairs to the car - the private use of the car is not relevant.

All the input tax will be reclaimed on fuel and the adjustment to private use will be made by charging output tax based on the fuel scale charge.

29 Alisa has to pay any VAT liability for the quarter ended 31 March 2023 by [7 May 2023] using [an electronic payment] method.

Alisa has to pay any VAT liability for the quarter ended 31 March 2023 by 7 May 2023 using an electronic payment method.

30 The correct answer is: The customer's VAT registration number

Section C

31 Joe

Workbook references

Employment income is covered in Chapter 3. The income tax computation is the subject of Chapter 2. National insurance contributions are dealt with in Chapter 12. Corporation tax is covered in Chapter 19.

Top Tips

A good start would be to look at the list of taxes in note 1 and consider whether they apply each of the two scenarios.

Easy marks

There were some easy marks for basic income tax and corporation tax computations. However, you needed to be methodical in the way in which you set out your computations.

Examining team's comments.

Although there were many good attempts at this question, various aspects consistently caused problems.

- It was often not clear as to which section of the scenario was being answered, particularly as regards the corporation tax calculations.
- The majority of candidates did not appreciate that where all of a company's profits are paid out as director's remuneration (and the related employer's class 1 NIC) then there is no corporation tax liability.
- Similarly, it was not appreciated that with director's remuneration of just £8,000 (which is below the NIC lower thresholds) then there were no NICs.
- Many candidates incorrectly calculated NICs on the dividends.

Marking guide	Marks	
Profits withdrawn as director's remuneration		
Income tax	1½	
Class 1 employee's NIC	1½	
Corporation tax	½	
Profits withdrawn as a mix of director's remuneration and dividends		
Income tax	3	
Class 1 NIC	1	
Corporation tax	1½	
Overall tax saving	1	
		10
Total		10

Joe – Income tax liability 2022/23 if just remuneration

	Non-savings income
	£
Director's remuneration/Net income	57,688
Less personal allowance	(12,570)

	Non-savings income
	£
Taxable income	45,118
Tax	
£37,700 @ 20%	7,540
£(45,118 – 37,700) = 7,418 @ 40%	2,967
Income tax payable	10,507

Joe – National insurance contributions 2022/23 if just remuneration

	£
£(57,688 – 50,270) = 7,418 @ 3.25%	241
£(50,270 – 12,570) = 37,700 @ 13.25%	4,995
Class 1 employee's NIC payable	5,236

There will be no corporation tax payable since the profits are entirely withdrawn as director's remuneration (including Class 1 employer's NIC).

Joe – Income tax liability 2022/23 if mix of remuneration and dividends

	Non-savings income	Dividend income	Total income
	£	£	£
Director's remuneration	8,000		
Dividends	–	46,170	
Net income	8,000	46,170	54,170
Less personal allowance	(8,000)	(4,570)	
Taxable income	0	41,600	41,600
Tax			
£2,000 @ 0% (dividend nil rate band)			0
£(37,700 – 2,000) = 35,700 @ 8.75%			3,124
£(41,600 – 37,700) = 3,900 @ 33.75%			1,316
Income tax payable			4,440

There will be no Class 1 NIC for either OK-Joe Ltd or Joe as the earnings are below the NIC employee's and employer's thresholds.

Corporation tax liability of OK-Joe Ltd for the year ended 5 April 2023 if mix of remuneration and dividends

	£
Trading profit	65,000
Less: Director's remuneration	(8,000)
Taxable trading profit	57,000
Corporation tax £57,000 @ 19%	10,830

Summary of tax and NIC liabilities

	Remuneration only	*Mix of remuneration and dividends*
	£	£
Income tax	10,507	4,440
Class 1 NIC employee's	5,236	0
Class 1 NIC employer's (given in question)	7,312	0
Corporation tax	0	10,830
Total tax and NIC	23,055	15,270

Therefore, the overall tax and NIC saving if Joe extracts profits using a mix of director's remuneration and dividends is £(**23,055** – 15,270) = £7,785.

32 Ashura

Workbook References

Assessable trading income is dealt with in Chapter 9, capital allowances in Chapter 8 and losses in Chapter 10. Employment income is dealt with in Chapters 3 and 4. Taxable income is covered in Chapter 2.

Top Tips

In part (d), note the difference between the tax treatment of occupational pension contributions (paid gross and deducted in the income computation giving tax relief at all rates) and personal pension contributions (basic rate relief given by being paid net and further tax relief being given by increasing the basic rate limit so not relevant to this question which only required a calculation of taxable income).

Easy marks

There were some easy marks in part (b) for straightforward adjustments to profit. Part (d) had some easy marks for dealing with the mileage allowance and subscriptions.

Examining team's comments

For part (a), the requirement was to state two advantages of the taxpayer choosing 5 April as an accounting date rather than a date early in the tax year such as 30 April. There were three obvious advantages, and many candidates correctly explained that the application of the basis period rules is more straightforward and that there will be no overlap profits. Less well-prepared candidates instead covered the advantages of a 30 April accounting date, so not surprisingly did not achieve high marks.

Part (b) required a calculation of the taxpayer's revised tax adjusted trading loss for the first period of account. This meant adjusting for pre-trading expenditure, use of one of the five rooms in the taxpayer's private house as an office, and capital allowances. There were many good answers to this section, although a common mistake was to not appreciate that each of the three adjustments increased (not decreased) the trading loss.

For part (c), candidates had to explain why it was not beneficial for the taxpayer to claim loss relief under the provisions giving relief to a loss incurred in the early years of trade. It should have been fairly obvious that such a claim would have wasted the personal allowance and not resulted in any tax saving. This section was not as well answered, with many candidates not appreciating that the loss could only be carried back for three years. Some candidates actually explained why a claim would be beneficial.

Part (d) required a calculation of the taxpayer's taxable income (on the basis that loss relief was claimed against total income). This meant taking account of two subscriptions (only one of which was deductible), a mileage allowance deduction for the use of a private car for business purposes, and pension contributions (both to an occupational scheme and a personal pension scheme). This section was generally well answered, although many candidates wasted time by calculating the tax liability. The occupational pension scheme contribution was often grossed up (such contributions are not paid net of tax). Many candidates made things more difficult than they needed to be by attempting this section before section (b).

Marking guide		Marks
(a) Two advantages of basis period ending on 5 April (one mark for each)		
		2
(b) Trading loss	2.5	
Capital allowances	3.5	
		6
(c) Early years loss relief		
		2
(d) Salary	0.5	
Mileage	1	
Pension	1	
Subscriptions	1	
Loss	1	
Personal allowance	0.5	
		5
Total		15

(a) **Advantages of choosing 5 April as accounting date rather than earlier date in tax year**

Any **two** of:

- The basis period rules are more straightforward.
- On commencement, there will be no overlap profits.
- On cessation, the final basis period will be a maximum of 12 months. If a date earlier in the tax year is chosen, the final basis period will be longer, up to 23 months with a 30 April year end.

(b) **Ashura – Trading loss for the nine-month period ended 5 April 2023**

		£
Trading loss		(3,300)
Less:	Pre-trading expenditure	(800)
	Use of office £4,350 × 1/5	(870)
	Capital allowance (W)	(2,960)
Adjusted trading loss		(7,930)

Working

Capital allowances

9 months to 5 April 2023	*AIA*	*Main pool*	*Car*		*Allowances*
	£	£	£		£
Additions					
Laptop	2,600				
AIA	(2,600)				2,600
Transfer to pool	0	0			
Car			25,600		
WDA @ 6% × 9/12		—	(1,152)	× 2,500/8,000	360
WDA c/f		0	24,448		—
Allowances					2,960

Tutorial note. The advertising expenditure incurred in January 2022 is pre-trading expenditure which is treated as incurred on the first day of trading. An adjustment is therefore required.

Tutorial note. Ashura's car has CO_2 emissions over 50g/km and therefore only qualifies for writing down allowance at the rate of 6%.

Tutorial note. The laptop computer purchased on 10 June 2022 is pre-trading capital expenditure and is therefore treated as incurred on the first day of trading.

(c) **Early years trading loss relief**

Under early years trading loss relief, the loss of £7,930 in 2022/23 would be relieved against her total income of £10,800 in 2019/20 since this is the earliest of the three years 2019/20, 2020/21 and 2021/22.

However, since Ashura's total income for 2019/20 is covered by her personal allowance of £12,570 (assumed), there would be no tax saving by making an early years loss relief claim.

(d) **Ashura – Taxable income 2022/23**

		£
Salary		56,600
Mileage allowance 3,400 × 10p (55p – 45p)		340
Pension contributions	Occupational	(2,800)
	Personal	(0)
Subscriptions	Professional	(320)
	Health club	(0)
Total income		53,820
Less: Loss relief against total income		(7,930)
Net income		45,890
Less: Personal allowance		(12,570)
Taxable income		33,320

ANSWERS

Tutorial note. The personal pension scheme contribution does not affect the calculation of taxable income but will instead increase Ashura's basic rate limit by the gross contribution of £3,400.

Tutorial note. The health club subscription is not an allowable deduction because membership is not a necessary expense for Ashura to carry out the duties of her employment.

Tutorial note. The loss relief cap does not apply because Ashura's trading loss is less than the greater of £50,000 and 25% of her total income.

33 Mable

Workbook references

The computation of taxable total profits is covered in Chapter 19. The adjustment to trading profits is dealt with in Chapter 7 and capital allowances in Chapter 8. Property business income is covered in Chapter 5.

Top tips

Be careful when working with short accounting periods. For example, in part (b) you needed to adjust the writing down allowance so that only six months of allowances were given.

Easy marks

There were some easy marks in part (b) for adjustments to profits which should have been well-known.

Examining team's comments

Part (a) was generally very well answered, requiring a calculation of the first company's taxable total profits for the final period of trading. This involved calculating the balancing charge on cessation (all of the items included in the company's main pool being sold), the chargeable gain on the sale of the company's freehold office building and the property business income in respect of one floor of the office building which had been let out. The company has also made qualifying charitable donations. The only consistent problem here was the capital allowances, with many candidates not appreciating that neither the annual investment allowance (a laptop computer had been purchased during the period) nor writing down allowances are given in the period of cessation. A few candidates ignored the cessation altogether and therefore did not calculate a balancing charge.

Part (b) was also well answered on the whole, requiring a calculation of the second company's tax adjusted trading profit for the initial period of trading. This involved adjusting for depreciation and amortisation, calculating the deduction in respect of a lease premium, calculating capital allowances for two cars (one car was used as a pool car by the company's employees, with the other having private use by a director) and deducting loan interest in respect of a loan made to the company by a director/owner. Some candidates attempted to calculate benefits in respect of the cars and loan which, although correct as regards the cars, had no relevance to the requirement. Perhaps not surprisingly, the deduction for the lease premium caused quite a few problems.

Marking guide		Marks	
(a)	Taxable total profits	2.5	
	Balancing charge	3	
	Property business income	1.5	
			7
(b)	Profit and add-backs	1.5	

Marking guide		Marks
Interest payable	1	
Lease premium	2.5	
Capital allowances	3	
		8
Total		15

(a) **Tenth Ltd – Taxable total profits for the four-month period ended 31 July 2022**

	£
Trading profits	52,400
Balancing charge (W1)	15,300
Adjusted trading profits	67,700
Property business income (W2)	1,500
Chargeable gain £(180,300 – 164,500)	15,800
Total profits	85,000
Less qualifying charitable donations	(800)
Taxable total profits	84,200

Workings

1 *Capital allowances*

	Main pool	Allowances
	£	£
TWDV brought forward	12,400	
Addition		
Laptop computer	1,800	
Disposal		
Main pool items £(28,200 + 1,300)	(29,500)	
Balancing charge	15,300	(15,300)

2 *Property business income*

	£
Rent receivable £1,200 × 4	4,800
Less: Impairment loss	(1,200)
Running costs £6,300 × 1/3	(2,100)
Property business income	1,500

(b) **Eleventh Ltd – Tax adjusted trading profit for the six-month period ended 31 March 2023**

		£
Operating profit		122,900
Add:	Depreciation	2,580
	Amortisation	2,000
Less:	Deduction for lease premium (W1)	(1,440)
	Interest payable £100,000 × 5% × 6/12	(2,500)
	Capital allowances (W2)	(14,334)
Tax adjusted trading profit		109,206

Workings

1 *Deduction for lease premium*

	£
Premium paid	60,000
Less: £60,000 × 2% × (15 –1)	(16,800)
Amount taxable on landlord as property business income	43,200
Deduction £43,200/15 x 6/12	1,440

2 *Capital allowances*

	FYA	*Main pool*	*Allowances*
	£	£	£
Addition not qualifying for FYA			
Car [1]		12,600	
WDA @ 18% × 6/12		(1,134)	1,134
Addition qualifying for FYA			
Car [2]	13,200		
FYA @ 100%	(13,200)		13,200
Transfer to pool	0	0	
TWDV carried forward		11,466	—
Allowances			14,334

Tutorial note. Car [1] has CO_2 emissions of below 50g/km. It therefore goes into the main pool and has writing down allowances at 18% scaled down for the short accounting period.

Tutorial note. Car [2] is new and has zero CO_2 emissions so therefore qualifies for the 100% first year allowance. This is not scaled down for the short accounting period. The private use of the car is not relevant for the company.

ACCA

Taxation (TX - UK)

Mock Exam 2

Specimen exam updated to FA 2022

Questions	
Time allowed	3 Hours
This exam is divided into three sections Section A – All 15 questions are compulsory and MUST be attempted Section B – All 15 questions are compulsory and MUST be attempted Section C – All THREE questions are compulsory and MUST be attempted	

DO NOT OPEN THIS EXAM UNTIL YOU ARE READY TO START UNDER EXAMINATION CONDITIONS

Mock exam 2

Section A

ALL 15 questions are compulsory and MUST be attempted

1 William is self-employed, and his tax adjusted trading profit for the year ended 5 April 2023 was £84,050. During the tax year 2022/23, William contributed £5,400 (gross) into a personal pension scheme.

What amount of Class 4 national insurance contributions (NIC) will William pay for the tax year 2022/23?

- O £5,126
- O £7,327
- O £4,962
- O £3,864

(2 marks)

2 You are a trainee Chartered Certified Accountant, and your firm has a client who has refused to disclose a chargeable gain to HM Revenue & Customs (HMRC).

From an ethical viewpoint, which TWO of the following actions could be expected of your firm?

- ☐ Reporting under the money laundering regulations
- ☐ Advising the client to make disclosure
- ☐ Informing HMRC of the non-disclosure
- ☐ Warning the client that your firm will be reporting the non-disclosure

(2 marks)

3 Martin is self-employed and for the year ended 5 April 2023 his trading profit was £109,400. During the tax year 2022/23, Martin made a gift aid donation of £800 (gross) to a national charity.

What amount of personal allowance will Martin be entitled to for the tax year 2022/23?

£ ______

(2 marks)

4 For the year ended 31 March 2023, Halo Ltd made a trading loss of £180,000.

Halo Ltd has owned 100% of the ordinary share capital of Shallow Ltd since it began trading on 1 July 2022. For the year ended 30 June 2023, Shallow Ltd will make a trading profit of £224,000.

Neither company has any other taxable profits or allowable losses.

What is the maximum amount of group relief which Shallow Ltd can claim from Halo Ltd in respect of the trading loss of £180,000 for the year ended 31 March 2023?

- O £180,000
- O £168,000
- O £45,000
- O £135,000

(2 marks)

5 For the year ended 31 March 2022, Sizeable Ltd had taxable total profits of £820,000, and for the year ended 31 March 2023 had taxable total profits of £970,000. The profits accrue evenly throughout the year.

Sizeable Ltd has had one 51% group company for many years.

How will Sizeable Ltd pay its corporation tax liability for the year ended 31 March 2023?

- O Nine instalments of £15,580 and a balancing payment of £28,500
- O Four instalments of £46,075
- O Four instalments of £38,950 and a balancing payment of £28,500
- O One payment of £184,300 **(2 marks)**

6 For the year ended 31 December 2022, Lateness Ltd had a corporation tax liability of £60,000, which it did not pay until 31 March 2024. Lateness Ltd is not a large company.

How much interest will Lateness Ltd be charged by HM Revenue & Customs (HMRC) in respect of the late payment of its corporation tax liability for the year ended 31 December 2022?

[▼]

Pull down list

- £2,438
- £325
- £488
- £975

(2 marks)

7 On 26 November 2022 Alice sold an antique table for £8,700. The antique table had been purchased on 16 May 2014 for £3,800.

What is Alice's chargeable gain in respect of the disposal of the antique table?

- O £4,500
- O £1,620
- O £4,900
- O £0 **(2 marks)**

8 On 14 November 2022, Jane made a cash gift to a trust of £800,000 (after deducting all available exemptions). Jane paid the inheritance tax arising from this gift. Jane has not made any other lifetime gifts.

What amount of lifetime inheritance tax would have been payable in respect of Jane's gift to the trust?

£ [ ] **(2 marks)**

9 During the tax year 2022/23, Mildred made four cash gifts to her grandchildren.

For each of the gifts listed below, click in the box to indicate whether the gift will be exempt or not exempt from inheritance tax under the small gifts exemption.

£400 to Alfred	**EXEMPT**	**NOT EXEMPT**
£140 to Minnie	**EXEMPT**	**NOT EXEMPT**
A further £280 to Minnie	**EXEMPT**	**NOT EXEMPT**
£175 to Winifred	**EXEMPT**	**NOT EXEMPT**

(2 marks)

10 For the quarter ended 31 March 2023, Faro had standard rated sales of £49,750 and standard rated expenses of £22,750. Both figures are exclusive of value added tax (VAT).

Faro uses the flat rate scheme to calculate the amount of VAT payable, with the relevant scheme percentage for her trade being 12%. The percentage reduction for the first year of VAT registration is not available.

How much VAT will Faro have to pay to HM Revenue & Customs (HMRC) for the quarter ended 31 March 2023?

- O £5,970
- O £3,888
- O £5,400
- O £7,164

(2 marks)

11 Which TWO of the following assets will ALWAYS be exempt from capital gains tax?

- ☐ A car suitable for private use
- ☐ A chattel
- ☐ A UK government security (gilt)
- ☐ A house

(2 marks)

12 Winston invested £8,000 into a cash individual savings account (ISA) during the tax year 2022/23. He now wants to invest into a stocks and shares ISA.

What is the maximum possible amount which Winston can invest into a stocks and shares ISA for the tax year 2022/23?

- O £20,000
- O £12,000
- O £0
- O £10,000

(2 marks)

13 Ming is self-employed.

For each of the types of records listed below, click in the box to indicate the date until which Ming must retain the records used in preparing her self-assessment tax return for the tax year 2022/23.

Business records	**31 JANUARY 2025**	**31 JANUARY 2029**
Non-business records	**31 JANUARY 2025**	**31 JANUARY 2029**

(2 marks)

14 Moon Ltd has had the following tax adjusted trading profits and losses:

The company does not have any other income.

Period	*Profit/(loss)*
	£
Year ended 31 December 2022	(105,000)
Four-month period ended 31 December 2021	43,000
Year ended 31 August 2021	96,000

How much of Moon Ltd's trading loss for the year ended 31 December 2022 can be relieved against its total profits of £96,000 for the year ended 31 August 2021?

- O £64,000
- O £96,000
- O £70,000
- O £62,000

(2 marks)

15 Nigel has not previously been resident in the UK, being in the UK for less than 20 days each tax year. For the tax year 2022/23, he has three ties with the UK.

What is the maximum number of days which Nigel could spend in the UK during the tax year 2022/23 without being treated as resident in the UK for that year?

- O 90 days
- O 182 days
- O 45 days
- O 120 days

(2 marks)

Section B

ALL 15 questions are compulsory and MUST be attempted

Delroy and Marlon

The following scenario relates to Questions 16 to 20.

Delroy and Grant

On 10 January 2023, Delroy made a gift of 25,000 £1 ordinary shares in Dub Ltd, an unquoted trading company, to his son, Grant. The market value of the shares on that date was £240,000. Delroy had subscribed for the 25,000 shares in Dub Ltd at par on 1 July 2008. Delroy and Grant have elected to claim gift holdover relief.

Grant sold the 25,000 shares in Dub Ltd on 18 March 2023 for £240,000. Dub Ltd has a share capital of 100,000 £1 ordinary shares. Delroy was the sales director of the company from its incorporation on 1 July 2008 until 10 January 2023. Grant has never been an employee or a director of Dub Ltd.

For the tax year 2022/23 Delroy and Grant are both higher rate taxpayers. They have each made other disposals of assets during the tax year 2022/23, and therefore they have both already utilised their annual exempt amounts for this year.

Marlon and Alvita

On 28 March 2023, Marlon sold a residential property for £497,000, which he had owned individually. The property had been purchased on 22 October 2005 for £152,600. Throughout the period of ownership, the property was occupied by Marlon and his wife, Alvita, as their main residence. One-third of the property was always used exclusively for business purposes by the couple. Business asset disposal relief is not available in respect of this disposal.

For the tax year 2022/23, Marlon is a higher rate taxpayer, but Alvita did not have any taxable income. This will remain the case for the tax year 2023/24. Neither of them has made any other disposals of assets during the year.

16 What is Grant's capital gains tax (CGT) liability for the tax year 2022/23 in respect of the disposal of the shares in Dub Ltd?

- O £43,000
- O £21,500
- O £0
- O £40,540

(2 marks)

---

17 Which TWO of the following statements would have been true in relation to the CGT implications if Delroy had instead sold the 25,000 shares in Dub Ltd himself for £240,000 on 10 January 2023, and then gifted the cash proceeds to Grant?

- ☐ Business asset disposal relief would have been available.
- ☐ The CGT liability would have been paid later.
- ☐ The cash gift would not have been a chargeable disposal.
- ☐ The cash gift would have qualified for gift holdover relief.

(2 marks)

---

18 What is Marlon's chargeable gain for the tax year 2022/23?

- O £229,600
- O £0
- O £114,800
- O £344,400

(2 marks)

19 What is the amount of CGT which could have been saved if Marlon had transferred 50% ownership of the residential property to Alvita prior to its disposal?

- O £3,444
- O £7,214
- O £3,770
- O £14,000

(2 marks)

---

20 What is the payment date for the capital gains tax payable on the disposal of the residential property on 28 March 2023?

[▼]

Pull down list

- 27 May 2023
- 31 January 2024
- 31 January 2025
- 31 May 2023

(2 marks)

(Total = 10 marks)

Opal

The following scenario relates to Questions 21 to 25.

You should assume that today's date is 15 March 2023.

Opal is aged 71 and has a chargeable estate for inheritance tax (IHT) purposes valued at £950,000.

She owns two investment properties respectively valued at £374,000 and £442,000. The first property has an outstanding repayment mortgage of £160,000, and the second property is owned outright with no mortgage.

Opal owes £22,400 in respect of a personal loan from a bank, and she has also verbally promised to pay legal fees of £4,600 incurred by her nephew. Opal expects the cost of her funeral to be £5,200, and this cost will be covered by the £6,000 she has invested in an individual savings account (ISA).

Under the terms of her will, Opal has left all of her estate to her children. Opal's husband is still alive.

On 14 August 2013, Opal had made a gift of £100,000 to her daughter, and on 7 November 2022, she made a gift of £220,000 to her son. Both these figures are after deducting all available exemptions.

The nil rate band for the tax year 2013/14 is £325,000.

You should assume that both the value of Opal's estate and the nil rate band will remain unchanged for future years.

21 What is the net value for the two properties, which will have been included in the calculation of Opal's chargeable estate of £950,000?

£ [ ]

(2 marks)

22 Which TWO of the following amounts will have been deducted in calculating Opal's chargeable estate of £950,000?

☐ Personal loan from a bank of £22,400

☐ Promise to pay legal fees of £4,600

☐ Funeral cost of £5,200

☐ ISA investment of £6,000 **(2 marks)**

---

23 What amount of IHT will be payable in respect of Opal's chargeable estate valued at £950,000 were she to die on 20 March 2023?

O £250,000

O £338,000

O £378,000

O £335,600 **(2 marks)**

---

24 By how much would the IHT payable on Opal's death be reduced if she were to live for another seven years until 20 March 2030, compared to if she were to die on 20 March 2023?

[▼]

Pull down list

- £0
- £128,000
- £40,000
- £88,000

(2 marks)

---

25 Which TWO of the following conditions must be met if Opal wants to make gifts out of her income, so that these gifts are exempt from IHT?

☐ The gifts cannot exceed 10% of income.

☐ The gifts must be habitual.

☐ Opal must have enough remaining income to maintain her normal standard of living.

☐ Opal must make the gifts monthly or quarterly. **(2 marks)**

(Total = 10 marks)

Glacier Ltd

The following scenario relates to Questions 26 to 30.

The following information is available in respect of Glacier Ltd's value added tax (VAT) for the quarter ended 31 March 2023:

(1) Invoices were issued for sales of £44,600 to VAT registered customers. Of this figure, £35,200 was in respect of exempt sales and the balance in respect of standard rated sales. The standard rated sales figure is exclusive of VAT.

(2) In addition to the above, on 1 March 2023 Glacier Ltd issued a VAT invoice for £8,000 plus VAT of £1,600 to a VAT registered customer in respect of a contract which will be completed on 15 April 2023. The customer paid for the contract in two instalments of £4,800 on 31 March 2023 and 30 April 2023.

(3) The managing director of Glacier Ltd is provided with free fuel for private mileage driven in her company car. During the quarter ended 31 March 2023, the total cost of fuel for business and private mileage was £720, of which £270 was for private mileage. The relevant quarterly scale charge is £406. All of these figures are inclusive of VAT.

For the quarters ended 30 September 2021 and 30 June 2022, Glacier Ltd was one month late in submitting its VAT returns and in paying the related VAT liabilities. All of the company's other VAT returns have been submitted on time.

26 What is the amount of output VAT payable by Glacier Ltd in respect of its sales for the quarter ended 31 March 2023?

[▼]

Pull down list

- £1,880
- £10,520
- £2,680
- £3,480

(2 marks)

---

27 Calculate the amounts required to complete the following sentence:

Glacier Ltd will include output VAT of £ [ ]

and input VAT of £ [ ]

on its VAT return for the quarter ended 31 March 2023 in respect of the managing director's company car. **(2 marks)**

---

28 What surcharge penalty could Glacier Ltd be charged if the company is one month late in paying its VAT liability for the quarter ended 31 March 2023?

- O 5% of the VAT liability
- O 2% of the VAT liability
- O There will be no penalty
- O 10% of the VAT liability **(2 marks)**

---

29 What is the minimum requirement which Glacier Ltd needs to meet in order to revert to a clean default surcharge record?

- O Submit four consecutive VAT returns on time
- O Submit any four VAT returns on time and also pay the related VAT liabilities on time
- O Pay four consecutive VAT liabilities on time
- O Submit four consecutive VAT returns on time and also pay the related VAT liabilities on time **(2 marks)**

30 Complete the following sentence by matching one of the 'types of supply' and one of the 'types of customer' into each target area.

Glacier Ltd will be required to issue a VAT invoice when (1) ▼ is made to

(2) ▼ .

Pull down list 1

- A standard rated supply
- Any type of supply

Pull down list 2

- A VAT registered customer
- Any customer

(2 marks)

(Total = 10 marks)

Section C

ALL three questions are compulsory and MUST be attempted

31 Sarah

You should assume that today's date is 1 March 2022.

Sarah is currently self-employed. If she continues to trade on a self-employed basis, her total income tax liability and national insurance contributions (NIC) for the tax year 2022/23 will be £11,487.

However, Sarah is considering incorporating her business on 6 April 2022. The forecast taxable total profits of the new limited company for the year ended 5 April 2023 will be £50,000 (before taking account of any director's remuneration). Sarah will pay herself gross director's remuneration of £30,000 and dividends of £10,000. The balance of the profits will remain undrawn within the new company.

Required

(a) Determine whether or not there will be an overall saving of tax and national insurance contributions (NIC) for the year ended 5 April 2023 if Sarah incorporates her business on 6 April 2023.

Notes.

1. You are expected to calculate the income tax payable by Sarah, the Class 1 NIC payable by Sarah and the new limited company, and the corporation tax liability of the new limited company for the year ended 5 April 2023.
2. The new limited company will not be entitled to the NIC annual employment allowance.
3. You should assume that the rates of corporation tax remain unchanged. **(8 marks)**

(b) Advise Sarah as to why her proposed basis of extracting profits from the new limited company is not optimum for tax purposes and suggest how the mix of director's remuneration and dividends could therefore be improved.

Note. You are not expected to calculate any revised tax or NIC figures. **(2 marks)**

(Total = 10 marks)

---

32 Simon

On 6 April 2022, Simon commenced employment with Echo Ltd. On 1 January 2023, he commenced in partnership with Art, preparing accounts to 30 April. The following information is available for the tax year 2022/23:

Employment

(1) During the tax year 2022/23, Simon was paid a gross annual salary of £23,940.

(2) Throughout the tax year 2022/23, Echo Ltd provided Simon with living accommodation. The company had purchased the property in 2010 for £89,000, and it was valued at £143,000 on 6 April 2022. The annual value of the property is £4,600. The property was furnished by Echo Ltd during March 2022 at a cost of £9,400. The living accommodation is not job related.

(3) On 1 December 2022, Echo Ltd provided Simon with an interest-free loan of £84,000, which he used to purchase a holiday cottage.

Partnership

(1) The partnership's tax adjusted trading profit for the four-month period ended 30 April 2023 is £29,700. This figure is before taking account of capital allowances.

(2) The only item of plant and machinery owned by the partnership is a car which cost £25,000 on 1 February 2023. The car has a CO_2 emission rate of 75 grams per kilometre. It is used by Art, and 40% of the mileage is for private journeys.

(3) Profits are shared 40% to Simon and 60% to Art. This is after paying an annual salary of £6,000 to Art.

Property income

(1) Simon owns a freehold house which is let out furnished. The property was let throughout the tax year 2022/23 at a monthly rent of £660, all of which was received during the tax year.

(2) During the tax year 2022/23, Simon paid council tax and water rates totalling £1,320 in respect of the property. He also replaced the property's washing machine during March 2023. The old washing machine was sold for £70, being replaced by a washer-dryer costing £970. The cost of a similar washing machine would have been £730.

Required

(a) Calculate Simon's taxable income for the tax year 2022/23. **(13 marks)**

(b) State **TWO** advantages for the partnership of choosing 30 April as its accounting date rather than 5 April. **(2 marks)**

(Total = 15 marks)

---

33 Naive Ltd

(a) You are a trainee accountant and your manager has asked you to correct a corporation tax computation which has been prepared by the managing director of Naive Ltd. The corporation tax computation is for the year ended 31 March 2023 and contains a significant number of errors:

Naive Ltd – Corporation tax computation for the year ended 31 March 2023

	£
Trading profit (working 1)	372,900
Loan interest received (working 2)	32,100
	405,000
Corporation tax (405,000 at 19%)	76,950

Workings

(1) *Trading profit*

	£
Operating profit before interest and taxation	287,220
Depreciation	15,740
Donations to political parties	400
Qualifying charitable donations	900
Accountancy	2,300
Legal fees in connection with the issue of loan notes (the loan was used to finance the company's trading activities)	5,700

	£
Entertaining suppliers	3,600
Entertaining employees	1,700
Gifts to customers (pens costing £40 each and displaying Naive Ltd's name)	920
Gifts to customers (food hampers costing £45 each and displaying Naive Ltd's name)	1,650
Capital allowances (working 3)	65,460
Trading profit	385,590

(2) *Loan interest received*

	£
Loan interest receivable	32,800
Accrued at 1 April 2021	10,600
Accrued at 31 March 2022	(11,300)
Loan interest received	32,100

The loan was made for non-trading purposes.

(3) *Capital allowances*

	Main pool	*Car*	*Special rate pool*	*Allowances*
	£	£	£	£
Written down value (WDV) brought forward	12,400		13,600	
Additions				
Machinery	42,300			
Car [1]	13,800			
Car [2]	–	14,000		
	68,500			
Annual investment allowance (AIA)	(68,500)			68,500
Disposal proceeds			(9,300)	
			4,300	
Balancing allowance			(4,300)	(4,300)
Written down allowance (WDA) – 18%	–	(2,520)	× 50%	1,260
WDV carried forward	0	11,480		–
Total allowances				65,460

- Car [1] has a CO^2 emission rate of 40 grams per kilometre.
- Car [2] has a CO^2 emission rate of 125 grams per kilometre. This car is used by the sales manager and 50% of the mileage is for private journeys.

- All of the items included in the special rate pool at 1 April 2021 were sold for £9,300 during the year ended 31 March 2022. The original cost of these items was £16,200.

Required

Prepare a corrected version of Naive Ltd's corporation tax computation for the year ended 31 March 2023.

Note. Your calculations should commence with the operating profit before interest and taxation figure of £287,220, and you should indicate by the use of zero (0) any items in the computation of the trading profit for which no adjustment is required. **(12 marks)**

(b) The managing director of Naive Ltd understands that the company will have to file its self-assessment corporation tax returns online, and that the supporting accounts and tax computations will have to be filed using the inline eXtensible Business Reporting Language (iXBRL). The managing director is concerned with how the company will be able to produce the documents in this format.

Required

Explain the options available to Naive Ltd regarding the production of accounts and tax computations in the iXBRL format. **(3 marks)**

(Total = 15 marks)

Answers

DO NOT TURN THIS PAGE UNTIL YOU HAVE COMPLETED THE MOCK EXAM

Mock exam 2

A plan of attack

If this were the real Taxation (TX – UK) exam and you had been told to turn over and begin, what would be going through your mind?

Perhaps you're having a panic. You've spent most of your study time on income tax and corporation tax computations (because that's what your tutor/BPP Workbook told you to do), plus a selection of other topics, and you're really not sure that you know enough. So calm down. Spend the first few moments or so **looking at the exam** and develop a **plan of attack**.

Looking through the exam.

Section A contains **15 Objective Test (OT) questions** each worth **2 marks**. These will cover all sections of the syllabus. Some you may find easy and some more difficult. For example, Question 13 on keeping records for tax should be easy marks and you just need to pick the right answers from the table. Don't spend a lot of time on anything you really don't know. For multiple choice questions you are not penalised for wrong answers, so you should answer all of them. If all else fails – guess!

Section B contains **three OT Case** scenarios. These each have **five questions** each worth **2 marks**. Make sure you read the scenario carefully before you start to answer the OTQs.

- **Questions 16 to 20** are about chargeable gains for individuals.In Question 19, note that you are asked for the amount of CGT which could have been **saved** if Marlon had transferred 50% ownership of the residential property to Alvita prior to its disposal so you need to think about how CGT is computed for Alvita bearing in mind that she has no taxable income or other disposals in the year.
- **Questions 21 to 25** concern inheritance tax (IHT). In Question 24, you need to consider how the seven year accumulation period works.
- **Questions 26 to 30** test topics in value added tax (VAT).For Question 26, you need to think about the tax point for the contract in part (2).

In Section C you have three constructed response (long) questions:

- **Question 31** for **10 marks** is about the potential tax saving by incorporating a sole trader business. You need to work out the individual's income tax, the national insurance contributions for an employee and corporation tax.
- **Question 32** for **15 marks** is an income tax computation and also deals with choice of accounting date.
- **Question 33** for **15 marks** is a corporation tax question and includes capital allowances. Part (b) is about how a company files its corporation tax return and supporting accounts.

Allocating your time

BPP's advice is always allocate your time **according to the marks for the question** in total and for the parts of the question. But **use common sense**.If you're confronted by an OTQ on a topic of which you know nothing, pick an answer and move on. Use the time to pick up marks elsewhere.

After the exam...**Forget about it**!

And don't worry if you found the exam difficult. More than likely other candidates will too. If this were the real thing you would need to **forget** the exam the minute you left the exam hall and **think about the next one**. Or, if it's the last one, **celebrate**!

Section A

1 The correct answer is: £4,962

	£
£(50,270 – 12,570) = £37,700 × 10.25%	3,864
£(84,050 – 50,270) = £33,780 × 3.25%	1,098
Class 4 NICs	4,962

The answer £5,126 includes Class 2 NIC. The answer £7,327 uses 10.25% throughout. The answer £3,864 is just the 10.25% band liability.

2 The correct answers are:

- Reporting under the money laundering regulations
- Advising the client to make disclosure

Your firm should advise the client to make disclosure. Your firm should make a report under the money laundering regulations.

You should not inform HMRC of the non-disclosure. Your firm also should not warn the client that it will be reporting the non-disclosure as this might constitute the criminal offence of 'tipping-off'.

3 £ 8,270

	£
Personal allowance	12,570
Less restriction £(109,400 – 800 – 100,000) = £8,600/2	(4,300)
Restricted personal allowance	8,270

4 The correct answer is: £135,000

	£
Lower of:	
Taxable total profits of Shallow Ltd for the corresponding accounting period (1.7.22 – 31.3.23)£224,000 × 9/12	168,000
Losses of Halo Ltd for the corresponding accounting period £180,000 × 9/12	135,000

5 The correct answer is: Four instalments of £46,075

Profits threshold £1,500,000/2 (related 51% company)	£750,000
Sizeable Ltd was therefore a large company in both years.	
Each instalment for the year to 31 March 2023 is £(970,000 @ 19%) = 184,300/4	£46,075

The answer nine instalments of £15,580 and a balancing payment of £28,500 is based on the previous accounting period's profits with each of the instalments being 10% of the liability. This is the VAT annual accounting schedule of payments. The answer instalments of £38,950 and a balancing payment of £28,500 again is based on the previous year's profits, similar to self-assessment for individuals. The answer £184,300 is the full amount of corporation tax which would be payable if Sizeable Ltd was not a large company.

6 £975

Interest runs from due date (1 October 2023) to the date of payment (31 March 2024) which is six months.

£60,000 × 3.25% × 6/12	£975

The answer £2,438 is for a 15-month period from 31 January 2023 to 31 March 2024. The answer £325 is for a two-month period from 31 January 2024 to 31 March 2024. The answer £488 is for a three-month period from the filing date of 1 January 2024 to 31 March 2024.

7 The correct answer is: £4,500

	£
Proceeds	8,700
Less cost	(3,800)
Gain	4,900

The maximum gain is 5/3 × £(8,700 – 6,000) = £4,500.

The chargeable gain is the lower of £4,900 and £4,500, so it is £4,500.

The answer £0 assumes that this is an exempt chattel.

8 £ 118,750

	£
Net chargeable transfer	800,000
Less nil rate band	(325,000)
	475,000
IHT £475,000 × 20/80 (donor paid tax)	118,750

9 The correct answers are:

£400 to Alfred		**NOT EXEMPT**
£140 to Minnie		**NOT EXEMPT**
A further £280 to Minnie		**NOT EXEMPT**
£175 to Winifred	**EXEMPT**	

Outright gifts to individuals totalling £250 or less per donee in any one tax year are exempt under the small gifts exemption. The £400 gift to Alfred is therefore not exempt under the small gifts exemption. If gifts total more than £250 the whole amount is chargeable. Therefore, neither of the gifts to Minnie which total £(140 + 280) = £420 are exempt under the small gifts exemption. The gift of £175 to Winifred is exempt under the small gifts exemption.

10 The correct answer is: £7,164

£(49,750 × 120/100) = 59,700 × 12% = £7,164

Under the flat rate scheme, a business calculates VAT by applying a fixed percentage to its tax inclusive turnover. However, the business cannot reclaim any input tax suffered.

11 The correct answers are:

- A car suitable for private use
- A UK government security (gilt)

A wasting chattel is exempt, as is a chattel sold for gross proceeds of £6,000 or less. Other chattels are chargeable assets. A house may be exempt if private residence relief applies but is otherwise a chargeable asset.

12 The correct answer is: £12,000

£(20,000 – 8,000) = £12,000

The answer £20,000 is the full ISA allowance. The answer £0 assumes that only one ISA can be opened in a tax year and so Winston cannot invest into a stocks and shares ISA having invested in a cash ISA. The answer £10,000 assumes that the ISA limit is divided equally between the two accounts.

13 The correct answers are:

Business records		**31 JANUARY 2029**
Non-business records		**31 JANUARY 2029**

Records must be retained until five years after the 31 January following the tax year where the taxpayer is in business. This applies to all of the records, not only the business records.

14 The correct answer is: £62,000

	£
Loss incurred in y/e 31.12.22	105,000
p/e 31.12.21	(43,000)
	62,000
y/e 31.8.21	
Lower of £96,000 × 8/12 = £64,000 and unused loss	(62,000)
C/f	0

Loss relief by deduction from total profits may be given by deduction from current period profits and from the previous 12 months. Therefore, relief can be given in the four-month period ended 31 December 2021 and for eight months of the year ended 31 August 2021.

The answer £64,000 is the time apportioned amount of profits. The answer £96,000 assumes that the earlier accounting period profits can be relieved first.

15 The correct answer is: 90 days

Nigel was not previously resident in the UK. He will be UK resident for 2022/23 with three UK ties if he spends at least 91 days in the UK during that tax year. Therefore, the maximum number of days that Nigel could spend in the UK during the tax year 2022/23 without being treated as UK resident for that year is 90 days.

Section B

Delroy and Marlon

Workbook references

Computing chargeable gains and computation of the CGT liability are covered in Chapter 13. Private residence relief is dealt with in Chapter 14. Business reliefs are the subject of Chapter 15.

Top Tips

Be careful to read all the information given in the scenario. In this case you were told that Grant had used his annual exempt amount, but that Alvita had not made any other disposals of assets during the year and so must still have her annual exempt amount available.

Easy Marks

There were easy marks in Question 16 for a basic gain computation leading to the calculation of CGT. Question 20 should have been quick and easy marks for identification of the correct statement.

16 The correct answer is: £43,000

	£
Ordinary shares in Dub Ltd	
Proceeds	240,000
Less cost	(25,000)
Gain	215,000
Less annual exempt amount (already used as stated in question)	(0)
Taxable gain	215,000
CGT: £215,000 × 20%	43,000

Tutorial note. The effect of the gift holdover relief election is that Grant effectively took over Delroy's original cost of £25,000.

Tutorial note. The disposal does not qualify for business asset disposal relief as Grant was neither an officer nor an employee of Dub Ltd and, in any case, had only owned the shares for just over two months (the minimum period for the conditions for the relief to be satisfied is two years).

The answer £21,500 assumes that business asset disposal relief applies to the disposal so the rate of tax is 10%. The answer £0 assumes this is an exempt disposal. The answer £40,540 deducts the annual exempt amount – read the question carefully!

17 The correct answers are:

- Business asset disposal relief would have been available.
- The cash gift would not have been a chargeable disposal.

Delroy's disposal would have qualified for business asset disposal relief because for at least two years prior to the disposal:

- Dub Ltd was Delroy's personal company as he owned at least 5% of the ordinary share capital
- Dub Ltd was a trading company
- Delroy was an officer or employee of Dub Ltd

There are no capital gains tax implications of a gift of cash.

18 The correct answer is: £114,800

	£
Residential property	
Proceeds	497,000
Less cost	(152,600)
Gain before PRR	344,400
Less PRR (W)	(229,600)
Gain after PRR	114,800

Working

One-third of the residential property was always used exclusively for business purposes, so the private residence relief exemption is restricted to £(344,400 × 2/3) = £229,600.

The answer £229,600 is the PRR. The answer £0 assumes this is an exempt disposal. The answer £344,400 is the gain before PRR.

19 The correct answer is: £7,214

		£
Annual exempt amount	£12,300 × 28%	3,444
Basic rate band	£37,700 × (28 – 18)%	3,770
Total tax saving		7,214

The 50% ownership of the house would have been transferred from Marlon to Alvita on a no gain, no loss basis. The effect of this is that 50% of the gain on disposal would accrue to Marlon and 50% to Alvita.

Transferring 50% ownership of the house to Alvita prior to its disposal would have enabled her annual exempt amount and basic rate tax band for 2022/23 to be utilised.

The answer £3,444 is just the annual exempt amount saving. The answer £3,770 is just the basic rate band saving. The answer £14,000 is the annual exempt amount and the basic rate band, all at 28%.

20 27 May 2023

The CGT on disposal of a residential property is due within 60 days of the disposal.

Opal

Workbook

Inheritance tax is cover in Chapter 18

Top tips

Try drawing a timeline and mark on it the date of Opal's death and the lifetime transfers. Then mark the date which is seven years before Opal's death. It will be clear that the lifetime transfer in 2013 falls more than seven years before Opal's death and is therefore exempt.

Easy marks

There were some easy marks for working out the IHT on the death estate in Question 23.

21 £ 656,000

	£	£
Property one	374,000	
Less repayment mortgage	(160,000)	
	442,000	214,000
Property two	0	442,000
Net value of two properties		656,000

22 The correct answers are:

- Personal loan from a bank of £22,400
- Funeral cost of £5,200

The promise to pay the nephew's legal fees is not deductible as it is not legally enforceable.

23 The correct answer is: £338,000

	£
Chargeable estate	950,000
105,000 (W) × 0%	0
845,000 × 40%	338,000
950,000	
IHT on death estate	338,000

Working

		£
Nil rate band at death		325,000
Less:	PET 14 August 2013	(0)
	PET 7 November 2022	(220,000)
Available nil rate band		105,000

The potentially exempt transfer on 14 August 2013 is exempt from inheritance tax as it was made more than seven years before 20 March 2023.

The answer £250,000 has an unrestricted nil rate band. The answer £378,000 assumes that the PET in 2013 becomes chargeable on Opal's death. The answer £335,600 deducts two annual exemptions from the gift in 2022.

24 £88,000

If Opal were to live for another seven years, then the potentially exempt transfer on 7 November 2022 would become exempt.

The inheritance tax payable in respect of her estate would therefore decrease by £(220,000 × 40%) = £88,000.

25 The correct answers are:

- The gifts must be habitual.
- Opal must have enough remaining income to maintain her normal standard of living.

ANSWERS

Glacier Ltd

Workbook references

Value added tax is covered in Chapters 24 and 25.

Top tips

The tax point is frequently examined and is relevant in Question 26. The basic tax point for a supply of services is the date when they are completed, but if a VAT invoice is issued or payment received before the basic tax point, then this becomes the actual tax point.

Easy marks

There were easy marks in Questions 28 and 29 concerning the default surcharge penalty.

26 £3,480

	£
Sales	
VAT registered customers £(44,600 – 35,200) = £9,400 × 20%	1,880
Additional contract (1 March 2023)	1,600
Output VAT	3,480

The tax point for the contract is when the VAT invoice was issued on 1 March 2023, which is earlier than both the basic tax point of 15 April and the receipt of cash on 31 March.

27 Glacier Ltd will include output VAT of £ 68

and input VAT of £ 120

on its VAT return for the quarter ended 31 March 2023 in respect of the managing director's company car.

Output VAT £406 × 20/120	£68
Input VAT £720 × 20/120	£120

28 The correct answer is: 5% of the VAT liability

Glacier Ltd was late in submitting VAT returns and paying the related VAT liability for two previous quarters. The late payment of VAT for the quarter ended 31 March 2023 will therefore result in a surcharge of 5% of the VAT liability for that period since this is the second default during the surcharge period.

29 The correct answer is: Submit four consecutive VAT returns on time and also pay the related VAT liabilities on time

30 Glacier Ltd will be required to issue a VAT invoice when a standard rated supply is made to a VAT registered customer .

Glacier Ltd will be required to issue a VAT invoice when a standard rated supply is made to a VAT registered customer.

Section C

ALL three questions are compulsory and MUST be attempted

31 Sarah

Workbook references

Employment income is covered in Chapter 3.

The income tax computation is the subject of Chapter 2.

National insurance contributions are dealt with in Chapter 12.

Corporation tax is covered in Chapter 19.

Top tips

Note 1 outlines the steps that you need to take to complete the question.

Easy marks

There were some easy marks for basic income tax and corporation tax computations.

Marking guide		Marks	
(a)	*Income tax liability*		
	Director's remuneration	0.5	
	Dividends	0.5	
	Personal allowance	0.5	
	Basic rate on earnings	0.5	
	Nil rate on dividends	0.5	
	Basic rate on dividends	0.5	
	National insurance contributions		
	Class 1 employee	1	
	Class 1 employer	1	
	Corporation tax		
	Trading profit	0.5	
	Director's remuneration	0.5	
	Employer's Class 1 NIC	0.5	
	Corporation tax	0.5	
	Total tax cost if incorporates	0.5	
	Additional tax	0.5	
			8
(b)	Salary attracting NICs	1	
	Restrict salary, take more dividends	1	
			2
Total			10

(a) **Sarah – Income tax liability 2022/23**

	Non-savings income	*Dividend income*	*Total income*
	£	£	£
Director's remuneration	30,000		
Dividends	—	10,000	
Net income	30,000	10,000	40,000
Less personal allowance	(12,570)	—	
Taxable income	17,430	10,000	27,430

Tax	
Non-savings income	
£17,430 @ 20%	3,486
Dividend income	
£2,000 @ 0%	0
£8,000 (10,000 – 2,000) @ 8.75%	700
Income tax liability	4,186

Sarah – National insurance contributions 2022/23

	£
Employee Class 1 £(30,000 – 12,570) = 17,430 @ 13.25%	2,309
Employer Class 1 £(30,000 – 9,100) = 20,900 @ 15.05%	3,145

Corporation tax liability of the new limited company for the year ended 5 April 2023

		£
Trading profit		50,000
Less:	Director's remuneration	(30,000)
	Employer's Class 1 NIC	(3,145)
Taxable trading profit		16,855
Corporation tax £16,855 @ 19%		3,202

The total tax and NIC cost if Sarah incorporates her business is £12,842 (4,186 + 2,309 + 3,145 + 3,202).

Therefore, if Sarah incorporated her business there would be additional tax and NIC payable as there would be an increase of £1,355 (12,842 – 11,487) compared to continuing on a self-employed basis.

Using the spreadsheet software in your CBE exam, your answer might look like this:

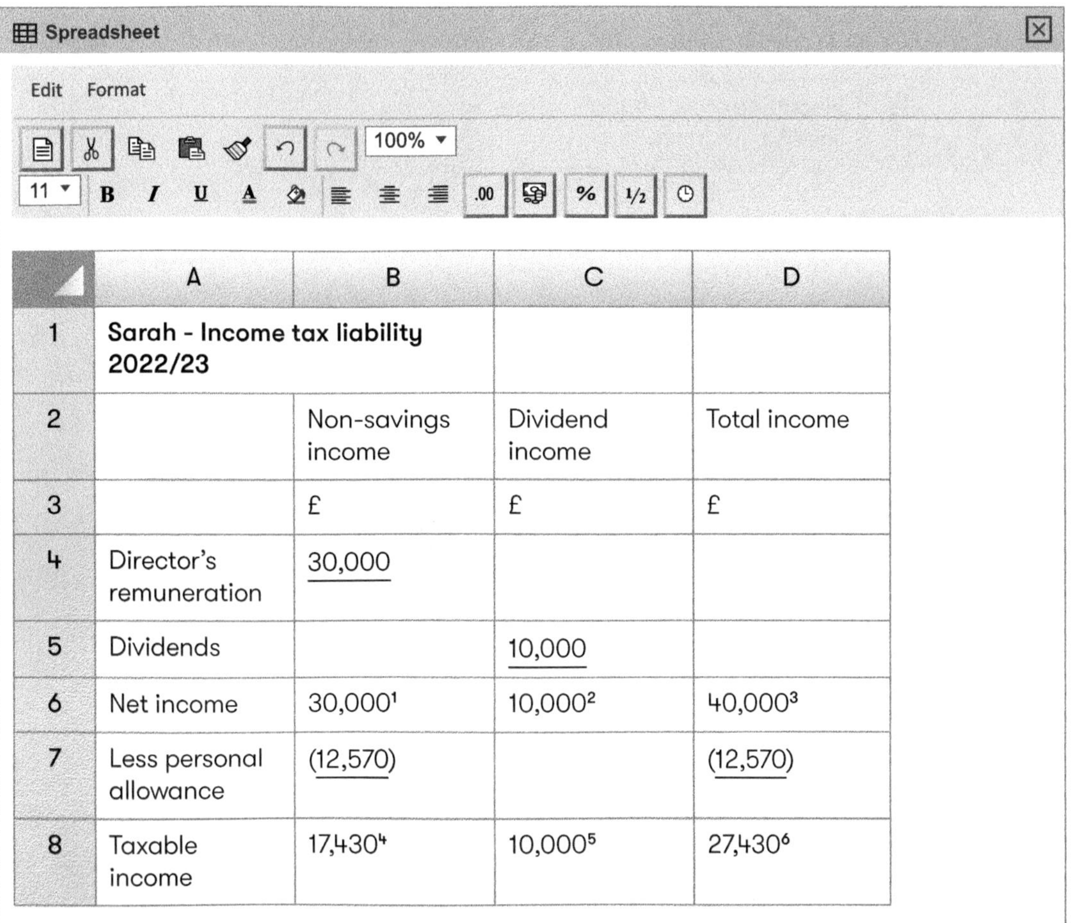

	A	B	C	D
1	**Sarah - Income tax liability 2022/23**			
2		Non-savings income	Dividend income	Total income
3		£	£	£
4	Director's remuneration	30,000		
5	Dividends		10,000	
6	Net income	30,000[1]	10,000[2]	40,000[3]
7	Less personal allowance	(12,570)		(12,570)
8	Taxable income	17,430[4]	10,000[5]	27,430[6]

[1] =SUM(B4:B5)

[2] =SUM(C4:C5)

[3] =SUM(B6:C6)

[4] =SUM(B6:B7)

[5] =SUM(C6:C7)

[6] =SUM(D6:D7)

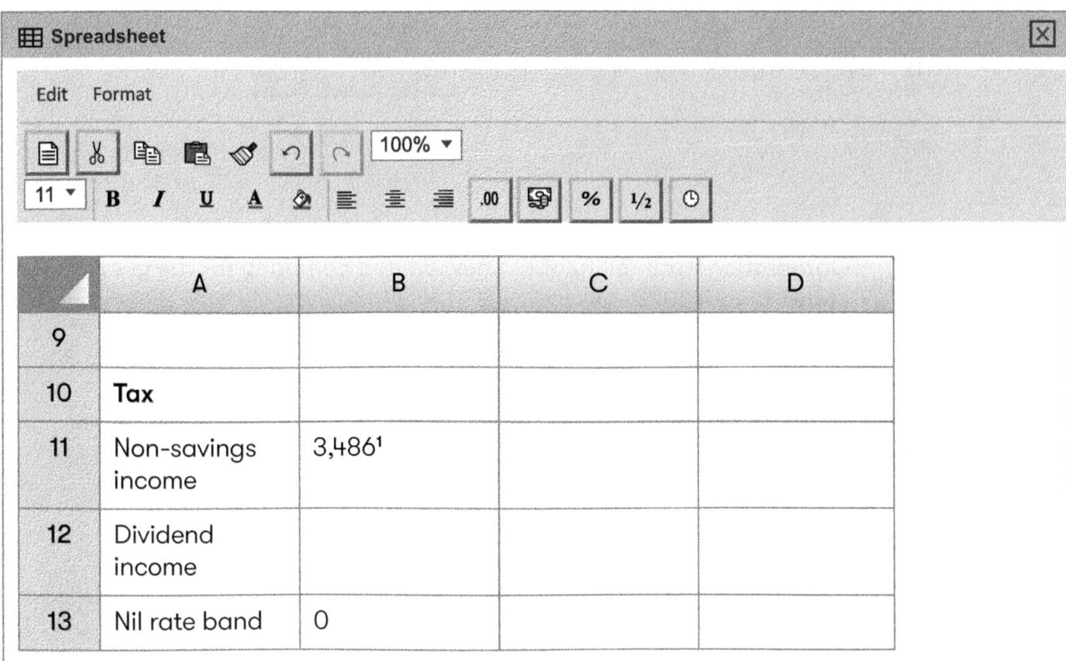

	A	B	C	D
9				
10	**Tax**			
11	Non-savings income	3,486[1]		
12	Dividend income			
13	Nil rate band	0		

	A	B	C	D
14		700[2]		
15	Income tax liability	4,186[3]		

[1] =B8*20%

[2] =(C8-2000)*8.75%

[3] =SUM(B11:B14)

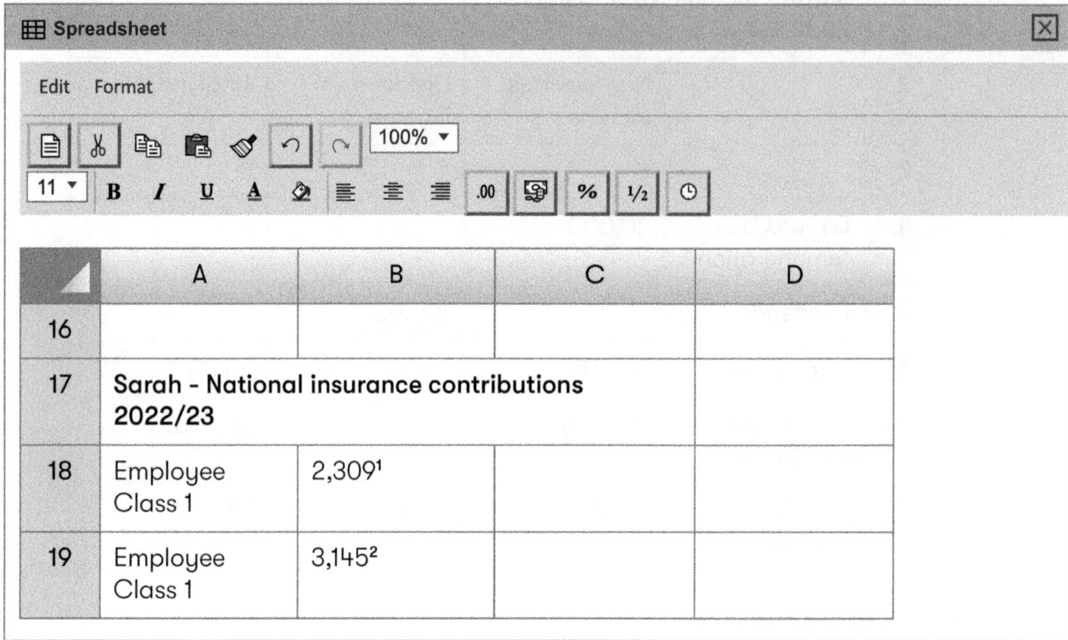

	A	B	C	D
16				
17	**Sarah - National insurance contributions 2022/23**			
18	Employee Class 1	2,309[1]		
19	Employee Class 1	3,145[2]		

[1] =(30000-12570)*13.25%

[2] =(30000-9100)*15.05%

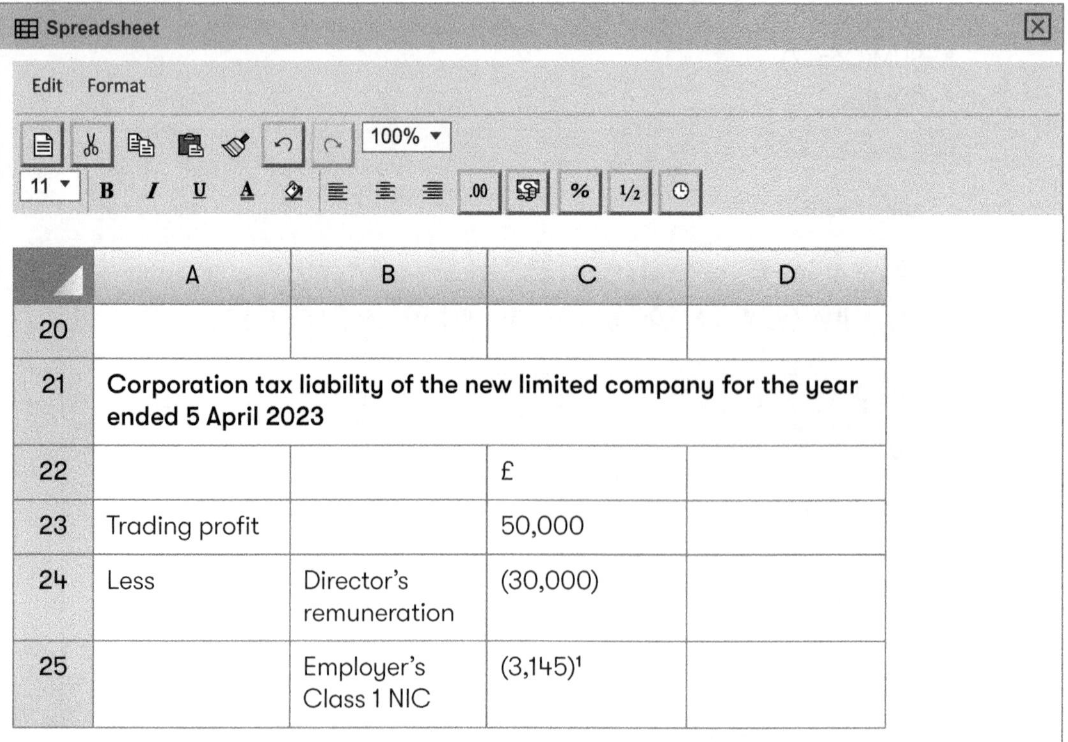

	A	B	C	D
20				
21	**Corporation tax liability of the new limited company for the year ended 5 April 2023**			
22			£	
23	Trading profit		50,000	
24	Less	Director's remuneration	(30,000)	
25		Employer's Class 1 NIC	(3,145)[1]	

	A	B	C	D
26	Taxable trading profit		16,855[2]	
27	Corporation tax		3,202[3]	
28			£	
29			12,842[4]	
30	Therefore, if Sarah incorporated her business there would be additional tax and NIC payable as there would be an increase of £1,355 (12,842 – 11,487) compared to continuing on a self-employed basis.			

[1] =-B19

[2] =SUM(C23:C25)

[3] =C26*19%

[4] =B15+B18+B19+C27

(b)

The relatively high tax cost of Sarah incorporating her business arises because of her salary attracting both employee and employer NICs.

Restricting the salary to around £8,000 and taxing a correspondingly higher amount of dividends, would significantly reduce her overall tax cost.

32 Simon

Workbook references

Employment income is dealt with in Chapters 3 and 4.

Trading income is covered in Chapter 7 and capital allowances in Chapter 8.

Property income is the subject of Chapter 6.

The computation of taxable income is covered in Chapter 2.

Assessable trading income is dealt with in Chapter 9.

Top tips

You should use the proforma taxable income computation and deal with more complicated computations in workings linked to the main computation.

Easy marks

There were some easy marks for computing employment benefits in part (a).

Marking guide		Marks
(a) Employment income	0.5	
Salary	0.5	
Living accommodation		
Annual value	1	
Additional benefit – market value	0.5	
Additional benefit – limit	0.5	
Additional benefit – benefit	0.5	
Furniture	1	
Loan benefit	1	
Trading income		
Accounts profit	0.5	
Capital allowances – addition	0.5	
Capital allowances – WDA	1.5	
Salary paid to Art	1	
Profit share	0.5	
Trading income 2022/23	1	
Property business income		
Rent receivable	0.5	
Council tax	0.5	
Furniture	1.5	
Personal allowance	0.5	
		13
(b) Payment of tax delayed	1	
Calculation of profits in advance of end of tax year	1	
		2
Total		15

(a) Simon – Taxable income 2022/23

	£
Employment income	
Salary	23,940
Living accommodation – annual value	4,600
Living accommodation – additional benefit (W1)	1,360
Living accommodation – furniture £9,400 × 20%	1,880
Loan benefit £84,000 × 2.0% × 4/12	560
	32,340
Trading income (W2)	8,220

	£
Property business income (W4)	5,940
Net income	46,500
Less personal allowance	(12,570)
Taxable income	33,930

Workings

1 *Living accommodation – additional benefit*

	£
Market value when first provided to Simon	143,000
Less limit	(75,000)
	68,000
Additional benefit £68,000 × 2.0%	1,360

Tutorial note. Where the property was acquired by the employer more than six years before first being provided to the employee, the market value when first so provided is used as the cost of providing the living accommodation.

2 *Trading income*

Simon's share of the partnership's trading profit for the period ended 30 April 2023 is £10,960 calculated as follows:

	£
Trading profit	29,700
Less capital allowances (W3)	(300)
	29,400
Less salary paid to Art £6,000 × 4/12	(2,000)
	27,400
Profit share £27,400 × 40%	10,960
Simon's trading income 2022/23 £10,960 × 3/4	8,220

Tutorial note. Simon's trading income for 2022/23 is for the period 1 January 2023 to 5 April 2023 as this is his first year of trading and the actual basis applies.

3 *Capital allowances*

Four-month period to 30 April 2023	*Car*		*Allowances*
	£		£
Addition	25,000		
WDA @ 6% × 4/12	(500)	× 60%	300
WDA c/f	24,500		

Tutorial note. The partnership's car has CO_2 emissions over 50 grams per kilometre and therefore qualifies for writing down allowances at the rate of 6%.

4 *Property business income*

	£	£
Rent received £660 × 12		7,920
Council tax and water rates	1,320	
Replacement furniture relief		
Washing machine £(730 – 70)	660	
		(1,980)
Property business income		5,940

> **Tutorial note.** No relief is given for that part of the cost of the washer-dryer which represents an improvement over the original washing machine. Relief is therefore restricted to the cost of a similar washing machine. This figure is then reduced by the proceeds from the sale of the original washing machine.

Using the spreadsheet software in your CBE exam, your answer might look like this:

Spreadsheet

Edit Format

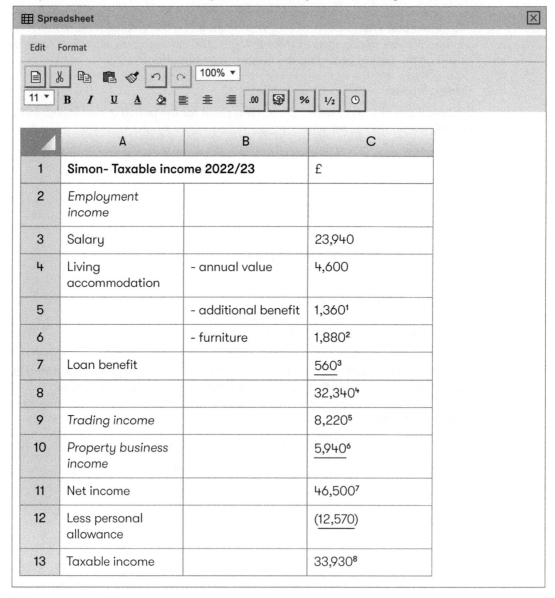

	A	B	C
1	**Simon- Taxable income 2022/23**		£
2	*Employment income*		
3	Salary		23,940
4	Living accommodation	- annual value	4,600
5		- additional benefit	1,360[1]
6		- furniture	1,880[2]
7	Loan benefit		560[3]
8			32,340[4]
9	*Trading income*		8,220[5]
10	*Property business income*		5,940[6]
11	Net income		46,500[7]
12	Less personal allowance		(12,570)
13	Taxable income		33,930[8]

[1] =(143000-75000)*2%

[2] =9400*20%

[3] =84000*2%*(4/12)

[4] =SUM(C3:C7)

[5] =C21

[6] =C27

[7] =SUM(C8:C10)

[8] =SUM(C11:C12)

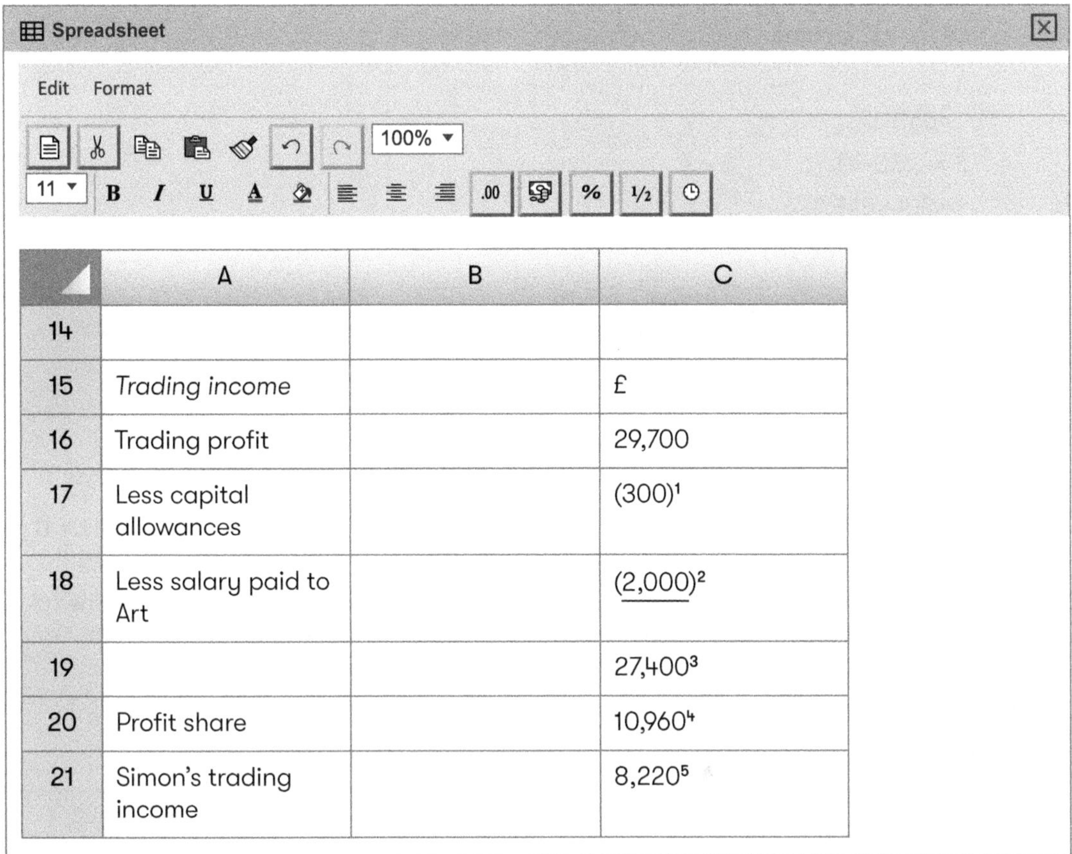

	A	B	C
14			
15	*Trading income*		£
16	Trading profit		29,700
17	Less capital allowances		(300)[1]
18	Less salary paid to Art		(2,000)[2]
19			27,400[3]
20	Profit share		10,960[4]
21	Simon's trading income		8,220[5]

[1] =25000*6%*(4/12)*60%

[2] =6000*(4/12)

[3] =SUM(C16:C18)

[4] =C19*40%

[5] =C20*(3/4)

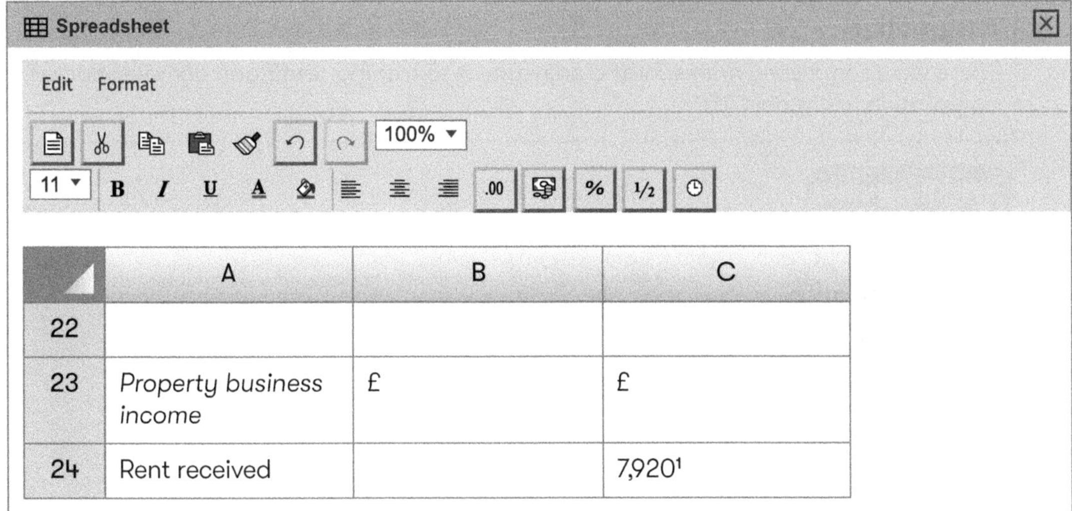

	A	B	C
22			
23	*Property business income*	£	£
24	Rent received		7,920[1]

	A	B	C
25	Council tax and water rates	(1,320)	
26	Replacement furniture relief	(660)[2]	(1,980)[3]
27	Property business income		5,940[4]

[1] =660*12

[2] =-(730-70)

[3] =SUM(B25:B26)

[4] =SUM(C24:C26)

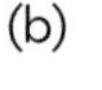

(b)

The interval between earning profits and paying the related tax liability will be 11 months longer. This can be particularly beneficial where profits are rising.

It will be possible to calculate taxable profits well in advance of the end of the tax year, making it much easier to implement tax planning and make pension contributions.

33 Naive Ltd

Workbook references

The computation of taxable total profits and the computation of the corporation tax liability are covered in Chapter 19. The adjustment to trading profits is dealt with in Chapter 7 and capital allowances in Chapter 8.

Top tips

The best approach to this style of question is to start new computations using the information given in the question, rather than trying to correct the wrong computations.

Easy marks

There were some easy marks for the adjustment to trading profit and computation of corporation tax in part (a).

Marking guide	**Marks**
(a) *Trading profit*	
Depreciation	0.5
Donations to political parties	0.5
Qualifying charitable donations	0.5
Accountancy	0.5

Legal fees	0.5	
Entertaining suppliers	0.5	
Entertaining employees	0.5	
Gift to customers – pens	0.5	
Gift to customers – food hampers	0.5	
Capital allowances brought from working	0.5	
Capital allowances		
WDV brought forward	1	
Annual investment allowance	1	
Addition – motor car [1]	0.5	
Addition – car [2]	0.5	
Disposal	0.5	
WDA @ 18%	0.5	
WDA @ 6%	1	
Loan interest	1	
Qualifying charitable donations	0.5	
Corporation tax	0.5	
		12
(b) HMRC software automatically to produce in iXBRL	1	
Other software automatically to produce in iXBRL	1	
Tagging services and software used by Naive Ltd to tag	1	
		3
Total		15

(a) **Naive Ltd – Corporation tax computation for the year ended 31 March 2023**

	£
Trading profit (W1)	248,706
Loan interest	32,800
Total profits	281,506
Less qualifying charitable donations	(900)
Taxable total profits	280,606
Corporation tax	
£280,606 × 19%	53,315

Workings

1 *Trading profit for the year ended 31 March 2023*

	£
Operating profit before interest and taxation	287,220
Add: Depreciation	15,740
Donations to political parties	400
Qualifying charitable donations	900

ANSWERS

	£
Accountancy	0
Legal fees	0
Entertaining suppliers	3,600
Entertaining employees	0
Gifts to customers – pens	0
Gifts to customers – food hampers	1,650
	309,510
Less capital allowances (W2)	(60,804)
Adjusted trading profit	248,706

2 *Capital allowances*

	FYA	*Main pool*	*Special rate pool*	*Allowances*
	£	£	£	£
WDV brought forward		12,400	13,600	
AIA additions				
Machinery (£42,300 × 130%)	54,990			
FYA @ 130%	(54,990)			54,990
Transfer to pool	0	0		
Non-AIA additions				
Car [1]		13,800		
Car [2]			14,000	
Disposal				
Special rate pool items		—	(9,300)	
		26,200	18,300	
WDA @ 18%		(4,716)		4,716
WDA @ 6%			(1,098)	1,098
WDV carried forward		21,484	17,202	—
Allowances				60,804

Tutorial note. Car [1] has CO_2 emissions between 1 and 50 grams per kilometre and therefore qualifies for writing down allowances at the rate of 18%. Cars do not qualify for the AIA.

Tutorial note. Car [2] has CO_2 emissions over 50 grams per kilometre and therefore qualifies for writing down allowances at the rate of 6%. The private use of the motor car is irrelevant since such usage will be assessed on the employee as a benefit.

Using the spreadsheet software in your CBE exam, your answer might look like this:

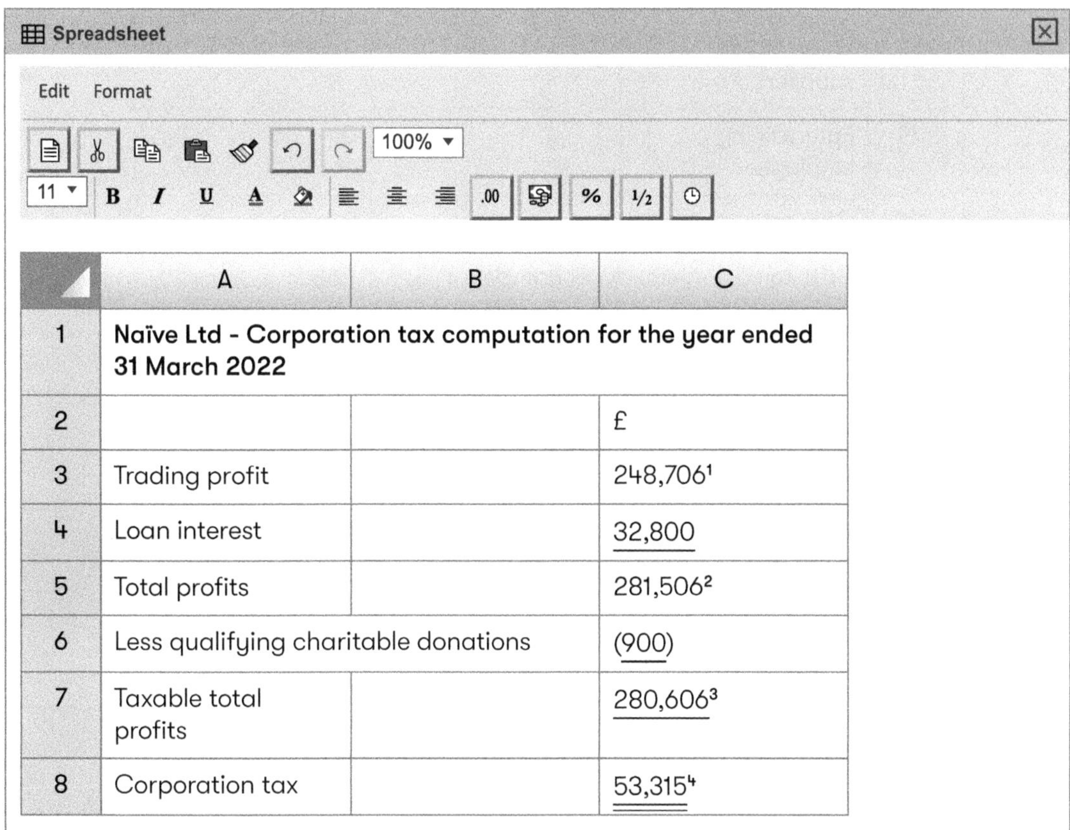

	A	B	C
1	**Naïve Ltd - Corporation tax computation for the year ended 31 March 2022**		
2			£
3	Trading profit		248,706[1]
4	Loan interest		32,800
5	Total profits		281,506[2]
6	Less qualifying charitable donations		(900)
7	Taxable total profits		280,606[3]
8	Corporation tax		53,315[4]

[1] =C24

[2] =SUM(C3:C4)

[3] =SUM(C5:C6)

[4] =C7*19%

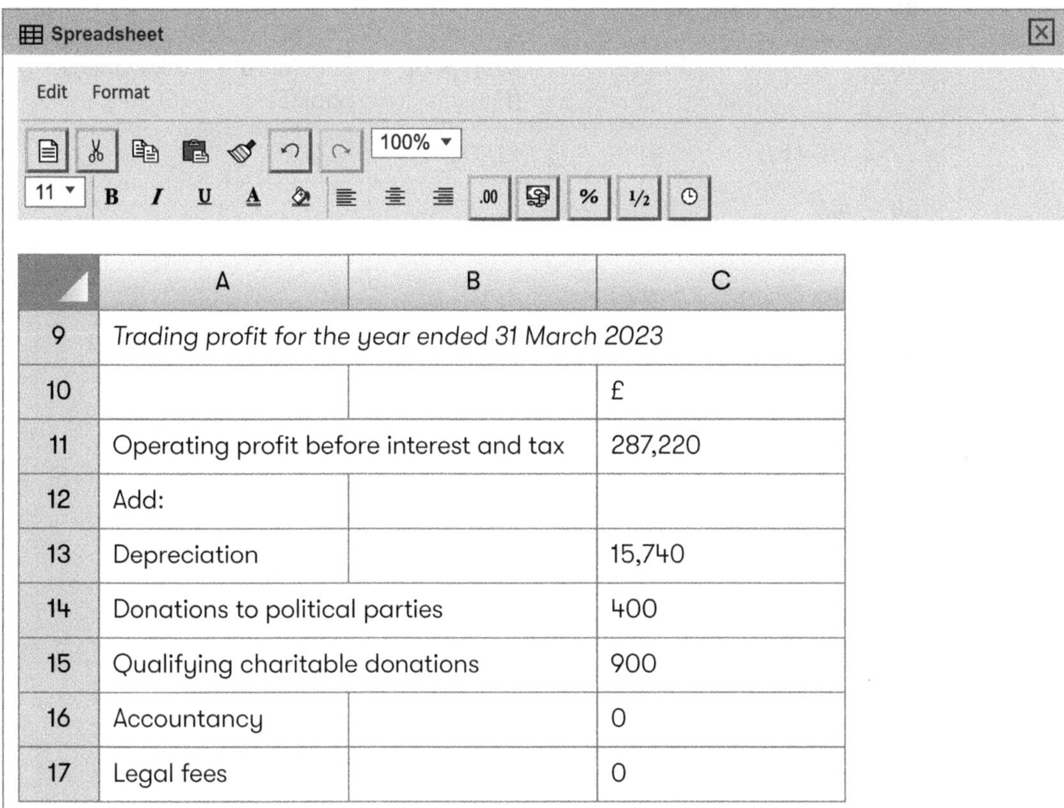

	A	B	C
9	*Trading profit for the year ended 31 March 2023*		
10			£
11	Operating profit before interest and tax		287,220
12	Add:		
13	Depreciation		15,740
14	Donations to political parties		400
15	Qualifying charitable donations		900
16	Accountancy		0
17	Legal fees		0

	A	B	C
18	Entertaining suppliers		3,600
19	Entertaining employees		0
20	Gifts to customers - pens		0
21	Gifts to customers - food hampers		1,650
22			309,510[1]
23	Less capital allowances		(60,804)[2]
24	Adjusted trading profit		248,706[3]

[1] =SUM(C11:C21)

[2] =E41

[3] =SUM(C22:C23)

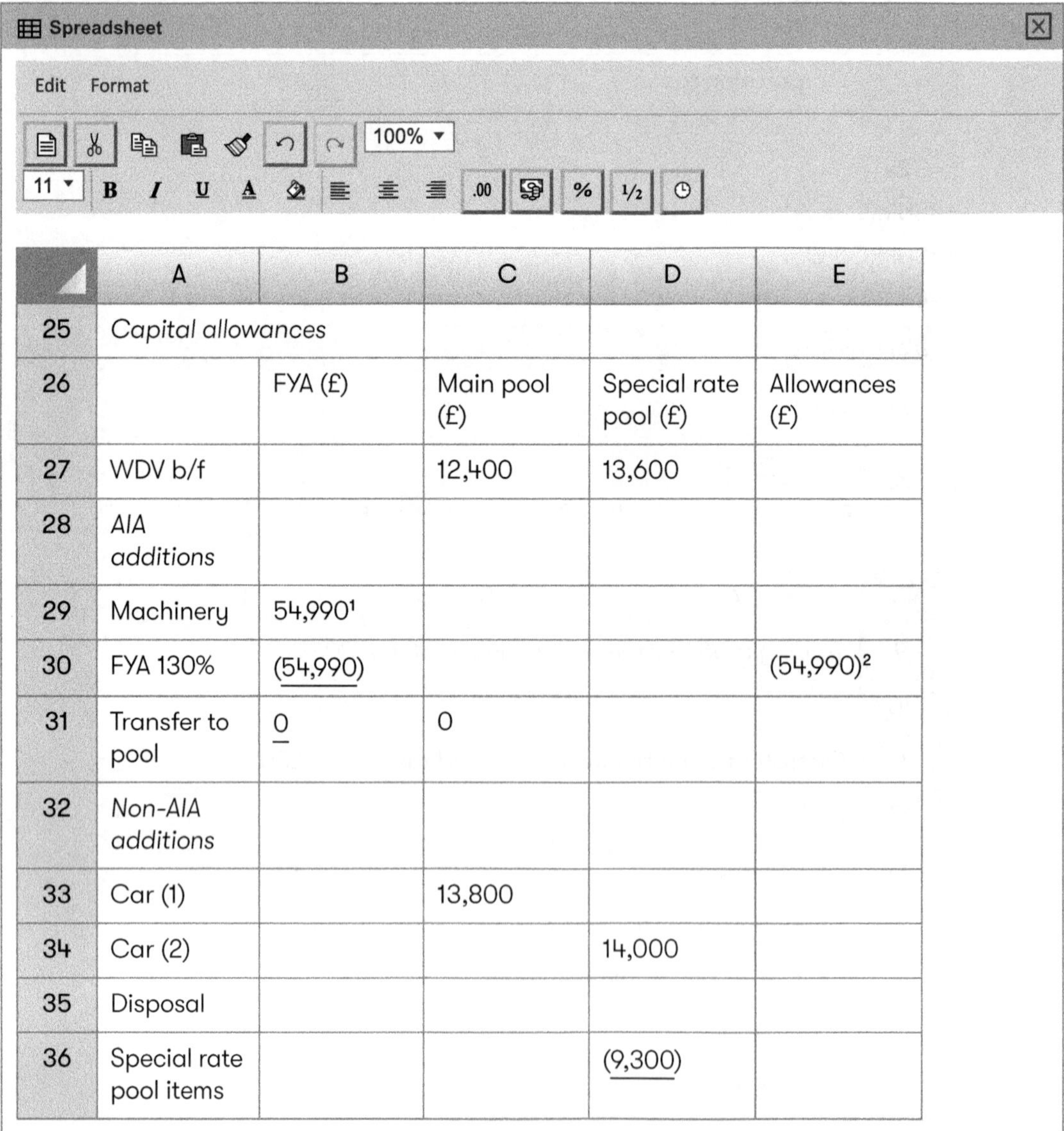

Spreadsheet

Edit Format

	A	B	C	D	E
25	*Capital allowances*				
26		FYA (£)	Main pool (£)	Special rate pool (£)	Allowances (£)
27	WDV b/f		12,400	13,600	
28	*AIA additions*				
29	Machinery	54,990[1]			
30	FYA 130%	(54,990)			(54,990)[2]
31	Transfer to pool	0	0		
32	*Non-AIA additions*				
33	Car (1)		13,800		
34	Car (2)			14,000	
35	Disposal				
36	Special rate pool items			(9,300)	

	A	B	C	D	E
37			26,200[3]	18,300[4]	
38	WDA@18%		(4,716)[5]		(4,716)[6]
39	WDA@6%			(1,098)[7]	(1,098)[8]
40	WDV c/f		21,484[9]	17,202[10]	
41	Allowances				(60,804)[11]

[1] =42300*130%

[2] =SUM(B30:D30)

[3] =SUM(C27:C36)

[4] =SUM(D27:D36)

[5] =-C37*18%

[6] =C38

[7] =-D37*6%

[8] =D39

[9] =SUM(C37:C39)

[10] =SUM(D37:D39)

[11] =SUM(E27:E40)

(b)

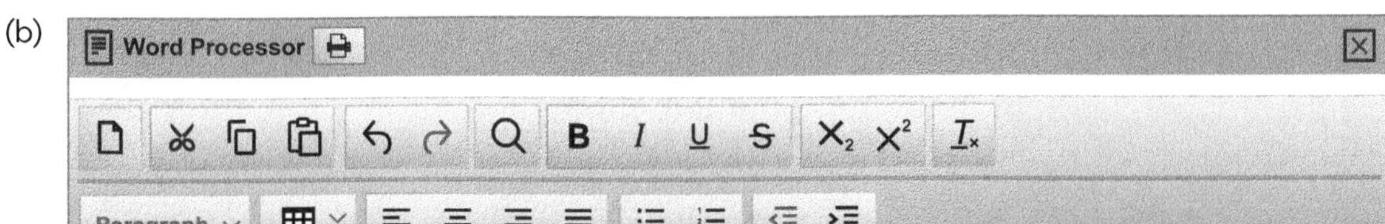

If Naive Ltd has straightforward accounts, it could use the software provided by HM Revenue & Customs. This automatically produces accounts and tax computations in the iXBRL format.

Alternatively, other software which automatically produces iXBRL accounts and computations could be used.

A tagging service could be used to apply the appropriate tags to the accounts and tax computations, or Naive Ltd could use software to tag documents itself.

ACCA

Taxation (TX - UK)

Mock Exam 3

December 2016 exam updated to FA 2022

Questions	
Time allowed	3 hours
This exam is divided into three sections: Section A - ALL 15 questions are compulsory and MUST be attempted. Section B - ALL 15 questions are compulsory and MUST be attempted. Section C - ALL THREE questions are compulsory and MUST be attempted.	

DO NOT OPEN THIS EXAM UNTIL YOU ARE READY TO START UNDER EXAMINATION CONDITIONS

Mock exam 3

Section A

ALL 15 questions are compulsory and MUST be attempted

1 Emil is registered for value added tax (VAT). For the quarter ended 31 March 2023, the input VAT incurred on his purchases and expenses included the following:

	£
Entertaining overseas customers	320
Purchase of new office equipment	1,250
Purchase of a new car for business and private use by one of Emil's employees	3,000

What is the amount of input VAT recoverable by Emil in the quarter ended 31 March 2023 in respect of the entertaining, office equipment and car?

£ [ ] **(2 marks)**

2 Acasta Ltd owns 75% of the ordinary share capital of Barge Ltd and 100% of the ordinary share capital of Coracle Ltd. Barge Ltd owns 75% of the ordinary share capital of Dhow Ltd. Coracle Ltd owns 51% of the ordinary share capital of Eight Ltd.

Which companies, along with Coracle Ltd, are within Acasta Ltd's chargeable gains group?

- O Barge Ltd, Dhow Ltd and Eight Ltd
- O Barge Ltd only
- O Barge Ltd and Dhow Ltd only
- O None of the other companies **(2 marks)**

3 Nadia died on 13 February 2004, leaving an estate valued at £275,400 for inheritance tax purposes. Nadia left 50% of her estate to her son and 50% to her husband, Tareq.

Tareq subsequently died on 17 January 2023. Tareq did not own a main residence at the date of his death.

Neither Nadia nor Tareq made any lifetime gifts.

The inheritance nil rate band for the tax year 2003/04 was £255,000.

What is the maximum available nil rate band which can be used when calculating the inheritance tax payable in respect of Tareq's estate?

- O £500,500
- O £474,500
- O £442,300
- O £462,700 **(2 marks)**

4 Habib purchased a copyright on 30 April 2006 for £31,320. The remaining life of the copyright at the date of purchase was 30 years. On 30 April 2022, Habib sold the copyright for £27,900.

What is Habib's chargeable gain or allowable loss for the tax year 2022/23 in respect of the disposal of the copyright?

- O (£3,420)
- O £11,196
- O £0
- O £13,284

(2 marks)

5 Which of the following is the correct definition of an extra-statutory concession?

- O A provision for the relaxation of the strict application of the law where it would lead to anomalies or cause hardship
- O Supplementary information providing additional detail in relation to the general principles set out in legislation
- O HM Revenue & Customs' interpretation of tax legislation
- O Guidance provided to HM Revenue & Customs' staff in interpreting and applying tax legislation

(2 marks)

6 Complete the following sentence relating to the length of time a sole trader is required to keep their accounting records after the end of a tax year in which a self-assessment tax return has been completed.

A sole trader is required to keep their accounting records for (1) ▼ months after the (2) ▼

Pull down list 1

- 12
- 60

Pull down list 2

- 31 January that follows the end of the tax year
- End of the tax year

(2 marks)

7 Sanjay commenced trading on 1 January 2022 and prepared his first set of accounts for the six-month period ended 30 June 2022. His second set of accounts were prepared for the year ended 30 June 2023.

Sanjay's tax-adjusted trading profits were:

Six-month period ended 30 June 2022	£10,500
Year ended 30 June 2023	£24,400

What are the class 4 national insurance contributions (NICs) which Sanjay should pay in respect of the tax year 2022/23?

- O £0
- O £1,038
- O £1,125
- O £1,213

(2 marks)

QUESTIONS

8 Modal Ltd lets out an unfurnished investment property.

During the year ended 31 December 2022, the company received rental income of £3,000 per month and paid electricity (relating to the rental property) of £200 per month. The electricity payment for December 2022 was not paid until 30 January 2023.

Modal Ltd also paid interest of £1,200 per month on a loan taken out to finance the purchase of the rental property.

What amount of property business income will be included in Modal Ltd's corporation tax computation for the year ended 31 December 2022?

- O £33,600
- O £19,200
- O £33,800
- O £19,400

(2 marks)

9 Which of the following will NOT cause Harper to be treated as automatically UK resident for the tax year 2022/23?

- O Harper spending 192 days in the UK during the tax year 2022/23
- O Harper renting a house in the UK to live in and then occupying it (as her only home) throughout the tax year 2022/23
- O Harper accepting a 15-month contract for a full-time job in the UK on 6 April 2022
- O Harper's husband living in the UK throughout the tax year 2022/23 and Harper staying with him when she visits the UK

(2 marks)

10 Somily Ltd filed its self-assessment corporation tax return for the year ended 31 December 2022 on 15 March 2024.

What is the deadline for HM Revenue & Customs (HMRC) to start a compliance check enquiry into Somily Ltd's corporation tax return for the year ended 31 December 2022?

- O 31 December 2024
- O 31 January 2025
- O 15 March 2025
- O 30 April 2025

(2 marks)

11 On 6 April 2022, Melinda rented out a furnished room in her house to Jenny at a rent of £720 a month. Jenny continued to rent the room on the same terms until 5 July 2023.

Melinda continued to live in the house and paid for all of the living expenses, of which £175 a month related to the room rented out to Jenny.

What is Melinda's property income for the tax year 2022/23, assuming that any beneficial elections are made?

- O £1,140
- O £0
- O £6,540
- O £2,760

(2 marks)

12 Three unconnected companies have the following results for corporation tax purposes:

Company	*Current accounting period*	*Number of 51% group companies*	*Taxable total profits (TTP)*	*TTP for previous 12-month period*
			£	£
Asher Ltd	Year ended 31 March 2023	3	700,000	600,000
Barton Ltd	Four-month period ended 31 December 2022	0	600,000	1,600,000
Chelfry Ltd	Year ended 30 November 2022	0	1,600,000	1,400,000

All the companies have had the same number of 51% group companies for many years. None of the companies have received any dividends.

Which of the three companies will NOT have to pay corporation tax by quarterly instalments for the current accounting period?

- O Asher Ltd only
- O Barton Ltd only
- O Chelfry Ltd only
- O Barton Ltd and Chelfry Ltd only

(2 marks)

13 David had the following taxable income (after deduction of his personal allowance) for the tax year 2022/23:

Non-savings income	£8,500
Savings income	£2,400
Dividend income	£4,250

What is David's total income tax liability for the tax year 2022/23?

Pull down list

- £2,177
- £2,352
- £2,377
- £2,552

(2 marks)

14 Gita died on 17 May 2022. On the date of her death, she owned the following assets:

	£
Investment property	390,000
Chattels and cash	70,000
Shares held in an individual savings account (ISA)	60,000

At the date of her death, Gita owed income tax of £25,000 in respect of the tax year 2022/23.

Gita left £100,000 of her estate to her husband, with the remainder of the estate left to her daughter.

What is Gita's chargeable estate for inheritance tax purposes?

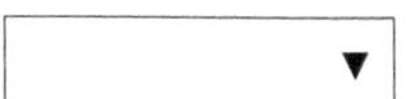

Pull down list

- £335,000
- £395,000
- £420,000
- £495,000

(2 marks)

15 Anika sold her entire holding of 3,000 £1 ordinary shares in Distribo Ltd, a trading company, to her son, Hemi, for £53,000 on 14 July 2022. The market value of the shares on that date was £98,000. Anika had purchased the 3,000 shares on 28 October 2007 for £41,500. She has never worked for Distribo Ltd.

Identify, by clicking on the relevant boxes in the table below, the amount of gift holdover relief (if any) that could be claimed in respect of the disposal of these shares, and Anika's chargeable gain for the tax year 2022/23 after taking account of any available relief.

Amount		
£0		Gift holdover relief
£11,500		Gain
£45,000		
£56,500		

(2 marks)

Section B

ALL 15 questions are compulsory and MUST be attempted

Zoyla

The following scenario relates to Questions 16 to 20.

Zoyla's capital gains tax (CGT) liability for the tax year 2022/23 is calculated as follows:

		Gain
		£
Ordinary shares in Minor Ltd		98,800
Ordinary shares in Major plc		44,400
Annual exempt amount		(12,300)
		130,900
CGT:	10,600 at 10%	1,060
	120,300 at 20%	24,060
		25,120

Minor Ltd is an unquoted trading company with an issued share capital of 200,000 £1 ordinary shares. Zoyla has been a director of this company since 1 April 2015. On 20 June 2022, Zoyla sold 20,000 of her holding of 45,000 ordinary shares in Minor Ltd. She had originally purchased 22,500 shares on 15 August 2021 for £117,000. On 12 December 2021, Minor Ltd made a 1 for 1 rights issue. Zoyla took up her allocation under the rights issue in full, paying £7.40 for each new share issued.

Major plc is a quoted trading company with an issued share capital of 2,000,000 £1 ordinary shares. Zoyla has been an employee of Major plc since 1 November 2021 when she acquired 16,000 ordinary shares in the company. On 6 March 2023, Zoyla sold her entire holding of ordinary shares in Major plc to her son for £152,000. On that date, shares in Major plc were quoted on the stock exchange at £9.62–£9.74.

Zoyla will not make any other disposals in the foreseeable future, and her taxable income will remain unchanged.

16 Complete the following sentences to explain why neither of Zoyla's share disposals during the tax year 2022/23 qualified for business asset disposal relief.

The disposal of shares in Minor Ltd did not qualifying for business asset disposal relief in the tax year 2022/23 due to:

The disposal of shares in Major plc did not qualifying for business asset disposal relief in the tax year 2022/23 due to:

Pull down list

- Holding period
- Size of shareholding

(2 marks)

17 What cost figure will have been used in calculating the chargeable gain on Zoyla's disposal of 20,000 ordinary shares in Minor Ltd?

- O £126,000
- O £104,000
- O £148,000
- O £252,000

(2 marks)

---

18 What proceeds figure will have been used in calculating the chargeable gain on Zoyla's disposal of 16,000 ordinary shares in Major plc?

- O £152,000
- O £154,400
- O £153,920
- O £154,880

(2 marks)

---

19 If Zoyla had delayed the sale of her 16,000 ordinary shares in Major plc until 6 April 2023, by how long would the related CGT liability have been deferred?

▼

Pull down list

- 1 month
- 11 months
- 12 months
- 6 months

(2 marks)

---

20 Assuming that the tax rates and allowances for the tax year 2022/23 continue to apply, how much CGT would Zoyla have saved if she had delayed the sale of her 16,000 ordinary shares in Major plc until the following tax year?

- O £1,060
- O £4,580
- O £3,520
- O £2,460

(2 marks)

(Total = 10 marks)

Roman and Paris

The following scenario relates to Questions 21 to 25.

Roman died on 7 August 2022, and his wife, Paris, died on 18 February 2023.

The couple had attempted to mitigate their inheritance tax (IHT) liabilities when they both made substantial gifts during 2020. These gifts made full use of their respective nil rate bands of £325,000, but unfortunately neither Roman nor Paris then survived long enough for any of the gifts to benefit from taper relief. Neither Roman nor Paris had made any previous lifetime gifts.

Roman

On 4 March 2020, Roman made a cash gift of £210,000 to his daughter. On 26 August 2020, he made a cash gift of £190,000 to a trust. No lifetime IHT arose in respect of the gift to the trust.

Roman's estate for IHT purposes was valued at £560,000. He did not own a main residence at the date of his death. Under the terms of his will, Roman left £300,000 to Paris (his wife) and the residue of his estate to his daughter.

Paris

On 12 December 2020, Paris made a gift of 75,000 £1 ordinary shares in Capital Ltd, an unquoted investment company, to her son. Before the transfer, Paris owned 100,000 of Capital Ltd's 250,000 ordinary shares. The market value of Capital Ltd's ordinary shares on 12 December 2020 was as follows:

Holding	Market value per share
10%	£5
30%	£6
40%	£8

Paris also made cash gifts of £80, £210, £195 and £460 to various friends during February 2021. The gifts of £80 and £195 were to the same friend.

Paris's estate for IHT purposes was valued at £840,000, including the inheritance from Roman (her husband). She did not own a main residence at the date of her death.

Under the terms of her will, Paris left a specific legacy of £20,000 to a friend and the residue of her estate to her grandchildren.

21 How much IHT will be payable in respect of the gift made to the trust by Roman as a result of his death?

- O £26,400
- O £30,000
- O £27,600
- O £13,200

(2 marks)

---

22 Who will be responsible for paying the IHT arising from Roman's gift to the trust as a result of his death, and when will the tax be due?

- O The personal representatives of Roman's estate on 30 April 2023
- O The personal representatives of Roman's estate on 28 February 2023
- O The trustees of the trust on 30 April 2023
- O The trustees of the trust on 28 February 2023

(2 marks)

---

23 For IHT purposes, what was the amount of the transfer of value as a result of Paris's gift of 75,000 ordinary shares in Capital Ltd?

- O £450,000
- O £600,000
- O £675,000
- O £425,000

(2 marks)

24 What is the amount of the cash gifts made by Paris to her friends during February 2021 NOT covered by the small gifts exemption?

- O £735
- O £460
- O £670
- O £0

(2 marks)

---

25 What is the amount of IHT payable in respect of Roman's and Paris's estates on death?

	Roman's estate	*Paris's estate*
O	£224,000	£336,000
O	£104,000	£336,000
O	£104,000	£328,000
O	£224,000	£328,000

(2 marks)

(Total = 10 marks)

Ardent Ltd

The following scenario relates to Questions 26 to 30.

Ardent Ltd was incorporated on 1 April 2022 and commenced trading on 1 January 2023. The company voluntarily registered for valued added tax (VAT) on 1 January 2023, preparing its first VAT return for the quarter ended 31 March 2023. Ardent Ltd's sales have been as follows:

		Standard rated	*Zero-rated*
		£	£
2023	January	24,800	30,100
	February	42,600	28,700
	March	58,300	22,700
		125,700	81,500

Where applicable, the above figures are stated exclusive of VAT.

During the period 1 April to 31 December 2022, Ardent Ltd incurred input VAT of £120 each month in respect of payments made for advertising services. The company also incurred input VAT totalling £400 (£200 each) in respect of the purchase of two laptop computers on 10 July 2022. One of the laptop computers was scrapped on 30 November 2022 at a nil value, and the other laptop was not used until Ardent Ltd commenced trading on 1 January 2023.

During the quarter ended 31 March 2023, Ardent Ltd received standard rated invoices totalling £56,400 (inclusive of VAT) in respect of purchases and expenses. As at 31 March 2023, £11,400 (inclusive of VAT) of the purchases were unsold and therefore included in inventory.

Ardent Ltd was late in submitting its VAT return for the quarter ended 31 March 2023, and in paying the related VAT liability. The company currently does not use either the VAT cash accounting scheme or the annual accounting scheme.

26 From what date would Ardent Ltd have been required to be compulsorily registered for VAT?

[▼]

Pull down list

- 1 April 2023
- 1 February 2023
- 1 March 2023
- 1 May 2023

(2 marks)

---

27 What amount of pre-registration input VAT was Ardent Ltd able to recover in respect of the inputs incurred prior to it registering for VAT on 1 January 2023?

O £920

O £1,120

O £1,480

O £1,280

(2 marks)

---

28 Ignoring pre-registration input VAT, what amount of VAT should Ardent Ltd have paid to HM Revenue & Customs in respect of the quarter ended 31 March 2023?

O £17,640

O £32,040

O £13,860

O £15,740

(2 marks)

---

29 How and by when should Ardent Ltd have filed its VAT return for the quarter ended 31 March 2023?

O Either on the HMRC website or by using Making Tax Digital software by 30 April 2023

O Using Making Tax Digital software by 7 May 2023

O Using Making Tax Digital software by 30 April 2023

O Either on the HMRC website or by using Making Tax Digital software by 7 May 2023

(2 marks)

---

30 Drag and drop the correct period and VAT scheme from the options below to correctly identify for which period after 31 March 2023 Ardent Ltd will need to avoid further defaults in order to revert to a clean default surcharge record, and which VAT scheme may help in avoiding such further defaults.

Options	Answer	Label
6 months		Period after 31 March 2023
12 months		VAT scheme

Cash accounting scheme

Annual accounting scheme

(2 marks)

(Total = 10 marks)

Section C

ALL three questions are compulsory and MUST be attempted.

31 Jack

You should assume that today's date is 15 March 2023 and that the tax rates and allowances for the tax year 2022/23 continue to apply.

Jack, aged 44, is a widower following the recent death of his wife. He has just cashed in a substantial share portfolio and is now considering what to do with the proceeds.

Gift to a trust

The value of Jack's estate is in excess of £1,000,000, and he is worried about the amount of inheritance tax which will be payable should he die. His wife's nil rate band was fully used when she died.

Jack is therefore planning to make an immediate lifetime cash gift of £300,000 to a trust with the funds then being held for the benefit of his two children aged 10 and 12. Jack has not made any previous lifetime gifts.

Personal pension contribution

The only pension contributions which Jack has made previously is the gross amount of £500 per month which he saves into a personal pension scheme. Jack has continued to make these contributions throughout the tax year 2022/23. Although Jack has been saving into this scheme for the previous 15 years, he is concerned that he is not saving enough for his retirement. Jack therefore wants to make the maximum possible amount of additional gross personal pension contribution for the tax year 2022/23, but only to the extent that the contribution will attract tax relief at the higher rate of income tax.

Jack is self-employed, and his trading profit for the tax year 2022/23 is £100,000. He does not have any other income and expects to make the same level of profit in future years.

Individual savings account (ISA)

Jack has never invested any amounts in ISAs. During the next 30 days he would like to invest the maximum possible amounts into stocks and shares ISAs.

Required

(a) Explain, with supporting calculations where necessary, why it is good inheritance tax planning for Jack to make the immediate lifetime cash gift of £300,000 to a trust.

Note. You are not expected to consider taper relief. **(3 marks)**

(b) (i) Advise Jack of the amount of additional gross personal pension contribution he can make for the tax year 2022/23 which will benefit from tax relief at the higher rate of income tax, and explain why this is a tax efficient approach to pension saving. **(4 marks)**

(ii) Calculate the amount of unused pension annual allowances which Jack will be able to carry forward to the tax year 2023/24 if the contribution in (i) above is made. **(1 mark)**

(c) Advise Jack as to the maximum possible amount which he can invest into stocks and shares ISAs during the next 30 days. **(2 marks)**

(Total = 10 marks)

32 Array Ltd

Array Ltd provides its employees with various benefits. It does not payroll benefits.

The benefits were all provided throughout the tax year 2022/23 unless otherwise stated.

Alice

Alice was provided with a petrol-powered car which has a list price of £24,600. The car has an official CO_2 emissions rate of 102 grams per kilometre. Alice made a capital contribution of £5,600 towards the cost of the car when it was first provided to her by Array Ltd.

Alice was also provided with fuel for her private journeys. The total cost to Array Ltd of fuel for the car during the tax year 2022/23 was £1,500.

During the tax year 2022/23, Alice drove a total of 12,000 miles, of which 8,000 were for business journeys.

Buma

Buma was provided with a loan of £48,000 on 1 October 2020, which she used to renovate her main residence. Buma repays £1,000 of the capital of the loan to Array Ltd each month, and by 6 April 2022 the amount of the loan outstanding had been reduced to £30,000. In addition, Buma paid loan interest of £180 to Array Ltd during the tax year 2022/23.

The taxable benefit in respect of this loan is calculated using the average method.

Claude

On 6 July 2022, Claude was provided with a mobile telephone. The telephone is a smartphone which is mainly used by Claude for personal internet access. It was purchased by Array Ltd on 6 July 2022 for £600.

On 6 January 2023, Claude was provided with a home entertainment system for his personal use. This was purchased by Array Ltd on 6 January 2023 for £3,200. The market value of the home entertainment system on 5 April 2023 was £2,400.

Denise

During May 2022, Array Ltd paid £10,400 towards the cost of Denise's removal expenses when she permanently moved to take up her new employment with Array Ltd, as she did not live within a reasonable commuting distance. The £10,400 covered both her removal expenses and the legal costs of acquiring a new main residence.

During February 2023, Array Ltd paid for £340 of Denise's medical costs. She had been away from work for three months due to an injury, and the medical treatment (as recommended by a doctor) was to assist her return to work.

Required

(a) State how employers are required to report details of employees' taxable benefits to HM Revenue & Customs following the end of the tax year, and the deadline for submitting this information for the tax year 2022/23. **(2 marks)**

(b) Calculate the taxable benefits which Array Ltd will have to report to HM Revenue & Customs in respect of each of its employees for the tax year 2022/23.

Note. Your answer should include an explanation for any benefits which are exempt or partially exempt. **(11 marks)**

(c) Calculate the class 1A national insurance contributions which Array Ltd would have had to pay in respect of its employees' taxable benefits for the tax year 2022/23, and state when this would have been due if paid electronically. **(2 marks)**

(Total = 15 marks)

33 Wretched Ltd

Wretched Ltd commenced trading on 1 August 2022, preparing its first accounts for the eight-month period ended 31 March 2023.

Wretched Ltd is incorporated in the United Kingdom, but its three directors are all non-resident in the United Kingdom. Board meetings are always held overseas.

The following information is available:

Trading loss

The trading loss based on the draft accounts for the eight-month period ended 31 March 2023 is £140,840. This figure is before making any adjustments required for:

(1) Advertising expenditure of £7,990 incurred during April 2022. This expenditure has not been deducted in arriving at the trading loss for the eight-month period ended 31 March 2023 of £141,200.

(2) The premium which was paid to acquire a leasehold office building on a ten-year lease.

(3) Capital allowances.

Premium paid to acquire a leasehold office building

On 1 August 2022, Wretched Ltd paid a premium to acquire a leasehold office building on a ten-year lease. The amount of premium assessed on the landlord as income was £34,440. The office building was used for business purposes by Wretched Ltd throughout the eight-month period ended 31 March 2023.

Plant and machinery

On 1 August 2022, Wretched Ltd purchased three new laptop computers at a discounted cost of £400 per laptop. The original price of each laptop was £850, but they were sold at the discounted price because they were ex-display.

Wretched Ltd also purchased three second-hand cars on 1 August 2022. Details are:

	Cost	*CO_2 emissions rate*
	£	
Car [1]	8,300	0 grams per kilometre
Car [2]	12,300	40 grams per kilometre
Car [3]	18,800	125 grams per kilometre

Property business income

Wretched Ltd lets out a warehouse which is surplus to requirements. The warehouse was let out from 1 August to 31 October 2022 at a rent of £1,400 per month. The tenant left on 31 October 2022, and the warehouse was not re-let before 31 March 2023.

During the eight-month period ended 31 March 2023, Wretched Ltd spent £2,100 on advertising for tenants.

Due to a serious flood, Wretched Ltd spent £5,900 on repairs during January 2023. The damage was not covered by insurance.

Loss on the disposal of shares

On 20 March 2023, Wretched Ltd sold its entire 1% shareholding of £1 ordinary shares in Worthless plc for £21,400. Wretched Ltd had purchased these shares on 5 August 2016 for £26,200.

The indexation factor from August 2016 to December 2017 is 0.052.

Other information

Wretched Ltd does not have any 51% group companies.

Wretched Ltd will continue to trade for the foreseeable future.

Required

(a) State, giving reasons, whether Wretched Ltd is resident or not resident in the United Kingdom for corporation tax purposes. **(1 mark)**

(b) Assuming that Wretched Ltd is resident in the United Kingdom, calculate the company's trading loss, property business loss and capital loss for the eight-month period ended 31 March 2023.

Note. You should assume that the company claims the maximum available capital allowances. **(11 marks)**

(c) Explain how Wretched Ltd will be able to relieve its trading loss, property business loss and capital loss for the eight-month period ended 31 March 2023. **(3 marks)**

(Total = 15 marks)

Answers

DO NOT TURN THIS PAGE UNTIL YOU HAVE COMPLETED THE MOCK EXAM

Mock exam 3

A plan of attack

If this were the real Taxation (TX – UK) exam and you had been told to turn over and begin, what would be going through your mind?

Perhaps you're having a panic. You've spent most of your study time on income tax and corporation tax computations (because that's what your tutor/BPP Workbook told you to do), plus a selection of other topics, and you're really not sure that you know enough. So calm down. Spend the first few moments or so **looking at the exam** and develop a **plan of attack**.

Looking through the exam.

Section A contains **15 Objective Test (OT) questions** each worth **2 marks**. These will cover all sections of the syllabus. Some you may find easy and some more difficult. For Question 5, make sure you carefully consider each statement about extra-statutory concessions before making your choice. Don't spend a lot of time on anything you really don't know. For multiple choice questions you are not penalised for wrong answers, so you should answer all of them. If all else fails – guess!

Section B contains **three OT Case** scenarios. These each have **five questions** each worth **2 marks**. Make sure you read the scenario carefully before you start to answer the OTQs.

- **Questions 16 to 20** are about chargeable gains for an individual. In Question 18, do you know how quoted shares are valued if there is an element of a gift?
- **Questions 21 to 25** tests your knowledge of inheritance tax (IHT). Don't forget to double check your calculations especially in Question 21.
- **Questions 26 to 30** concerns value added tax (VAT). Question 29 should be easy marks about payment of VAT.

In **Section C** you have **three constructed response (long) questions**:

- **Question 31** for **10 marks** covers a number of areas of tax planning. These are inheritance tax lifetime gifts, pensions and individual savings accounts.
- **Question 32** for **15 marks** is an income tax computation which also tests national insurance contributions. The scenario involves the provision of employment benefits.
- **Question 33** for **15 marks** is a corporation tax question. The test for UK residence is examined, the calculation of losses for companies and the use of those losses.

All of these questions are compulsory.

This means that you do not have to waste time wondering which questions to answer.

Allocating your time

BPP's advice is always allocate your time **according to the marks for the question** in total and for the parts of the question. But **use common sense.** If you're confronted by an OTQ on a topic of which you know nothing, pick an answer and move on. Use the time to pick up marks elsewhere.

After the exam...**Forget about it**!

And don't worry if you found the exam difficult. More than likely other candidates will too. If this were the real thing you would need to **forget** the exam the minute you left the exam hall and **think about the next one**. Or, if it's the last one, **celebrate**!

Section A

1 £ 1,570

	£
Entertaining overseas customers	320
Purchase of new office equipment	1,250
Input tax recoverable	1,570

Note the difference between entertaining overseas customers (input tax recoverable) and UK customers (input tax not recoverable). Input tax is not usually recoverable on cars with any private use – this could be by the owner of the business or an employee.

2 The correct answer is: Barge Ltd and Dhow Ltd only

Companies are in a chargeable gains group if at each level there is a 75% holding and the top company has an effective interest of over 50% in the group companies.

There is a 75% holding of Barge Ltd by the top company Acasta Ltd so this is in Acasta Ltd's chargeable gains group.

There is a 75% holding of Dhow Ltd by Barge Ltd and an effective interest of over 50% (75% × 75% = 56.25%) by Acasta Ltd in Dhow Ltd so Dhow Ltd is also in Acasta Ltd's chargeable gains group.

Coracle Ltd is in Acasta Ltd's chargeable gains group (given in question). However, there is no 75% holding between Coracle Ltd and Eight Ltd so Eight Ltd cannot be in Acasta Ltd's chargeable gains group.

ACCA Examining Team's Comments

This question tested candidates' knowledge of the group relationship which is necessary for chargeable gains purposes. The most popular answer was the second option, with candidates appreciating that Barge Ltd was included because of the 75% group relationship with Acasta Ltd (and that Eight Ltd was correspondingly excluded). However, Dhow Ltd is also included in the chargeable gains group because the 75% group relationship need only be met at each level, subject to Acasta Ltd having an effective interest of over 50% (and 75% of 75% is 56.25%). So the correct answer was the third option.

This demonstrates the need to carefully consider each alternative – not just quickly jumping to the most obvious one.

3 The correct answer is: £474,500

	£
Nil rate band (NRB) at Nadia's death in 2003/04	255,00
NRB used at Nadia's death	(137,700)
Unused NRB available for transfer	117,300
Tareq's NRB 2022/23	325,000
Nadia's transferred NRB adjusted for 2022/23 rate	
$£117,300 \times \dfrac{325,000}{255,000}$	149,500
Total NRB available for Tareq's estate	474,500

4 The correct answer is: £13,284

	£
Proceeds	27,900
Less cost £31,320 × $\frac{14}{30}$	(14,616)
Gain	13,284

5 The correct answer is: A provision for the relaxation of the strict application of the law where it would lead to anomalies or cause hardship

6 A sole trader is required to keep their accounting records for [60] months after the [31 January that follows the end of the tax year]

7 The correct answer is: £1,038

	£
2022/23	
Second year: basis period first 12 months of trading	
1.1.22 to 30.6.22	10,500
1.7.22 to 31.12.22 6/12 × £24,400	12,200
Taxable profit	22,700
Class 4 NICs £(22,700 × 12,570) = 10,130 @ 10.25%	1,038

The answer £0 uses £10,500 as the taxable profit. The answer £1,125 uses the accruals basis to give £23,550 as the taxable profits. The answer £1,213 uses £24,400 as the taxable profit.

8 The correct answer is: £33,600

	£
Rent receivable £3,000 × 12	36,000
Less electricity payable £200 × 12	(2,400)
Property business income	33,600

The electricity expense is deductible on an accruals basis (companies always use this basis) so the late payment for December 2022 does not affect the deduction. Finance costs for a company are a loan relationship and so not deducted in computing the property business income. They are also not subject to the finance cost restriction which only applies to individuals.

9 The correct answer is: Harper's husband living in the UK throughout the tax year 2022/23 and Harper staying with him when she visits the UK

The first three answers are automatic UK residency tests. The last answer is a combination of two of the sufficient ties tests and so is not an automatic UK residency test.

10 The correct answer is: 30 April 2025

The corporation tax return should have been filed by 31 December 2023. It was therefore filed late. The deadline for HM Revenue & Customs (HMRC) to start a compliance check enquiry is therefore the quarter day following the first anniversary of the actual filing date of 15 March 2024 so is 30 April 2025.

11 The correct answer is: £1,140

	£
Rent receivable £720 × 12	8,640
Less rent a room limit	(7,500)
Property business income	1,140

This is less than the normal basis of assessment which would be £8,640 × (175 × 12) = £6,540.

12 The correct answer is: Chelfry Ltd only

Asher Ltd was a large company in the current period and the previous period as its TTP exceeded the limit of £1,500,000/(3 + 1) = £375,000 in both periods and so will have to pay corporation tax by quarterly instalments for the current period.

Barton Ltd was a large company in the current period and the previous period as its TTP exceeded the limit of £1,500,000 in the previous period and £1,500,000 × 4/12 = £500,000 in the current period and so will have to pay corporation tax by quarterly instalments for the current period.

Chelfry Ltd was a large company in the current period as its TTP exceeded the limit of £1,500,000 but was not a large company in the previous period as its TTP did not exceed the limit. It is therefore not required to pay corporation tax by quarterly instalments for the current period.

13 £2,177

	£
Non-savings income	
£8,500 @ 20%	1,700
Savings income	
£1,000 @ 0%	0
£1,400 (2,400 – 1,000) @ 20%	280
Dividend income	
£2,000 @ 0%	0
£2,250 (4,250 – 2,000) @ 8.75%	197
Income tax liability	2,177

The answer £2,352 omits the dividend nil rate band. The answer £2,377 omits the savings income nil rate band. The answer £2,552 omits both the savings income nil rate band and the dividend nil rate band.

14 £395,000

	£
Investment property	390,000
Chattels and cash	70,000
Shares in an ISA	60,000
Income tax owed	(25,000)
Total estate	495,000
Less spouse exemption	(100,000)
Chargeable estate	395,000

Remember that the ISA exemptions only apply for income tax and capital gains tax.

15 The correct answers are:

Amount	
£45,000	Gift holdover relief
£11,500	Gain

	£
Proceeds (MV)	98,000
Less cost	(41,500)
Gain before relief	56,500
Gift holdover relief (balancing figure)	(45,000)
Gain = actual proceeds minus original cost £(53,000 × 41,500)	11,500

Section B

Zoyla

Workbook references

CGT business reliefs are covered in Chapter 15. Shares and securities are the subject of Chapter 16. The calculation of CGT liability and the payment date are dealt with in Chapter 13.

Top Tips

The conditions for business asset disposal relief are often tested so make sure that you know them!

Easy Marks

There were easy marks in Question 19 for identifying the deferral period for the capital gains tax (CGT) liability based on the payment dates for each tax year.

16 The disposal of shares in Minor Ltd did not qualifying for business asset disposal relief in the tax year 2022/23 due to:

Holding period

The disposal of shares in Major plc did not qualifying for business asset disposal relief in the tax year 2022/23 due to:

Size of shareholding

A disposal of shares in a company qualifies for business asset disposal relief if the company is the individual's personal company, which is one where the shareholder owns at least 5% of the ordinary share capital of the company, the company is a trading company and the shareholder is an officer or employee of the company. These conditions must be satisfied for at least two years prior to the disposal of the shares.

The shares in Minor Ltd were acquired on 15 August 2021 and disposed of on 20 June 2022 and so the conditions were not satisfied for at least two years.

The shares in Major Ltd were a shareholding of (16,000/2,000,000 × 100) = 0.8% and so Major Ltd was not Zoyla's personal company due to the size of the shareholding.

17 The correct answer is: £126,000

Date	*Transaction*	*No. of shares*	*Cost*
			£
15 August 2021	Acquisition	22,500	117,000
12 Dec 2021	Rights issue 1 new share for every 1 original share held @ £7.40	22,500	166,500
		45,000	283,500
20 June 2022	Sale	(20,000)	(126,000)
c/f		25,000	157,500

18 The correct answer is: £154,880

The actual proceeds are £152,000 but this must be compared with the market value of the shares to see if this is a sale at an undervalue. The market value per share is £9.62 + 1/2(9.74 ×9.62) = £9.68. The total market value is therefore £9.68 × 16,000 = £154,880 which is used as the proceeds for capital gains tax purposes.

19 | 12 months |

The date of the CGT liability on the sale of Major Ltd shares on 6 March 2023 (tax year 2022/23) was 31 January 2024. If Zoyla had delayed the sale until 6 April 2023 the disposal would have been in the tax year 2023/24 and so the CGT liability would have been due on 31 January 2025 thus deferring the payment by 12 months.

20 The correct answer is: £3,520

	£
Tax saved due to availability of another annual exempt amount: £12,300 × 20%	2,460
Tax saved due to part of the gain being taxed at basic rate instead of higher rate: £10,600 ×(20% ×10%)	1,060
Total CGT saving	3,520

The answer £1,060 is just the higher rate tax saving. The answer £4,580 uses 20% for both calculations. The answer £2,460 is just the annual exempt amount saving.

Roman and Paris

Workbook references

Inheritance tax is the subject of Chapter 18.

Top Tips

A gift of shares in an unquoted company will usually involve a computation of the amount by which the donor's estate decreases as in Question 23. You need to compare the value of the shareholding before the gift and after the gift.

Easy marks

There were easy marks in Question 22 for identifying the persons responsible for paying the inheritance tax on death on the chargeable lifetime transfer and the date of payment.

21 The correct answer is: £26,400

	£	£
4 March 2020		
Gift	210,000	
Less: Annual exemption 2019/20	(3,000)	
Annual exemption 2018/19 b/f	(3,000)	
Potentially exempt transfer		204,000
26 August 2020		
Gift	190,000	
Less: Annual exemption 2020/21	(3,000)	
Annual exemption 2019/20 b/f	(0)	
Chargeable lifetime transfer		187,000
7 August 2022		
Nil rate band at death	325,000	

ANSWERS

	£	£
Less PET now chargeable and within seven years of CLT	(204,000)	
Available nil rate band for CLT	121,000	
IHT on CLT:		
£121,000 @ 0%		0
£66,000 @ 40%		26,400
£187,000		26,400

The calculation above is for teaching purposes to show in detail how the computation works. In the exam you could simplify it to:

£((190,000 – 3,000) – (325,000 – (210,000 – 3,000 – 3,000))) @ 40% = £26,400

ACCA Examining Team's Comments

This question caused particular problems. The requirement was to establish how much inheritance tax was payable in respect of a chargeable lifetime transfer as a result of the donor's death. The chargeable lifetime transfer had been preceded by a potentially exempt transfer. In selecting the most popular alternative, candidates failed to take account of the £3,000 annual exemptions which were available. In selecting the second most popular alternative, candidates did not appreciate that the two gifts were made in consecutive tax years, meaning that three annual exemptions were available rather than the two used in this option.

This demonstrates just how careful candidates need to be in using each piece of information given, be it a date, number or fact.

22 The correct answer is: The trustees of the trust on 28 February 2023

23 The correct answer is: £675,000

	£
Before: 100,000 @ £8	800,000
After: 25,000 @ £5	(125,000)
Transfer of value	675,000

Before the transfer, Paris owned a 100,000/250,000 × 100 = 40% shareholding and after the transfer she owned a 25,000/250,000 × 100 = 10% shareholding.

24 The correct answer is: £735

	£
Gifts to same friend exceeding £250 in tax year £(80 + 195)	275
Gift exceeding £250	460
Gifts not covered by small gifts exemption	735

25 The correct answer is:

Roman's estate	***Paris's estate***
£104,000	£336,000

Roman's estate

	£
Death estate	560,000
Less spouse exemption	(300,000)
Chargeable death estate	260,000
Nil rate band used by lifetime transfers	
£260,000 @ 40%	104,000

Paris's estate

	£
Chargeable death estate	840,000
Nil rate band used by lifetime transfer	
£840,000 @ 40%	336,000

There is no exemption for legacies on death to another person other than a spouse or civil partner.

Ardent Ltd

Workbook references

Value added tax is covered in Chapters 24 and 25.

Top tips

In Question 27, note the different time limits for pre-registration input tax to be recovered. The time limit for services is six months before registration but for goods it is four years before registration.

Easy marks

There were easy marks in Question 29 for the filing requirement and date.

26 1 April 2023

	£
January 2023 £(24,800 + 30,100)	54,900
February 2023 £(42,600 + 28,700)	71,300
	126,200

Note that all taxable supplies (here standard rated and zero rated) are taken into account when working out whether the registration threshold has been exceeded.

The registration threshold of £85,000 is exceeded by 28 February 2023. Ardent Ltd should therefore have notified HMRC by 30 March 2023, with registration effective from 1 April 2023.

27 The correct answer is: £920

	£
Advertising: £120 × 6 months (max) before registration	720
Computer acquired in four years before registration and still held at registration	200
Input tax reclaimable	920

28 The correct answer is: £15,740

	£
Output tax £125,700 @ 20%	25,140
Less input tax £56,400 × 1/6	(9,400)
VAT payable to HMRC	15,740

It is not relevant whether the purchases are still held in inventory.

29 The correct answer is: Using Making Tax Digital software by 7 May 2023

30 The correct answers are:

12 months	Period after 31 March 2023
Annual accounting scheme	VAT scheme

A trader must submit one year's returns on time and pay the VAT shown on them on time in order to break out of the surcharge liability period and the escalation of surcharge percentages.

The annual accounting scheme may help because only one VAT return is required each year so there are fewer occasions to trigger a default surcharge.

Section C

31 Jack

Workbook references

Inheritance tax is the subject of Chapter 18. Pension contributions are covered in Chapter 5. The ISA limits are dealt with in Chapter 2.

Top tips

There are three marks for part (a) so you should be making three relevant points to obtain these marks. It is important to attempt all three parts of the question to gain a reasonable overall mark.

Easy marks

There were some easy marks in part (b)(i) for working out the available annual allowances and in part (c) for identifying the ISA limits. The basic information required is in the tax rates and allowances provided in the examination.

Examiner's comments

This question proved difficult for many candidates, with some aspects consistently causing problems:

(1) As regards part (a), long, detailed, computations were often provided when the answer was quite straightforward. For example, the gift would have reduced the taxpayer's death estate by £300,000, so the inheritance tax saving was simply £120,000 (£300,000 at 40%). There was no need for before and after computations.

(2) As regards part (b), few candidates appreciated that restricting the amount of personal pension contributions to the amount qualifying for tax relief at the higher rate minimises the cost of pension saving because each £100 saved effectively only costs £60 (£100 less 40% tax relief).

(3) As regards part (c), very few candidates realised that the 30-day period fell into two tax years, so the taxpayer could invest £20,000 by 5 April 2023, and then another £20,000 (using the tax year 2023/24 limit) on or after 6 April 2023.

Marking guide		Marks	
(a)	Chargeable lifetime transfer	1	
	No inheritance tax	1	
	Inheritance tax saving	1	
			3
(b) (i)	Higher rate income	1	
	Available annual allowances	2	
	Minimising cost of pension saving	1	
			4
(ii)	Unused annual allowances		
			1
(c)	ISA limits	1	
	Maximum investments	1	
			2
Total			10

(a) The gift will be a chargeable lifetime transfer of £294,000 (£300,000 less annual exemptions of £3,000 for 2022/23 and 2021/22).

No lifetime inheritance tax will be payable because this is less than the nil rate band, and if Jack survives for seven years, there will be no additional inheritance tax liability either.

The value of Jack's estate will therefore be reduced by £300,000, which will mean an eventual inheritance tax saving of £120,000 (£300,000 at 40%).

Tutorial note. Although it might itself be fully exempt, the chargeable lifetime transfer will have to be taken into account when calculating any inheritance tax liability arising on any further lifetime transfers which may be made within the following seven years. After seven years, a further gift can be made to a trust.

(b) (i) For 2022/23, £(100,000 – 12,570 – (37,700 + (500 × 12))) = £43,730 of Jack's income is currently taxable at the higher rate of income tax.

This is less than the available annual allowances of £(40,000 × 4 – ((500 × 12) × 4))= £136,000 for 2022/23.

Restricting the amount of personal pension contributions to the amount qualifying for tax relief at the higher rate will minimise the cost of pension saving because each £100 saved will effectively only cost £60 (£100 less 40% tax relief).

Tutorial note. Unused annual allowances can be carried forward for up to three years.

Tutorial note. Although Jack's approach to pension saving will maximise the available tax relief, it will mean that some carried forward annual allowances are wasted.

(ii) Jack will have unused allowances of £68,000 being £(40,000 – 6,000) = £34,000 from 2020/21 and the same amount for 2021/22 to carry forward to 2023/24.

Where an annual allowance is exceeded with contributions made in a tax year the current year AA is used first and then the unused AA from the previous three years can be used on a first-in, first out basis. The £44,000 contribution would therefore be set against the 2022/23 AA first and then £10,000 would be used from 2019/20, leaving £34,000 from each of 2020/21 and 2021/22 to carry forward as follows.

Tax year	Annual allowance	Already used (£500 x 12)	Additional contribution in 2022/23	Carry forward to 2023/24
2019/20	£40,000	(£6,000)	(£10,000)	0
2020/21	£40,000	(£6,000)		£34,000
2021/22	£40,000	(£6,000)		£34,000
2022/23	£40,000	(£6,000)	(£34,000)	

(c) Jack can invest in an ISA for 2022/23 by 5 April 2023, and another ISA for 2023/24 between 6 April 2023 and 5 April 2024.

The maximum possible amount which he can invest into stocks and shares ISAs during the next 30 days is therefore £20,000 × 2 = £40,000.

32 Array Ltd

Workbook references

Employment income is dealt with in Chapter 3 and 4.

Top tips

Make sure you know the filing dates for the main forms that need to be submitted to HMRC and the payment dates for payments that need to be made to HMRC.

Easy marks

There were easy marks in part (b) for standard benefit computations.

However, you must be very accurate in your computations to obtain all the marks available.

Examiner's comments

This was the income tax question. It was well answered.

In part (a), many candidates appreciated that reporting is done using form P11D, but the submission deadline was often not known. Less well-prepared candidates often discussed (at length) submission details for self-assessment tax-returns.

There were many exceptional answers to part (b). Common mistakes included:

- For the car and fuel benefits, not ignoring the fuel cost and the mileage figures – both of which were irrelevant to the benefit calculations.
- For the beneficial loan, not commencing calculations with the amount of the loan outstanding at the start of the tax year – this figure was given – but instead trying to work from the original loan amount.
- For the home entertainment system, using the value at the start of tax year rather than the original purchase price.

Part (c) was reasonably well answered, although a few candidates included employee salaries when calculating the class 1A national insurance contributions.

Marking guide		Marks	
(a)	Form P11D	1	
	Submission deadline	1	
			2
(b)	*Alice*		
	Car benefit percentage	1	
	Car use taxable benefit	2	
	Fuel taxable benefit	1	
	Buma		
	Interest benefit	2	
	Deduction for interest paid by employee	0.5	
	Claude		
	Mobile phone	1	
	Home entertainment system	1.5	
	Denise		
	Relocation costs	1	
	Medical costs	1	
			11

Marking guide		Marks
(c) Class 1A NIC	1	
Payment date	1	
		2
Total		15

(a) Details of employees' taxable benefits are reported to HM Revenue & Customs (HMRC) using a form P11D for each employee.

The P11D submission deadline for 2022/23 is 6 July 2023.

(b) **Alice**

The relevant percentage for the car benefit is 16% + 9% ((100 – 55)/5) = 25%.

The car was available throughout 2022/23, so the taxable benefit is £(24,600 – 5,000) × 25% = £4,900.

The fuel benefit is £(25,300 × 25%) = £6,325.

> **Tutorial note.** The amount of capital contribution which can be used to reduce the list price when calculating a car benefit is restricted to £5,000.
>
> **Tutorial note.** The proportion of business mileage is not relevant to the calculation of the car benefit.

Buma

	£
$\frac{30{,}000 + (30{,}000 - (1{,}000 \times 12))}{2} \times 2.0\%$	480
Less: interest paid	(180)
Taxable benefit	300

Claude

The provision of one mobile telephone does not give rise to a taxable benefit even if the telephone is a smartphone.

The taxable benefit for the use of the home entertainment system is £(3,200 × 20% × 3/12) = £160.

> **Tutorial note.** The home entertainment system has not been given to Claude, so the market value on 5 April 2023 is irrelevant.

Denise

Only £8,000 of the relocation costs is exempt, so the taxable benefit is £(10,400 – 8,000) = £2,400.

The payment of medical costs of up to £500 does not result in a taxable benefit provided the medical treatment is recommended in writing by a medical professional to assist an employee to return to work following a period of absence due to ill-health or injury lasting at least 28 days.

(c) The employer's Class 1A NIC payable by Array Ltd for 2022/23 is £(4,900 + 6,325 + 300 + 160 + 2,400) = 14,085 @ 15.05%) = £2,120.

If paid electronically, this would have been payable by 22 July 2023.

33 Wretched Ltd

Workbook references

Company residence is covered in Chapter 19. The calculation of losses is also covered in Chapter 19 and the use of losses is dealt with in Chapter 21.

Top tips

All companies which are UK incorporated are UK resident for corporation tax purposes.

If a company is not incorporated in the UK, it is resident in the UK only if its central control and management are exercised in the UK.

Easy marks

The capital allowances computation in part (b) should have produced easy marks provided that you used the standard layout.

Examiner's comments

For part (a), candidates were required to state whether the company was resident or not resident in the UK for corporation tax purposes.

This requirement resulted in a very surprising number of incorrect answers, with at least half the candidates deciding that the company was not resident because of its central management and control being exercised overseas.

Part (b) was generally very well answered, although there were a couple of consistent problems. Firstly, it was often not appreciated that a second-hand car does not qualify for the 100% first year allowance. And secondly, indexation allowance was often used to increase the capital loss.

Part (c), provided candidates appreciated that it was the company's first period of trading, was then well answered. However, candidates who overlooked this basic fact spent a lot of time discussing all the various (irrelevant) loss reliefs, with a few candidates discussing the income tax relief for a loss incurred in the early years of a trade.

Marking guide	Marks	
(a) Company residence		
		1
(b) *Trading loss*		
Pre-trading expenditure	1	
Deduction for lease premium	1.5	
Capital allowances		
Additions qualifying for AIA	1	
AIA	0.5	
Car [1]	1	
Car [2]	0.5	
Car [3]	0.5	
WDA main pool	1	
WDA special rate pool	1	
Property business loss		
Rent receivable	0.5	
Advertising	0.5	
Repairs	0.5	

ANSWERS

Marking guide		Marks
Capital loss		
Proceeds	0.5	
Cost	0.5	
Indexation allowance	0.5	
		11
(c) Trading loss relief	1	
Property business loss relief	1	
Capital loss relief	1	
		3
Total		15

(a) Companies which are incorporated in the UK such as Wretched Ltd are resident in the UK regardless of where their central management and control is exercised.

(b) **Wretched Ltd – period ended 31 March 2023**

Trading loss

	£
Trading loss	(140,840)
Advertising expenditure	(7,990)
Deduction for lease premium £(34,440/10) × 8/12	(2,296)
Capital allowances (W)	(4,784)
Revised trading loss	(155,910)

> **Tutorial note.** The advertising expenditure incurred during April 2022 is pre-trading and is treated as incurred on 1 August 2022. It is therefore deductible, and an adjustment is required.

Working

Capital allowances

	FYA	*Main pool*	*Special rate pool*	*Allowances*
	£	£	£	£
Additions qualifying for AIA				
Laptops ((£400 × 3) × 130%	1,560			
FYA @ 130%	(1,560)			1,560
Transfer to pool	0	0		
Additions not qualifying for AIA				
Car [1]		8,300		
Car [2]		12,300		
Car [3]		—	18,800	
		20,600		

	FYA	Main pool	Special rate pool	Allowances
	£	£	£	£
WDA @ 18 × 8/12		(2,472)		2,472
WDA @ 6% × 8/12			(752)	752
		—	—	
TWDVs carried forward		18,128	18,048	—
Allowances				4,784

Tutorial note. The original cost of the laptops is irrelevant.

Tutorial note. Although car [1] has zero CO_2 emissions, it is second hand and therefore does not qualify for the 100% first year allowance. It instead qualifies for writing down allowances at the rate of 18%.

Tutorial note. Car [2] has CO_2 emissions between 1 and 50 grams per kilometre and therefore qualifies for writing down allowances at the rate of 18%.

Tutorial note. Car [3] has CO_2 emissions over 50 grams per kilometre and therefore qualifies for writing down allowances at the rate of 6%.

Property business loss

		£
Rent receivable £1,400 × 3		4,200
Less:	Advertising	(2,100)
	Repairs	(5,900)
Property business loss		(3,800)

Capital loss

		£
Disposal proceeds		21,400
Less:	Cost	(26,200)
	Indexation allowance	(0)
Capital loss		(4,800)

Tutorial note. Where a company makes a capital loss, then no indexation allowance is available because it cannot be used to increase a loss.

(c) The trading loss of £155,910 will be carried forward and relieved against the total profits of the next accounting period (and then subsequent accounting periods if there is any unrelieved loss). The company can decide how much of the loss is to be relieved in each accounting period.

The property business loss of £3,800 will be carried forward and relieved against total profits in the same way as the trading loss.

The capital loss of £4,800 will be carried forward and relieved against the first available chargeable gains.

TWDVs carried forward

Allowances

Tutorial note. The original cost of the laptop is irrelevant.

ACCA

Taxation (TX - UK)

Mock Exam 4

March/June 2022 amended

<table>
<tr><td colspan="2">Questions</td></tr>
<tr><td>Time allowed</td><td>3 hours</td></tr>
<tr><td colspan="2">This exam is divided into three sections:
Section A - ALL 15 questions are compulsory and MUST be attempted.
Section B - ALL 15 questions are compulsory and MUST be attempted
Section C - ALL THREE questions are compulsory and MUST be attempted</td></tr>
</table>

DO NOT OPEN THIS EXAM UNTIL YOU ARE READY TO START UNDER EXAMINATION CONDITIONS

Mock exam 4

Section A

ALL 15 questions are compulsory and MUST be attempted

1 Simon has been a sole trader since 2012, preparing accounts to 30 June each year. In the year to 30 June 2022, he had trading profits of £60,000 and in the year to 30 June 2023 he had trading profits of £66,000.

What is the amount of Class 4 National Insurance Contributions (NIC) that Simon will have to pay for the tax year 2022/23?

£ [ ] **(2 marks)**

2 Which TWO of the following statements about tax appeals are correct?

- ☐ The First Tier Tribunal deals with straightforward cases such as the imposition of fixed filing penalties
- ☐ The Crown Prosecution Service (CPS) conducts tax appeals against taxpayers
- ☐ The taxpayer must apply for an internal review by HM Revenue and Customs (HMRC) before making an appeal to the Tax Tribunal
- ☐ The Upper Tribunal hears appeals against decisions of the First Tier Tribunal **(2 marks)**

3 Kate sold a flat in November 2022, realising a gain of £31,800. The flat had always been rented out to tenants and was the only chargeable asset that Kate owned. Kate had taxable income of £31,500 in the tax year 2022/23. She made a gross Gift Aid donation of £800 in December 2022.

What is Kate's capital gains tax liability for the tax year 2022/23?

- O £4,840
- O £8,204
- O £3,200
- O £4,760 **(2 marks)**

4 Melton plc prepared accounts for the 12-month period to 31 July 2022. There will not be a compliance check into this accounting period.

Complete the following sentence about the retention of records for Melton plc by matching the date of retention and the maximum penalty into the relevant target area.

Melton plc will be liable for a penalty of up to (1) ▼ if it does not retain its records until (2) ▼ .

Pull down list 1

- £1,000
- £3,000

Pull down list 2

- 31 July 2024
- 31 July 2028

(2 marks)

5 Nicola bought a residential property on 6 April 2022. She let it out immediately at an annual rent of £2,000 per month, all of which was received in the tax year 2022/23. Nicola had bought the property using an interest-only mortgage. The interest paid in the tax year 2022/23 was £9,500. She paid £2,400 in the year to a managing agent.

For many years Nicola's only income has been employment income of £60,000.

What is Nicola's additional income tax liability in respect of her property business income in the tax year 2022/23?

O £8,640

O £7,700

O £6,740

O £4,840

(2 marks)

6 Shona had always been resident in the UK before the tax year 2022/23. She spent more than 90 days in the UK in every tax year up to 2022/23.

Shona's only relative is her father who is UK resident in 2022/23. Shona owns a house in the UK which is available to her for the whole of 2022/23. On 6 April 2022, Shona bought an overseas house where she spent 260 days during 2022/23. She lived in her UK house for the remaining 105 days. Shona is neither employed nor self-employed.

How many ties does Shona have with the UK for the tax year 2022/23 for the purposes of the sufficient ties test for UK residence?

[▼]

Pull down list

- Four
- One
- Three
- Two

(2 marks)

7 Ronald is self-employed. He purchased a house and lived in it for two years. The house was then unoccupied for five years because Ronald went to work outside the UK. He then lived in the house for three years. Ronald then went to live with his mother and the house was unoccupied for six and a half years. Finally, Ronald lived in the house for the last six months of his ownership.

How many months of Ronald's 17-year period of ownership of the house will be exempt for the purposes of private residence relief?

O 66 months

O 150 months

O 153 months

O 165 months

(2 marks)

8 Charlotte's tax payable for the tax years 2021/22 and 2022/23 is as follows:

	2021/22	*2022/23*
	£	£
Income tax on trading income	9,000	10,600
Class 2 NIC	159	164

	2021/22	2022/23
	£	£
Class 4 NIC	1,350	1,800
Capital gains tax	1,750	4,970

Charlotte made the appropriate payments on account on 31 January 2023 and 31 July 2023.

What is the amount payable due on 31 January 2024 in respect of the tax year 2022/23?

O £2,050

O £7,184

O £7,020

O £5,275

(2 marks)

9 On 1 December 2023, Devonte was issued by HM Revenue & Customs (HMRC) with a notice to file his tax return for the tax year 2022/23. Devonte submitted his return online on 20 February 2024. HMRC wishes to conduct a compliance check into this return.

Complete the following sentence about the submission of the online return and the date by which HMRC will have to notify Devonte of a compliance check into the return by matching the date of submission of the tax return and the date of notification of the compliance check into the relevant target area.

The due date for the submission of the return was [▼] and HMRC must notify Devonte by [▼] of a compliance check into the return.

Pull down list

- 20 February 2025
- 28 February 2024
- 28 February 2025
- 30 April 2024
- 31 January 2024
- 31 January 2025

(2 marks)

10 Caster plc sold the whole of its 4% shareholding in Antics Ltd on 15 November 2022. Caster plc had purchased 10,000 shares in Antics Ltd on 16 July 2010 for £20,000. There was a 1 for 2 rights issue at £2.50 per share in December 2017 and Caster plc took up all its rights.

The indexation factor between July 2010 and December 2017 was 0.190.

What is the indexed cost of the shares sold in November 2022?

£ [ ]

(2 marks)

11 On 12 August 2018, Patience made a gross chargeable transfer (after all exemptions) of £175,000.

On 24 November 2022, she gave £180,000 to a trust.

Patience agreed to pay any lifetime inheritance tax (IHT) due.

How much IHT will be payable by Patience on the November 2022 transfer of value?

- O £6,000
- O £4,800
- O £7,500
- O £4,500

(2 marks)

12 Alberto died on 3 September 2022. His only asset was his main residence valued at £525,000 which he left to his daughter. Alberto had made a potentially exempt transfer (after all exemptions) of £40,000 in July 2020. He had been divorced for several years.

What is the inheritance tax (IHT) liability on Alberto's death estate?

- O £26,000
- O £10,000
- O £96,000
- O £0

(2 marks)

13 Rebecca started trading on 1 January 2021 and her taxable turnover for the first 12 months of trading was £5,500 a month.

For the first seven months of 2022 her taxable turnover was as follows:

	£
January 2022	8,100
February 2022	8,300
March 2022	8,400
April 2022	9,200
May 2022	9,500
June 2022	10,300
July 2022	10,600

What was the date by which Rebecca must have notified HM Revenue & Customs (HMRC) that she was liable to be registered for value added tax (VAT)?

[▼]

Pull down list

- 30 August 2022
- 30 July 2022
- 30 June 2022
- 30 September 2022

(2 marks)

14 Which TWO of the following are required for a full value added tax (VAT) invoice to be valid?

- ☐ Customer's VAT registration number
- ☐ Supplier's email address
- ☐ Date of invoice
- ☐ Total invoice price excluding VAT

(2 marks)

15 Wogan Ltd started trading on 1 April 2021 and made a trading loss of £70,000 in the year ended 31 March 2022. It had no other income or gains in the accounting period and made no qualifying charitable donations.

In the year ended 31 March 2023, Wogan Ltd had the following taxable total profits:

	£
Trading profits	50,000
Chargeable gain	1,800
Total profits	51,800
Less: qualifying charitable donation	(1,500)
Taxable total profits	50,300

Assuming that Wogan Ltd uses its trading loss in the most tax efficient manner, what is the company's unused trading loss carried forward at 1 April 2023?

- O £19,700
- O £20,000
- O £21,500
- O £18,200 **(2 marks)**

Section B

ALL 15 questions are compulsory and MUST be attempted

Jaquetta

The following scenario relates to Questions 16 to 20.

Jaquetta started in business as a sole trader on 1 February 2007. She prepared accounts to 30 September each year and had overlap profits on commencement of £1,800.

On 31 December 2022, Jaquetta sold her business to Richard. Her results to the date of cessation **after** capital allowances were as follows:

	£
Year ended 30 September 2021	48,000
Year ended 30 September 2022	36,000
Period ended 31 December 2022	6,000

Jaquetta had a main pool for capital allowances with a tax written-down value of £8,600 at 1 October 2022. She purchased a car with emissions of 35g CO^2/km on 15 October 2022 at a cost of £900.

Jaquetta sold the following assets of her business to Richard on 31 December 2022:

	Proceeds	*Cost*
	£	£
Goodwill	15,000	0
Plant and machinery in main pool	7,800	13,690
Freehold shop	50,000	43,000

Jaquetta had no other chargeable assets and had property business income in addition to her trading income such that she was a higher rate taxpayer in 2022/23.

Richard commenced trading on 1 January 2023 and will prepare accounts to 30 June each year, the first accounts being prepared for the 18-month period to 30 June 2024.

Richard anticipates that he will have a trading loss for the tax year 2023/24.

He was previously employed with employment income of at least £50,000 each tax year since 2014/15.

16 What is the amount of trading income assessable on Jaquetta for the tax year 2022/23?

£ ☐ **(2 marks)**

---

17 What balancing allowance was deducted from Jaquetta's trading profits for the period ended 31 December 2022?

- O £656
- O £1,700
- O £764
- O £1,624

(2 marks)

18 What is Jaquetta's capital gains tax liability for the tax year 2022/23?

- O £1,940
- O £381
- O £970
- O £2,200 **(2 marks)**

---

19 Complete the following sentence about Richard's basis period for the tax year 2023/24 by matching the start date of the basis period and the end date of the basis period into the relevant target area.

Richard's basis period for the tax year 2023/24 will start on [▼] and end on [▼].

Pull down list

- 1 January 2023
- 1 July 2023
- 30 June 2024
- 31 December 2023
- 5 April 2024
- 6 April 2023

(2 marks)

---

20 Which TWO of the following are possible uses by Richard of his trading loss for the tax year 2023/24?

- ☐ Early years loss relief against general income in 2020/21, 2021/22 and 2022/23 in that order
- ☐ Carry forward against general income in 2024/25
- ☐ Early years loss relief against general income in 2022/23, 2021/22 and 2020/21 in that order
- ☐ Against general income in 2022/23 and/or 2023/24 **(2 marks)**

(Total = 10 marks)

Diggory Ltd

The following scenario relates to Questions 21 to 25.

Diggory Ltd is a manufacturing company which owns 78% of another manufacturing company, Chang Ltd. Both companies have been registered for value added tax (VAT) for many years. The companies do not currently have a group registration. Both only make standard-rated supplies.

The following information is available in respect of Diggory Ltd's value added tax (VAT) for the quarter ended 31 December 2022:

(1) Output VAT of £36,500 has been charged in respect of sales. This figure includes output VAT of £700 where an invoice was issued on 2 January 2023 for goods supplied on 29 December 2022 and output VAT of £500 where an invoice was issued on 24 December 2022 for goods supplied on 5 January 2023.

(2) In addition to the above, Diggory Ltd also charged output VAT of £460 on sales to Chang Ltd.

(3) Input VAT included the following:

	£
Entertaining UK customers	210
Entertaining overseas customers	330
Redecorating a room in the managing director's house	500
Building a wall around Diggory Ltd's car park	2,300

In the quarter to 31 March 2023, Diggory Ltd supplied goods to a customer in another country which operates a valued added tax on certain goods. The goods had a VAT-exclusive price of £1,200. The rate of VAT in the other country on the goods supplied is 15%. Diggory Ltd has evidence of the export in the form required by HM Revenue and Customs.

Diggory Ltd is considering expanding its business. It will either acquire part of the business of a sole trader, John, or will acquire 100% of the shares in Downs Ltd. Both John and Downs Ltd are registered for VAT. Downs Ltd makes largely zero-rated supplies. If Diggory Ltd acquires part of the business of John, this will satisfy the requirements to be a transfer of a going concern. John will continue to run the remainder of his business. Diggory Ltd is considering entering into a group registration.

21 What is the amount of output VAT should be charged on the sales in (1) and (2) for the quarter to 31 December 2022?

- O £36,960
- O £36,260
- O £35,300
- O £35,760

(2 marks)

---

22 What is the amount of input VAT recoverable on the expenses in (3) for the quarter to 31 December 2022?

- O £2,300
- O £330
- O £2,630
- O £3,130

(2 marks)

---

23 What is the amount of VAT that Diggory Ltd will charge on the sale of the goods to the customer in another country?

- O £180
- O £0
- O £240
- O £200

(2 marks)

---

24 Which TWO of the following statements about Diggory Ltd's acquisition of part of the business of John as a transfer of a going concern are correct?

- ☐ Diggory Ltd will automatically be liable for any outstanding VAT penalties incurred by John in respect of the part of the business acquired
- ☐ The acquisition of the part of the business of John is outside the scope of VAT
- ☐ If the VAT chargeable on the acquisition is less than £1,000 it need not be paid
- ☐ John will not need to register again for VAT

(2 marks)

25 Which TWO of the following statements about Diggory Ltd group's possible VAT group registration are correct?

- ☐ The Diggory Ltd group must appoint one of the group companies to be a representative member which is solely liable for paying the group VAT liability
- ☐ Downs Ltd should not be included in the group registration because it is largely making zero-rated supplies
- ☐ Supplies of services by Diggory Ltd to Chang Ltd will be disregarded for VAT purposes if they are both within the group registration
- ☐ Each of the companies in the Diggory Ltd group will have to make separate VAT returns

(2 marks)

(Total = 10 marks)

Christophe

The following scenario relates to Questions 26 to 30.

You should assume that the current date is 22 April 2023.

On 10 December 2019, Christophe was appointed as a director of an investment company, Custard Ltd, and he acquired a 3% shareholding of the company at a cost of £10 per share. On 5 April 2022, he acquired a further 48% shareholding in Custard Ltd at a cost of £80 per share.

Due to unexpected ill-health, Christophe wished to reduce his involvement in Custard Ltd and on 1 April 2023, he resigned his directorship and gave a 49% shareholding in Custard Ltd to his son, Dexter.

The values of the shares on 1 April 2023 were as follows:

Shareholding	*Value per share*
%	£
51–75	120
26–50	90
1–25	30

Custard Ltd has always had 10,000 shares in issue. Christophe has no other chargeable assets.

Christophe has been told by a friend that he ought to have waited until 6 April 2023 to make the gift of the Custard Ltd shares to Dexter as this would have been beneficial for capital gains tax (CGT). If Christophe had delayed the gift until 6 April 2023, the values of the shares in Custard Ltd would have been the same as on 1 April 2023.

Christophe is considering making regular payments of £250 to his granddaughter each month, starting on 30 April 2023, to cover some of her living costs while she is at university. He will not make any other gifts in the tax year 2023/24. You have advised Christophe that the gifts to his granddaughter will be exempt from inheritance tax (IHT).

The following information is available about the income and expenses of Christophe:

Tax year	*Gross income*	*Expenses*
	£	£
2022/23	60,000	25,000
2023/24	20,000	18,000

Christophe was married to Leah for many years. Leah died in March 2009 and in her will she left her estate of £250,000 to Christophe. The IHT nil rate band in 2008/09 was £312,000. Leah had made a potentially exempt transfer of £20,000 (after all exemptions) to her sister in August 2005.

Assume the tax rates and allowances in 2022/23 also apply in future years.

26 What is the IHT transfer of value made by Christophe on 1 April 2023?

£ [ ] **(2 marks)**

---

27 What is Christophe's gain chargeable to CGT on 1 April 2023?

- O £216,176
- O £56,000
- O £70,000
- O £69,176

(2 marks)

---

28 Which TWO of the following statements about the CGT advantages of Christophe delaying his gift until 6 April 2023 are correct?

- ☐ He would have been able to set the annual exempt amounts for both 2022/23 and 2023/24 against the chargeable gain
- ☐ Payment of the CGT liability would have been postponed for 12 months
- ☐ He would have been chargeable to CGT at 10% instead of 20% on some of the taxable gain
- ☐ He would have been entitled to business asset disposal relief on the disposal

(2 marks)

---

29 Which of the following IHT exemptions applies to the gifts made by Christophe to his granddaughter?

- O Normal expenditure out of income exemption
- O Small gifts exemption
- O Annual exemption 2023/24
- O Annual exemption 2022/23

(2 marks)

---

30 What amount of Leah's unused nil rate band can Christophe's personal representatives claim to reduce the IHT payable on his death?

- O £260,417
- O £292,000
- O £304,167
- O £308,333

(2 marks)

(Total = 10 marks)

Section C

ALL three questions are compulsory and MUST be attempted

31 Fleur (March/June 2022) (18 mins)

This scenario relates to one requirement.

You should assume that today's date is 25 March 2022.

You are a trainee Chartered Certified Accountant dealing with the tax affairs of Fleur. Fleur has been self-employed since 6 April 2007 and has previously asked you to calculate whether it would be beneficial to incorporate her business on 6 April 2022.

The new limited company was to be called Flower Ltd.

Fleur operating as a sole trader

Her forecast tax adjusted trading profit was £100,000 for the year ending 5 April 2023.

Fleur operating as a limited company

Flower Ltd's forecast tax adjusted trading profit for the year ending 5 April 2023 was £100,000. After taking account of Fleur's director's remuneration of £35,000 and the related employer's class 1 national insurance contributions (NICs) of £3,898, this was to be £61,102 (£100,000 – £35,000 – £3,898).

Fleur would then have withdrawn £45,000 of the company's profits as dividends. Fleur has no other source of income.

Based on these figures, you established that there was no tax benefit to incorporating Fleur's business since the tax and NIC costs were higher.

The supporting tax liabilities and NICs which you had correctly calculated were:

Operate as sole trader	£	*Operate as limited company*	£
Income tax	27,432	Income tax	15,681
Class 2 NICs	164	Employee class 1 NICs	2,972
Class 4 NICs	5,480	Employer's class 1 NICs	3,898
Total	33,076	Corporation tax	11,609
		Total	34,160

Change to the forecast figures

Fleur has just signed a contract with a new customer and has revised her forecast for the year ending 5 April 2023.

Operating as a sole trader

She now forecasts that her tax adjusted trading profit for the year ending 5 April 2023 will be £135,000 rather than £100,000.

Operating as a limited company

The forecast tax adjusted trading profit for the year ending 5 April 2023 will be £135,000 rather than £100,000. Director's remuneration will remain at £35,000, but Fleur will increase the dividends taken from Flower Ltd to £70,000.

Fleur wants to know whether the additional £35,000 of profit will now mean it is beneficial to incorporate her business on 6 April 2022.

Required

Based on the increased tax adjusted trading profit of £135,000, calculate revised figures for each of the seven tax and national insurance contributions (NICs) figures already calculated for the year ending 5 April 2023, and show if there will be an overall cost or saving if she incorporates the business on 6 April 2022.

Notes.

1 For each of the seven tax and NIC figures already calculated, you should show the revised amounts, stating if any remain unchanged.

2 For the income tax figures, you are expected to produce full income tax computations.

3 You should assume that the rate of corporation tax remains unchanged. **(10 marks)**

32 Poppy (March/June 2022) (27 mins)

This scenario relates to three requirements.

Poppy is employed by Zune plc and she is also a member of a partnership. The following information is available:

Employment

(1) During the tax year 2022/23, Poppy was paid a gross annual salary of £65,000 in respect of her employment with Zune plc.

(2) During the period from 1 August 2022 to 5 April 2023, Zune plc provided Poppy with a diesel car which has a list price of £21,800. The car cost Zune plc £20,600, and it has an official CO_2 emission rate of 70 grams per kilometre. The car does not meet the real driving emissions 2 (RDE2) standard. Poppy was not provided with any fuel for private use.

(3) Throughout the tax year 2022/23, Zune plc provided Poppy with two mobile telephones. The telephones had each cost £480 when purchased by the company in March 2022.

(4) All of the taxable benefits provided by Zune plc to Poppy are payrolled.

Partnership

(1) Poppy has been in partnership with Rose and Teasel since 6 April 2013, but Teasel resigned as a partner on 6 July 2022. The partners have always shared profits equally.

(2) For the year ended 5 April 2023, the partnership had a tax adjusted trading loss of £19,500. This figure is before taking account of capital allowances.

(3) The only item of plant and machinery owned by the partnership is a car with a CO2 emission rate of 90 grams per kilometre. The car was used by Poppy and 70% of the mileage was for private journeys. The written down value of the car as at 6 April 2022 was £8,400. The car was sold on 31 July 2022 for £5,400 and was not replaced.

UK Government securities (gilts)

On 1 January 2023, Poppy purchased, for £50,000, gilts with a nominal value of £40,000. The gilts paid interest at the rate of 3%, with interest paid half-yearly on 30 June and 31 December based on the nominal value. Poppy sold the gilts on 31 March 2023 for £50,300 (including accrued interest).

Balancing payment for tax year 2021/22

Poppy filed her self-assessment tax return for the tax year 2021/22 by the filing date, but did not make the balancing payment of £2,600 until 31 August 2023. She was not required to make any payments on account.

Required

(a) Assuming that Poppy claims loss relief against her total income for the tax year 2022/23, calculate her taxable income for this tax year. **(10 marks)**

(b) Explain how Poppy's income tax liability in respect of her taxable benefits for the tax year 2022/23 will have been collected, and if any forms containing details of these benefits will have been reported to HM Revenue and Customs (HMRC). **(2 marks)**

(c) Advise Poppy of the interest and penalties that will be charged by HM Revenue and Customs (HMRC) as a consequence of her not making the balancing payment for the tax year 2021/22 until 31 August 2023. **(3 marks)**

(Total = 15 marks)

33 Mixture Ltd (March/June 2022) (27 mins)

This scenario relates to five requirements.

Mixture Ltd is a large company and therefore has to make quarterly instalment payments in respect of its corporation tax liability.

For the year ended 31 March 2023, Mixture Ltd has taxable total profits of £470,000 and dividends from a non-group company of £45,000. The company had the same level of profits for the year ended 31 March 2022.

Mixture Ltd has had two 51% group companies for many years.

Capital expenditure

Mixture Ltd incurred the following capital expenditure during the year ended 31 March 2023:

(1) A new freehold office building was purchased. The purchase price included £22,200 for a staircase linking the two floors of the building, £16,400 for sprinkler equipment and the fire alarm system, £18,700 for doors and windows and £27,100 for the ventilation system.

(2) Machinery was purchased for £76,600. At the same time, a further £9,200 was spent on building alterations which were necessary for the installation of this machinery.

(3) Movable partition walls were purchased for £33,800. Mixture Ltd uses these to divide up its open plan offices, and the partition walls are moved around on a regular basis.

(4) A new decorative wall was constructed around the boundary of Mixture Ltd's business premises at a cost of £44,700.

Property business income

Mixture Ltd lets out a warehouse which is surplus to requirements, although the property was empty between 1 September 2022 and 28 February 2023. The following income and expenditure relates to the year ended 31 March 2023:

Date received/(paid)		£
1 January 2022	Insurance for the year ended 31 December 2022	(1,700)
28 March 2022	Rent for the quarter ended 30 June 2022	7,800
4 July 2022	Rent for July and August 2022	5,200
5 December 2022	Advertising for tenants	(900)
1 January 2023	Insurance for the year ended 31 December 2023	(1,900)
1 March 2023	Premium for the grant of a five-year lease	18,000
1 March 2023	Rent for the quarter ended 31 May 2023	8,400

Required

(a) (i) Explain why Mixture Ltd is classed as a large company for the year ended 31 March 2023. **(2 marks)**

(ii) Calculate Mixture Ltd's corporation tax liability for the year ended 31 March 2023, and explain when this will have been paid.

Note. You should assume that Mixture Ltd's profits accrued evenly throughout the year.

(3 marks)

(b) List the expenditure incurred by Mixture Ltd during the year ended 31 March 2023 which will have qualified as plant and machinery for capital allowance purposes.

Notes.

1 Your answer should indicate by the use of zero (0) any item of expenditure which does not qualify as plant and machinery.

2 You are not expected to calculate the capital allowances or to state the rate of capital allowance available. **(4 marks)**

(c) Explain why a company may wish to make a short-life asset election for capital allowance purposes. **(2 marks)**

(d) Calculate the property business income figure which will have been included in Mixture Ltd's taxable total profits of £470,000 for the year ended 31 March 2023. **(4 marks)**

(Total = 15 marks)

Answers

DO NOT TURN THIS PAGE UNTIL YOU HAVE COMPLETED THE MOCK EXAM

Mock exam 4

A plan of attack

If this were the real Taxation (TX – UK) exam and you had been told to turn over and begin, what would be going through your mind?

Perhaps you're having a panic. You've spent most of your study time on income tax and corporation tax computations (because that's what your tutor/BPP Workbook told you to do), plus a selection of other topics, and you're really not sure that you know enough. So, calm down. Spend the first few moments or so **looking at the exam** and develop a **plan of attack**.

Looking through the exam.

Section A contains **15 Objective Test (OT) questions** each worth **2 marks**. These will cover all sections of the syllabus. Some you may find easy and some more difficult. In Question 2, where you are asked to identify the true statement, read the possible answers at least twice before you decide which one to select. Don't spend a lot of time on anything you really don't know. For multiple choice questions you are not penalised for wrong answers, so you should answer all of them. If all else fails – guess!

Section B contains **three OT Case** scenarios. These each have **five questions** each worth **2 marks**. Make sure you read the scenario carefully before you start to answer the OTQs.

- **Questions 16 to 20** test your knowledge of trading income taking in basis periods, balancing adjustments and losses. Question 20 is a relatively quick question as you don't need to do any calculations.
- **Questions 21 to 25** concern VAT for companies in a small group. Make sure to double check your calculations to avoid losing marks for simple mistakes. A couple of knowledge questions with no calculations should save you some time here.
- **Questions 26 to 30** are about inheritance tax (IHT). Read the questions carefully to make sure you answer the question set. For example, in Question 26 you are considering IHT and in Q27 CGT on the same gift.

In Section C you have three constructed response (long) questions:

- **Question 31** for **10 marks** is about whether there is a tax advantage for self-employed Fleur by remaining self-employed over the business being incorporated. The question demonstrates that sometimes you can quickly identify extra taxes due without the need for a whole computation, whereas in other situations the whole computation is required.
- **Question 32** for **15 marks** is an income tax question based on Poppy who is employed by Zune plc and also a member of a partnership. It looks at taxable benefits, accrued interest and a trading loss, as well as the consequences of making a late balancing payment.
- **Question 33** for **15 marks** is a corporation tax question dealing with a large company, expenditure qualifying for capital allowances, short-life asset elections and property income. With five different parts to this question, it's important to keep an eye on the time and not spend too long on any one part.

Allocating your time

BPP's advice is always allocate your time **according to the marks for the question** in total and for the parts of the question. But **use common sense**. If you're confronted by an OTQ on a topic of which you know nothing, pick an answer and move on. Use the time to pick up marks elsewhere.

After the exam...**Forget about it**!

And don't worry if you found the exam difficult. More than likely other candidates will too. If this were the real thing you would need to **forget** the exam the minute you left the exam hall and **think about the next one**. Or, if it's the last one, **celebrate**!

Section A

1 £ 4,180

	£
£(60,000 – 50,270) = 9,730 × 3.25%	316
£(50,270 – 12,570) = 37,700 × 10.25%	3,864
Class 4 contributions	4,180

Class 4 NICs are based on the trading profits for the period of account ending in the tax year.

2 The correct answers are:

- The First Tier Tribunal deals with straightforward cases such as the imposition of fixed filing penalties
- The Upper Tribunal hears appeals against decisions of the First Tier Tribunal

HMRC conducts tax appeals against taxpayers. The CPS provides legal advice and institutes and conducts criminal prosecutions in England and Wales where there has been an investigation by HMRC.

The taxpayer does not have to use the internal review procedure before making an appeal to the Tax Tribunal.

3 The correct answer is: £4,760

	£
Chargeable gain	31,800
Less annual exempt amount	(12,300)
Taxable gains	19,500
Tax	
£((37,700 + 800) – 31,500) = 7,000 × 18%	1,260
£(19,500 – 7,000) = 12,500 × 28%	3,500
Total capital gains tax	4,760

The residential property rates apply.

The answer £4,840 does not adjust for Gift Aid. The answer £8,204 does not deduct the annual exempt amount. The answer £3,200 uses the rates of 10% and 20% which apply to other assets.

4 Melton plc will be liable for a penalty of up to £3,000 if it does not retain its records until 31 July 2028 .

5 The correct answer is: £6,740

	£
Rent received	24,000
Less: Agent's fees	(2,400)
Property business income	21,600

	£
£21,600 × 40%	8,640
Less	
Finance costs tax reducer £9,500 × 20%	(1,900)
Income tax liability on property business income	6,740

The answer £8,640 does not make any adjustment for the finance costs. The answer £7,700 does not deduct the agent's fees in the computation of property business income. The answer £4,840 allows full deduction of the finance costs in the property business income computation.

6 Two

The two ties are: available accommodation in the UK, in which she spends at least one night in the tax year, and more than 90 days spent in the UK in either or both of the previous two tax years.

Shona's father is not treated as close family (not a spouse/civil partner or child under the age of 18) so that tie does not apply. She does not have substantive UK work. She is not present in the UK at midnight for at least an equal number of days in the tax year as in any other country.

7 The correct answer is: 153 months

	Exempt months	*Chargeable months*	*Total months*
Actual occupation	24		24
Deemed occupation – up to 4 years self-employed overseas, plus 1 year any reason	60		60
Actual occupation	36		36
Deemed occupation – remaining 2 years up to 3 years any reason	24		24
Unoccupied		51	51
Last 9 months of ownership	9	–	9
Totals	153	51	204

The answer 66 months is the actual occupation. The answer 150 months ignores the last 9 months of ownership rule and only gives 6 months of actual occupation. The answer 165 months treats the overseas period as fully exempt – this only applies if the taxpayer is employed (rather than self-employed) outside the UK.

8 The correct answer is: £7,184

	£
Income tax £(10,600 – 9,000 payments on account)	1,600
Class 2 NIC	164
Class 4 NIC £(1,800 – 1,350 payments on account)	450
Capital gains tax	4,970
Amount payable on 31 January 2024 for 2022/23	7,184

There are no payments on account for Class 2 NIC or capital gains tax.

The answer £2,050 is just the income tax and the Class 4 NIC. The answer £7,020 ignores the Class 2 NIC. The answer £5,275 treats the Class 2 NIC and the capital gains tax as having payments on account.

9 The due date for the submission of the return was **28 February 2024** and HMRC must notify Devonte by **20 February 2025** of a compliance check into the return.

The notice to file a return was issued after 31 October 2023 so the due filing date was the last day of the three-month period starting with the issue. Because the return was made on or before the due date, the date for notification of the compliance check is the first anniversary of the actual filing date.

10 £ **36,300**

	£
July 2010 shares	20,000
Add: Indexation to December 2017	
0.190 × £20,000	3,800
December 2017 shares	
10,000/2 × £2.50	12,500
Total indexed cost	36,300

Indexation is frozen at December 2017 so there is no further indexation allowance on either the original shares or the rights issue shares.

11 The correct answer is: £6,000

	£
Gift	180,000
Less AE × 2 (2022/23 and 2021/22 b/f)	(6,000)
	174,000
Less nil rate band available £(325,000 – 175,000)	(150,000)
	24,000
IHT @ $^{20}/_{80}$	6,000

The answer £4,800 uses the rate of 20%. The answer £7,500 does not deduct the annual exemptions. The answer £4,500 deducts annual exemptions again from the brought forward transfer.

12 The correct answer is: £26,000

	£
£175,000 @ 0% (residence nil rate band)	0
£285,000 @ 0% (£(325,000 – 40,000) nil rate band)	0
£65,000 @ 40%	26,000
£525,000	26,000

The residence nil rate band is the lower of the maximum (2022/23) of £175,000 and the value of the main residence.

The answer £10,000 applies the full nil rate band. The answer £96,000 does not apply the residence nil rate band. The answer £0 assumes that the residence nil rate band is £525,000 and so there is no liability on the estate.

Since Alberto was divorced there can be no transfer of the residence nil rate band nor the nil rate band between spouses.

13 | 30 July 2022 |

Rebecca was required to notify HMRC within 30 days of exceeding the £85,000 registration threshold ie 30 July 2022 (30 days after the year to 30 June 2022 when her cumulative 12-month turnover was £86,800).

14 The correct answers are:

- Date of invoice
- Total invoice price excluding VAT

The customer's VAT registration number is not required, only the supplier's VAT registration number. The supplier must give a business name and address but is not required to give an email address.

15 The correct answer is: £19,700

	£
Loss brought forward	70,000
Used in y/e 31.3.23	(50,300)
Loss carried forward at 1.4.23	19,700

The loss brought forward is set against total profits but the claim can be restricted to leave total profits of £1,500 in charge to preserve tax relief on the qualifying charitable donation.

The answer £20,000 sets the brought forward loss against trading profits only. The answer £21,500 sets the brought forward loss against trading profits only but restricts the loss used to leave trading profits in charge to cover the qualifying charitable donation. The answer £18,200 does not restrict the claim to leave total profits in charge to cover the qualifying charitable donation.

Section B

Jaquetta

16 £ 40,200

	£
y/e 30.9.22	36,000
p/e 31.12.22	6,000
Less overlap profits	(1,800)
Trading income	40,200

17 The correct answer is: £1,700

	Main pool
	£
TWDV b/f	8,600
Addition	900
	9,500
Disposal	(7,800)
Balancing allowance	1,700

There is no annual investment allowance or writing down allowance in the period to cessation.

The answer £656 gives an annual investment allowance of £900 and 12-month writing down allowance of £144 so the balance of the pool is £656. The answer £764 gives an annual investment allowance of £900 and 3-month writing down allowance of £36 so the balance of the pool is £764. The answer £1,624 gives just a 3-month writing down allowance of £76 so the balance of the pool is £1,624.

18 The correct answer is: £970

	£
Goodwill £(15,000 – 0)	15,000
Plant and machinery	0
Freehold shop £(50,000 – 43,000)	7,000
	22,000
Less annual exempt amount	(12,300)
Taxable gains	9,700
CGT @ 10% (business asset disposal relief applies)	970

As the plant and machinery on which capital allowances have been obtained are sold at a loss, the result is no gain and no loss. This is because relief for the loss has already been given through the capital allowances computation.

The answer £1,940 uses the 20% rate. The answer £381 deducts the loss on the plant and machinery. The answer £2,200 does not deduct the annual exempt amount.

19 Richard's basis period for the tax year 2023/24 will start on | 6 April 2023 | and end on | 5 April 2024 |.

The tax year 2023/24 is Richard's second year of trading. There is no period of account ending in that tax year, so the basis period is the tax year itself.

20 The correct answers are:

- Early years loss relief against general income in 2020/21, 2021/22 and 2022/23 in that order
- Against general income in 2022/23 and/or 2023/24

Carry forward loss relief is against trading income of the same trade.

Early years loss relief is against earlier years before later years.

Diggory Ltd

21 The correct answer is: £36,260

	£
Output VAT	
Sales £(36,500 – 700)	35,800
Sale to Chang Ltd (no group registration)	460
Output VAT	36,260

The tax point for the goods supplied on 29 December 2022 is 2 January 2023 (invoice within 14 days) and so the output tax is not due for payment in the 31 December 2022 quarter. However, the tax point for the goods supplied on 5 January 2023 is the issue of the invoice on 24 December 2022 and so no adjustment is needed for this supply.

The answer £36,960 does not adjust for the 29 December 2022 supply. The answer £35,300 omits the sales to Chang Ltd and adjusts for both the 24 and 29 December 2022 supplies. The answer £35,760 adjusts for the 24 and 29 December 2022 supplies.

22 The correct answer is: £2,630

	£
Entertaining UK customers	0
Entertaining overseas customers	330
Redecoration	0
Wall	2,300
	2,630

Input VAT on business entertaining is only recoverable if it relates to the cost of entertaining overseas customers. No input tax is recoverable on expenditure on domestic accommodation for directors. There is no distinction between capital and revenue expenditure for VAT so input tax is recoverable on the building of the new wall (capital).

The answer £2,300 disallows all the input VAT except on the wall. The answer £330 disallows all the input VAT except on the overseas entertaining. The answer £3,130 disallows UK customer entertaining only.

23 The correct answer is: £0

Diggory Ltd will charge VAT at zero rate because there is general zero-rating where a UK VAT registered trader exports goods.

The answer £180 charges VAT at the rate in the other country – this is not relevant for UK VAT. The answer £240 charges the supply at the UK standard rate. The answer £200 treats the supply as VAT-inclusive and charges the supply at the UK standard rate.

24 The correct answers are:

- The acquisition of the part of the business of John is outside the scope of VAT
- John will not need to register again for VAT

Diggory Ltd is not taking over the registration of John and so is not liable for his VAT penalties and John will not have to re-register for VAT.

The rule that if the VAT chargeable is less than £1,000 it need not be paid applies on deregistration.

25 The correct answers are:

- Downs Ltd should not be included in the group registration because it is largely making zero-rated supplies
- Supplies of services by Diggory Ltd to Chang Ltd will be disregarded for VAT purposes if they are both within the group registration

This is because Downs Ltd is in a repayment position and will continue to benefit from cash flow repayments by completing monthly VAT returns.

All members of the Diggory Ltd group will be jointly and severally liable for any VAT due from the representative member.

The Diggory Ltd group will make one VAT return.

Christophe

26 £ 606,000

	£
Before: (3% + 48%) = 51% 5,100 shares @ £120	612,000
After: (51% – 49%) = 2% 200 shares @ £30	(6,000)
Transfer of value	606,000

27 The correct answer is: £69,176

	£
Proceeds (49%) 4,900 shares @ £90 per share	441,000
Less: Cost (W)	(371,824)
Gain	69,176

Working

	No. of shares	*Cost*
		£
10 December 2019 @ £10 per share	300	3,000
5 April 2022 @ £80 per share	4,800	384,000
	5,100	387,000

	No. of shares	Cost
		£
	(4,900)	(371,824)
1 April 2023 disposal	200	15,176

The answer £216,176 uses £120 per share as the proceeds. The answer £56,000 does not pool the shares and treats the 5 April 2022 shares as sold first. The answer £70,000 does not pool the shares and treats the 10 December 2019 shares as sold first.

28 The correct answers are:

- Payment of the CGT liability would have been postponed for 12 months
- He would have been chargeable to CGT at 10% instead of 20% on some of the taxable gain

The payment date for the disposal on 1 April 2023 (2022/23) is 31 January 2024 and on a disposal on 6 April 2023 (2023/24) would be 31 January 2025.

Christophe is a higher rate taxpayer in 2022/23 since his income exceeds the total of the personal allowance and the basic rate band £(12,570 + 37,700) = £50,270. In 2023/24 (assuming 2022/23 rates and allowances) his income is within that total, so some of the taxable gain would have been chargeable at 10% instead of 20%.

Christophe would only have been able to set the annual exempt amount for 2023/24 against the chargeable gain on 6 April 2023. It is not possible to carry forward CGT unused annual exempt amounts, unlike IHT annual exemptions.

He would not have been entitled to business asset disposal relief on the disposal because Custard Ltd is an investment company. Business asset disposal relief for shares only applies to those in trading companies.

29 The correct answer is: Annual exemption 2023/24

The normal expenditure out of income exemption cannot apply because Christophe only has excess income of £(20,000 – 18,000) = £2,000 which is insufficient to cover the gifts of £(250 × 12) = £3,000. The small gifts exemption only applies to gifts up to £250 per donee in a tax year; once exceeded all of the gifts to the same donee are chargeable. The annual exemption for 2022/23 has been used against the gift on 1 April 2023 and, in any case, the current year exemption is used first.

30 The correct answer is: £304,167

$$\frac{£(312{,}000-20{,}000)}{312{,}000} \times £325{,}000 = £304{,}167$$

The answer £260,417 treats the exempt estate passing to Christophe as the unused nil rate band. The answer £292,000 does not deal with the increase in the nil rate band. The answer £308,333 treats the PET as being reduced by 20% taper relief. Remember that taper relief reduces death tax on a lifetime transfer, not the transfer itself.

ANSWERS

Section C

31 Fleur (March/June 2022)

Workbook references

Income tax is covered in Chapter 2. National insurance is covered in Chapter 12. Corporation tax is covered in Chapter 19.

Top tips

This question contains three notes that you must read carefully. Apart from the two income tax computations, workings should be carried out at the margin. For example, for Class 4 national insurance, the increase in the amount due, is the increase in profit @3.25%. Don't forget to consider the personal allowance.

Easy marks

The class 2 and class 1 NIC figures do not change with the new profit level and therefore provide easy marks.

Examining team's comments

Many candidates did not appreciate that the £2,000 dividend nil rate band counts towards the £37,700 basic rate band. Some candidates produced the four-line income tax calculation within one cell. This is not good practice and very difficult to follow. Those candidates who attempted to recalculate all of the tax and NIC figures already given, wasted a considerable amount of time.

Fleur

Remain self employed

		£
Income tax	(Working 1)	46,460
Class 2 NICs	(Unchanged)	164
Class 4 NICs	(5,480 + (35,000 at 3.25%))	6,618
Total		53,242

Incorporation

		£
Income tax	(Working 2)	25,243
Employee class 1 NICs	(Unchanged)	2,972
Employer's class 1 NICs	(Unchanged)	3,898
Corporation tax	(11,609 + (35,000 at 19%)	18,259
		50,372

Conclusion

Given the increased forecast trading profit of £135,000, incorporating her business will now result in an overall tax and NIC saving of £2,870 (53,242 – 50,372) for Fleur.

Workings

1 ***Income tax***

		£
Trading profit		135,000
Personal allowance		0
Taxable income		135,000
Income tax		
£37,700	@ 20%	7,540
£97,300	@ 40%	38,920
£135,000		
Income tax liability		46,460

2 ***Income tax***

		£
Director's remuneration		35,000
Dividend income		70,000
		105,000
Personal allowance	(Working 3)	10,070
Taxable income		94,930
Income tax		
£24,930	(35,000 - 10,070) @ 20%	4,986
£2,000	@ 0%	0
£10,770	(37,700 - 24,930 - 2,000) @ 8.75%	942
£57,230	(70,000 - 2,000 - 10,770) @ 33.75%	19,315
£94,930		
Income tax liability		25,243

3 ***Personal allowance***

		£
Personal allowance		12,570
Reduction	((105,000 - 100,000) / 2)	(2,500)
Reduced personal allowance		10,070

ANSWERS

32 Poppy (March/June 2022)

> **Workbook references**
>
> Gilts are covered in Chapter 2. Benefits are covered in Chapter 4. Trading losses are covered in Chapter 10. Partnerships are covered in Chapter 11.
>
> **Top tips**
>
> Remember that the relevant figures for calculating accrued interest are the nominal value and the interest rate.
>
> **Easy marks**
>
> The calculation of the car benefit and 20% for the mobile phone provide easy marks.
>
> **Examining team's comments**
>
> A number of candidates struggled to correctly allocate the trading loss. The interaction of capital allowances and loss relief was a particular issue. The calculation of the accrued gilt income also caused problems.

(a) Poppy - Taxable income 2022/23

Employment income		£
Salary		65,000
Car benefit	(21,800 × (19% + 4%) × 8/12)	3,343
Mobile phone	(480 × 20%)	96
		68,439
Savings income	(40,000 at 3% × 3/12)	300
		68,739
Loss relief	(Working 1)	(9,350)
Personal allowance		(12,570)
Taxable income		46,819

Notes.

1 The exemption for mobile telephones does not apply to the second telephone.

2 Under the accrued income scheme, Poppy must include the accrued interest from the gilts as savings income for 2022/23, even though she has not received any actual interest.

Working

Trading loss

		£
Trading loss		19,500
Balancing allowance	((8,400 - 5,400) × 30%)	900
Revised trading loss		20,400
Profit share		
6 April 2022 to 5 July 2022	20,400 × 3/12 × 1/3	1,700
6 July 2022 to 5 April 2023	20,400 × 9/12 × 1/2	7,650
		9,350

(b) Because Poppy's benefits are payrolled, the related income tax liability will have been collected under PAYE along with the tax on her salary.

Payrolled benefits do not have to be reported to HMRC on form P11D or otherwise.

(c) Interest will be charged for the period 31 January 2023 to 31 August 2023, so the charge will be £49 (2,600 × 3.25% × 7/12).

Two penalties of £130 (2,600 at 5%) will be imposed on the balancing payment, one when it is one month late and the other when it is six months late.

33 Mixture Ltd

Workbook references

Computing taxable total profits (including property income) and corporation tax are covered in Chapter 19. Large companies and instalments are covered in Chapter 23. Capital allowances are covered in Chapter 8.

Top tips

Remember that dividends received from other companies are not included in taxable total profits. For part (b), list all the assets and include a value for expenditure that does qualify and a zero for expenditure that does not qualify. Note that the cash basis for property income is not relevant for limited companies.

Easy marks

There were easy marks for calculating the corporation tax liability, dividing it by four and stating that it was due on the 14th of each month.

Examining team's comments

The corporation tax question was generally reasonably well answered, especially parts (a)(i), (b) and (d) which accounted for 10 of the marks. For part (c), few candidates seemed to appreciate that there is no benefit in making a short life asset election where the 100% annual investment allowance can be claimed, or if the super deduction of 130% is available.

Negative figures should be included by entering them as such on the spreadsheet. It is very difficult for markers to pick up negative figures if all figures are shown positive, with the total calculated within the cell on the lines of A1 + A2 – A3 + A4. It is also very easy to make mistakes using this approach. If negative figures are entered, the total is simply SUM(A1:A4).

(a) (i) Mixture Ltd is classed as a large company for the year ended 31 March 2023 because its profits of £515,000 (470,000 + 45,000) exceed the threshold of £500,000 (1,500,000/3).

Notes.

1 The threshold is divided by three because Mixture Ltd has two 51% group companies.

2 No exception applies because Mixture Ltd would have also been a large company for the year ended 31 March 2022.

(ii) Mixture Ltd's corporation tax liability for the year ended 31 March 2023 is £89,300 (470,000 at 19%).

The company will have paid this in four quarterly instalments of £22,325 (89,300/4).

The instalments will have been due on the 14th of October 2022, January 2023, April 2023 and July 2023.

(b) **Expenditure qualifying as plant and machinery**

	£
Staircase	0
Sprinkler equipment and fire alarm system	16,400

ANSWERS

	£
Doors and windows	0
Ventilation system	27,100
Machinery	76,600
Building alterations	9,200
Moveable partition walls	33,800
Decorative wall	0

Note. The costs of building alterations necessary for the installation of plant and machinery are treated as plant and machinery for the purposes of the capital allowances legislation.

(c) Short-life asset election:

(1) A short-life asset election will be beneficial when an asset is disposed of for less than its tax written down value within eight years of the accounting period in which it was purchased.

(2) However, there is no benefit to a short-life asset election where the 100% annual investment allowance can be claimed in respect of the asset or if the super deduction of 130% is available.

(3) The balancing allowance given when the asset is disposed of accelerates the allowances rather than these being given on a reducing balance basis.

Any of these three points up to a maximum of 2.

(d) Mixture Ltd - Property business income for the year ended 31 March 2023

	£
Premium received	18,000
Less: 18,000 × 2% × (5 - 1)	(1,440)
	16,560
Rent receivable (7,800 + 5,200 + (8,400 × 1/3))	15,800
	32,360
Advertising	(900)
Insurance ((1,700 × 9/12) + (1,900 × 3/12)	(1,750)
Property business income	29,710

Tax Tables

Supplementary information

(a) Calculations and workings need only be made to the nearest £.

(b) All apportionments should be made to the nearest month.

(c) All workings should be shown in section C.

Tax rates and allowances

The following tax rates and allowances are to be used in answering the questions.

Income tax

		Normal rates	Dividend rates
Basic rate	£1 – £37,700	20%	8.75%
Higher rate	£37,701 – £150,000	40%	33.75%
Additional rate	£150,001 and over	45%	39.35%
Savings income nil rate band	– Basic rate taxpayers		£1,000
	– Higher rate taxpayers		£500
Dividend nil rate band			£2,000

A starting rate of 0% applies to savings income where it falls within the first £5,000 of taxable income.

Personal allowance

	£
Personal allowance	12,570
Transferable amount	1,260
Income limit	100,000

Where adjusted net income is £125,140 or more, the personal allowance is reduced to zero.

Residence status

Days in UK	Previously resident	Not previously resident
Less than 16	Automatically not resident	Automatically not resident
16 to 45	Resident if 4 UK ties (or more)	Automatically not resident
46 to 90	Resident if 3 UK ties (or more)	Resident if 4 UK ties
91 to 120	Resident if 2 UK ties (or more)	Resident if 3 UK ties (or more)
121 to 182	Resident if 1 UK tie (or more)	Resident if 2 UK ties (or more)
183 or more	Automatically resident	Automatically resident

Child benefit income tax charge

Where income is between £50,000 and £60,000, the charge is 1% of the amount of child benefit received for every £100 of income over £50,000.

Car benefit percentage

The relevant base level of CO_2 emissions is 55 grams per kilometre.

The percentage rates applying to petrol cars (and diesel cars meeting the RDE2 standard) with CO_2 emissions up to this level are:

51 grams to 54 grams per kilometre	15%
55 grams per kilometre	16%

The percentage for electric cars with zero CO_2 emissions is 2%.

For hybrid-electric cars with CO_2 emissions between 1 and 50 grams per kilometre, the electric range of the car is relevant:

Electric range	
130 miles or more	2%
70 to 129 miles	5%
40 to 69 miles	8%
30 to 39 miles	12%
Less than 30 miles	14%

Car fuel benefit

The base figure for calculating the car fuel benefit is £25,300.

Company van benefits

The company van benefit scale charge is £3,600, and the van fuel benefit is £688.

Vans producing zero emissions have a 0% benefit.

Individual savings accounts (ISAs)

The overall investment limit is £20,000.

Pension scheme limits

Annual allowance	£40,000
Minimum allowance	£4,000
Income limit	£240,000
Lifetime allowance	£1,073,100

The maximum contribution that can qualify for tax relief without any earnings is £3,600.

Approved mileage allowances: cars

Up to 10,000 miles	45p
Over 10,000 miles	25p

Capital allowances: rates of allowance

Plant and machinery

Main pool	18%
Special rate pool	6%

Cars

New cars with zero CO_2 emissions	100%

CO_2 emissions between 1 and 50 grams per kilometre	18%
CO_2 emissions over 50 grams per kilometre	6%

Annual investment allowance

Rate of allowance	100%
Expenditure limit	£1,000,000

Enhanced capital allowances for companies

Main pool super deduction	130%
Special rate pool first year allowance	50%

Structures and buildings allowance

Straight line allowance	3%

Cash basis accounting

Revenue limit	£150,000

Cap on income tax reliefs

Unless otherwise restricted, reliefs are capped at the higher of £50,000 or 25% of income.

Corporation tax

Rate of tax: Financial year 2022	19%
Financial year 2021	19%
Financial year 2020	19%
Profit threshold	£1,500,000

Value added tax (VAT)

Standard rate	20%
Registration limit	£85,000
Deregistration limit	£83,000

Inheritance tax: nil rate bands and tax rates

		£
Nil rate band		325,000
Residence nil rate band		175,000
Rate of tax on excess over nil rate band	– Lifetime rate	20%
	– Death rate	40%

Inheritance tax: taper relief

Years before death	Percentage reduction
More than 3 but less than 4 years	20%
More than 4 but less than 5 years	40%
More than 5 but less than 6 years	60%
More than 6 but less than 7 years	80%

Capital gains tax: tax rates

	Normal rates	Residential property
Lower rate	10%	18%
Higher rate	20%	28%
Annual exempt amount		£12,300

Capital gains tax: business asset disposal relief and investors' relief

Lifetime limit – business asset disposal relief	£1,000,000
– investors' relief	£10,000,000
Rate of tax	10%

National insurance contributions

Class 1 Employee	£1 to £12,570 per year	Nil
	£12,571 to £50,270 per year	13.25%
	£50,271 and above per year	3.25%
Class 1 Employer	£1 – £9,100 per year	Nil
	£9,101 and above per year	15.05%
	Employment allowance	£5,000
Class 1A		15.05%
Class 2	£3.15 per week	
	Lower profits limit	£12,570
Class 4	£1 to £12,570 per year	Nil
	£12,571 to £50,270 per year	10.25%
	£50,271 and above per year	3.25%

Rates of interest (assumed)

Official rate of interest	2.00%
Rate of interest on underpaid tax	3.25%
Rate of interest on overpaid tax	0.50%

Standard penalties for errors

Taxpayer behaviour	Maximum penalty	Minimum penalty – unprompted disclosure	Minimum penalty – prompted disclosure
Deliberate and concealed	100%	30%	50%
Deliberate but not concealed	70%	20%	35%
Careless	30%	0%	15%

Tell us what you think

Got comments or feedback on this book? Let us know.
Use your QR code reader:

Or, visit:
https://bppgroup.fra1.qualtrics.com/jfe/form/SV_cuphESF344D68Mm